FUNCTIONAL RESPONSIBILITY OF INTERNATIONAL ORGANIZATIONS

This book provides a novel approach to the allocation of international responsibility in a multilayered structure like the European Union. Introducing a new concept of functional international responsibility, this study finds that in international economic law the focus of international dispute settlement bodies is not on the responsible party, but on a party best placed to bear responsibility. The book offers a comprehensive analysis of international rules of responsibility and international dispute settlement practice, primarily that of the World Trade Organization and investment arbitration. The study offers a practically applicable approach to questions of international responsibility, which will assist international adjudicators, EU and Member States' officials and third country government agents who negotiate economic agreements and are involved in international economic disputes. The book is also relevant to those interested in the governance and accountability questions under the new EU–UK Trade and Cooperation Agreement.

EMILIJA LEINARTE is a British Academy Postdoctoral Fellow at the Lauterpacht Centre for International Law, University of Cambridge. Prior to this, she was awarded the Fulbright grant (LLM, the University of Texas at Austin) and an AHRC scholarship (PhD, the University of Cambridge). Emilija has taught EU and international law at the University of Cambridge and Sciences Po Law School in Paris.

Functional Responsibility of International Organizations

THE EUROPEAN UNION AND INTERNATIONAL ECONOMIC LAW

EMILIJA LEINARTE
University of Cambridge

CAMBRIDGE
UNIVERSITY PRESS

CAMBRIDGE
UNIVERSITY PRESS

University Printing House, Cambridge CB2 8BS, United Kingdom

One Liberty Plaza, 20th Floor, New York, NY 10006, USA

477 Williamstown Road, Port Melbourne, VIC 3207, Australia

314–321, 3rd Floor, Plot 3, Splendor Forum, Jasola District Centre, New Delhi – 110025, India

103 Penang Road, #05–06/07, Visioncrest Commercial, Singapore 238467

Cambridge University Press is part of the University of Cambridge.

It furthers the University's mission by disseminating knowledge in the pursuit of education, learning, and research at the highest international levels of excellence.

www.cambridge.org
Information on this title: www.cambridge.org/9781108838887
DOI: 10.1017/9781108979085

First published 2021

A catalogue record for this publication is available from the British Library.

Library of Congress Cataloging-in-Publication Data
NAMES: Leinarte, Emilija, author.
TITLE: Functional responsibility of international organizations : the European Union and international economic law / Emilija Leinarte, University of Cambridge.
OTHER TITLES: Functional responsibility of international organizations
DESCRIPTION: Cambridge, United Kingdom ; New York, NY : Cambridge University Press, 2021. | Includes bibliographical references and index.
IDENTIFIERS: LCCN 2021017682 (print) | LCCN 2021017683 (ebook) | ISBN 9781108838887 (hardback) | ISBN 9781108979085 (ebook)
SUBJECTS: LCSH: International agencies. | European Union. | International agencies – European Union countries. | Court of Justice of the European Union. | World Trade Organization – European Union countries. | Foreign trade regulation – European Union countries.
CLASSIFICATION: LCC KZ4850 .L45 2021 (print) | LCC KZ4850 (ebook) | DDC 341.23–dc23
LC record available at https://lccn.loc.gov/2021017682
LC ebook record available at https://lccn.loc.gov/2021017683

ISBN 978-1-108-83888-7 Hardback

To my Mother

Contents

Preface

The past century – a belle epoque of international organizations – saw the creation of multilateral institutions as an instrument to prevent war, maintain global economic stability and enhance cooperation between nations. In recent years, however, some states have taken a step back from multilateralism in the name of sovereignty suggesting that an end of honeymoon for international institutions is in sight. The United Kingdom withdrew its membership from the European Union (EU) and the United States cut funding to the United Nations (UN) agencies and programmes, questioned its relationship with the World Health Organization and its Supreme Court opened doors to litigate against multilateral banks over damage caused by their lending activities.[1] Notwithstanding, international law fails to set clear rules of responsibility of international organizations. This unsatisfactory state of affairs is, most likely, to the detriment of international bodies themselves which are increasingly subjected to unilateral sanctions from states which helped create them.

This book is based on a doctoral thesis which was submitted to the Law Faculty of the University of Cambridge in September 2018. It explores one dimension of the broad topic of responsibility of international organizations – responsibility of the European Union in international economic law. The topic first sparked my interest in the spring of 2012. Three years prior, after gaining a law degree in the United States, I joined a Baltic law firm. I spent much of my legal practice assisting the government of Lithuania in the implementation of the so-called EU's Third Energy Package aimed at liberalizing Member States' energy markets.[2] The Third Energy Package listed

[1] *Jam* v. *International Finance Corp.*, No. 17–1011, United States Supreme Court, 27 February 2019.

[2] Directive 2009/72/EC of the European Parliament and of the Council of 13 July 2009 concerning common rules for the internal market in electricity and repealing Directive 2003/54/EC and Directive 2009/73/EC of the European Parliament and of the Council of 13 July 2009

alternative methods of unbundling gas supply and generation from the operation of transmission networks in order to ensure fair competition. The Lithuanian government chose the strictest model under the EU directive – full ownership unbundling of integrated gas companies, which effectively meant that no supply or production company is allowed to hold a majority of shares or have any influence over the work of the transmission system operator. The Russian company OAO Gazprom, which owned the majority of shares of a company providing gas services in the country, threatened to bring an investment claim against Lithuania. A question arose: if a Member State implements an EU measure which results in a violation of an international obligation, who is to bear responsibility? What sounded like a narrow and practical question back in 2012 proved to be only a tiny edge of a much larger and highly complex topic of international responsibility.

The question of the international responsibility of the EU is a legal mosaic of global governance, with numerous elements which must be correctly placed to see a whole picture. Looking at these elements in isolation will point to a wrong direction, as has happened to me numerous times during the course of writing this book. Once I linked all the tiny pieces into one interconnected order, I came to an unexpected but clear conclusion which is convincing because it reflects common sense. This perhaps explains why my argument – that international responsibility is allocated to the EU or its Member State(s) depending on who is best placed to remedy the breach – is simple and yet novel. The concept of functional responsibility, which this book presents, does not reject the approach taken by the International Law Commission (ILC). Quite the opposite, it helps rebuke some of the criticism that its rules of responsibility are insufficiently comprehensive to address the allocation of responsibility between various types of organizations and their members, by suggesting that allocation of responsibility in multilayered and multicomposite structures falls outside the scope of the ILC framework (whether that is good or bad is another question). It should be born in mind that apart from this and some other normative findings, which may be applicable to all international organizations, this book does not offer a general theory of allocation of responsibility of international organizations and is focused on the peculiar case of the EU. While it is likely that functional international responsibility applies to other international institutions, I neither claim nor reject this. Instead I leave this question open for further research.

concerning common rules for the internal market in natural gas and repealing Directive 2003/55/EC.

Acknowledgements

First and foremost, I am grateful to my supervisor Professor Michael Waibel. Ever since I stepped on the grounds of the University of Cambridge as a master's student in 2013, he has guided me through the labyrinths of academia. His insights, suggestions and challenges to my ideas have been very helpful while writing this book. Most importantly, his kindness and ability to reassure in times of difficulty helped me to stay focussed.

I owe special thanks to Professor Catherine Barnard, who has been and continues to be my mentor. Working alongside her on multiple projects over the last years has been truly inspiring and her impeccable work ethic has taught me a great deal about the academic profession. I am also very grateful to Professor James Crawford, who supervised my master's thesis which formed the starting point of my doctoral research. Discussions with him played a significant role in framing the topic of this book. As his student and, later, research assistant, I received lessons which have shaped me as an international lawyer.

I owe special thanks to Professors Jan Wouters and Eyal Benvenisti, my doctoral thesis examiners, for their invaluable comments and suggestions. They have been instrumental in preparing this book. I am also very grateful to Dr Lorand Bartels and Dr Markus Gehring for their constructive criticism during the examination of my first-year dissertation.

I thank Dr Claire Fenton Glynn, Professor Alicia Hinarejos, Professor Albertina Albors-Llorens and Professor Sarah Nouwen for being women who help other women. I am also immensely grateful to Professors Egidijus Kūris, Vytautas Pakalniškis and John R Hays Jr who supported me while finding my way to Cambridge.

I had the great luck of discussing my research with experts whose insights were essential in forming my arguments: Jai Motwane (US Trade Representative), James Flett and Ramón Vidal Puig (European Commission Legal Service), Colin Brown (European Commission DG Trade), Ioannis

Zervas (EU Mission to the WTO), Stéphane Lambert and Karl van Kessel (Mission of Canada to the EU).

This book would not have been possible without the generous financial assistance of the Arts and Humanities Research Council and the Trinity College Bursary. I am truly lucky to have been able to be part of the rich and stimulating academic community of the Trinity College and the Lauterpacht Centre for International Law, and I am also very grateful to the Cambridge–Harvard Link and the Hollond Fund (Trinity College) for the opportunity to conduct a significant part of research at Harvard Law School.

Thanks are also due to my two anonymous reviewers of Cambridge University Press. Their constructive and very useful comments helped me improve the final product. I am grateful to Tom Randall, Becky Jackaman and Malini Soupramanian at the Cambridge University Press for their professionalism.

The process of writing of this book has been joyful thanks to the many friends I made at the Cambridge Law Faculty and Trinity College. While life of a doctoral student may at times feel lonely, I never experienced this thanks to my loving family: Dalyte, Nicolas, Viktoria, Simas and my two rocks, Gilles and Jonas. I dedicate this book to my mother, an extraordinary woman who has given me a room of my own.

Table of Cases

COURT OF JUSTICE OF THE EUROPEAN UNION

C-77/69 *Commission of the European Communities* v. *Kingdom of Belgium* [1970] ECR 237

C-22-70 *Commission of the European Communities* v. *Council of the European Communities* [1971] ECR 273 (ERTA case)

C-21-24/72, *International Fruit Company NV et autres contre Produktschap voor Groenten en Fruit* [1972] ECR

C-104/81 *Hauptzollamt Mainz* v. *C.A. Kupferberg & Cie KG a.A.* [1982] ECR 3641

C-175/84 *Krohn & Co Import-Export GmbH & Co KG* v. *Commission* [1986] ECR 753

C-12/86 *Demirel* v. *Stadt Schwäbisch Gmünd* [1987] ECR 3719

C-188-89 A. *Foster and others* v. *British Gas plc.* [1990] ECR I-3313

C-316/91 *Parliament* v. *Council of the European Union* [1994] ECR 661

C-265/95 *Commission of the European Communities* v. *French Republic* [1997] ECR I-6959

T-184/95 *Dorsch Consult Ingenieurgesellschaft mbH* v. *Council of the European Union and Commission of the European Communities* [1998] ECR II-667

C-53/96 *Hermès International* v. *FHT Marketing Choice BV* [1998] ECR I-3603

C-13/00 *Commission of the European Communities* v. *Ireland* [2001] ECR I-02943

C-425/01 *Ospelt* v. *Schlössle Weissenberg Familienstiftung* [2003] ECR I-9743

C-284/16 *Slowakische Republik* v. *Achmea* BV [2018]

Opinions

Opinion 1/76 *Pursuant to Article 228 (1) of the EEC Treaty – 'Draft Agreement Establishing a European Laying-Up Fund for Inland Waterway Vessels'* [1977] ECR 754

Opinion 2/94 *Accession of the Community to the European Human Rights Convention* [1996] ECR I-1759

Opinion 2/15 *Free Trade Agreement with Singapore* [2017]; Opinion of AG Sharpston delivered on 21 December 2016

Rulings

Ruling 1-78 *re Convention on the Physical Protection of Nuclear Materials, Facilities and Transports* [1978] ECR 2151

EUROPEAN COURT OF HUMAN RIGHTS

M. & Co. v. *the Federal Republic of Germany* App no 13258/87 (ECtHR 9 February 1990)

Drozd and Janousek v. *France and Spain* App no 12747/87 (ECtHR 26 June 1992)

Heinz v. *Contracting States and Parties to the European Patent Convention* App no 21090/92 (ECtHR 16 December 1992)

Cantoni v. *France* App no 17862/91 (ECtHR 15 November 1996)

Matthews v. *the United Kingdom* App no 24833/94 (ECtHR, 18 February 1999) (*Matthews* v. *the United Kingdom*)

Beer and Regan v. *Germany* App no 28934/95 (ECtHR 18 February 1999)

Waite & Kennedy App no 26083/94 (ECtHR 18 February 1999) (*Waite & Kennedy*)

T.I. v. *the United Kingdom* App no 43844/98 (ECtHR 7 March 2000)

Streletz, Kessler and Krenz v. *Germany* App nos 34044/96, 35532/97 & 44801/98 (ECtHR 22 March 2001)

S.A. *Dangeville* v. *France*, App no. 36677/97 (ECtHR 16 April 2002)

Bosphorus Hava Yollari Turizm Ve Ticaret Anonim Sirketi v. *Ireland* App no 45036/98 (ECtHR 30 June 2005) (*Bosphorus*)

Commission Decisions

Hess v. *United Kingdom* App no 6231/73 (Commission decision 28 May 1975)

Confédération française démocratique du travail v. *the European Communities* App no 8030/77 (Commission decision 10 July 1978)

Dufay v. *European Communities* App no 13539/88 (Commission decision 19 January 1989)

WORLD TRADE ORGANIZATION DISPUTE-SETTLEMENT

WTO Panel Report, *US – Taxes on Petroleum and Certain Imported Substances*, BISD 34S/136, adopted 17 June 1987 (*US – Superfund*)
WTO Panel Report, *United States – Standards for Reformulated and Conventional Gasoline*, *WT/DS2*, adopted 29 January 1996
WTO Panel Report, *European Communities – Regime for the Importation, Sale and Distribution of Bananas*, WT/DS27/RW/USA, and WT/DS27/AB/RW/USA and Corr.1, adopted 22 May 1997; Appellate Body Report adopted 9 September 1997; Decision of the Arbitrators, adopted 9 April 1999, WT/DS27/ARB (*EC –Bananas III*)
WTO Appellate Body Report, *United States – Measures Affecting Imports of Woven Wool Shirts and Blouses from India*, WT/DS33, adopted 25 April 1997
WTO Appellate Body Report, *European Communities – Hormones*, WT/DS26/AB/R, adopted 13 February 1998 (*EC – Hormones*)
WTO Panel Report, *Argentina – Measures Affecting Imports of Footwear, Textiles, Apparel and Other Items*, WT/DS56, adopted 25 November 1997
WTO Panel Report, *European Communities – Computer Equipment*, WT/DS62/R, WT/DS67/R, WT/DS68/R, adopted 22 June 1998 (*EC – Computer Equipment*)
WTO Panel Report, *European Communities – Measures Affecting Asbestos and Products Containing Asbestos*, WT/DS135, adopted 18 September 2000 (*EC – Asbestos*)
WTO Appellate Body Report, *United States – Import Measures on Certain Products from the European Communities*, WT/ DS165, adopted 11 December 2000
WTO Panel Report, *United States – Countervailing Duties on Certain Corrosion-Resistant Carbon Steel Flat Products from Germany*, WT/DS213, adopted 3 July 2002; Appellate Body Report, adopted 28 November 2002 (*US – Carbon Steel*)
WTO Panel Report, *Chile – Price Band System and Safeguard Measures Relating to Certain Agricultural Products*, WT/DS207, adopted 3 May 2002; Appellate Body Report, adopted 23 September 2002, (*Chile – Price Band System*)
WTO Panel Report, *European Communities – Geographical Indications (US)*, WT/DS174/ R, adopted 20 April 2005 (*EC – Geographical Indications*)
WTO Panel Report, *European Communities – Measures Affecting Trade in Commercial Vessels*, WT/DS301/R, adopted 22 April 2005 (*EC – Commercial Vessels*)

WTO Panel Report, *European Communities – Measures Affecting the Approval and Marketing of Biotech Products*, WT/DS291, adopted 29 September 2006 (*EC – Biotech Products*)

WTO Panel Report, *European Communities – Selected Customs Matters*, WT/DS315/R, adopted 11 December 2006 (*EC – Selected Customs Matters*)

WTO Appellate Body Report, *European Communities – Customs Classification of Frozen Boneless Chicken Cuts*, WT/DS269, adopted 12 September 2005 (*EC – Boneless Chicken*)

WTO Panel Report, *European Communities and Certain Member States – IT Products*, WT/DS375/R, WT/DS376/R, WT/DS377/R, adopted 21 September 2010 (*EC and Certain Member States – IT Products*)

WTO Panel Report, *European Communities – Measures Affecting Trade in Large Civil Aircraft*, WT/DS316/R, adopted 30 June 2010; Appellate Body Report adopted 18 May 2011 (*EC – Large Civil Aircraft*)

WTO Panel Report, *China – Payment Services*, WT/DS413/ R, adopted 31 August 2012

WTO Panel Report, *Canada – Measures Relating to Exports of Wheat and Treatment of Imported Grain*, WT/DS276, adopted 6 April 2004; Appellate Body Report adopted 30 August 2004 (*Canada – Wheat Exports and Grain Imports*)

INVESTMENT ARBITRATION

Metalclad Corporation v. *The United Mexican States* (Award, 30 August 2000) ICSID Case No. ARB(AF)/97/1 (*Metalclad* v. *Mexico*)

Middle East Cement Shipping and Handling Co. S.A. v. *Arab Republic of Egypt*, (Award, 12 April 2002) ICSID Case No. ARB/99/6

Técnicas Medioambientales Tecmed, S.A. v. *The United Mexican States* (Award, 29 May 2003) ICSID Case No. ARB (AF)/00/2 (*Tecmed* v. *Mexico*)

Nykomb Synergetics Technology Holding AB v. *The Republic of Latvia*, (Award, 16 December 2003), SCC (*Nykomb* v. *Latvia*)

Waste Management, Inc. v. *United Mexican States ('Number 2')* (Award, 30 April 2004), ICSID Case No. ARB(AF)/00/3 (*Waste Management* v. *Mexico*)

Petrobart Limited v. *The Kyrgyz Republic* (Award, 29 March 2005) SCC Case No. 126/2003, 82

CMS Gas Transmission Company v. *Argentina*, (Award 12 May 2005), ICSID Case No. ARB/01/8 (*CMS Gas* v. *Argentina*)

Desert Line Projects LLC v. *The Republic of Yemen* (Award, 6 February 2008) ICSID Case No ARB/05/17 (*Desert Line* v. *Yemen*)

Plama Consortium Limited v. *Republic of Bulgaria* (Award, 27 August 2008) ICSID Case No. ARB/03/24 (*Plama Consortium* v. *Bulgaria*)

Merrill & Ring Forestry LP v. *Canada*, (Award, 31 March 2010), ICSID Case No. UNCT/07/1 (*Merrill* v. *Canada*)

ATA Construction v. *The Hashemite Kingdom of Jordan* (Award, 18 May 2010) ICSID Case No ARB/08/2 (*ATA Construction* v. *Jordan*)

AES Summit Generation Limited and AES-Tisza Erömü Kft v. *The Republic of Hungary* (Award, 23 September 2010) ICSID Case No. ARB/07/22 (*AES Summit* v. *Hungary*)

AbitibiBowater Inc. v. *Government of Canada* (Award, 15 December 2010) ICSID Case No. UNCT/10/1

Vattenfall AB, Vattenfall Europe AG, Vattenfall Europe Generation AG v. *Federal Republic of Germany* (Award, 11 March 2011) ICSID Case No. ARB/09/6 (*Vattenfall I* v. *Germany*)

Electrabel S.A. v. *Republic of Hungary, Decision on Jurisdiction, Applicable Law and Liability* (Decision on Jurisdiction, Applicable Law and Liability, 30 November 2012) ICSID Case No. ARB/07/19 (*Electrabel* v. *Hungary*)

Ioan Micula, Viorel Micula, S.C. European Food S.A, S.C. Starmill S.R.L. and S.C. Multipack S.R.L. v. *Romania* (Final Award, 11 December 2013) ICSID Case No. ARB/05/20 (*Micula* v. *Romania*)

Hrvatska Elektroprivreda d.d. v. *Republic of Slovenia* (Award, 17 December 2015) ICSID Case No. ARB/05/24 (*Hrvatska Elektroprivreda* v. *Slovenia*)

RREEF Infrastructure (G.P.) Limited and RREEF Pan-European Infrastructure Two Lux S.à r.l. v. *Kingdom of Spain* (Decision on Jurisdiction, 6 June 2016) ICSID Case No. ARB/13/30 (*RREEF Infrastructure* v. *Spain*)

Charanne and Construction Investments v. *Kingdom of Spain* (Final Award, 16 March 2017), SCC Case No. V 062/2012 (*Charanne* v. *Spain*)

Abbreviations and Acronyms

ACP States	African, Caribbean and Pacific Group of States
AG	Advocate General
ARIO	Articles on the Responsibility of International Organizations
ARSIWA	Articles on Responsibility of States for Internationally Wrongful Acts
BIT	Bilateral Investment Treaty
CCP	Common Commercial Policy
CETA	Comprehensive Economic and Trade Agreement
CJEU	Court of Justice of the European Union
CPTPP	Comprehensive and Progressive Agreement for Trans-Pacific Partnership
DSB	Dispute Settlement Body
DSU	Dispute Settlement Understanding
ECHR	European Convention on Human Rights and Fundamental Freedoms
ECJ	European Court of Justice
ECT	Energy Charter Treaty
ECtHR	European Court on Human Rights
EEA	European Economic Area
EEC	European Economic Community
EPA	EU–Japan Economic Partnership Agreement
EUSFTA	EU–Singapore Free Trade Agreement
FDI	Foreign Direct Investment
FTA	Free Trade Agreement
GATS	General Agreement on Trade in Services
GATT	General Agreement on Tariffs and Trade
GCEU	General Court of European Union
ICJ	International Court of Justice

ICS	Investment Court System
ICSID	International Centre for Settlement of Investment Disputes
ILC	International Law Commission
ILO	International Labour Organization
IMF	International Monetary Fund
INTERPOL	International Criminal Police Organization
ISDS	Investor-State Dispute Settlement
MIC	Multilateral Investment Court
PCIJ	Permanent Court of International Justice
REIO	Regional Economic Integration Organization
SHARES	Research Project on Shared Responsibility in International Law
TEU	Treaty on European Union
TFEU	Treaty on the Functioning of the European Union
TPP	Trans-Pacific Partnership
TRIPS	Agreement on Trade-Related Aspects of Intellectual Property Rights
TTIP	Transatlantic Trade and Investment Partnership
UN	United Nations
UNCLOS	United Nations Convention on the Law of the Sea
UNESCO	United Nations Educational, Scientific and Cultural Organization
UNFCCC	United Nations Framework Convention on Climate Change
WHO	World Health Organization
WTO	World Trade Organization

1

Introduction

It is undisputed that international organizations may have legal personality. In the landmark Opinion of the International Court of Justice (ICJ) in the *Reparation for Injuries*, the ICJ concluded that the United Nations (UN) is an international person capable of possessing international rights and duties.[1] Leaving aside the debate on the rationales underlying the ICJ's conclusion and how it applies to different legal theories on international legal personality,[2] Klabbers notes a presumptive approach which holds that as soon as an organization performs acts which can only be explained on the basis of international legal personality, it is presumed that it possesses international legal personality.[3] The Union's legal personality has been provided for in Article 210 of the European Economic Community (EEC) Treaty and is now found in Article 47 of the Treaty of Lisbon. While the drafters of the Union Treaties never expressly clarified whether that personality covers *international* legal personality, already in 1971 the Court of Justice of the European Union (the Court or CJEU) held that Article 210 of the EEC Treaty was supposed to also mean 'international' legal personality.[4]

Stemming from this international legal personality is the capacity of organizations to assume international rights and obligations. Article 6 of the 1986 Vienna Convention on the Law of Treaties between states and international organizations or between international organizations establishes that their

1 Reparation for Injuries Suffered in the Service of the United Nations (Advisory Opinion) [1949] ICJ Rep 174, 179.

2 Two main theories can be noted – the will theory and the objective theory; see Jan Klabbers, *An Introduction to International Organizations Law* (Cambridge University Press 2015), 46–50.

3 Jan Klabbers, 'Presumptive Personality: The European Union in International Law', in Martti Koskenniemi (ed), *International Law Aspects of the European Union* (Martinus Nijhoff Publishers 1998), 231–253.

4 Case 22–70 *Commission of the European Communities* v. *Council of the European Communities* [1971] ECR 273, para 13–14.

capacity to conclude treaties is governed by the rules of that organization. Article 216(1) of the Treaty on the Functioning of the European Union (TFEU) sets express and implied powers of the European Union (EU) to conclude international agreements.[5] The EU enjoys capacity to conclude international economic treaties which fall within its competence in the area of the common commercial policy.[6] It has become a usual practice in the EU to conclude international agreements alongside its Member States when agreements also cover areas which fall outside the EU's exclusive competence. The Court concluded in *Opinion 2/15* that agreements which cover commitments that fall within a competence shared between the EU and the Member States cannot be concluded by the Union alone.[7] Treaties to which both the EU and some or all of the Member States are party are called 'mixed agreements'. Most of the EU's major economic and environmental treaties are mixed, including the World Trade Organization Agreements (the WTO Agreements), the United Nations Convention on the Law of the Sea (UNCLOS), the Kyoto Protocol to the Climate Change Convention, the EU's association agreements,[8] free trade agreements[9] (except the EU-UK Trade and Cooperation Agreement which is an EU-only treaty) and the European Economic Area Agreement (EEA Agreement).

The power to conclude international agreements comes with responsibility. An early principle of international law, formulated by the Permanent Court of International Justice in the famous *Chorzów Factory* case, is that a violation of international law entails responsibility and the obligation to make

5 Art 216(1) of TFEU provides that 'the Union may conclude an agreement with one or more third countries or international organisations where the Treaties so provide or where the conclusion of an agreement is necessary in order to achieve, within the framework of the Union's policies, one of the objectives referred to in the Treaties, or is provided for in a legally binding Union act or is likely to affect common rules or alter their scope'. The implied power stems from the ERTA doctrine; see Case 22–70 *Commission of the European Communities* v. *Council of the European Communities* [1971] ECR 273. The Court expanded the implied powers doctrine to include those areas where the EU has not yet legislated internally; see Opinion 1/76 *Pursuant to Article 228 (1) of the EEC Treaty – 'Draft Agreement establishing a European laying-up fund for inland waterway vessels'* [1977] ECR 754.

6 Art 3(1)(e) TEU.

7 Opinion 2/15 *Free Trade Agreement with Singapore* [2017] EU:C:2017:376, paras 243–244. However, note that the Court also noted that this conclusion is nothing more than acknowledgement of the fact that there was no possibility of the required majority being obtained within the Council for the Union to be able to exercise alone the external competence that it shares with the Member States in the area under consideration (non-direct foreign investment), see Case C-600/14 *Federal Republic of Germany* v. *Council of the European Union* [2017] EU:C:2017:935, para 67–68.

8 For example, the EU-Ukraine Association Agreement.

9 For example, CETA.

reparation.[10] Nevertheless, the question of the international responsibility of organizations has puzzled legal scholars since the middle of the twentieth century. In his extensive work on international responsibility in the 1950s, Eagleton, for example, did not consider that international organizations may incur international responsibility.[11] While the principle that organizations may be responsible for breach of their obligations is no longer seriously contested, the exact functioning of responsibility of international organizations remains a matter of great confusion. Alvarez rightly notes that it is not clear how the traditional doctrine of state responsibility, if it is relevant at all, ought to apply to organizations.[12] The complexity of the question stems from the limited capacity enjoyed by international bodies – organizations may act only in those areas where they have been empowered to act by their founding members. A number of commentators have suggested that the 2011 International Law Commission's (ILC) Articles on Responsibility of International Organizations (ARIO)[13] are inadequate to address the different types and forms of international organizations. The root of this criticism lies in the fact that the ARIO rules are based on the 2001 Articles on Responsibility of States for Internationally Wrongful Acts (ARSIWA),[14] ignoring that states and organizations are essentially different subjects of international law.

The question of the international responsibility of the EU is particularly complex. On the one hand, unlike other organizations it is a supranational body with extensive, state-like powers. On the other hand, the EU's multilevel implementation system has its origins in the limited resources that its Member States put at its disposal necessary to exercise its competences.[15] To overcome this imbalance between power and means the EU has adopted the so-called system of executive federalism, whereas authorities of the Member States implement Union policies. In this system decisions which will often bind Member States can be taken by majority vote, and so, as Klabbers rightly notes, it is entirely possible that a Member State will have to adopt a certain course of

10 *Factory at Chorzów (Germany v. Poland), Jurisdiction* [1927] PCIJ Series A – No. 8, para 55. The PCIJ held that 'It is a principle of international law that the breach of an engagement involves an obligation to make reparation in an adequate form'.

11 Clyde Eagleton, 'Purchase Access International Organization and the Law of Responsibility' (1950) 76 Recueil Des Cours 323, 345.

12 José E Alvarez, *International Organizations as Law-Makers* (Oxford University Press 2010), 129.

13 Articles on the Responsibility of International Organizations, ILC Report on the Work of its Sixty-third Session, UNGAOR 66th Sess., Supp. No. 10, UN Doc. A/66/10 (2011).

14 Articles on Responsibility of States for Internationally Wrongful Acts, ILC Yearbook 2001/II(2).

15 Jan Klabbers, *An Introduction to International Institutional Law* (2nd edn, Cambridge University Press 2009), 279.

conduct which it itself vehemently opposes.[16] How then do we determine international responsibility for violations of joint obligations in such multi-layered governance structure? By the term 'joint obligations' I primarily mean obligations held by both the EU and its Member States under mixed agreements.

The European Union proposes its answers. The central idea is that the EU is a *sui generis* entity and so subject to a special regime of international responsibility.[17] The applicable *lex specialis*, according to the European Commission, must be based on the internal division of competences between the EU and its Member States.[18] The competence-based approach to international responsibility holds that the EU is responsible for violations of obligations in its areas of competence, irrespective of who carried out the conduct in question. Gaja, Special Rapporteur for the ARIO project, seemed to agree with the European Commission on what he referred to as a 'problem' of determining responsibility in the EU by addressing the following example:

> *Member State customs authorities follow a policy of tariff classification which is alleged to be contrary to the trade provisions of an agreement that has been concluded by the EC and its member States together. The question of apportionment of the obligation and of responsibility would have to be decided in favour of the EC, since trade policy is an exclusive competence of the EC which has been wholly transferred by the member States to it. It would seem to be impossible in such a situation to say that the action by member States' customs authorities should nonetheless lead to the attribution of the conduct to the member States, since they are not the carriers of the obligation any longer.*

Gaja suggested that the articles '*should probably make room for the internal rules of the organization*' as an element that is important not only to the question of the attribution of conduct but also – and perhaps foremost – for the question of the apportionment of responsibility.[19]

Opinions which have emerged during the debate can be broadly divided into two groups. A first group of legal scholars suggests that the responsibility of the EU cannot be regulated solely on the basis of the rules of the organization because they are internal rules. While the need to accommodate the special

16 Klabbers 2015, 26.

17 Comments and Observations Received from Governments and International Organizations, A/CN.4/556 (ILC 2005), 31.

18 Comments A/CN.4/556, 32.

19 Comments and Observations Received from International Organizations, A/CN.4/545 (ILC 2004), 26.

nature of the EU legal order is acknowledged, the argument is that rules of responsibility must sit comfortably within international law.[20] A second group of authors stress the *sui generis* nature of the EU, a one-of-a-kind supranational organization. They suggest that law of international responsibility should provide space for the rules of the organization which governs the division of competences between the EU and Member States.[21] To use the phrase of Kuijper and Paasivirta, this is the 'inside looking out' approach.[22]

While determining international responsibility on the basis of internal rules conveniently accommodates the special nature of the Union, there is nothing in international dispute-settlement practice which would indicate that courts and tribunals support or apply the competence-based responsibility of the EU. To the best of my knowledge there has been no international economic dispute where responsibility was allocated to the EU or its Member States solely on the basis of competence. International adjudicators do not engage in the complex task of untangling the internal institutional functioning of the EU. Rather, as will be argued in this book, the EU and its

[20] For example, Stefan Talmon, 'Responsibility of International Organizations: Does the European Community Require Special Treatment?', in Maurizio Ragazzi (ed), *International Responsibility Today* (Martinus Nijhoff 2005), 415; Christiane Ahlborn, 'The Rules of International Organizations and the Law of International Responsibility', ACIL Research Paper No. 2011–03 (SHARES Series); Jean D'Aspremont, 'A European Law of International Responsibility? The Articles on the Responsibility of International Organizations and the European Union', in Vicky Kosta, Nikos Skoutaris and Vassilis Tzevelekos (eds), *The EU Accession to the ECHR* (Hart Publishing 2014), 75–86; Joni Heliskoski, *Mixed Agreements as a Technique for Organizing the International Relations of the European Community and Its Member States* (Kluwer Law International 2001); Pieter Jan Kuijper, 'Amsterdam Center for International Law: Introduction to the Symposium on Responsibility of International Organizations and of (Member) States: Attributed or Direct Responsibility or Both?' (2010) 7 IOLR 9; Andrés Delgado Casteleiro, *The International Responsibility of the European Union: From Competence to Normative Control* (Cambridge University Press 2016); Malcolm Evans and Phoebe Okawa, 'Approaches to Responsibility in International Courts', in Panos Koutrakos and Piet Eeckhout (eds), *The International Responsibility of the European Union: European and International Perspectives* (Hart Publishing 2013), 101–138.

[21] For example, Esa Paasivirta, 'Responsibility of a Member State of an International Organization: Where Will It End? Comments on Article 60 of the ILC Draft on the Responsibility of International Organizations' (2010) 7 IOLR 49; Pieter Jan Kuijper and Esa Paasivirta, 'EU International Responsibility and Its Attribution: From the Inside Looking Out', in Malcolm Evans and Panos Koutrakos (eds), *The International Responsibility of the European Union: European and International Perspectives* (Hart Publishing 2013), 35–72; Frank Hoffmeister, 'Litigating against the European Union and Its Member States – Who Responds under the ILC's Draft Articles on International Responsibility of International Organizations?' (2010) 21 EJIL 723.

[22] Kuijper and Paasivirta 2013.

Member States remain independently responsible for violations of their joint obligations, irrespective of the internal transfer of powers. The question then is what governs the distribution of international responsibility between the EU and its Member States in, as is more specifically asked in this book, international economic law?

The relevance of the topic stems from the steady expansion of the Union's role in the global economy. While the EU has been a player in international trade since its inception in the form of the European Coal and Steel Community in 1951, a significant impetus for its common commercial action was given in 2009 with the adoption of the Treaty of Lisbon. Among other things, competence in the field of foreign direct investment was transferred from Member States to the Union. Having acquired these new powers, the EU commenced the development of a European international investment policy by adopting a Communication titled 'Towards a comprehensive European international investment policy' of 7 July 2010 (Communication).[23] The European Commission set out two major goals for the new investment policy and is currently working along two parallel lines to achieve them. First, the EU is seeking to ensure that EU investors abroad enjoy a level playing field, which assures both uniform and optimal conditions for investment through the progressive abolition of restrictions and protection of investors' rights. To this end the Union announced in the Communication that the EU would gradually replace bilateral investment treaties (BITs) concluded by its Member States and third countries with those of its own. The second goal indicated in the Communication is the enforcement of investment commitments. It is stated in Part 3(d) of the Communication that future EU trade and investment protection agreements should include a new investor-state dispute-settlement mechanism.

To achieve its goals the European Commission is currently negotiating a number of free trade agreements (FTAs) with third countries.[24] From 2016 to 2018 it has finalized negotiations with several partners, including the EU-Canada Comprehensive Economic and Trade Agreement (CETA),[25] the

[23] European Commission, 'Communication: Towards a Comprehensive European International Investment Policy, COM 343'. In this book, I will refer to earlier bilateral investment treaties concluded by the Member States as first-generation treaties.

[24] For the status of current negotiations, see European Commission's document 'Overview of FTA and Other Trade Negotiations', available at http://trade.ec.europa.eu/doclib/docs/2006/december/tradoc_118238.pdf, last visited 2 August 2018.

[25] CETA was signed on 30 October 2016. It entered into force provisionally on 21 September 2017. National/regional parliaments will have to approve CETA before it can take full effect. Canadian side ratified the treaty on 16 May 2017.

EU-Singapore Free Trade Agreement (EUSFTA),[26] the EU-South Korea Free Trade Agreement and the EU-Japan Economic Partnership Agreement (EPA).[27] The following analysis refers to these treaties as 'new-generation' FTAs, a term also employed by the European Commission.[28] The new agreements, *inter alia*, cover trade liberalization and investment protection. They also establish dispute-settlement mechanisms to deal with trade and investment claims.

The expansion of the EU's external action in the global economy demands accountability. The issues of responsibility have not (yet) given rise to serious contention. That is so because, rather than looking for routes to escape responsibility, the EU has proved to be a willing respondent in international economic disputes. That does not make the question of this book moot. On the contrary, it calls for an investigation into the EU's approach to international responsibility and how this approach fits within international law.

This book presents a concept of functional international responsibility of the EU for violation of international economic obligations. Reference to the word 'functional' is not, however, made to present a connection with the general theory of functionalism in international institutional law.[29] This term is used to argue that responsibility in a multilayered structure like the EU is distributed based on the adjudicative function which is defined by the treaty regime in question. At the same time, this study does not reject that there may be, at a deeper level, a connection with the broader concept of functionalism in the law of international organizations.

1.1 SCOPE OF RESEARCH

This book explores the allocation of international responsibility for violations of joint economic obligations in the context of a multilayered structure where sovereignty is shared among different subjects of international law. By

[26] The EU and Singapore completed the negotiations for a comprehensive FTA on 17 October 2014, text available at http://trade.ec.europa.eu/doclib/press/index.cfm?id=961, last visited 2 August 2018. The treaty needs now to be formally approved by the European Commission and then agreed upon by the Council of Ministers and ratified by the European Parliament.

[27] The negotiations were finalized on 8 December 2017. After the legal verification and translation processes, the European Commission can then submit the agreement for the approval of the European Parliament and EU Member States.

[28] For example, see 2013 press release of the European Commission, available at http://europa.eu/rapid/press-release_MEMO-13-576_en.htm, last visited 2 August 2018.

[29] Jan Klabbers, 'The Emergence of Functionalism in International Institutional Law: Colonial Inspirations' (2014) 25 EJIL 3, 645–675.

reference to 'shared sovereignty' I mean a common governance arrangement, whereas the EU policies are implemented through authorities of Member States, a feature stemming from its limited resources. Analysis is primarily focused on the EU and its Member States, but the normative findings of the present research are relevant to the institutional law of international organizations and law of international responsibility more broadly.

The book aims to answer three main questions: what, how and why.

First, the book aims is to identify *what* legal basis governs the allocation of international responsibility between the EU and its Member States. It searches for the underlying rationales which guide international dispute-settlement bodies when faced with violation(s) of economic obligations held jointly by the EU and its Member States.

Second, the book seeks to extrapolate *how* international courts and tribunals apply this legal basis in practice. Does the reasoning of international courts and tribunals differ depending on the treaty regime in question? How do these differences correlate with the patterns of distribution of shared responsibility between the EU and its Member States?

Third, the book aims to explain *why* the distribution of shared responsibility differs across treaty regimes. How can we explain the factors that shape the role of the EU and its Member States in international dispute-settlement practice?

It must be emphasized that this book explores the question of the international responsibility of the EU in international economic law only. To specify further, it explores the question in the context of joint economic obligations of the EU and its Member States, primarily under mixed agreements. I have chosen to explore the question of responsibility primarily in the context of two major economic frameworks, namely the Energy Charter Treaty (ECT) and the WTO Agreements. Both the ECT and the WTO Agreements are mixed, that is they bind both the EU and its Member States, and their dispute-settlement bodies provide a great case study to explore allocation of international responsibility in a multilayered body.

Under EU law, international economic obligations fall under the category of Common Commercial Policy (CCP) which is an exclusive competence of the EU (Article 3 of the TFEU). That is, the right of decision-making in the area of CCP belongs to the EU, while Member States are prevented from taking action unless mandated by the Union. One may question to what extent the normative findings of this book are applicable in the context of other EU competences or whether they are limited to the narrow case of the EU's exclusive competence in trade.

This work does not address international responsibility for violations of obligations in areas other than CCP. Accordingly, it does not expressly answer whether and how the normative findings of this research are applicable in fields that do not fall under the category of exclusive competences of the EU, such as shared competences in the field of environment, development cooperation or immigration, and ancillary competence in, for example, public health. However, this book addresses CCP not because my intention was to focus exclusively on trade matters but simply because the EU's action in trade offers valuable case law under the ECT and the WTO dispute-settlement mechanisms which is not present, at least to the same extent, in other fields.

Here I should like to note one important point. Functional international responsibility, which is presented in this book, may or may not apply to other areas of EU action. While this book does make any specific conclusions in this regard, the central claim presented herein implicitly suggests that the categorization of competence is largely irrelevant to the question of allocation of international responsibility between the EU and its Member States. The (in)applicability of functional international responsibility to other areas of EU action will depend not on the type of competence (i.e. shared or exclusive) but on the nature of an international obligation in question.

First, this book suggests that the *type of competence* is not always relevant – as it is not relevant in the area of CCP – for the allocation of international responsibility between the EU and its Member States. For the purposes of international responsibility, the nature of competence is not instructive of who is bound by an international obligation. This is a question of mixity, that is, whether Member States are parties to an international treaty in addition to the EU (and, in some cases, the question of obligations erga omnes). Member States may be bound by international obligations in the areas of exclusive EU competence if they are parties to an international treaty alongside the EU. This may, and does, happen when a treaty covers both areas of exclusive and shared competences. Whether a mixed treaty contains trade or environmental obligations is, in this respect, irrelevant – the very purpose of mixity is to avoid categorizing obligations as belonging to the sphere of Member States versus the EU. In this sense, there is no difference between international obligations under mixed agreements in the area of CCP and obligations under mixed agreements in areas of shared competence – it will be argued in Chapter 3 that in both cases Member States are independently responsible for all obligations under a given mixed agreement, irrespective of whether that obligation falls under a shared or exclusive competence.[30] The typology of a given competence is largely irrelevant from an international law perspective. The only relevance that the category of a specific competence plays in the context of international responsibility is that it informs of who is likely to be bound by an international obligation in the context of that competence – the EU, its Member States or both. In the context of shared competences, mixed agreements are a dominant form of treaty-making precisely because there has been no full transfer of powers to the EU. Given that both the EU and its Member States are bound by treaties which contain obligations in the fields of shared competence (e.g. environmental treaties such as the Paris Agreement adopted under the United Nations Framework Convention on Climate Change), the question of allocation of international responsibility may be particularly relevant in the context of shared competences.

Second, whether functional international responsibility is applicable in areas other than CCP depends not on the type of competence but on the *nature of the obligation* in question. This book argues that it is the obligation, rather than the internal categorization of competences, which dictates the underlying rationale for the allocation of international responsibility. The nature of an obligation and the typology of competences are related but independent concepts: that a specific obligation falls under a certain competence (shared or exclusive) is not determinative of its nature. By 'nature' I mean the inherent features of the commitment. As it will be argued in this book, international economic obligations differ essentially from other types of international obligations because of their consensual nature and the restorative, rather than retributive, function of remedies that protect them. It will be suggested that in international economic law, attribution of conduct is irrelevant for the allocation of responsibility in a multilayered structure where sovereignty is shared between different subjects of international law. What international courts and tribunals ask is not who is responsible for a breach but rather who is best placed to bear responsibility. The answer to this question depends on the nature of the obligation in question.

It may thus be that the functional approach to international responsibility will not apply in case of obligations which are essentially different from international economic law. While it is not possible, at least within the scope of the present book, to differentiate various international obligations according to their characteristics, a brief reference to one example illustrates the point. It is unlikely that attribution of conduct will be irrelevant in

30 An in-depth analysis of the principle of independent responsibility of the EU and its Member States is provided in Chapter 3.

the context of responsibility for violations of human rights, international humanitarian law or international criminal law. As will be explained in Chapter 5, obligations in the latter areas are not, or not always, consensual in nature, and the purpose of remedies is retribution rather than restoration.[31] Accordingly, it is questionable whether the normative findings of this book will be applicable to the EU action in areas such as the European Common Security and Defence Policy (CSDP) which is part of the European Common Foreign and Security Policy (CFSP). While the EU does not have an army of its own, it is nevertheless an active player in global security, defence and crisis response. The EU conducts military and civilian missions and operations, such as training missions (EUTM), capacity building missions (EUCAP) and advisory missions (EUAM) in conflict or post-conflict countries, for example, in Mali, Iraq and Libya.[32]

It is important to re-emphasize that the likely inapplicability of the normative findings of this book to responsibility arising in the context of the CFSP is determined not by the type of competence in the field of the CFSP but by the characteristics of international obligations undertaking in this field. With respect to the CFSP activities, the nature of EU competence is not straightforward.[33] The sole relevance of competence category in this context is that it may instruct us of whether the Member States are likely to be bound by international obligations in the field of CFSP. While the CFSP is not categorized neither as exclusive nor as shared competence under the EU treaties, Wessel nevertheless suggests that it is closest to the latter because both the Union and the Member States have roles to play.[34] Therefore, international treaties in the context of the CFSP are likely to be mixed, binding both the EU and its Member States. Moreover, conduct in the area of security, defence and crisis response is not necessarily treaty-based and may concern obligations erga omnes or arise out of peremptory norms which bind Member States irrespective of whether they are parties to an international treaty. Therefore, Member States are likely to be bound by international obligations in the context of CSDP making the question of distribution of

31 The restorative versus punitive nature of remedies is addressed in more detail in Chapter 5.

32 For more information on ongoing and completed missions, see https://eeas.europa.eu/headquarters/headquarters homepage/430/military-and-civilian-missions-and-operations_en, last visited 15 September 2019.

33 Article 2(4) TFEU merely states that 'The Union shall have competence, in accordance with the provisions of the Treaty on European Union, to define and implement a common foreign and security policy, including the progressive framing of a common defence policy'.

34 Ramses A Wessel, 'Common Foreign, Security and Defence Policy', in D Patterson and A Södersten (eds), A *Companion to European Union Law and International Law* (Wiley-Blackwell 2016), 394–412.

shared responsibility relevant in this field too.[35] There have so far been no cases which would indicate that the functional approach to distribution of shared responsibility applies in the context of human rights, international humanitarian law or international criminal law, that is, there have been no cases which would indicate that international responsibility is allocated to the party which is best placed to bear responsibility rather than to the party which carried out the conduct in question. Quite the opposite, some cases suggest that allocation of international responsibility in multilayered structures for violations of human rights, international humanitarian law or international criminal law is likely to follow attribution of conduct.[36] A further analysis of questions of international responsibility in the context of human rights, international humanitarian law or international criminal law falls outside the scope of this book.

Importantly, the present work is limited to identifying and explaining the underlying rationales for the distribution of shared responsibility between the EU and its Member States. I do not evaluate the normative findings of this book from a policy perspective. The purpose of my research is to provide a valuable contribution to a pivotal aspect of the law of responsibility of international organizations, namely the relationship between the organization and its Member States. This book nevertheless concludes by raising some critical questions which may assist further debate on policy implications of functional international responsibility suggested here.

1.2 SOURCES AND RESEARCH METHOD

This book is heavily based on analysis of legal scholarship and the main primary sources. First, it is based on the ILC doctrine of the law on international responsibility, including *travaux préparatoires* of the ARSIWA and the ARIO projects dating back to 1957. Part I of this book explores the commonly accepted hypothesis that answers to the question of the allocation of international responsibility in the multilayered structure of the EU is governed by the ILC framework of international responsibility, primarily the rules of attribution. In my analysis I employ a deductive research method to test this hypothesis by relying on the ILC framework of international

[35] For a detailed account of international obligations of the EU in the field of CSDP, see Frederik Naert, *International Law Aspects of the EU's Security and Defence Policy, With Particular Focus on the Law of Armed Conflict and Human Rights*, doctoral thesis submitted to the Faculteit Rechtsgeleerdheid, Katholieke Universiteit Leuven, 2018.

[36] For example, The Decision of the Appeals Court of The Hague in *Nuhanovic* v. *the State of the Netherlands*, Case no. 200.020.174/01, 5 July 2011.

responsibility as well as a large body of international dispute-settlement practice. This study is based on the analysis of the *travaux préparatoires* of the ILC framework on responsibility for both the ARSIWA and the ARIO projects, which include reports of Special Rapporteurs, ILC reports, reports by the drafting committees and summary records of ILC meetings.

Second, Part II, which relies on inductive reasoning, is based on an extensive body of publicly available international economic dispute-settlement documents, including disputes under the WTO and the ECT regimes where the EU and its Member States have been respondents. Leaving aside the aforementioned hypothesis, the book delves into international dispute-settlement practice to extrapolate and explain the underlying rationales of the distribution of shared responsibility between the EU and its Member States. Identifying grounds for the distribution of shared responsibility of the EU and its Member States in international dispute-settlement practice was complex. The patterns formulated in this book are novel and, to the best of my knowledge, have not been identified in the existing literature. I have analysed fifty-nine WTO disputes which involve the EU. I have also analysed publicly available procedural documents of investment arbitration under the ECT which involve the EU. Pinpointing the relevant elements and placing them in a systemic explanation was difficult for two main reasons. First, the findings presented in this book are counterintuitive in that dispute-settlement bodies do not allocate responsibility on some predetermined structural element. Second, applying an inductive method to WTO case law and investment awards is particularly complicated. Distribution of shared responsibility between the EU and its Member States is rarely contentious and is almost never discussed directly, which made it difficult to locate the relevant elements scattered within hundreds of pages of technical reports and rulings, particularly in WTO law. Importantly, while the title of the case indicates parties to the dispute, it is not conclusive as to who the actual respondents in the dispute are. The exercise often resembled a painstaking task of finding a needle in a haystack. Panels are free to include or exclude persons from its recommendations, irrespective of the title of the dispute. Skimming through the documents was not possible because I was searching for an explanation of the adjudicators' determination of the proper respondent, rather than looking for statements which support/reject some preconceived legal basis. Instead of looking for proof for a hypothesis, I had to formulate a hypothesis by extrapolating invisible general patterns from detailed and technical documents.

Third, this study employed qualitative semi-structured informal interview as an interdisciplinary method to collect data for Chapter 9 which discusses the question of international responsibility in the context of new-generation

FTAs. For this purpose, I have received generous funding from the Arts and Humanities Research Council (AHRC) to conduct over fifteen hours of semi-structured informal interviews with EU and third-party officials based in the United States, Brussels and Geneva who participated in the negotiation of the discussed treaties. My interlocutors, whom I met in autumn 2017, include representatives of the Legal Service of the European Commission, the Directorate General for Trade, the EU Mission in the WTO, the Mission of Canada to the EU and the United States Trade Representative.[37] These meetings provided insight into the process of negotiation of the dispute-settlement mechanism under new FTAs and the approach to the distribution of shared responsibility of the EU and its Member States adopted by both the EU and its trading partners. I did not conduct my research in the form of formal interviews because the FTAs in question had not yet come into force at the time of research and so the information provided was sensitive.

1.3 BOOK STRUCTURE

This book is divided into two parts. Part I explores the legal foundations of the international responsibility of the EU. Building on the normative findings extrapolated in the first part of this book, Part II then lays out a concept of functional international responsibility. Part I consists of Chapters 2, 3 and 4. Part II consists of Chapters 5, 6, 7, 8 and 9.

Chapter 2 of this book explores the ILC framework of international responsibility. The aim of the analysis is to identity rules which govern the allocation of international responsibility in a multilayered structure where sovereignty is shared between different subjects of international law. It will be argued that the purpose of both the ARIO and the ARSIWA is to determine whether a subject of international law *is* internationally responsible. If the question of responsibility arises in the context of a multilayered structure such as that of the EU, additional questions arise. The allocation of international responsibility within an international body falls outside the scope of the ARIO framework. Instead, this book suggests looking for guidance in the rules of organization and the international dispute-settlement practice in which these rules operate.

Chapter 3 looks at the rules of organization. This book concludes that the European Commission's claim that international responsibility follows the internal division of competences does not find support in international dispute-settlement practice. The findings presented in this book reveal that the EU and its Member States are independently responsible for their joint

[37] All opinions, as well as errors, expressed in this book remain mine.

obligations. The central argument is that while states are free to transfer their powers to an organization, their international obligations are non-transferable.

The principle of joint responsibility takes me only halfway to solving the question of the international responsibility of the EU. That the EU and its Member States are independently responsible for their joint obligations does not necessarily mean that a breach will result in their joint and several responsibilities. Chapter 4 accordingly addresses the exclusive responsibility of the EU and its Member States. The book explores the hypothesis suggested by the European Commission that authorities of the EU act as *de facto* organs of the Union when they implement EU law. For this purpose I delve into the *travaux préparatoires* of the ILC rules of responsibility to search for the concept of an organ and agent. It is suggested that while the ILC adopts a broad reading of these terms, international dispute-settlement practice does not support the European Commission's claim that conduct of Member States' organs is attributed to the EU when they carry out EU policies.

Part I thus concludes that (i) the ILC framework does not govern the allocation of responsibility in the multilayered structure of the EU, (ii) the EU and its Member States are independently responsible for their joint obligations and (iii) there is no evidence which supports attribution of conduct of Member States' organs to the EU. Accordingly, the book rejects the hypothesis that the ILC rules of attribution of conduct (or breach in case of derived responsibility) allocate responsibility to the EU when a violation occurs in the areas of EU competence.

Having set aside the aforementioned hypothesis, Part II examines international dispute-settlement practice in order to identify the basis for the allocation of exclusive responsibility within the EU. I approach the case law, primarily that in the fields of trade and investment, with the following enquiry: is attribution of conduct or breach at all relevant to the determination of responsibility in international economic law, and if it is not, what is relevant? My answer results in the formulation of what I call functional international responsibility.

Chapter 5 explores the nature of international economic obligations. It will be suggested that remedies in international economic regimes have a restorative rather than punitive purpose. This book argues that attribution of breach may not be relevant, or that relevant, in the international economic law context. It posits that what international courts and tribunals ask is not *who is responsible for a breach* but rather *who is best placed to bear responsibility*. In international economic law shared responsibility typically raises the question of the proper respondent(s).

Chapter 6 then examines how tribunals determine the proper respondent in the trade and investment regimes. It focuses on WTO law and the ECT regime because their mixed form provides a relevant context in which to explore responsibility of the EU and its Member States for joint obligations. In light of an extensive case-law analysis, this book extrapolates patterns in the tribunals' reasoning. It will be argued that WTO dispute-settlement employs what I call 'the positive solution test' to identify the proper respondent. Arbitral tribunals operating under the ECT, on the other hand, allocate responsibility to the subject which is the proximate cause of harm.

The aim of Chapter 7 is to explain the patterns identified in Chapter 6. In particular, it looks into the characteristics of the WTO and the ECT treaty regimes to explain why the EU is the optimal respondent in trade disputes, whereas Member States are exclusive respondents in investment arbitration.

Chapter 8 adds to Chapter 7 by examining the special WTO cases of multiple respondents. It argues that Member States act as co-respondents when their restorative actions are necessary for compliance purposes. That depends on the nature and scope of the claim which, in turn, defines the remedy.

Chapter 9 attempts to apply the normative findings of this book to new-generation FTAs concluded by the EU, primarily to CETA. My analysis is based on the data gathered during the discussions with officials involved in the negotiation of these agreements. It explains how the new FTAs establish primacy of procedural rules which place the EU at the forefront of dispute resolution. Finally, in my conclusions, I propose some critical questions with the aim of opening further debate on the policy implications of functional international responsibility.

In this book I refer to the European Union as the EU or the Union. Where appropriate I also refer to the European Communities, Community or the EC.

PART I

THE LEGAL FOUNDATIONS OF THE INTERNATIONAL RESPONSIBILITY OF THE EUROPEAN UNION

It is intuitive to start the analysis of the allocation of international responsibility within the European Union (EU) with the International Law Commission's (ILC's) rules of international responsibility. The Articles on the Responsibility of International Organizations (ARIO) govern attribution of conduct and breach to an international organization and determine whether an organization is responsible for a violation of its international obligations. However, attempts to identify the right legal basis for the delimitation of international responsibility between an organization and its Member States in the ILC framework lead to an impasse. Whichever angle one tries to adopt in the analysis, failure is the inevitable outcome of every attempt to solve this legal Rubik's Cube.

The reason for an impasse is simple and yet identifying it proved to be a complex task. This book reaches a counter-intuitive but highly significant conclusion regarding the governing law for the delimitation of responsibility between the EU and its Member States. Re-reviewing and re-analysing multiple times the ILC rules and their commentaries and, importantly, the extensive body of *travaux préparatoires* of both the ARIO and the Articles on Responsibility of States for Internationally Wrongful Acts (ARSIWA), dating back as early as 1957, leads to the conclusion that the ILC framework does not govern this question. While the ARIO is often criticized for being insufficiently comprehensive to address the allocation of responsibility between various types of organizations and their Member States, this chapter argues that the allocation of responsibility falls outside the scope of the ILC framework.

The purpose of Chapter 2 is to explain the reasoning behind this conclusion. It is suggested that the purpose of both the ARIO and the ARSIWA is to determine whether a subject of international law *is* internationally responsible. If the question of responsibility arises in the context of a multilayered structure where sovereignty is shared among separate subjects of international law, additional questions arise. As it was mentioned in the introduction, 'shared sovereignty' means a governance arrangement, such as that of the EU where competences are implemented through Member States' authorities. The 'interwovenness' of international organizations and their Member States begs the question of who bears responsibility when institutional activity offends international law.[1] I conclude Chapter 2 with a suggestion to look at the rules of organization and how those rules operate in international dispute-settlement practice.

Chapter 3 will then explore the EU's approach to the delimitation of international responsibility. It will be suggested that the European Commission's claim for competence-based responsibility does not find support in international dispute-settlement practice. Instead, I it will be argued that both the EU and its Member States are independently responsible for their joint obligations. The main argument of Chapter 3 is that while states can transfer their powers to an international body, their international obligations are non-transferable. This argument will be substantiated with reference to an extensive case law.

A finding that the EU and its Member States are independently responsible for their joint obligations provides only a halfway solution to the question of the international responsibility of the EU. That responsibility of both the EU and its Member States *can* be invoked does not tell us whether the EU, its Member States or both *will* be responsible in a given situation. Chapter 4 thus explores the concept of an organ and agent with the aim of identifying exclusive responsibility of the EU and its members. It will be argued that the EU's claim that Member States act as de facto organs of the EU when they implement Union law does not find support in international dispute-settlement practice. Part It will be argued with a suggestion that the answer may lie outside the rules of attribution of conduct (or breach, in case of derived responsibility). I introduce my hypothesis that allocation of responsibility may instead be remedy-based. On the basis of an extensive analysis of international trade and investment disputes and economic treaty regimes, Part II explains functional international responsibility.

Before proceeding to Chapter 2, I would like to make a brief note regarding the terminology employed in this book. A number of verbs can be used to refer

[1] Ana Sofia Barros, Cedric Ryngaert and Jan Wouters, 'Member States, International Organizations and International Responsibility', in Ana Sofia Barros, Cedric Ryngaert and Jan Wouters (eds), *International Organizations and Member State Responsibility: Critical Perspectives* (Brill Nijhoff 2017), 1.

to the act of dividing responsibility for breach of joint obligations in the context of a multilayered structure of an international body, such as allocation, distribution, delimitation, apportionment or attribution. I have not identified a normative difference in meaning among these verbs, neither in the relevant legal literature, nor in the practice of international courts and tribunals, nor in the ILC's *travaux préparatoires*. Similarly, Nollkaemper and Jacobs suggest that the term 'distribution', on a basic level, refers to the 'allocation' or 'division' of something between multiple persons or entities. According to them, 'distribution' addresses the normative foundations for the actual choices that are made in terms of thinking of the allocation of responsibility among several wrongdoing entities.[2] Since differentiating these terms does not seem to add value, they will be used interchangeably. I will not, however, employ the term 'attribution' to refer to the allocation of responsibility in a multilayered structure of an organization in order to avoid confusion with a common usage of this word in the ILC's framework to refer to an act of prescribing conduct (or breach) to a legal person as an element of responsibility.[3]

2 André Nollkaemper and Dov Jacobs, 'Introduction: Mapping the Normative Framework for the Distribution of Shared Responsibility', in André Nollkaemper and Dov Jacobs (eds), *Distribution of Responsibilities in International Law* (Cambridge University Press 2015), 2.

3 ARIO Art 4 and ARSIWA Art 2.

2

The Governing Law

2.1 INTRODUCTION

Various international organizations and states have criticized the ILC's ARIO project. A first central and recurring theme in the comments to the articles was that the ARIO is insufficient to cater to the many structural and functional differences of various international organizations as it does not take into consideration their special orders.[4] A second main critique of the ARIO framework concerns its lack of clear general rules for 'member' responsibility, that is, responsibility arising out of membership in an international organization.[5] There is an ongoing search for principles that govern the allocation of responsibility between an international organization and its Member States. Third, many suggest that the drafters of the ARIO followed the ARSIWA too closely which resulted in the creation of rules for international organizations which were originally tailored for another subject of international law.[6] Because of the essential differences between international

4 For example, for remarks of the European Commission, ILO, IMF and for the joint submission of other organizations, see Comments and Observations Received from International Organizations, A/CN.4/637 (ILC 2011), para 26. Some organizations suggested that the articles are tailored specifically to the UN and are inapt to address activities other than peacekeeping; see comments of the UNESCO, Comments and Observations Received from International Organizations, A/CN.4/568 (ILC 2006), 128; for comments of the IMF, see Comments and Observations Received from International Organizations, A/CN.4/582 (ILC 2007), 20. Gaja himself noted that 'the main difficulty in reaching a satisfactory definition of international organizations is related to the great variety that characterizes organizations that are currently considered to be 'international'. One aspect of this variety concerns their membership'; see First Report on Responsibility of International Organizations, by Mr Giorgio Gaja, Special Rapporteur (ILC 2003), 109, para 14.

5 Barros, Ryngaert and Wouters 2017, 1.

6 Some authors emphasize on a lack of practice of international organizations; see Vincent-Joël Proulx, 'An Uneasy Transition? Linkages between the Law of State Responsibility and the Law Governing the Responsibility of International Organizations', in Maurizio Ragazzi (ed), *Responsibility of International Organizations: Essays in Memory of Sir Ian Brownlie*

organizations and states, some members of the ILC were sceptical about over-reliance on the ARSIWA framework as a template for the ARIO.[7]

This book does not aim at providing an evaluation of the ILC's rules of responsibility of international organizations in toto. This chapter's more limited purpose is to address one central, contested issue – namely which law governs the complex question of delimitation of responsibility in a multilayered structure where sovereignty is shared among separate legal entities. While the purpose of the current discussion is to shed light on the EU's international responsibility, findings of this chapter are relevant to other international organizations as well.

Section 2.2 will define the concept of 'act of an organization'. Section 2.3 will analyse the subject matter of the ILC's draft rules of responsibility of an international body in order to assess whether these rules govern the delimitation of responsibility according to the internal structure of the organization. It will be suggested that the division of powers and an institutional structure of an organization – questions central to the concept of an act of an organization – fall outside the scope of the ARIO subject matter. Section 2.4 will suggest that the rules of the organization should be taken into consideration for the distribution of responsibility among the EU and its Member States.

2.2 THE ILC FRAMEWORK – (IN)SUFFICIENT?

The crux of the debate as to whether the ARIO takes sufficient regard of the differences of various international organizations lies in the essential difference between states and international organizations. While states are unitary subjects of international law with general competencies, international organizations are not. Remarks by ILC member Pambou-Tchivounda on the ARIO project provide one of the many examples of this approach. According to him, international organizations differ from states in the manner in which they were established, their areas of competence and the degree of their powers, but especially by virtue of their means of implementing their policies as set out in the rules of organization.[8] As will be explained in the following section, these

(Martinus N, Martinus Nijhoff Publishers 2013); José Manuel Cortés Martín, 'European Exceptionalism in International Law? The European Union and the System of International Responsibility', in Maurizio Ragazzi (ed), *Responsibility of International Organizations: Essays in Memory of Sir Ian Brownlie* (Martinus Nijhoff Publishers 2013).

7 For example, see comments by Mr Matheson, Summary Record of the 2800th Meeting, A/CN.4/SR.2800 (ILC 2004), 69, para 17.

8 Summary Record of the 2801st Meeting, A/CN.4/SR.2801 (ILC 2004), 75, para 21.

aspects are important to the question of international responsibility, in particular to the application of the rules of attribution.

Responsibility of states is governed by the principle of unity which requires that actions or omissions of every individual or collective member of the state machinery be treated in the same way as actions or omissions of the state at the international level.[9] According to Crawford, for ARSIWA, separate personality of territorial units does not prevent their actions from being attributed to a state.[10] Accordingly, the ARSIWA is not preoccupied with determining the exact position of an organ in a state's institutional structure. Crawford's predecessor Ago considered the discussions on the exact delimitation of powers of state organs to be pointless because, irrespective of the conclusion, the conduct will still be attributed to the state.[11] States possess general capacity and so conduct which can be characterized as governmental will, in most cases, be treated as state conduct. In practice, what becomes decisive is not the title or place of the organ in the state's institutional structure but whether or not that conduct breached one of the state's obligations.[12] For example, when we deal with the state's failure to ensure law and order, our purpose is not to determine attribution of such conduct to the state's law enforcement officers. We are rather seeking to determine omission, the result of which could have been produced by any other organ of the state.

Since the ARSIWA is not concerned with the internal institutional structures of a state, the question whether an individual in question is in fact an organ of the state becomes less important. Precisely because states are unitary entities, determining who is an organ of a state has not caused too much debate in the ARSIWA context. As a general rule, municipal law is not binding under international law. However, international law considers the status of an international organization's organ as a fact because there is no intention on the part of international law to insert into the state machinery 'organs' which the state itself has not designated as such.[13] Commonly, attribution to the state is established whenever the conduct in question breaches one of the state's international obligations. Of course, an individual who carried out the

[9] First Report on State Responsibility, by Mr James Crawford, Special Rapporteur (ILC 1998), 38, para 188.

[10] Crawford First Report, 38, para 188.

[11] Third Report on State Responsibility, by Mr Roberto Ago, Special Rapporteur, the Internationally Wrongful Act of the State, Source of International Responsibility (ILC 1971), para 142.

[12] Ago Third Report, para 161. Ago suggested that '[t]he sole criterion in this matter is that the organ must be engaged, through its functions in an activity in which it can enter the field of an international obligation of the State, and possibly obligation by its conduct'.

[13] Ago Third Report, para 119.

conduct in question must be part of the state's machinery – or otherwise related to it as discussed in other rules of attribution – but that will generally be the case. The position of such an organ in the distribution of powers and in the internal hierarchy is irrelevant. Ago noted that since the state, as a legal entity, is not physically capable of conduct, it is obvious that all that can be imputed to a state is the act or omission of an individual, whatever its composition may be.[14]

The context when dealing with international organizations is essentially different. Amerasinghe rightly notes that states generally have international responsibility because their duties flow from the control they have over territory, airspace, persons or other, whereas international organizations generally have no control of such elements.[15] The question with respect to international organizations is not only whether an individual has acted in a governmental capacity but also in whose capacity – that of an organization or its member state. To give a fictional example, let us assume that the EU and its Member State X have both signed an international treaty obliging not to discriminate against foreign workers. The EU adopts a directive which calls on Member States to implement legislation regarding retirement plans for foreign workers and provides Member States with alternatives, some of which are discriminatory. The Ministry of Social Affairs of the state X adopts the discriminatory policy under the directive. Multiple complex questions arise. Does the Ministry, in implementing legislation of the EU, act as an organ or agent of the State X or of the EU? If the regulation of retirement policies is a competence of the EU, can the implementation of the discriminatory laws be attributed to the State X? Would the reply to this question change if one of the alternatives provided in the directive did not lead to a breach of international obligations but the State X nevertheless chose to adopt the discriminatory option? What if the competence is shared? If the Ministry exceeded the competence, would it amount to an ultra vires act of an organization or turn into a competence of Member States? If Member States have transferred their competence in social affairs to the EU, does State X have an international obligation under the treaty or does the obligation belong to the EU alone? Who is to make reparation for violations of international obligations? Who is to act as respondent in a dispute?

[14] Second Report on State Responsibility, by Roberto Ago, Special Rapporteur – the Origin International Responsibility (1970), A/CN.4/233, para 37.

[15] CF Amerasinghe, *Principles of the Institutional Law of International Organizations* (2nd edn, Cambridge University Press 2005), 239.

These and other questions, which commonly do not arise when dealing with state responsibility, dominate when faced with responsibility of international organizations. I shall return to these questions in Part II. The following sections will first explore whether the ILC rules of international responsibility govern the aforementioned enquiries. It will be argued that allocation of international responsibility falls outside the scope of the ILC framework.

2.3 ATTRIBUTION VERSUS ALLOCATION OF INTERNATIONAL RESPONSIBILITY

The ARIO is based on the rules of responsibility of states because the latter codify general rules of international responsibility. The rationale of Special Rapporteur Gaja was to duplicate aspects that did not call for a different regulation. However, as was suggested earlier, states and international organizations are essentially different subjects of international law. In addition, there is a high degree of variation between international organizations themselves. The *travaux préparatoires* to the ARIO reveal that both international organizations and governments were doubtful that one, almost identical, set of rules will effectively apply to all of these subjects.

One may suggest a counterargument to the aforementioned criticism. Rules of state responsibility do not differentiate between different characteristics of states. Small or big, authoritarian or democratic, presidential or parliamentary – general rules apply to them all as long as they are subjects of international law and are able to bear international obligations. That same single requirement is stated for the application of the rules of responsibility of international organizations.[16] If the ARSIWA provides a codification of the general rules of international responsibility of states irrespective of their institutional structure, why would a different rationale underlie the same exercise only with respect to international organizations?

The debate regarding the (in)sufficiency of the ARIO rules stems from the notion that draft articles govern, or should govern, the allocation of responsibility between international organizations and their member states. There is an expectation that rules of international responsibility must solve the conundrum of dividing responsibility in situations when the conduct in question is somehow related to membership in an organization, a puzzle which has so far

16 ARIO Art 2 defines international organization as an organization 'established by a treaty or other instrument governed by international law and possessing its own international legal personality [. . .]'.

remained unresolved. Some organizations have thus voiced a need for a more nuanced approach to attribution which would reflect the complexity of their institutional set-up. For example, International Criminal Police Organization (INTERPOL) noted that the draft rules should qualify the double-hatted functioning of the national central bureaus which, even though they are generally classified as organs or at least agents of INTERPOL, in some cases act as local law enforcement authorities and thus in such situations do not constitute an act of INTERPOL.[17]

I question this expectation by addressing two points. First, the purpose and subject matter of the rules of attribution is to determine whether an entity *is* internationally responsible. This is different from 'allocation' of responsibility according to the internal structure of an international body. Allocating responsibility is not about determining whether a subject of international law *is* responsible, but rather to establish *which* subject is responsible. Second, one should question whether the ILC framework governs the allocation of international responsibility between an international organization and its member states in the first place. If, for example, a court or tribunal is faced with a case of environmental damage and needs to determine whether an international organization, its member states or both bear responsibility, it would apply the ILC rules of international responsibility to determine whether, first, there exists responsibility of the member states and, second, whether there exists responsibility of the organization. Responsibility is not allocated to the subjects of international law but rather its existence is determined for each subject individually. If elements of international responsibility are present with respect to both, shared responsibility is established.

That does not mean, however, that allocation of responsibility is irrelevant – in order to determine whether X *is* internationally responsible, one first needs to identify X. All that is suggested here is that this latter enquiry falls outside the scope of the ILC draft articles. This point will be explained further by addressing the purpose and subject matter of the ILC rules of attribution.

2.3.1 *The Purpose and Subject Matter of the Rules of Attribution*

For international responsibility to arise, two main elements must be established:[18] (i) there must be an attribution of the wrongful conduct to a state or international organization and (ii) that conduct must constitute

[17] Comments and Observations Received from Governments and International Organizations, A/CN.4/556 (ILC 2005), 38.

[18] ARIO Art 4, ARSIWA Art 2.

a breach of an international obligation of that state or international organization.[19] International responsibility in some cases can be indirect (derived), that is, arise without attribution of conduct but on the basis of attribution of breach, for example, if a state or international organization aids or assists (Article 14), directs and controls (Article 15) or coerces (Article 16) another entity to commit an internationally wrongful act.

Except in cases of indirect responsibility, wrongful conduct must be attributed to a subject of international law for responsibility to arise. The meaning of the word *attribution*, both in legal and common dictionaries, is an act of ascribing a characteristic or quality.[20] If an international legal person has a characteristic provided in the rules of attribution of conduct, the conduct in question will be considered as its own conduct. Thus, the purpose of the rules of attribution is to determine the existence of responsibility of a subject of international law, not to allocate it among several subjects. The process of attribution of conduct (or breach) does not determine the question of allocation of responsibility. The two points regarding the application of the rules of attribution which prove this statement will be addressed.

2.3.2 *Rules of Attribution Apply Only to Separate Legal Persons*

International rules of responsibility apply only with respect to responsibility of subjects of international law with separate legal personality.[21] This is undisputed as it flows logically from the conditions for the existence of international responsibility. If for international responsibility to arise there needs to be a breach by an entity of its international obligation, that entity must be a separate legal person. This is so because only subjects of international law may possess international obligations of their own.[22] Also, if rules of attribution only deal with the consequences of conduct carried out by the organs of such entities, it must be that these rules only deal with

19 Crawford preferred using the 'attribution of conduct to the state under international law' instead of a less informative 'act of the state'; see Crawford First Report, 147. During the early stages of the ARSIWA project Ago used the word *imputation* to refer to what now is 'attribution' of conduct.

20 For example, Bryan Garner's *A Dictionary of Modern Legal Usage* (2nd edn, Oxford University Press 1996) defines attribution as 'the act or an instance of ascribing a characteristic or quality'. Another definition of the verb 'attribute' is to 'accredit with, assign, consider as belonging to'; see William Burton, *Burtons Legal Thesaurus 5th Edition: Over 10,000 Synonyms, Terms, and Expressions Specifically Related to the Legal Profession* (5th edn, McGraw-Hill Education 2013).

21 Gaja First Report, para 15.

22 Gaja First Report, para 15.

separate legal persons – a non-person can have no organs in the sense of the draft articles.[23] The ARIO expressly notes this requirement in Article 2 (a) in its definition of an international organization.

States are generally separate legal persons, and it has been recognized that international organizations can also have this status.[24] However, it is not sufficient for an international organization to simply *have* a status of a separate legal person listed in its constituent documents. What is important is that an international organization, in the exercise of the functions transferred to it by the constituent documents, may be considered as separate from its member states.[25] Otherwise its actions might be considered as actions carried out by the organs of the member states and would be attributed to the latter. In his First Report to the ARIO project, Special Rapporteur Gaja emphasized this point by noting that

> *[f]or an organization to be held potentially responsible it should not only have legal personality and thus some obligation of its own under international law. What is required is also that in the exercise of the relevant functions the organization may be considered as a separate legal entity from its members and that thus the exercise of these functions must be attributed to the organization itself.*[26]

Existence of international personality is a question of fact – an international organization must be sufficiently independent from its member states so that it cannot be regarded as acting as an organ common to the members.[27] Accordingly, for intergovernmental organizations like the EU, it is not enough to point to Article 47 of the Treaty on European Union (TEU) which establishes its legal personality. A further enquiry into whether responsibility in a given situation is allocated to the 'legal person Member State' or the 'legal person the EU' is necessary. The same must be true of other state members of international organizations. These questions relate to the different positions of states in relation to their organizations.[28] These questions will be addressed in

[23] 'Draft Articles on Responsibility of States for Internationally Wrongful Acts, with Commentaries, commentary to Art 57', para 2.

[24] Reparation for Injuries Suffered in the Service of the United Nations (Advisory Opinion) [1949] ICJ Rep 174, para 179.

[25] Gaja First Report, para 27.

[26] Gaja First Report, para 15.

[27] Gaja First Report, para 19.

[28] Wessel and Dekker suggest exploring the question not through the lens of capacity but through the idea that states may have different positions and identities in relation to their international organization; see Wessel RA and Dekker IF, 'Identities of States in International Organizations', in Ana Sofia Barros, Cedric Ryngaert and Jan Wouters

Chapter 3. Suffice it to say now that both an international organization and its member states may have international personality, but they will each have capacity to act only in limited spheres – member states transfer to international organization only so much capacity and what they have transferred, they have lost.

2.3.3 *Rules of Attribution Do Not Govern Allocation of Responsibility*

The second point to be made relates to the subject matter of the rules of attribution. According to Anzilotti, attribution of an act to a state is a process of linking an action or omission to its author.[29] This exercise is necessarily a legal operation that has nothing in common with the link of natural causality because states are fictional categories which act through individuals.[30] Imputation is a process of determining what individual conduct can be attributed to the state for the purposes of responsibility and in what conditions such conduct must have taken place in order for that attribution to be possible.[31] An act so attributed is an 'act of a state'. The same reasoning applies to international organizations.

As a general rule, what is attributed to a state (and an international organization) are the acts of persons or groups of persons who form part of its 'organization', in other words acts of its organs or agents.[32] Acts of various types of individuals who are not part of the official state structure can also lead to attribution to the state, such as persons exercising elements of governmental authority (Article 5 of the ARSIWA) and organs placed at the disposal of the state by another state or international organization (Article 6 of the ARSIWA).

Rules of attribution do not tell us '*whether* an individual is an organ of the state' (or an international organization) but rather deal with the consequences '*if* that individual is an organ' by stating that such conduct is then

(eds), *International Organizations and Member State Responsibility : Critical Perspectives* (Brill Nijhoff 2017).

29 Ago Second Report, para 37. Anzilotti also stressed that the meaning given to the term 'imputability' in international law by no means corresponds to that sometimes attached to it in municipal law, when imputability denotes the state of mind of the agent as a basis for responsibility; see Ago Second Report, para 37.

30 Ago Second Report, para 38.

31 Ago Third Report, para 58.

32 Ago Third Report, para 107. ARIO Art 2 defines 'organ' as any person or entity which has that status in accordance with the rules of the organization. The articles define 'agent' as an official or other person or entity, other than an organ, who is charged by the organization with the carrying out, or helping to carry out, one of its functions, and thus through whom the organization acts.

attributed to the state for the purposes of international responsibility. Ago emphasized that a state machinery is always a fact for the international legal systems and its structures are not 'received' into that system and do not acquire the character of legal structures in it, even if international law takes them into consideration.[33]

The implication of these two points is that the subject matter of the rules of attribution is unrelated to the process of allocation of international responsibility between an organization and its member states. The purpose of the rules of attribution is different – they determine whether a subject of international law *is* internationally responsible. The ILC rules do not touch upon the delimitation of powers and institutional structures of an organization. This latter task must precede the application of the ILC framework. In order to apply the rules of attribution to determine whether an organization *is* in fact responsible in a given situation, one must first delimit the sovereignty of that organization from that of its member states in the exercise of their institutional activities.

The conclusion that ILC rules do not govern allocation of responsibility between an international organization and its members begs a closer look at what exactly is allocation of responsibility.

2.3.4 *The Notion of Allocation of International Responsibility*

If wrongful conduct can only be attributed to separate legal persons, it must be true that at the time of attribution of conduct or breach, a member state and an international organization are already institutionally detached from one another. That is, their conduct is regarded as that of separate entities as if they had no organizational ties (in those types of membership where such ties exist, as is the case in the EU). It seems then that responsibility must somehow be delimited between these interrelated subjects of international law. The purpose of the following discussion is to question whether such basis exists under international law or whether the governing law sits outside international law.

First, there is no general rule of international law which provides for the international responsibility of a state for the obligations of an international organization solely based on its membership in the organization.[34] The Commentary to the ARIO Article 61 clearly states that membership does not

[33] Ago Third Report, para 117.

[34] Rosalyn Higgins, 'The Legal Consequences for Member States of the Non-Fulfilment by International Organizations of Their Obligations toward Third Parties', *Yearbook of the Institute of International Law (Paris), part I (Session of Lisbon, Preparatory works)* (1995), 445: 'there is no general rule of international law whereby States members are, and solely to

as such entail international responsibility for member states when the organization commits an internationally wrongful act. The comments provided by various international organizations to the draft articles also reveal that organizations themselves do not consider member states to be responsible for the wrongful conduct of international organizations. According to the International Labour Organization (ILO), for example, while constituent instruments of certain international organizations do make provisions for the shared responsibility between an organization and its member states, this is not the case of the majority of them and there is no practice to show the existence of such concurrent or subsidiary responsibility.[35]

Other organizations are of a similar opinion.[36] In Chapter 3 of its 2006 report to the General Assembly, the ILC asked states whether members of an international organization that is not responsible for an internationally wrongful act have an obligation to provide compensation to the injured party, should the organization not be in a position to do so.[37] With only a few exceptions, the great majority of states responded negatively.[38] Of course, as noted by the ILO and other organizations, special provisions regarding member state liability can be envisaged in the constituent instruments and treaties, but that would constitute *lex specialis*. For example, charters of international banks often limit the liability of their members and shareholders to the value of their paid-in and payable shares.[39] Some constituent documents provide for member state liability but only *vis-à-vis* the organization itself.[40] A similar internal obligation can be found in Article 216(2) of the Treaty on the Functioning of the European Union (TFEU) which states that international agreements concluded by the Union are binding on the Member States.

their membership, liable concurrently or subsidiarily, for the obligations of an international organization of which they are members'.

35 Comments by ILO; see 'Comments and Observations Received from International Organizations, A/CN.4/568', 148.

36 For example, UNESCO suggested that there is no member state responsibility as such, unless a specific provision exists, Comments A/CN.4/568, 144.

37 Yearbook of International Law Commission, A/CN.4/SER.A/2006/Add 1 (Part 2) (2006), 21, para 28 (a).

38 'Fifth Report on Responsibility of International Organizations, by Mr. Giorgio Gaja, Special Rapporteur', para 27.

39 For example, the Articles of Agreement of the International Bank for Reconstruction and Development (Art II, sect 6), the Bank for International Settlements' Statutes (Art 11) and the Agreement establishing the European Bank of Reconstruction and Development (Art 5, para 7).

40 For example, Art 40(2) of the Convention on the Grant of European Patent.

Like with direct responsibility based on attribution of conduct, there is no general rule of international responsibility which would base indirect responsibility on membership in an organization. According to Gaja, it would be tantamount to denying separate personality of an international organization if responsibility for its conduct would be attributed to a member state because of the roles that a member state may have within the organs of an international organization.[41] In fact, rules of indirect responsibility of a state in connection with an act of an international organization that is listed in Part V of the drafts articles have been added to the ARIO project as an addition to the rules on state responsibility. The ARSIWA only covered indirect responsibility by one state in connection to conduct of another state and left out indirect responsibility for acts of an international organization.[42] Rules of indirect responsibility contained in the ARIO fill this gap. The reasoning behind indirect responsibility of states for conduct of an international organization is identical to the rules of indirect responsibility of the state for acts of another state and so do not relate to membership in an organization. Conditions for indirect responsibility attest to this.

For indirect responsibility to arise, a state must act as a legal person that is separate from the organization.[43] As Gaja noted in his Fourth Report on the ARIO project, the state that aids or assists, directs and controls, or coerces an international organization may or may not be a member state as long as it acts as a separate legal person.[44] For example, when a member state donates money to an international organization for technical assistance, indirect responsibility could arise in case this money is used to carry out a wrongful conduct. For responsibility to arise, a state has to be a member of an organization because only a member can donate funds for technical assistance. However, responsibility, if it were to arise, would in this case be based on the wrongfulness of a donation, not on its membership in the organization. Furthermore, for indirect responsibility to arise it is insufficient that a state simply participates in the decision-making process or day-to-day functioning of an organization according to the rules of that organization.[45] The wrongful acts of a state, and an international organization in this case, are different. As noted by Crawford, despite the nature of the coercion as a form of an

41 Fourth Report on Responsibility of International Organizations, by Mr. Giorgio Gaja, Special Rapporteur (ILC 2006), para 67.

42 Gaja Fourth Report, para 55.

43 Gaja Fourth Report, para 62.

44 Gaja Fourth Report, para 62.

45 Gaja Fourth Report, para 62; Seventh Report on Responsibility of International Organizations, by Mr. Giorgio Gaja, Special Rapporteur (ILC 2009), para 74.

imposition of will on the part of the coercing state, the act of the coerced state remains its own act – an act of coercing and an act committed by a coerced state against a third state are not identical.[46] A further condition is that a state can only be indirectly responsible for acts which would have been wrongful if it had carried out these acts itself.[47]

The ARIO provides for two cases in which a state's responsibility for acts of an international organization is expressly related to its membership. Article 62 states that a state member of an international organization is responsible for the wrongful conduct of that organization if it has accepted that responsibility towards a third party or it has led the injured party to rely on its responsibility.[48] Such responsibility is subsidiary. But here again, responsibility would arise, not based on membership but because of the state's own conduct towards the injured party. No allocation of responsibility takes place – an organization is still responsible for the wrongful conduct in question, and a state carries a separate subsidiary responsibility for the conduct of an organization but that responsibility is based on the state's own acts.

A second case is Article 61 which addresses circumvention of international obligations of a state member of an organization.[49] A member state incurs international responsibility if, by taking advantage of the fact that the organization has competence in relation to the subject matter of one of state's international obligations, it circumvents that obligation by causing an organization to commit an act that, if committed by a state, would have constituted a breach of the obligation. Similar to Article 62, a member state in this case incurs responsibility, not because of its membership but because of its own actions – the taking of disadvantage of a separate legal personality of an organization to avoid compliance with its own obligation.[50]

It is important to distinguish between the secondary rules of responsibility under the draft articles and international obligations set out in the primary

46 Eighth Report on State Responsibility, by Mr Roberto Ago, Special Rapporteur – the Internationally Wrongful Act of the State, Source of International Responsibility (1979) A/CN.4/318 and Add.1–4, para 205. Ago was of a somewhat different position – he suggested that there is no parallel responsibility. According to Ago, indirect responsibility assumed by one state for an internationally wrongful act of another state replaces the responsibility of that other state and is not additional to it; see Ago Eighth Report, para 45.

47 Second Report on State Responsibility, by Mr James Crawford, Special Rapporteur (ILC 1999), para 202.

48 Assumption of responsibility as the basis for indirect responsibility was discussed during the early stages of the ARSIWA project; see Ago Eighth Report, para 44. According to Ago, a state is free to assume responsibility for the conduct of another state which serves as a kind of treaty guarantee towards third states.

49 Circumvention by a member state will be addressed in Chapter 3.

50 Gaja Fourth Report, para 117.

rules.[51] Primary rules, which are not covered by the ARIO, can and do state obligations for members of international organizations. That, however, is different from attribution of direct or indirect responsibility. To provide a simple example, let us assume that under the rules of organization X, its Member State Y has an obligation to provide technical assistance to that organization.[52] If the state Y fails to provide assistance its responsibility will be invoked, not because state Y is a member of organization X but because the breach of the primary rule will be attributed to it.[53]

It must thus be concluded that the purpose of the rules of international responsibility is to determine whether a subject of international law *is* internationally responsible. The draft articles only deal with persons whose sovereignty has been delimited from that of other persons within a multilayered structure. Rules of attribution do not govern delimitation of powers in the internal structure of the organization, a task which must precede the application of the rules of attribution. Furthermore, there is no general rule of international responsibility under which responsibility would arise solely on the basis of membership in an international organization. The absence of such rules does not, of course, prevent the inclusion of provisions in the *lex specialis*, such as constituent documents or headquarters agreements. Under the general rules of international responsibility codified by the ILC a member state can be held indirectly responsible for the conduct of an international organization, but in each case its responsibility would arise not because it is a member of an organization but because of its own conduct.

If allocation of responsibility must precede the application of the ILC framework, what governs this primary enquiry? I suggest looking at the rules of organization.

2.4 THE RULES OF ORGANIZATION

The fact that the ARIO does not govern the delimitation of powers and institutional structures within the internal order of an international

[51] Ago Second Report, para 7.

[52] There is a debate in the ILC whether breach of obligations under the rules of organization should be covered by the articles. It is clear from the comments of the international organizations that the status of the rules of organization is controversial; see Comments A/CN.4/568. It has been agreed that the status of the rules of organization (internal as opposed to international) depends on the rules themselves; see Third Report on Responsibility of International Organizations, by Mr. Giorgio Gaja, Special Rapporteur (2005) A/CN.4/553, paras 18–24.

[53] For more discussion on this, see Second Report on Responsibility of International Organizations, by Mr. Giorgio Gaja, Special Rapporteur (2004) A/CN.4/541, paras 15–18.

organization does not mean, however, that this question is moot.[54] In the context of international organizations where separate legal persons exercise shared sovereignty in a common institutional structure, some other rules outside the draft articles must identify which of these persons will be the object of the ILC draft rules of international responsibility. In other words, some other rules must trigger the application of the ILC framework.

It can be seen from the comments to the ARIO that there is a general consensus among governments and international organizations that general rules of attribution should provide reference to the rules of organization.[55] Representatives of the Democratic Republic of the Congo, for example, noted the principle of specialty governing international organizations and claimed the need for reference to the rules of organizations.[56] The EC in turn suggested that the rules of organization define the powers and the scope of the 'organs' or 'institutions' of an international organization and of its officials or persons acting on its behalf.[57] According to the EC, reference to these rules are necessary for ensuring that an international organization, as a subject of international law, shall be held responsible for the conduct of all its organs, instrumentalities and officials which form part of the organization and act in that capacity.[58] The EC affirmed that the rules of organization are important for the attribution of a specific conduct to the international organization.[59] It seems thus that rules of organization must be considered before the application of the ILC rules of attribution – they delimit the powers between an organization and its member states regarding the conduct in question and determine which of them is the proper subject of international law for the application of the draft articles.

Gaja also recognized the importance of the rules of organization. According to him, institutional rules are likely to affect, to a certain extent,

54 In its comments to ARIO, Italy provides a helpful account of domestic case law which reveals the problem of identifying the organs of an international organization; see Comments and Observations Received from Governments, A/CN.4/547 (ILC 2004), 25. In ft 20 Italy referred to *Cristiani* v. *Istituto italolatino-americano*, the Court of Cassation held that the organs of an international organization which is endowed with international legal personality are to be distinguished for legal purposes from the organs of Member States, and at the same time they cannot be equated with joint organs of the Member States.

55 Comments and Observations Received from International Organizations, A/CN.4/545 (ILC 2004), paras 26–27, the International Atomic Agency, the IMF, the UN Secretariat, the WHO and other organizations unanimously suggested that the general rules of attribution should contain a reference to the rules of the organization.

56 Comments A/CN.4/556, 46.

57 Comments by the EC, see Comments A/CN.4/545, 26, para 1.

58 See EC's comments, Comments A/CN.4/545, 26, para 1.

59 Comments A/CN.4/545, 26, para 1.

the application of the rules of international responsibility in the relations between an international organization and its members.[60] Paragraph 2 of the general rule of attribution under Article 6 expressly states that the rules of organization apply in the determination of the functions of its organs and agents. In addition, Article 65 of the draft articles states that the applicable rules of international law continue to govern questions concerning the responsibility of an international organization or a state for an internationally wrongful act to the extent that they are not regulated by these draft articles. Rules of organization for the purposes of the application of the rules of attribution are to be defined in the broad sense, including practice of the organization.[61]

To briefly note for the purpose of clarity, there is some confusion among organizations regarding the status of the rules of organization in the context of international responsibility. A majority of international organizations consider that the rules of organizations are *lex specialis* in relation to the ILC draft articles.[62] For example, the International Monetary Fund (IMF) remarked that the rules of organizations are *lex specialis* under international law in determining obligations of international organizations.[63]

Two misunderstandings are inherent in this approach. First, as has been stressed elsewhere in this chapter, the ILC draft articles are secondary norms, whereas obligations are governed by primary rules.[64] Second, the ILC rules do not govern delimitation of powers within the organization. Therefore, in both cases rules of organization are not *lex specialis* to the draft articles because they govern questions falling outside the subject matter of the ARIO. This is of course not to say that the rules of organizations cannot be *lex specialis* in relation to the ARIO. The rules of organization would gain special status in relation to the draft articles if they were to set out special rules of international responsibility, for example, limited responsibility for

[60] Gaja Seventh Report, para 123.

[61] For example, according to the WHO, the role of the practice of the organization in the delimitation or specification of attribution cannot be ignored and should be given forma status through inclusion in the concept of 'rules of the organization'; see Comments A/CN.4/545, 27. The EC suggested that the concept of rules of organization should encompass court rulings, for example the CJEU's case law which offers guidelines on the apportionment of responsibility as between the EC and its Member States; see Comments A/CN.4/545, 27, para 3.

[62] Comments A/CN.4/637, 9.

[63] Comments by the IMF; see Comments A/CN.4/582, 21.

[64] This point has been acknowledged by the World Bank, which noted that the articles should expressly state that they do not cover the content of obligations which is governed by the primary rules; see Comments A/CN.4/637, 14, paras 1–2.

a wrongful act carried out by the organs of the member states to the share of financial contribution.[65]

In addition, if rules of organization regulate obligations *vis-à-vis* third parties, they are undoubtedly part of international law. Article 6 of the 1982 draft articles on the law of treaties between states and international organizations or between international organizations provides that the capacity of an international organization to conclude treaties is governed by the relevant rules of that organization. If, on the other hand, they relate to issues of a purely internal nature, such as staff regulations, they are internal rules of the organization, similar to the domestic law of a state. It is clear that the status of the rules of organizations is dynamic and depends on the nature of the question they regulate. As to the issues we are concerned with here, that is, the delimitation of powers between international organizations and member states for the purposes of the application of international rules of attribution, internal rules serve as a fact. However, rules of organizations are *res inter alios acta* and therefore cannot as such be asserted against third parties.[66] The distinction between the internal and external application of the rules of organization rests on whether the rule in question touches upon the rights of third parties.[67]

I leave aside the question of whether internal allocation of responsibility for joint international obligations should have been governed by the ILC's draft articles.[68] My conclusion is limited, namely, that the ILC framework does not govern the delimitation of international responsibility within the EU. I suggest looking for answers in the rules of organization and dispute-settlement practice in which these rules are applied.[69]

65 For example, under the IMF rules, Member States' responsibility to third parties is limited to the amount of the financial contribution or guarantees of those Member States, similarly to corporate shareholders' liability; see Comments A/CN.4/545, 24 para 3.

66 In this regard, Gaja distinguishes between obligations towards Member States and obligations towards third parties. According to him, in relations with non-members, the rules of organization are like internal law of the state; see Gaja Fifth Report, para 33.

67 The IMF argued that 'the law of obligations cannot validly make a distinction between obligations resulting from external engagements and obligations resulting from the internal rules of the organization. Rather, it would seem that the responsibility will be determined by the substance of the obligation that is breached. If the purpose of the obligation is to protect the subjective rights of third parties, the consequences of breaches cannot be governed by anything other than the law of responsibility for acts that are wrongful under international law'; see 'Comments and Observations Received from Governments and International Organizations, A/CN.4/556', 46.

68 Comments A/CN.4/568, 127. For the position of the EU, see Comments A/CN.4/556, 43.

69 For example, as noted by the North Atlantic Treaty Organization, it may be that the fundamental rule governing the functioning of the organization – that of consensus decision-making – is to be found neither in the treaties establishing NATO nor in any other

2.5 CONCLUSION

A closer look at the rules of attribution under the draft articles reveals that the purpose of the ILC framework is to determine whether a subject of international law *is* responsible for a violation of an international obligation. These rules do not regulate allocation of international responsibility between an organization and its member states. In fact, as this chapter reveals, there are no general rules of responsibility which call for a direct or indirect responsibility based solely on a membership in an international body.

This chapter suggests examining whether rules of organization determine allocation of responsibility. It is noted that rules of organization are *res inter alios acta*, and it is therefore necessary to also examine how they are interpreted by international courts and tribunals.

Chapter 3 will thus look into the EU rules of organization for the delimitation of international responsibility. The European Commission's argument for competence-based responsibility will be explained. The chapter will then provide an in-depth analysis of dispute-settlement practice to test whether and how these rules are applied in practice in relation to third parties. The case law reveals that competence-based responsibility is not reflected in dispute-settlement practice. Instead, it will be argued that the EU and its Member States are independently responsible for their joint obligations, irrespective of their internal division of competences.

formal rules and is rather the result of the practice of the organization, Comments A/CN.4/637, 40.

3

Independent Responsibility of the EU and Its Member States

3.1 INTRODUCTION

Chapter 2 took a closer look at the rules of attribution under the Articles on the Responsibility of International Organizations (ARIO). It was suggested that the purpose of the draft articles is to determine whether a subject of international law *is* internationally responsible for breach of international obligations. The rules deal with organizations as separate legal persons, the shared sovereignty of which has already been delimited from that of its member states. The chapter further suggested looking at the rules of organization and international dispute-settlement practice for guidance on how to allocate international responsibility between an organization and its member states. The questions of the allocation of responsibility within an international body fall outside the scope of the International Law Commission (ILC) framework.

This chapter will explore the European Union (EU) rules for allocation of international responsibility between the EU and its Member States. Section 3.2 will address the competence-based approach to responsibility under EU law. It will then be argued in Section 3.3 that international dispute-settlement practice does not support this position. It is so, because competence-based responsibility calls for the transfer of international obligations within an internal legal order, which is not recognized under international law. Organizations and their members are individually responsible for their own conduct. The rule of non-circumvention prevents states and organizations from arbitrarily transferring their joint obligations in accordance with their internal division of powers.

3.2 COMPETENCE-BASED INTERNATIONAL RESPONSIBILITY

The functioning of the EU is based on the principle of conferral in accordance to which competences not conferred upon the Union in the Treaties remain with the Member States.[1] The Treaty of Lisbon introduced categories of competences, listing areas of exclusive EU competence which prevent Member States' action (e.g. trade),[2] competences shared with Member States (e.g. environment and transport)[3] and supporting, coordinating and supplementing competences (e.g. culture and tourism). Article 216 of the Treaty on the Functioning of the European Union (TFEU) establishes the power of the EU to conclude international agreements. Article 3(2) provides that the Union enjoys treaty-making powers not only with respect to expressly listed exclusive competences but also because it has implied exclusive treaty-making powers.[4] An in-depth analysis of the confusing and intertwined web of EU/Member States competences is beyond the scope of this book. Suffice it to say that Delgado Casteleiro is right to suggest that because of the complex competence system of the EU, it is almost impossible to link the EU's responsibility to its division of competences.[5]

Nevertheless, the European Commission has on a number of occasions expressed its position that under the internal rules of the EU, the Union and its Member States each assume international responsibility with respect to their own competences.[6] In its comments on the ARIO, the European Commission emphasized that the EU is regulated by a legal order of its own, establishing a common market and organizing the legal relationship between its members.[7] Responsibility is to follow the division of competences between the EU and its Member States rather than be based on the attribution of conduct. That is, the EU would bear exclusive responsibility in areas of its exclusive competences, whereas responsibility would be shared in areas of shared competences. For example, even though Member States carry out tariff classifications, the EU is responsible for breach of relevant international obligations since it holds exclusive competence with respect to the customs union.[8]

1 Opinion 2/94 *Accession of the Community to the European Human Rights Convention* [1996] ECR I-1759, para 23.
2 Art 5 TFEU.
3 Art 4 TFEU.
4 Art 3(2) TFEU codifies the ECJ's case law on implied exclusive treaty-making powers. The so-called AETR (Accord Européen sur les Transports Routiers) doctrine establishes implied competences if the conclusion of the agreement in question 'may affect common rules or alter their scope'.
5 Andrés Delgado Casteleiro, *The International Responsibility of the European Union: From Competence to Normative Control* (Cambridge University Press 2016), 30.
6 Comments A/CN.4/545, 21, para 3.
7 Comments A/CN.4/545, 21, para 4.
8 Comments A/CN.4/545, 26, para 4.

The European Commission's support for competence-based responsibility is evident from its statements in international disputes, for example, in the World Trade Organization (WTO). Both the EU and its Member States are parties to the WTO Agreements. In *EC – Computer Equipment*, the European Commission took the view that the actions of customs authorities should be attributed to the Union and emphasized its readiness to assume responsibility for all measures within the particular field of tariff concessions, whether they are taken at the EU or the Member State level.[9] The European Commission declared that it was ready to assume (the entire) international responsibility on its own for all measures in the area of tariff concessions because it was exclusively competent for the subject matter concerned.[10] The European Commission used strong language to respond to the claimants' rebuttal that the internal division of competences is irrelevant with respect to the distribution of international responsibility.[11] It responded that '*the transfer of sovereignty had been recognized by Members, and that the EC was more than a simple customs union. The EC was ready to assume its international obligations, but was not ready to allow an attack on its constitution in the WTO*'.[12]

Similarly, in *EC – Geographical Indications*, the European Commission suggested that the United States was right in bringing the claim against the Union since the subject matter of the dispute fell within the exclusive competence of the EU.[13] In *EC and Certain Member States – IT Products*, the European Commission sought to assume full responsibility and stand as the sole respondent in proceedings because of its exclusive competence

9 Oral pleadings of the European Commission at the second substantive meeting of the panel, 10 July 1997, para 6. See also 'Replies to the Question' posed during the first substantive meeting of the panel, 20 June 1997, in particular reply to question 1 of the WTO Panel Report, *European Communities – Computer Equipment*, WT/DS62/R, WT/DS67/R, WT/DS68/R, adopted 22 June 1998 (*EC – Computer Equipment*); see also Oral pleadings, paras 4 and 11.

10 Comments A/CN.4/637, 24, comment to Art 8.

11 WTO Panel Report, *EC – Computer Equipment*, para 4.13, the United States claimed that 'Moreover, the Commission appeared to suggest that a transfer of sovereignty within the internal legal framework of the EC had resulted in fewer rights and obligations being allotted to the member States. That might be the case in the internal legal framework of the Communities, but that framework was not at issue in this dispute. What was at issue were the WTO rights of the United States and the WTO obligations of the EC, Ireland and the United Kingdom'.

12 *EC – Computer Equipment*, PR, para 4.15.

13 *EC – Protection of Trademarks and Geographical Indications for Agricultural Products and Foodstuffs* (*EC – Geographical Indications*) WT/DS174, PR adopted 15 March 2005. First written submission of the European Communities, 25 May 2004, Annex B-2, B-69, para 255.

with respect to all tariff matters.[14] Similarly, in *EC – Large Civil Aircraft*, a case which concerned subsidy measures for civil aircraft, the European Commission claimed to be the sole respondent in the dispute[15] and stressed that it was not 'representing' its Member States but rather 'takes full responsibility' for their actions.[16] An analogous internal law-based approach of the European Commission to assume international responsibility in disputes regarding measures which fall under its competences was expressed in *EC – Commercial Vessels* which concerned the legality of subsidies.[17]

Similar to its stance in WTO dispute-settlement proceedings, the European Commission calls for competence-based responsibility in disputes under the Energy Charter Treaty (ECT). Like the WTO Agreements, the ECT is also silent on the division of competences between the EU and its Member States. However, with its accession to the ECT the European Commission did provide a declaration which calls for a competence-based approach to responsibility by stating that '*The European Communities and their Member States have both concluded the Energy Charter Treaty and are thus internationally responsible for the fulfilment of the obligations contained therein, in accordance with their respective competences*'.[18] For example, in its written statement in *Electrabel* v. *Hungary*, an ICSID (International Centre for Settlement of Investment Disputes) arbitration concerning Hungary's termination of power purchase agreement, the European Commission stated that the Union and Member States were responsible for breaches of the ECT '*in accordance with their respective competences*'.[19] The European Commission submitted that responsibility for preventing unlawful state aid lies with the EU and not with Member States, and therefore Spain is the wrong party named by the claimant for the termination of power purchase agreement.[20] According to the European Commission, the

[14] Letter from the Delegation of the European Commission, 4 February 2009, reproduced in *EC and Certain Member States – IT Products*, WT/DS375/R, WT/DS376/R, WT/DS377/R, PR adopted 21 September 2010 (*EC and Certain Member States – IT Products*), 49, para 7.80.

[15] *EC – Measures Affecting Trade in Large Civil Aircraft*, WT/DS316/R, PR adopted 30 June 2010, Letter of the EC dated 23 May 2008 (*EC – Large Civil Aircraft*).

[16] *EC – Large Civil Aircraft*, Letter of the European Communities dated 6 October 2005.

[17] *Commercial Vessels*, WT/DS301/R, First submission of the EC, para 93, see *European Communities – Measures Affecting Trade in Commercial Vessels*, WT/DS301/R, PR adopted 22 April 2005 (*EC – Commercial Vessels*).

[18] Statement submitted by the EC to the Secretariat of the ECT pursuant to Art 26 (3) (b) (ii) of the ECT, OJL 336, 23 December 1994, 115.

[19] *Electrabel S.A.* v. *Republic of Hungary, Decision on Jurisdiction, Applicable Law and Liability* (Decision on Jurisdiction, Applicable Law and Liability, 30 November 2012) ICSID Case No. ARB/07/19 (*Electrabel* v. *Hungary*), para 3.18.

[20] *Electrabel* v. *Hungary*, European Commission's Submission, para 41, as reproduced in Decision on jurisdiction, para 4.170.

Communities and the Member States could, if necessary, determine among themselves who is the respondent party to arbitration proceedings.[21]

Thus, under the Union's internal rules international responsibility is to follow the division of competences between the EU and its Member States. But does international law accept such, to use Delgado Casteleiro's phrase, 'Europeanization' of an international agreement which entails the expansion of EU constitutional principles to that agreement?[22] The following section argues that the Union's internal rules on international responsibility are incompatible with the principle of independent responsibility and are not supported by international dispute-settlement practice.

3.3 THE NON-TRANSFERABILITY OF INTERNATIONAL OBLIGATIONS

The European Commission's call for competence-based responsibility relates international responsibility to the Union's constitutional architecture. The transfer of competences from a Member State to the Union, as understood by the European Commission, has the effect of transferring the respective international obligations.

This position ignores a disconnect under international law between the transfer of powers by a state to an international body and the transfer of obligations. It is argued that while states are free to create international organizations for the latter to carry some of their functions, the corresponding obligations are non-transferable.[23] In other words, when a state assumes international obligations, these obligations remain the responsibility of that state even if the state later transfers these respective sovereign powers to an international body. States can only shift their powers, not their international obligations. The conclusion is the same irrespective of whether an international organization has also assumed that same obligation. Separateness of the legal personality of an international organization stipulates that it can only have responsibilities which it has itself assumed. Thus, international law tolerates an arrangement where a state has obligations in a certain field of activity, but the power to act in that field is no longer within that state's autonomy. It is for states to ensure that they do not breach their obligations, whether they act on their own or through an international body.

21 *Electrabel* v. *Hungary*, Decision on Jurisdiction, para 3.18.

22 Delgado Casteleiro 2016, 41.

23 The book does not cover questions of transfer of obligations arising out of state succession and other cases and is limited to issues arising out of relationships between international organizations and their Member States.

This section considers the non-transferability of international obligations by addressing two rules of international law. First, the rule of non-circumvention shows that states and international organizations cannot escape their international obligations by acting indirectly through another entity. Second, unless expressly provided otherwise, both international organizations and their members are subject to all obligations under international treaties they sign (such as in the case of mixed agreements signed and ratified by both the EU and its Member States), irrespective of the internal division of competences and limits of their autonomy. I refer to such obligations as joint obligations.[24]

3.3.1 *The Rule of Non-circumvention*

The problem of circumvention of international obligations arises when subjects of international law breach their obligations but do so through the conduct of another legal person. Such a situation may arise when states establish international organizations to which they transfer part of their sovereign powers. A two-way route for circumvention of obligations may open. States may acquire certain international obligations with regard to some of their functions and then transfer those functions to an international body which is itself free of associated obligations. An international organization, in turn, may acquire international obligations and then bind members to implement decision which can result in a breach of those obligations.

The problem of circumvention of international obligations thus arises when the entity which is empowered to act in a certain field of activity does so without breaching one of its international obligations. Special Rapporteur for the ARIO Gaja initially considered addressing this issue in the ARIO Article 15 which governs a situation when an international organization directs and controls a state in the commission of an internationally wrongful act. Such an approach, however, appeared to be problematic.[25] For Article 15 to apply, the definition of control would have to cover normative control, which was rejected by the drafters of an analogous provision of the Articles on Responsibility of States for Internationally Wrongful Acts (ARSIWA)[26] and

[24] See, for example, Joni Heliskoski, *Mixed Agreements as a Technique for Organizing the International Relations of the European Community and Its Member States* (Kluwer Law International 2001); Allan Rosas, 'Mixed Union – Mixed Agreements', in Allan Rosas and Martti Koskenniemi (eds), *International Law Aspects of the European Union* (Kluwer Law International, 1998), 142.

[25] Gaja Third Report, 35.

[26] Yearbook of the International Law Commission, A/CN.4/SER.A/2001/Add.1 (Part 2), 69, para 7.

was also seen as too complex to define by the ILC itself.[27] An additional limitation of Article 15 was that both the controlling organization and the controlled state must be bound by the same international obligation, which does not solve the problem of circumvention.[28]

Gaja noted the need to address the problem of circumvention in a separate provision.[29] Subject to criticism of some international organizations,[30] the ARIO Article 17 provides that international organizations should be held responsible if an act that would be wrongful if committed by the organization directly was in fact committed by a Member State on the basis of the organization's binding decision.[31] Support was also expressed for the current Article 61 which governs a reverse situation when a state that is a member of an international organization uses the separate personality of that organization to carry out conduct which breaches one of its obligations.[32] In his Fourth Report Gaja noted that while the practical relevance of this case depends on the fact that the organization is not bound by the obligation, it is certainly not a requirement.[33] Though enshrined in separate provisions, the two rules are intertwined and embody the principle of non-circumvention which governs a circular relationship: a member state transfers competences to an international organization, which, in the exercise of those competences, makes binding decisions on that member state. The purpose is to avoid double circumvention of obligations. On the one hand, it prevents states from shielding themselves from their responsibilities by transferring their competences to an international body. On the other hand, it also prevents the latter from escaping responsibility for obligations it has assumed when it 'outsources' wrongful conduct back to its members. The core premise is that states and

27 Comments A/CN.4/568, 135. The EC illustrates the difficulty of defining normative control by describing its legal instruments (directives and regulations).

28 Gaja Third Report, 36.

29 Gaja noted that the fact of being able to require Member States to take a certain act would otherwise put the organization in a position to achieve indirectly what is directly prohibited, Gaja Third Report, 36.

30 For example, the IMF suggesting deleting the rule from the articles altogether, Comments A/CN.4/582, 23, sect I. See also comments by the International Criminal Police Organization, see Comments A/CN.4/556, 50, sect N.2.

31 The Commentary to ARIO Art 17 states that the term 'circumvention' implies an intention on the part of the international organization to take advantage of the separate legal personality of its members in order to avoid compliance with an international obligation. Delgado Casteleiro suggests that the complexity of proving intent makes the provision hardly applicable with respect to the EU; see Delgado Casteleiro 2016.

32 For example, Ireland – 13th meeting, para 33; Switzerland: 13th meeting, para 45, see A/C.6/60/SR.13.

33 Gaja Fourth Report, para 74.

international organizations, being separate legal persons, assume obligations of their own and should be prevented from escaping those obligations by relocating competences or conduct to another body.

In its comments on the ARIO, the European Commission expressed its reservation regarding the current Article 17, especially in cases when responsibility of an organization is interpreted to arise out of recommendations made to the states.[34] It is unclear why the EU opposes the rule while at the same time it promotes an even broader principle of competence-based responsibility. After all, with respect to the EU's responsibility both principles would essentially have the same effect: non-circumvention and competence-based responsibility suggest that if, in the exercise of its competences, the EU assumes an obligation, it must be held responsible when it breaches that obligation, be it through its own actions or those of its Member States. The European Commission's negative reception of the reverse case – responsibility of state members of an international organization under Article 61 – is less surprising. Its call for the competence-based responsibility eliminates the possibility of holding Member States responsible for any conduct in the areas of the Union competences, while Article 61 would prevent such arrangement by tying Member States to their obligations even when they transfer respective powers to an international body.[35]

3.3.2 *The ECtHR Case Law*

Whether consistent or not with the Union's internal legal order, the principle of non-circumvention is applicable law. The case law of the European Court on Human Rights (ECtHR) supports the principle[36] of

34 Comments A/CN.4/637, 28.

35 The ILO expressed concern that under the rule 'the mere fact of adopting a decision binding on a member State of international organization to commit an act of the wrongful nature described, without the act actually being taken on the part of the member State'; see Comments A/CN.4/568, 136. Similar concern was expressed by the European Commission; see Comments A/CN.4/582, 25, sect S. For more comments by the European Commission on the rule of non-circumvention, see Comments A/CN.4/568, 135. A similar concern was expressed by the IMF: 'This proposition suggests that the act of taking a binding decision alone constitutes wrongful conduct. [...] As such, this proposition is inconsistent with the fundamental principle that there must be conduct constituting breach of an international obligation for responsibility to arise', see Comments A/CN.4/582, 23, sect I. This interpretation, however, conflates the difference between the primary and secondary rules. The responsibility in this case arises not because of the act of 'circumvention' as such, which would be subject to regulation by primary rules, but because of an indirect breach of an obligation which an organization owns.

36 I refer to non-circumvention as a 'principle' rather than 'rule' because I have not found a direct reference to ILC articles which establish the rule of non-circumvention in the discussed case law.

non-circumvention.[37] In *Waite & Kennedy*, the Court refused to absolve states from their obligations under the Convention Protection of Human Rights and Fundamental Freedoms (ECHR) when they transfer their competences to an international organization.[38] The case concerned employment rights of two German citizens who performed services to the European Space Agency at the European Space Operations Centre in Germany. Arguing that they were in an employment relationship with the Agency, they brought the Agency before the German courts for the termination of their employment contract. The European Space Agency claimed immunity from jurisdiction, which the Federal Constitutional Court upheld. The applicants subsequently brought the case before the ECtHR. Though the Court finally rejected the applicants' claims, it nevertheless stated the principle of non-circumvention:

> *The Court is of the opinion that where States establish international organizations in order to pursue or strengthen their cooperation in certain fields of activities, and where they attribute to these organizations certain competences and accord them immunities, there may be implications as to the protection of fundamental rights. It would be incompatible with the purpose and object of the Convention, however, if the Contracting States were thereby absolved from their responsibility under the Convention in relation to the field of activity covered by such attribution.*[39]

The Court restated the principle in another case under analogous circumstances, *Beer and Regan* v. *Germany*.[40]

Matthews v. *the United Kingdom* is another seminal ECtHR case on the principle of non-circumvention.[41] The dispute concerned the right of the

37 It should be noted that the case law mainly concerns responsibility of the Member States and is silent on the responsibility of the EU, since only Member States, and not the Union, are parties to the ECHR. Even as a holder of transferred power, an organization is not itself held responsible under the ECHR for the decisions of its organs, as long as it is not a Contracting Party; see Gaja Third Report, 14, para 33. See also *Matthews* v. *United Kingdom* App no 24833/94 (ECtHR 18 February 1999) (*Matthews* v. *the United Kingdom*), para 32; *M. & Co.* v. *the Federal Republic of Germany* App no 13258/87 (ECtHR 9 February 1990) (*M. & Co.* v. *Germany*); *Confédération française démocratique du travail* v. *the European Communities* App no 8030/77 (Commission decision 10 July 1978); *Dufay* v *European Communities* App no 13539/88 (Commission decision 19 January 1989).

38 *Waite & Kennedy* App no 26083/94 (ECtHR 18 February 1999) (*Waite & Kennedy*).

39 *Waite & Kennedy*, para 67.

40 *Beer and Regan* v. *Germany* App no 28934/95 (ECtHR 18 February 1999), 78, para 55.

41 *Matthews* v. *the United Kingdom*, see Ana Sofia Barros, '6 Responsibility, 6.3 Matthews v. United Kingdom, ECtHR, App. no 24833/94, 18 February 1999', in Cedric Ryngaert and others (eds), *Judicial Decisions on the Law of International Organizations* (Oxford University Press 2016).

Gibraltar citizen to vote at the elections to the European Parliament. The United Kingdom argued that it cannot be held responsible under the Convention for the lack of elections to the European Parliament in Gibraltar because the claim concerned elections to a constitutional organ of the Community itself over which the United Kingdom had no control. The ECtHR observed that the Convention does not exclude the transfer of competences to international organizations, provided that Convention rights continue to be 'secured'. Member states' responsibility therefore continues even after such transfer.[42] The fact that the United Kingdom may not have effective control over the conduct under examination was irrelevant in the determination of its responsibility.[43]

T.I. v. *the United Kingdom* provides yet another example of the ECtHR's affirmation of the principle of non-circumvention of international obligations. The case concerned an allegation that the United Kingdom violated Article 3 of the Convention by ordering the removal of the applicant to Germany from where he may be sent to Sri Lanka and be exposed to torture.[44] The United Kingdom based its decision on the Dublin Convention concerning the attribution of responsibility between European countries for deciding asylum claims. The Court noted that the United Kingdom cannot rely automatically on the arrangement under the Dublin Convention. According to the Court, where states establish international organizations, or *mutatis mutandis* international agreements, to pursue cooperation in certain fields of activities, there may be implications for the protection of fundamental rights. The ECtHR concluded that '*it would be incompatible with the purpose and object of the Convention if Contracting States were thereby absolved from their responsibility under the Convention in relation to the field of activity covered by such attribution*'.

The Court's adherence to the rule of non-circumvention is not limited to cases involving Community measures. *Drozd and Janousek* concerned two persons sentenced to imprisonment for burglary, who alleged the responsibility of France for detaining them following an allegedly unfair conviction by Andorran courts.[45] The Court noted that it does not have jurisdiction to review observance of Andorran legal procedures.[46] The ECtHR, having

42 *Matthews* v. *the United Kingdom*, 265, para 32.

43 *Matthews* v. *the United Kingdom*, 265, para 34.

44 *T.I.* v. *the United Kingdom* App no 43844/98 (ECtHR 7 March 2000), Decision as to the Admissibility.

45 *Drozd and Janousek* v. *France and Spain* App no 12747/87 (ECtHR 26 June 1992) (Drozd and Janousek).

46 Drozd and Janousek, para 107.

balanced the benefits of international cooperation and ensuring accountability for violations of the Convention, expressed its unwillingness to compromise the latter. The Court noted that the Convention does not require the contracting parties to impose their standards on third states and so France was not obliged to verify whether the proceedings which resulted in the conviction were compatible with all the requirements of the Convention.[47] According to the Court, to require such a review would thwart the current trend towards strengthening international cooperation in the administration of justice. At the same time, the Court emphasized that '*States are obliged to refuse their co-operation if it emerges that the conviction is the result of a flagrant denial of justice*'.

In its decision as to the admissibility in *M. & Co.* v. *Germany*, the European Commission for Human Rights faced the question whether Germany could be held responsible for issuing a writ of execution of the judgment of the European Court of Justice (ECJ) which upheld its decision to impose a fine on the applicant for violations of the Community's antitrust law.[48] The European Commission for Human Rights refused to accept that by granting executory power to a judgment of the ECJ, the competent German authorities acted quasi as Community organs and were to that extent beyond the scope of control exercised by the Convention's organs. According to the European Commission for Human Rights, Member States are responsible for all acts and omissions of their domestic organs which violate the Convention regardless of whether the act or omission in question is a consequence of domestic law or of the necessity to comply with international obligations.[49]

While the ECtHR is clear on its stance on the non-circumvention of obligations, it also acknowledges the benefits of international cooperation, including that under EU law.[50] The Court employs the principle of 'equivalent protection' to balance the right of states to create international organizations and the need to prevent circumvention of their obligations. States are free to transfer their powers to international bodies as long as equivalent protection of the ECHR rights is secured. In *Waite & Kennedy*, the Court noted that a material factor in assessing immunity of the European Space Agency from the German jurisdiction was whether the applicants had available to them reasonable alternative means to effectively protect their rights under the Convention.[51] Similarly, in *Matthews* v. *the United Kingdom*, the

47 Drozd and Janousek, para 110.

48 *M. & Co.* v. *Germany*, 145.

49 See also *Hess* v. *United Kingdom* App no 6231/73 (Commission decision 28 May 1975), 72.

50 S.A. *Dangeville* v. *France*, App no 36677/97 (ECtHR 16 April 2002), paras 47 and 55.

51 *Waite & Kennedy*, para 68.

Court analysed whether under the Union law the applicant had voting rights equivalent to those required under the Convention and concluded that the applicant, as a citizen of Gibraltar, was completely denied any opportunity to express her opinion in the choice of the members of the European Parliament.[52] In *M & Co.* v. *Germany* it was ruled that the transfer of powers to an international organization was not incompatible with the Convention provided that within that organization, fundamental rights will receive equivalent protection.[53] The principle of equivalent protection was restated in *Heinz* v. *the Contracting Parties* and other cases.[54]

The most notable post-2000 case where the ECtHR articulated the criterion of equivalence in more general terms is its 2005 judgment in *Bosphorus*.[55] The Irish government impounded an aircraft which the applicant had leased from the Yugoslav Airlines pursuant to the UN Security Council's sanctions regime. The applicant maintained that the manner in which Ireland had implemented the sanctions regime was a reviewable exercise of discretion. The Grand Chamber stated the approach expressed in earlier decisions that the Convention does not prohibit contracting parties from transferring sovereign power to an international organization in order to pursue cooperation in a certain field of activity.[56] According to the Court, the Community's judicial organs are better placed to interpret and apply Union law.[57] At the same time the Court kept its earlier line of reasoning and stated that absolving contracting states completely from their Convention responsibility in the areas covered by such a transfer would be incompatible with the object and purpose of the ECHR.[58] The Court noted that its role is confined in ascertaining whether the effects of Community adjudication are compatible with the Convention.[59]

52 *Matthews* v. *the United Kingdom*, para 64.

53 At the same time, the European Commission for Human Rights noted that it would be contrary to the very idea of transferring powers to an international organization to hold a Member State responsible for examining each case before issuing a writ of execution for a judgment of the European Court of Justice, whether Art 6 was respected in the underlying proceedings.

54 *Heinz* v. *Contracting States and Parties to the European Patent Convention* App no 21090/92 (ECtHR 16 December 1992), 125.

55 *Bosphorus Hava Yollari Turizm Ve Ticaret Anonim Sirketi* v. *Ireland* App no 45036/98 (ECtHR 30 June 2005) (*Bosphorus*).

56 *Bosphorus*, para 152.

57 *Bosphorus*, para 143.

58 *Bosphorus*, para 154. AG Jacobs' Opinion noted that Community law cannot release Member States from their obligations under the ECHR and that the essential question was whether the interference with the applicant company's possession of the aircraft was a proportionate measure in the light of the aims of general interest that the regulation sought to achieve.

59 See also *Streletz, Kessler and Krenz* v. *Germany* App nos 34044/96, 35532/97, and 44801/98 (ECtHR 22 March 2001).

The Grand Chamber then restated the principle of equivalent protection as set out in *M. & Co.* v. *Germany*. According to the Court, if '*such equivalent protection is considered to be provided by the organization, the presumption will be that a State has not departed from the requirements of the Convention when it does no more than implement legal obligations flowing from its membership of the organization*'.[60]

3.3.3 *The ECT Case Law*

Investment tribunals dealing with cases under the ECT also support the principle of non-circumvention. As a rule, they approach the question of non-circumvention through conflict of law principles. Part II of this book will investigate how investment tribunals deal with the distribution of responsibility in disputes involving the EU. The following paragraphs are limited to providing examples of how tribunals apply the principle of non-circumvention.

In *AES Summit* v. *Hungary*, the investor argued that reintroduction of administrative pricing for electricity breached its rights under the investment treaty. One of Hungary's defences was an initiation by the European Commission of an investigation of the power purchase agreement based on a concern that it contained unlawful state aid.[61] The Tribunal agreed with the claimant that the Community law was not an excuse for Hungary's breaches of the ECT.[62] It refused to analyse Hungary's obligations under EU law and concluded that the dispute was about the conformity or nonconformity of Hungary's acts and measures with the ECT.[63] The Tribunal noted that the question of '*whether Hungary was, may have been, or may have felt obliged under the EU law to act as it did, is only an element to be considered when determining the "rationality," "reasonableness," "arbitrariness" and "transparency" of the reintroduction of administrative pricing*'.[64]

Similarly, in *Micula* v. *Romania*, Romania argued that its obligations under EU law and, eventually, the EU-Romania Accession Treaty were relevant in the evaluation of its conduct because, *inter alia*, they were binding under

60 *Bosphorus*, para 156.

61 *AES Summit Generation Limited and AES-Tisza Erömü Kft* v. *The Republic of Hungary* (Award 23 September 2010) ICSID Case No. ARB/07/22 (*AES Summit* v. *Hungary*), para 10.2.3.

62 *AES Summit*, Award, para 7.3.1.

63 *AES Summit*, Award, para 7.6.9.

64 *AES Summit*, Award, para 7.6.9.

Romanian law.[65] The Tribunal rejected this view and noted that the relevant bilateral investment treaty (BIT) did not contain reference to EU accession and '*the Tribunal cannot therefore assume that by virtue of the EU, either Romania, or Sweden, or the EU sought to amend, modify or otherwise detract from the application of the BIT*'.[66] The Tribunal further noted that there is no reason to assume that Sweden and Romania had any intent to defeat their obligations under any applicable treaties when they signed the Accession Treaty.[67]

In another case under the ECT, *RREEF Infrastructure* v. *Spain*, the claimant rejected Spain's invocation of the supremacy of EU law where EU Member States have transferred their competences to the EU.[68] The Tribunal found that the ECT binds both the EU and its Member States on the one hand, and non-EU States on the other hand, and the EU law is *res inter alios acta* which cannot prevail over the ECT.[69] Refusing to accept Spain's defence that EU law shields it from responsibility under the ECT, the Tribunal referred to the ECT as its 'constitution' and concluded that it prevails over any other norm (apart from *ius cogens*).[70]

In some cases tribunals avoid the question of non-circumvention by focusing on Member State implementation of the binding decision of the EU. The Tribunal in *Electrabel* v. *Hungary* did not pronounce on non-circumvention and left open the question of responsibility of the EU for violating investors' rights by adopting decisions which bind its Member States. It noted that the ECT accepts that the Union can make binding decisions on the Member States in which case investors' rights would not be protected *as against that Member State*.[71] However, according to the Tribunal, the dispute is not about the binding character of an EU decision itself, but about the alleged incorrect enforcement of that decision by the Member State within its permitted margin of appreciation under EU law.[72] Therefore, according to the Tribunal, the

65 *Ioan Micula, Viorel Micula, S.C. European Food S.A, S.C. Starmill S.R.L. and S.C. Multipack S.R.L.* v. *Romania* (Final Award 11 December 2013) ICSID Case No. ARB/05/20 (*Micula* v. *Romania*), para 3.15.

66 *Micula* v. *Romania*, para 321.

67 *Micula* v. *Romania*, para 326.

68 *RREEF Infrastructure (G.P.) Limited and RREEF Pan-European Infrastructure Two Lux S.à r. l.* v. *Kingdom of Spain* (Decision on Jurisdiction 6 June 2016) ICSID Case No. ARB/13/30 (*RREEF Infrastructure* v. *Spain*), para 59.

69 *RREEF Infrastructure* v. *Spain*, para 74.

70 *RREEF Infrastructure* v. *Spain*, para 75.

71 *Electrabel S.A.* v. *Republic of Hungary, Decision on Jurisdiction, Applicable Law and Liability* (Decision on Jurisdiction, Applicable Law and Liability 30 November 2012) ICSID Case No. ARB/07/19 (*Electrabel* v. *Hungary*), para 4.169.

72 *Electrabel* v. *Hungary*, para 4.169.

analysis '*leaves open the responsibility of the European Union under the ECT*'.[73]

Similarly to the balancing exercise undertaken by the ECtHR which was addressed earlier, investment tribunals also seek to establish equilibrium between the '*protection of rights of foreign investors and the economic integration of the EU Member States*'.[74] In somewhat similar tone to the principle of equivalent protection, investment tribunals apply the rule of 'harmonious interpretation', though emphasizing that it applies specifically and uniquely when dealing with the Member States' implementation of Community law. In *Electrabel* v. *Hungary* the European Commission called for the application of the *Bosphorus* test to evaluate whether EU law afforded protection equivalent to the ECT, in which case Hungary's termination of the power purchase agreement would have been in conformity with the ECT.[75] The Tribunal rejected that there exists a general principle of international law compelling the harmonious interpretation of different treaties.[76] However, it noted that '*the situation here is somewhat special, with the European Union and its Member States so closely involved in and parties to the ECT. In the Tribunal's view, the ECT's historical genesis and its text are such that the ECT should be interpreted, if possible, in harmony with the EU*'.[77] Drawing on the historical analysis of the common goals of the EU and the ECT, the Tribunal concluded that foreign investors in the EU Member States cannot have acquired any legitimate expectations that the ECT would necessarily shield their investments from the effects of EU law as regards anticompetitive conduct.[78] Contrary to the position in *Electrabel* v. *Hungary*, the Tribunal in *RREEF Infrastructure* v. *Spain* established that the principle of harmonious interpretation applies not only with respect to the EU, but generally whenever there is a conflict between an obligation under the ECT and those under other treaties.[79]

3.3.4 *Binding Decisions of an Organization*

The principle of non-circumvention applies with respect to breaches of obligations through *binding* decisions of an organization which leave *no*

73 *Electrabel* v. *Hungary*, para 4.170.
74 *Electrabel* v. *Hungary*, para 4.113.
75 *Electrabel* v. *Hungary*, para 4.102.
76 *Electrabel* v. *Hungary*, para 4.130.
77 *Electrabel* v. *Hungary*, para 4.130.
78 *Electrabel* v. *Hungary*, para 4.141.
79 *RREEF Infrastructure* v. *Spain*, para 76.

discretion to the Member State.[80] Gaja noted that if Member States have discretion so that they may comply with the decision without breaching an international obligation, the organization cannot be held responsible.[81] With respect to non-binding decisions, such as recommendations and authorizations, the Special Rapporteur suggested that the organization's responsibility could be invoked if such authorizations and recommendations are made in furtherance of the organization's own interest[82] and, more ambiguously, based on the extent of its involvement in the act.[83] Gaja noted that responsibility would be justified only if the recommended or authorized act was actually taken and would be in breach of an organization's obligation.[84] While some international organizations rejected the possibility that in certain cases they could be responsible for an authorization issued to its members,[85] other states nevertheless supported such reasoning.[86] The French representative, for example, suggested that the extent of latitude the state was allowed by the organization's request was of relevance in such cases.[87]

In *Bosphorus*, the ECtHR considered the responsibility of Member States arising out of mandatory EU law. The Court also noted that if a Member State was acting outside its strict legal obligations under the Union law, it would be

80 The commentary applies both with respect to ARIO Art 17 and a reverse rule under ARIO Art 61, i.e. both with respect to circumvention of obligations by organizations and states. However, as noted by Gaja, it is unlikely that states authorize or recommend organizations to carry out acts, and therefore the discussion here is more relevant with respect to Art 17 – circumvention by international organizations, see Gaja Fourth Report, 117, para 68.

81 Gaja Third Report, 14, para 30. See comments of INTERPOL and the WHO supporting this limitation of non-circumvention rule, Comments A/CN.4/568, 136, sect I.

82 Gaja Third Report, 16, para 41.

83 Gaja Third Report, 16, para 41.

84 Gaja Third Report, 16, para 41. The IMF rejected this interpretation suggesting that states are independent actors and it makes its own determination whether to carry out recommendations and authorizations; see Comments A/CN.4/582, 23, sect I. INTERPOL also expressed concern over the possibility to hold an international organization responsible for authorizing or recommending a state to carry out conduct.

85 For example, the IMF illustrated its criticism with an example: when a Member State requests to use IMF resources, the IMF may indicate that the member needs to reduce the net present value of its sovereign debt. While the member might decline to do so or might do so in a variety of ways, one of the choices being to unilaterally default on its debt thereby breaching the member's international obligations. The IMF's concern was that responsibility in this case could be interpreted from the fact that the member is pursuing an objective of the IMF; see Comments A/CN.4/556, 51, sect N.3. It is questionable whether the IMF's concerns are well placed, since in this case the IMF itself does not hold the obligation against debt holders and therefore its responsibility would not arise under Art 17, in the example provided by the IMF.

86 See Gaja Third Report, ft 61.

87 Summary Record of the 22nd Meeting, A/C.6/59/SR.22 (ILC 2004), 3, para 13.

fully responsible under the Convention.[88] It was, however, not the case in the present dispute. The Court agreed with the European Commission that the Supreme Court of Ireland had no real discretion and had to implement the ECJ ruling.[89] *Cantoni* v. *France* provides another relevant example. The case concerned criminal proceedings brought against the applicant for unlawfully selling pharmaceutical products. The ECtHR agreed with the applicant's position that the notion of medicinal product, as defined in the provision on which his conviction has been based, was not sufficiently clear to enable him to determine with accuracy what acts would incur criminal liability.[90]

The qualification that only binding decisions call for responsibility of an organization is also confirmed by investment tribunals. In *Electrabel* v. *Hungary*, the Tribunal noted that the claimant alleged incorrect enforcement of the EU decision within the permitted margin of appreciation under EU law.[91] Accordingly, the EU's responsibility would be invoked if the claim concerned the Union's decision itself, whereas in this case claims related only to certain measures by Hungary, some resulting from the Union law and some with no link to it.[92] In *AES Summit* v. *Hungary*, Hungary argued that one of the reasons for the introduction of disputed price decrees was the pressure of the European Commission's investigations and foreseeable obligation to recover state aid that the decision would impose. The Tribunal replied that as long as the European Commission's state aid decision was not issued, Hungary had no legal obligation to act in accordance with what it believed could be the result of that decision.[93]

Though dealing with the internal law of the Union rather than international obligations, the position of the ECJ also supports that the determining factor in deciding the question of responsibility of the EU and its Member States is whether the European Commission's instruction was binding or whether it left a degree of discretion to the Member State.[94] In *Krohn & Co.*, an action for

88 *Bosphorus*, para 157.

89 *Bosphorus*, para 147.

90 *Cantoni* v. *France* App no 17862/91 (ECtHR 15 November 1996), para 26.

91 *Electrabel* v. *Hungary*, para 4.168.

92 *Electrabel* v. *Hungary*, para 4.171.

93 *AES Summit* v. *Hungary*, paras 10.3.15–10.3.16.

94 Moshe Hirsch, *The Responsibility of International Organizations Toward Third Parties: Some Basic Principles* (Martinus Nijhoff Publishers 1995), 83. See also Jean Groux and Philippe Manin, *The European Communities in the International Order* (Office for Official Publications of the European Communities 1995), 143–144. Giorgio Gaja, 'Some Reflections on the European Community's International Responsibility', in Henry G Schermers, Ton Heukels and Philip Mead (eds), *Non-Contractual Liability of the European Communities* (Martinus Nijhoff Publishers 1988), 172.

damages suffered as a result of the refusal of the Bundesanstalt,[95] acting on instructions given by the European Commission to grant import licences, the ECJ found that '*the unlawful conduct alleged by the applicant in order to establish its claim for compensation is to be attributed not to the Bundesanstalt, which was bound to comply with the Commission's instructions, but to the Commission itself*'.[96] A similar principle was applied by the Court of First Instance in *Dorsch Consult* v. *Council*, only this time with regard to the relations between the European Community and the United Nations. The Court said that '*[T]he alleged damage cannot, in the final analysis, be attributed to Regulation No. 2340/90 but must, as the Council has in fact contended, be attributed to United Nations Security Council Resolution No. 661 (1990) which imposed the embargo on trade with Iraq*'.[97]

With respect to the ECtHR case law, the European Commission's stance on the principle of non-circumvention is unknown because the Union is not a party to the ECHR and has therefore not been a party to the disputes in cases when breaches were related to its decisions. The European Commission did express a positive attitude to the principle of equivalent protection as formulated by the ECtHR in *Bosphorus* in some of its *amicus curiae* briefs in the disputes under the ECT.[98] At the same time the European Commission noted the difficulty of drawing a line between binding decisions of the EU and

[95] The German Federal Office for the Organization of Agricultural Markets.

[96] C-175/84 *Krohn & Co Import-Export GmbH & Co KG* v. *Commission* [1986] ECR 753, 768, para 23. The approach of the Court in apportioning liability either to the European Community or to a Member State, but not to both, even when there are reasons for holding responsibility to be concurrent, was underlined by Manuel Perez Gonzalez, 'Les Organisations Internationales et Le Droit de La Responsabilité' (1998) 92 RGDIP 63, 89. Interestingly, differently from its stance on international responsibility in disputes under the WTO system, in C-175/84 *Krohn & Co Import-Export GmbH & Co KG* v. *Commission* [1986] ECR 753, the European Commission contended that the authority of national decisions is not weakened by the fact that the European Commission is empowered to give instructions regarding them; see p 767, para 16.

[97] T-184/95 *Dorsch Consult Ingenieurgesellschaft mbH* v. *Council of the European Union and Commission of the European Communities* [1998] ECR II-667, 694, para 73.

[98] In its comments the European Commission stated that 'At the very least, it would have to be clarified that there is no "circumvention" if a State transfers powers to an international organization which is not bound by the State's own treaty obligations, but whose legal system offers a comparable level of guarantees; see Comments A/CN.4/582, 28. Also, the European Commission's support for the principle of equivalent protection expressed in its third-party submission in *Bosphorus*, para 122. The European Commission's support seems to be based on its willingness to free Member States from a requirement to review for Convention compliance an act of the Union before implementing it, as this would pose a threat to the very foundation of the Community, para 124. For endorsement of principle of equivalent protection in investment cases, see the European Commission's statement in *Electrabel* v. *Hungary*, paras 4.103, 4.144.

discretion left to the Member States. The Commission explained that under the Community law, secondary Community legislation may be binding in its entirety and directly applicable in all Member States (regulations) or only binding as to the result to be achieved (directives) or binding only upon those to whom it is addressed (decisions). It is suggested that an obligation of result (such as in a directive) comes very close to a binding decision but nevertheless may leave a certain discretion to the Member State.[99]

Following the aforementioned case-law analysis it may be concluded that the principle of non-circumvention does not sit comfortably with the European Commission's call for competence-based responsibility. Human rights law practice as well as investment arbitration does not support the European Commission's approach that international responsibility follows the transfer of competence from Member States to an international body. The following section addresses the rule of joint obligations which further undermines the EU's claim that responsibility is to be allocated in accordance to the division of competences between an organization and its members.

3.3.5 *The Principle of Joint Obligations*

The rule of non-circumvention ensures accountability for breaches of international obligations when states and organizations act indirectly through another state or organization. The latter may or may not be bound by that same obligation, though in practice the rule is usually triggered when the acting entity is not itself a holder of an obligation. Thus, in practice the question of circumvention arises either under EU-only or Member State-only agreements.

With respect to cases when both the EU and its Member States are parties to a treaty, two types of arrangements can be observed. Some treaties provide a declaration of competences, in which case obligations are allocated (*vis-à-vis* third parties) to the EU and its Member States. For example, with respect to the United Nations Convention for the Law of the Sea (UNCLOS), the EU and its Member States have expressly stated that they are bound by the obligations to the extent of their respective competences, a limitation which was stressed both during the accession process[100] and in the text of the

[99] Comments A/CN.4/568, 135, sect I.

[100] See Letter Dated 10 September 1976 from the Representative of the Netherlands to the President of the Conference (1976), A/CONF.62/48. See André Nollkaemper, 'The European Community and International Environmental Co-Operation: Legal Aspects of External Community Powers' (1987) 14 LIEI 55, 68; Albert Koers, 'Participation of the European Economic Community in a New Law of the Sea Convention' (1979) 73 AJIL 426, 437.

UNCLOS itself.[101] A similar division is prescribed with respect to rights in order to prevent double benefitting.[102] In some cases, even when a treaty requires an organization to deposit a declaration of competences, it still allows the organization to decide internally the respective responsibilities for the performance of obligation.[103] Third parties are not always fully comfortable to enter into treaties with an organization which lacks full autonomy with respect to the fulfilment of obligations, even if a declaration of competences is in place.[104]

With respect to mixed agreements without declarations of competences, the position of the European Commission and third parties regarding international responsibility diverges. Following its competence-based approach to responsibility, the European Commission often seeks to assert itself as the sole respondent claiming that the measure in question falls under its field of competence, irrespective of whether that measure was implemented by the organs of the Union or its Member States. Third parties, on the other hand, are often unwilling to leave the matter to the internal division of powers. This trend can be observed in the WTO case law. These cases will be addressed in detail in Part II, and therefore only references to the relevant parts will be provided in the present discussion. It must be noted that the ECJ has itself ruled that the Union and its Member States are jointly liable to the third states for the fulfilment of every obligation arising from the commitments undertaken.[105]

3.3.6 *The WTO Case Law*

In *EC and Certain Member States – IT Products*, the complainants (United States, Japan and Chinese Taipei) called for the participation as respondents

101 Declaration concerning the competence of the European Community with regard to matters governed by the UNCLOS of 10 December 1982 and the Agreement of 28 July 1994 relating to the implementation of Part XI of the Convention state that 'By depositing this instrument, the Community has the honour of declaring its acceptance, in respect of matters for which competence has been transferred to it by those of its Member States which are parties to the Convention, of the rights and obligations laid down for states in the Convention and the Agreement'.

102 Heliskoski 2001, 135.

103 For example, Art 14 and 13(2) of the *Vienna Convention for the Protection of the Ozone Layer*, signed 22 March 1985.

104 See John Lang Temple, 'The Ozone-Layer Convention: A New Solution to the Question of Community Participation in "Mixed" International Agreements' (1986) 23 CML Rev. 157, 163.

105 C-316/91 *Parliament* v. *Council of the European Union* [1994] ECR 661; Opinion of AG Jacobs delivered on 10 Nov 1993, para 29.

of both the EU and certain Member States.[106] The case concerned customs classification of certain information technology products, and the claimants considered that both the EC and certain Member States played a role in the application of customs duties. The European Commission, on the other hand, wished to be a sole respondent and bear full responsibility because the role of the Member States was reduced to the application of measures previously enacted by the EU.[107]

Similarly, in *EC – Computer Equipment* the European Commission argued that it is the only respondent in the dispute because Member States have transferred their powers in this area to the Union.[108] The United States, however, disagreed with such position and required that both Ireland and the United Kingdom participate in the dispute as respondents.[109] According to the United States, '*[A]s independent Members, Ireland and the United Kingdom hid behind no other Member. Nothing in the text of the GATT 1994 or the DSU limited the scope of application of the provisions of these two agreements with respect to either Member as to its status in a dispute brought under these agreements*'.[110] According to the United States, the internal legal framework of the EU could in no way result in fewer rights and obligations being allotted to the Member States.[111]

Similarly, in *EC – Commercial Vessels*, a WTO case which concerned subsidization measures of the EC and certain Member States affecting trade in commercial vessels, Korea argued that its claim was against both the EC and certain Member States.[112] The European Commission, on the other hand, asserted that it '*considers that it is the "proper respondent" for the measures at issue and states that it "takes full responsibility under international law" for measures taken by EC member States pursuant to the TDM Regulation, and that for the purposes of WTO law, such measures are taken by the European Communities as a Member of the WTO*'.[113] In *EC – Large Civil Aircraft*, a WTO case which concerned a United States' claim that the EC's so-called launch aid was in breach of the WTO obligations, the European Commission too stated that the claim related to matters for which the EC bears responsibility in the WTO and thus the EC is a proper respondent.[114]

106 *EC and Certain Member States – IT Products*, PR, para 7.81.
107 *EC and Certain Member States – IT Products*, PR, para 7.80.
108 *EC – Computer Equipment*, PR, para 4.9–4 .10, also 4.15.
109 *EC – Computer Equipment*, PR, para 4.12.
110 *EC – Computer Equipment*, PR, para 4.13.
111 *EC – Computer Equipment*, PR, para 4.14.
112 *EC – Commercial Vessels*, PR, para 4.32.
113 *EC – Commercial Vessels*, PR, para 7.32, ft 163, referring to First submission of the EC, 93.
114 *EC – Large Civil Aircraft*, PR, para 7.172, ft 2037.

A similar pattern can be observed under the ECT regime. In *Electrabel* v. *Hungary* the claimant argued that Hungary violated its rights under a power purchase agreement.[115] The European Commission, in its *amicus curiae*, submitted a jurisdictional objection stating that the claim against the termination of the power purchase agreement should have been brought against the Community rather than Hungary.[116] According to the Commission, the fact that there is no declaration of competences under the ECT does not mean that Member States have competence for all areas under the ECT.[117] The European Commission stated that '*the responsibility for preventing unlawful State aid lies with the European Union and not with EU Member States; and therefore the Respondent is the wrong party named by the Claimant for its PPA Termination Claim. However, as the Commission asserts, it 'would trigger the [European Union's] responsibility if contrary to the ECT'*.[118]

The position of third parties in the intra-EU BIT cases (i.e. disputes between two EU Member States) is also relevant to the present discussion as it shows unwillingness of the third parties to compromise the binding nature of the ECT on the basis of the supremacy of the Community law. In intra-EU BIT cases, investors often dispute the European Commission's tendency to dispute the jurisdiction of the tribunals and assert the supremacy of the Community law. For example, in *RREEF Infrastructure* v. *Spain*, the claimant argued that the ECT's recognition of the existence of a regional organization does not deprive investors of their ECT rights. According to the claimants, the reference to the regional economic integration organizations in Articles 1(2), 1(3) and 1(10) of the ECT serves to ensure that a claim can be brought against a regional economic integration organization regarding a dispute arising out of an investment made in that area, and it by no means suggests that the multilateral treaty does not apply within the regional organization absent a disconnection clause.[119]

International courts and tribunals reject the competence-based approach advocated by the European Commission in support of the principle of joint obligations. In a WTO case *EC – Computer Equipment*, the Panel stressed that while it was not clear in this initial phase which exact

[115] *Electrabel* v. *Hungary*, para 4.52.

[116] *Electrabel* v. *Hungary*, para 5.10.

[117] *Electrabel* v. *Hungary*, para 5.20.

[118] *Electrabel* v. *Hungary*, para 4.170, referring to para 41 of the European Commission's Submission.

[119] *RREEF Infrastructure* v. *Spain*, para 58. A disconnection clause is provisions in a multilateral treaty which ensure that certain parties are not required to apply the provisions of the treaty because other relevant rules have already been agreed to among themselves.

measures were at issue '*the European Communities, Ireland and the United Kingdom are all bound by their tariff commitments under Schedule LXXX, our examination will focus, in the first instance, on whether customs authorities in the European Communities, including those located in Ireland and the United Kingdom, have or have not deviated from the obligations assumed under that Schedule*'.[120]

In the *EC and Certain Member States – IT Products* dispute, the Panel also agreed with the complainant that EU Member States are individually bound by the obligations under the WTO Agreements.[121] In a similar line of reasoning, the Panel in *EC – Large Civil Aircraft* first rejected the European Commission's submission that the violations alleged all relate to matters for which the EC bears responsibility under the WTO and instead stated that each Member State is a member of the WTO in its own right, with all rights and obligations stemming from this treaty.[122] According to the Panel, '*whatever responsibility the European Communities bears for the actions of its member States does not diminish their rights and obligations as WTO Members, but is rather an internal matter concerning the relations between the European Communities and its member States*'.[123] The fact that these states are members of the European Communities was irrelevant in the Panel's conclusion that Member States hold an individual status as members of the WTO against whom another member has brought a claim.

Though the EU representation of Member States in WTO disputes will be addressed in detail in Part II, it is useful to note that WTO the Dispute Settlement Body (DSB) suggests that whether Member States are represented by the Union in a given dispute or whether they participate themselves has no impact on their rights and obligations. In *EC – Large Civil Aircraft*, in which a claim was brought against the Community and certain Member States, the Panel noted that whether Member States participate in the dispute themselves or whether they are represented by the European Commission is irrelevant to their rights and obligations.[124] The Panel indicated that the title and participation in the dispute proceedings does not affect Member States' obligations under the WTO:

> *We need not and do not decide whether the European Communities "represents" the member States in this dispute in some formal sense. Nor does the title*

[120] *EC – Computer Equipment*, PR, para 8.16.

[121] *EC and Certain Member States – IT Products*, PR, para 7.86.

[122] *EC – Large Civil Aircraft*, PR, para 7.174.

[123] *EC – Large Civil Aircraft*, PR, para 7.175.

[124] *EC – Large Civil Aircraft*, PR, para 7.174.

> *given to the dispute have any legal significance with respect to the rights and obligations of Members against whom claims are made, or with respect to their individual or direct participation in the dispute.*[125]

According to the Panel, the fact that Member States have chosen not to participate in this dispute does not affect their status as respondents.[126] In fact, the Panel provided a list of cases where the title of the case did not correspond to the actual respondent parties.[127] To illustrate its refusal to provide a legal status to the concept of 'representation' in the WTO dispute-settlement system, the Panel noted that it is unaware of any dispute involving claims against the EC and one or more of its Member States in which a Member State has made submissions and representations separate or in addition to those made by the EC.[128] An analogous approach can be observed in *EC – Computer Equipment*. Here the United States had requested that the title of the panel be changed to read 'European Communities, Ireland and the United Kingdom – Increases in Tariffs on Certain Computer Equipment' to reflect the status of Member States as respondent parties.[129] The Panel refused to do so for practical reasons but noted that '*title of a particular dispute is given for the sake of convenience in reference and in no way affects the substantive rights and obligations of the parties to the dispute*'.[130]

3.3.7 *The CJEU Case Law*

Interestingly, the case law of the Court of Justice of the European Union (CJEU) itself supports the approach of third states rather than one advocated by the European Commission. It should be noted, however, that the Court's case law conflates the concepts of joint obligations and joint responsibility, the difference between which is addressed later. In any case, since there can be no joint responsibility without joint obligations, the case law is relevant to the current discussion.

The cases are well known and will be only briefly summarized. The case law of the CJEU adheres to the position that both the EU and its Member States assume responsibility for all obligations within the agreement they sign,

125 EC – *Large Civil Aircraft*, PR, para 7.176. See ft 2047 for a list of case law.
126 EC – *Large Civil Aircraft*, PR, para 7.176.
127 EC – *Large Civil Aircraft*, PR, para 7.176, ft. 2047.
128 EC – *Large Civil Aircraft*, PR, para 7.176, ft. 2047.
129 EC – *Computer Equipment*, PR, para 8.17.
130 EC – *Computer Equipment*, PR, para 8.17.

irrespective of the internal allocation of competences. In *Ruling 1/78*, the Court said that it is not necessary to set out and determine, as regards other contracting parties to the IAEA Convention on the Physical Protection of Nuclear Materials, Facilities and Transports, the division of powers in this respect between the Community and the Member States, particularly as it may change in the course of time.[131] It is sufficient for the Union to communicate to the other contracting parties that the matter gives rise to a division of powers within the Community, whereas the exact nature of the division is a domestic question in which third parties have no need to intervene. In *Demirel*, the Court noted that in ensuring respect for commitments arising from an agreement concluded by the Community institutions, the Community had assumed responsibility for the due performance of the agreement.[132] In *Kupferberg*, the Court also stated that the effect of provisions of an agreement cannot vary according to who is responsible for the implementation of the treaty.[133]

The CJEU has affirmed its position in later cases. In *Parliament* v. *Council*, which concerned financial assistance under the fourth Lomé Convention, the Court noted the bilateral nature of the Convention and concluded that in the absence of express derogations in the Lomé Convention, the Community and its Member States as partners of the African, Caribbean and Pacific Group of States are jointly liable to those latter States for the fulfilment of every obligation arising from the commitments undertaken, including those relating to financial assistance.[134] The Court followed Advocate General (AG) Jacobs's Opinion that under a mixed agreement the Community and the Member States are jointly liable unless the provisions of the agreement point to the opposite conclusion.[135] Even though AG Jacobs appeared to call for joint responsibility with respect to all mixed agreements, it is not clear whether the Court adhered to such a broad interpretation because the Court referred specifically to the Lomé Convention. Furthermore, the case concerned development aid which is a shared competence.

131 Ruling 1-78 re Convention on the Physical Protection of Nuclear Materials, Facilities and Transports [1978] ECR 2151, para 35. At the same time, the Union may inform the other parties of the internal division of powers by, for example, indicating which (in some cases dual) legal basis the decision approving a mixed treaty is based on; see judgment in case C-94/03 *Commission of the European Communities* v. *Council of the European Union* [2006] EU:C:2005:308, para 55.

132 C-12/86 *Demirel* v. *Stadt Schwäbisch Gmünd* [1987] ECR 3719, para 11.

133 C-104/81 *Hauptzollamt Mainz* v. *C.A. Kupferberg & Cie KG a.A.* [1982] ECR 3641, para 12.

134 C-316/91 *Parliament* v. *Council of the European Union* [1994] ECR 661 (*Parliament* v. *Council*), para 29.

135 *Parliament* v. *Council*, Opinion of AG Jacobs, para 69.

Similarly, in *Hermès International* AG Tesauro noted that Member States and the Community constitute, *vis-à-vis* contracting non-member states, a single contracting party or at least contracting parties bearing equal responsibility in the event of failure to implement the agreement.[136] According to AG Tesauro, the line dividing the competences of the Member States and the EU is often not easy to establish and the provisions are often interconnected.[137] An exception to this trend is AG Mischo's Opinion in *Commission* v. *Ireland*, where he suggested that the '*very fact that the Community and its Member States had recourse to the formula of a mixed agreement announces to non-member countries that that agreement does not fall wholly within the competence of the Community and that, consequently, the Community is, a priori, only assuming responsibility for those parts falling within its competence*'.[138] AG Mischo's reasoning, however, disregards the interests of third parties. If the very purpose of mixity is to avoid the express delimitation of competences between the EU and its Member States, then it would be illogical, if not unfair, to require third parties to draw a line which the European Commission itself is unable or unwilling to determine.

The prevailing view in the legal scholarship also supports the default position that both the organization and its Member States are bound by all obligations within a treaty they sign, irrespective of the internal division of powers.[139] Bartels notes the distinction between autonomy and responsibility and suggests that Article XI:1 of the WTO Agreement, which allows for the possibility that original WTO members will not have autonomy in all matters covered by the WTO Agreements, is unrelated to the question of responsibility.[140] Nollkaemper also supports the majority opinion that, from the international law perspective, both the EU and its Member States are bound by all obligations under mixed agreements, except where declaration of competences or an alternative scheme is laid out.[141] Similarly, Tomuschat

136 C-53/96 *Hermès International* v. *FHT Marketing Choice BV* [1998] ECR I-3603 (*Hermès International*) Opinion of AG Tesauro, para 14.

137 *Hermès International*, Opinion of AG Tesauro, para 20.

138 C-13/00 *Commission of the European Communities* v. *Ireland* [2001] ECR I-02943, para 30.

139 See Eric Stein, 'External Relations of the European Community: Structure and Process', in Andrew Clapham (ed), *European Community Law, Collected Courses of the Academy of European Law* (Martinus Nijhoff 1991), vol. I-1, 162.

140 Lorand Bartels, 'The UK's Status in the WTO after Brexit' [2016]. Available at SSRN: https://ssrn.com/abstract=2841747, 4–5.

141 André Nollkaemper, 'Joint Responsibility between the EU and Member States for Non-Performance of Obligations Under Multilateral Environmental Agreements', in Elisa Morgera (ed), *The External Environmental Policy of the European Union* (Cambridge University Press 2012), 22–23. Nollkaemper suggests that in addition to mixed agreements, joint responsibility may arise in cases when conduct of the EU and its Member States is so

reasons that if the European Commission and Member States refrain from publicizing the demarcation line between their respective areas of jurisdiction, their partners cannot be expected to make necessary inquiries themselves.[142] Dolmans suggests that in such cases, it is preferable for third parties to regard the Community and its Member States as jointly liable.[143] For example, during the negotiations of the Galileo/GPS Agreement between the United States and the EU, the United States argued for joint and several liability because the internal allocation of competences was unknown to it.[144]

If states and international organizations are bound by all obligations under a treaty they sign, irrespective of the limits of their powers, the question is how can entities assume international obligations without having autonomy to do so? Gaja explains that it does not follow from the indivisibility of rights and obligations under international law that the Community and its Member States cannot respect the partition of competences internally.[145] Similarly, Tomuschat rejects that joint obligations extend the scope of the EU's powers beyond the limits established by the EU treaties. It only means that third states could eventually address claims to the Community as such, while internally the distribution of powers would in no way be affected.[146] Dolmans disagrees with the theory of 'implicit modification' proposed by Bleckmann,[147] according to which once the Community and Member States enter into an agreement, the EU treaties are implicitly modified so as to extend in its entirety the competences in the areas covered by that agreement to both the Community and its Member States.[148] Rather, Dolmans rightly sets aside the Community

closely intertwined that it is impossible to allocate responsibility between them, for example in case of the EU financing of a construction project which resulted in damage, 304.

142 Christian Tomuschat, 'Liability for Mixed Agreements', in David O'Keeffe and Henry G Schermers (eds), *Mixed Agreements* (Kluwer Law & Taxation Publishers 1983), 130.

143 Maurits JFM Dolmans, *Problems of Mixed Agreements: Division of Powers Within the EEC and the Rights of Third Parties* (Asser Instituut 1985), 82.

144 Peter M Olson, 'Mixity from the Outside: The Perspective of a Treaty Partner', in Christophe Hillion and Panos Koutrakos (eds), *Mixed Agreements Revisited: The EU and Its Member States in the World* (Hart Publishing 2010), 343.

145 Giorgio Gaja, 'The European Community's Rights and Obligations under Mixed Agreements', in David O'Keeffe and Henry G Schermers (eds), *Mixed Agreements* (Kluwer Law & Taxation Publishers 1983), 137.

146 Tomuschat 1983, 131.

147 Albert Bleckmann, 'The Mixed Agreements of the EEC in Public International Law', in David O'Keeffe and Henry G Schermers (eds), *Mixed Agreements* (Liability for Mixed Agreements 1983). Similar approach is that of Weiler, who suggests that external competences could perhaps be conceived as being broader than internal competences, Joseph HH Weiler, 'The External Legal Relations of Non-Unitary Actors', in David O'Keeffe and Henry G Schermers (eds), *Mixed Agreements* (Kluwer Law and Taxation Publishers 1983).

148 Dolmans 1985, 74.

law and suggests that joint responsibility in such cases would be based on *ultra vires* conduct by the Community and/or Member States which entails international responsibility unless third states have or should have knowledge of the violation of the rules on division of competences.[149]

In sum, international obligations are assumed by states and organizations in their capacity as independent legal persons. The internal division of competences and transfer of powers do not affect the status of international obligations. States and international organizations are prevented from escaping (even unintentionally) their international obligations by transferring powers or outsourcing conduct to another entity. The rule of non-circumvention and the principle of joint obligations find extensive support in international human rights and economic law dispute-settlement practice. It must therefore be concluded that international organizations and their members are independently responsible for breaches of their international obligations.

3.4 THE PRINCIPLE OF INDEPENDENT RESPONSIBILITY

The fact that both an organization and its member states are bound by all obligations under a treaty they enter does not mean that a breach of that treaty will result in their joint and several responsibility.[150] Joint responsibility arises in cases when several entities are responsible for the same internationally wrongful act, for example, when two or more states together carry out an internationally wrongful act in circumstances where they may be regarded as acting jointly in respect of the entire operation.[151] Joint responsibility refers to situations when persons who are jointly and severally liable for obligations are each responsible for the whole damage caused to third parties. In that case the injured party can hold each responsible state to account for the wrongful conduct as a whole. Other cases where responsibility may be joint are when several states establish a joint organ or when an international organization and one of its members participate in a common endeavour, such as a peacekeeping operation.[152] The rules of international responsibility provide for joint responsibility,[153] even though these have attracted criticism for lack of

149 Dolmans 1985, 77.

150 It seems that Delgado Casteleiro arrived at a similar conclusion; see Delgado Casteleiro 2016, 66.

151 Yearbook of the International Law Commission, A/CN.4/SER.A/2001/Add.1 (Part 2), 124, para 2.

152 Gaja Second Report, 4, para 7.

153 ARSIWA Art 47, ARIO Art 48.

clarity.[154] In his reports, Gaja has indicated on a number of occasions that attribution is not exclusive and conduct can result in the responsibility of several entities.[155]

According to Gaja, joint responsibility can also arise when both the organization and its members have jointly undertaken the same obligation towards a third party and the obligation is breached.[156] In his reports, the Special Rapporteur expressly noted that breach of the EU's mixed agreements, which is silent on the declaration of competences, can result in joint responsibility of the EU and its Member States.[157] Gaja's statement that joint obligations under mixed agreements can result in joint responsibility is certainly correct. There could be situations where conduct is attributed both to the EU and its Member States or where they both contribute to a common endeavour. According to Nollkaemper joint responsibility can result in the rare cases of undivided injury when the EU and the Member States both contribute to an injury and it is not possible for third parties to determine who caused what.[158]

However, notwithstanding such cases, the general principle in international law is that in the absence of agreement to the contrary, each state or international organization is independently responsible for conduct attributable to it.[159] The general rule in international law is that of separate responsibility of a state for its own wrongful acts. In fact, Nollkaemper provides practical examples which suggest that joint responsibility often results in individualized responsibility.[160] As Noyes and Smith rightly note, even in situations of joint responsibility there is a tendency to make a single assertion of responsibility against the most blatant and perhaps politically accessible or responsive wrongdoer.[161]

[154] André Nollkaemper, 'Introduction', in André Nollkaemper and Ilias Plakokefalos (eds), *Principles of Shared Responsibility in International Law: An Appraisal of the State of the Art* (Cambridge University Press 2014), 14. Nollkaemper notes that in some respects, the law even complicates or even impedes application of shared responsibility, Nollkaemper's Introduction, 3.

[155] Gaja Second Report, 4, para 6. See also Summary Record of the 2802nd Meeting, A/CN.4/SR.2802 (ILC 2004), 84, para 21, for comment by Economides, and p 82, para 3, for comment by Kolodkin. Pellet represented a minority position by suggesting that the very purpose of the rules of attribution was to avoid joint responsibility; see Summary Record of the 2801st Meeting, A/CN.4/SR.2801, 74, para 12.

[156] 'Sixth Report on Responsibility of International Organizations, by Mr. Giorgio Gaja, Special Rapporteur', 23, para 24.

[157] Gaja Second Report, 5, para 8; Gaja Sixth Report, 23, para 24, ft 31.

[158] Nollkaemper 2012, 310.

[159] Yearbook of the International Law Commission, A/CN.4/SER.A/2001/Add.1 (Part 2), 124, para 3.

[160] Nollkaemper 2012, 304.

[161] John E Noyes and Brian D Smith, 'State Responsibility and the Principle of Joint and Several Liability' (1988) 13 Yale J. Int'l L. 225, 232.

Furthermore, the principle of joint obligations means that obligations are binding on all parties to the treaty. However, as Talmon and Nollkaemper note, being bound to the same obligation is a necessary but not a sufficient condition for responsibility to arise.[162] The second condition under the ILC rules of international responsibility is the attribution of a wrongful conduct.[163] As the majority of the EU's mixed agreements do not provide an express statement on joint, or joint and several, responsibility of the EU and its Member States, the default rule is independent responsibility.[164]

3.5 CONCLUSION

To recap the discussion, the non-transferability of international obligations when states create international organizations and transfer to them part of their sovereign powers has two important implications for the international responsibility. First, states and international organizations are not allowed to circumvent their obligations by acting indirectly. States are not relieved from their obligations solely on the basis that they were merely carrying out the decisions of an international organization whose member they are. Organizations are also prevented from escaping accountability when they make binding decisions on their members who carry out the unlawful activity. In cases when both a state and an international organization assume international obligations, such as under mixed agreements, both an organization and its members are bound individually by all obligations under that agreement, unless expressly noted otherwise. It is concluded that the EU and its Member States are independently responsible for their joint obligations, irrespective of their internal division of competences.

The principle of independent responsibility, however, provides only part of the answer to the conundrum of the responsibility of the EU and its Member States because independent responsibility does not necessary result in joint responsibility. If an organization and its members are independently responsible for their joint obligations, how does one determine which subject is responsible in a given situation?

This follow-up question is particularly complex in the context of the EU. Under the constitutional architecture of the Union, Member States often

162 Stefan Talmon, 'Responsibility of International Organizations: Does the European Community Require Special Treatment?', in Maurizio Ragazzi (ed), *International Responsibility Today* (Martinus Nijhoff 2005); Nollkaemper 2012, 330.

163 ARIO Art 4; ARSIWA Art 2.

164 Heliskoski 2001, 150. There are exceptions, e.g. the Declaration of the EU to the Kyoto Protocol states that the EC and its Member States will fulfil the commitments jointly.

implement decisions and policies of the Union. In case Member States' measures result in a violation of a mixed agreement, how does one determine whose conduct was in breach of their joint obligations? Are Member States acting independently and so their actions must be attributed to them? Or are they acting as organs or agents of the Union in which case the EU is solely responsible? Or are they, instead, jointly responsible for a breach to which they both contributed? The following chapter thus addresses the concept of an organ and agent for the purpose of determining exclusive responsibility in the EU's multilayered structure.

4

The Concept of an Organ and Agent of the EU

4.1 INTRODUCTION

It was suggested in Chapter 2 that the International Law Commission (ILC) framework does not determine the allocation of responsibility in a multilayered structure such as that of the European Union (EU). The purpose of the International Law Commission's (ILC) framework is to establish whether a subject of international law *is* internally responsible. The draft articles do not address the internal allocation of responsibility within the EU. They apply to conduct which has already been detached from that of other subjects of international law with whom they share a common organizational structure. It was instead suggested that the legal basis for the allocation of responsibility is found in the rules of the organization and the international dispute-settlement practice in which those rules operate.

Accordingly, Chapter 3 looked into the EU's rules for the allocation of international responsibility. Based on an extensive analysis of international trade, investment and human rights case law, it was argued that the European Commission's claim for competence-based responsibility lacks support in international law. Instead, the chapter suggested suggested that both the EU and its Member States are independently responsible for breach of their joint obligations, irrespective of the internal division of competences.

It was also noted that the principle of independent responsibility for joint obligations does not necessarily mean that a breach will result in joint and several responsibility. That both the EU and its Member States *may* be held responsible for a breach of their joint obligations does not tell us which of them (or both of them) *will* be responsible in a given situation.

How then do we determine exclusive responsibility in situations where the EU and its Member States exercise shared sovereignty in a common governance arrangement, whereas the EU competences are implemented through Member States' authorities? In the context of such complex institutional structure, how do we separate the conduct of the EU from that of its Member States? As Wessel and Decker rightly note, state members of an international organization possess different identities, and it is difficult to identify '*where the State ends and the member State of an organization begins*'.[1] Klabbers suggests that one cannot approach this question '*in terms of a zero-sum game between the organization and its members, where powers exercised by the members on Monday may be transferred to the organization on Tuesday only to flow back again to the members on Wednesday, and so on and so forth*'.[2]

I return to the ILC framework to search for guidance on the attribution of conduct. A significant nuance must be explained. The ILC rules of attribution refer to broad *categories*[3] of individuals, that is organs and agents.[4] The general rule of attribution laid down in Article 6 of the Articles on the Responsibility of International Organizations (ARIO) state that '*the conduct of an organ or agent of an international organization in the performance of functions of that organ or agent shall be considered an act of that organization under international law, whatever position the organ or agent holds in respect of the organization*'. The ARIO does not specify which entity is an organ or agent of an organization. In other words, the ARIO tells us that *if* agent X is an organ of organization Y, that organization will be responsible for a breach committed by X. It does not tell us whether agent X is in fact an organ of Y. The ARIO framework is silent on this latter question because, as was argued in Chapter 2, the ILC rules do not deal with the internal arrangements and sovereignty sharing in the institutional structure of an international body. The *allocation* of responsibility within the EU is outside the ARIO framework.

While the ILC framework does not define an organ or agent of an international organization, the ILC's *travaux préparatoires* provide significant guidance in this regard. Accordingly, the following analysis will focus on the ILC rules as a source of international law to define the concept of an organ or agent of an international organization. I will thus not *apply* the ILC rules of attribution but will use this framework as guidance on how international law defines organic relationships within an organization. The aim of the present chapter is to determine when authorities of an EU Member State act as organs

1 Ramses A Wessel and Ige F Dekker, 'Identities of States in International Organizations', in Ana Sofia Barros, Cedric Ryngaert and Jan Wouters (eds), *International Organizations and Member State Responsibility: Critical Perspectives* (Brill Nijhoff 2017), 12.

2 Jan Klabbers, *An Introduction to International Institutional Law* (2nd edn, Cambridge University Press 2009), 309.

3 Ago himself refers to the term 'categories'; see Ago Third Report, 233.

4 The terminology used under the internal law is not decisive – what is decisive is not whether an entity is formally defined as an 'organ' but whether it in fact acts as one; see Gaja Third Report (n 75), 14.

or agents of the EU or that Member State. The ARIO bases for attribution of conduct determine whether a subject, whose sovereignty has already been detached from that of other legal persons, *is* responsible for a given breach. They can thus only be applied (specifically to the EU or its Member State) once responsibility has been allocated within the EU.

4.2 ILC DOCTRINE

States and international organizations act through individuals. The most common category – an organ – is a person who belongs to the formal structure of a state or an organization. An agent, on the other hand, is not part of the official machinery but acts on behalf of a state or an organization. As noted by the ILC member Reuter, an organ is a person that a statute formally established to be part of a state, whereas an agent possesses that status 'functionally'.[5] The ILC has employed conceptually different approaches with respect to the organic relationships between states and international organizations for the purposes of attribution of conduct. They will be examined in turn.

4.2.1 *The ARSIWA Framework*

In the early days of the ILC project on the Articles on Responsibility of States for Internationally Wrongful Acts (ARSIWA), the terms agent and organ were used interchangeably to refer to persons who form part of the internal machinery of the state.[6] A lack of a clear definition of the term organ has been noted by the Special Rapporteur Ago and other members of the ILC.[7] In his Third Report on the ARSIWA, Ago listed a number of earlier cases which defined an act of the state as one carried out by its agents, without making a distinction between different types of individuals who act on behalf of the state.[8] As was noted by ILC member Tammes during the discussions of the ARSIWA draft, all persons acting on behalf of the state, whether regular or *ad hoc*, temporary or *de facto*, were part of the same kind of organ in the Kelsian sense of 'organon'.[9] Ago also relied on Article 15 of the draft Convention on the international responsibility of states for injuries of aliens, prepared by the

5 Summary Record of the 1212th Meeting, A/CN.4/SR.1212 (ILC 1973), 53, para 46.
6 Ago Third Report, 238, para 122.
7 Summary Record of the 1261st Meeting, A/CN.4/SR.1261 (ILC 1974), 50–51, paras 11–23.
8 Ago Third Report, 329, para 124.
9 Summary Record of the 1253rd Meeting, A/CN.4/SR.1253 (ILC 1974), 13, para 6.

Harvard Law School in 1961, which conflated acts of 'organs, agencies, officials or employees' of the state into one base of attribution.[10]

At the time of the drafting of the ARSIWA Article 5 (now Article 4), which provides a general rule of attribution of acts of its organs to the state, the term 'organ' was not yet defined and the opinions of the ILC members differed on the matter.[11] Ago himself initially did not make a distinction between the two categories of 'organ' and 'agent'. He used the terms interchangeably to refer to persons who participate in the organization of the state and who are considered state organs according to the internal legal order.[12] Several ILC members suggested differentiating between formal and *de facto* state organs.[13] For example, according to Wallat, the term 'agent' could be used to refer to a person having the status of an agent of the state, but it could also be used in its more ordinary sense of a person acting as an agent in a specific case, whereas the general rule of attribution only dealt with persons regarded as organs of the state.[14]

During the consideration of Ago's Third Report it was agreed to exclude the term 'agent' from draft Article 5 as it seems '*to denote, especially in English, a person acting on behalf of the State rather than a person having the actual status of an organ*'.[15] Though without using the word 'agent', the latter category of persons was covered by what at the time was draft Article 8. The latter rule of attribution addressed persons to whom Ago referred as *de facto* officials, in other words persons who in principle were not state officials but who in special circumstances were called upon to perform state functions.[16]

The Special Rapporteur Crawford maintained the distinction between the categories of organ and agent based on whether or not a person is part of the structure of the state (organ), or whether they are acting on behalf of the state by reason of some mandate or direction (agent).[17] In his First Report

10 Ago Third Report, 240, para 126.

11 Summary Record of the 1226th Meeting, A/CN.4/SR.1226 (ILC 1973), 121, paras 17–19.

12 Summary Record of the 1210th Meeting, A/CN.4/SR.1210 (ILC 1973), 45, para 54.

13 Summary Record of the 1258th Meeting, A/CN.4/SR.1258 (ILC 1974), 34, para 18, for comments by Tammes; Summary Record of the 1255th Meeting, A/CN.4/SR.1255 (ILC 1974), 19, para 24, for comments by Ushakov.

14 Summary Record of the 1212th Meeting, A/CN.4/SR.1212, 53, 58–59.

15 Report of the International Law Commission on the Work of Its Twenty-Fifth Session, 7 May – 13 July 1973, Official Records of the General Assembly, Twenty-Eighth Session, Supplement, A/9010/Rev.1, 193, para 13.

16 Summary Record of the 1258th Meeting, A/CN.4/SR.1258, 32, para 3.

17 Crawford First Report, 35, para 162. Per Crawford, direction and control of a state as the basis for attribution, which was initially noted by the ICJ in *Military and Paramilitary Activities in*

Crawford noted that it was difficult to typologize persons who act on behalf of the state but were not part of its official structure. He noted that the origin of Article 7 can be found in the work of the 1930 Hague Conference for the Codification of International Law, where reference was made to proliferation and variety of '*autonomous institutions which exercise public functions of a legislative or administrative character*' and that their real common feature was the exercise of specified functions which are akin to those normally exercised by organs of the state.[18] The concept of autonomous institutions which exercise public functions of a legislative or administrative character was understood to cover any type of body or entity of whatever nature, the focus being on the empowerment to exercise functions normally exercised by organs of the state.[19] With respect to the latter category, Crawford remodelled draft Article 8 into what is now found in Article 5 of the ARSIWA under the heading 'Conduct of persons or entities exercising elements of governmental authority'.

States supported the inclusion of *de facto* agents of the state in the rules of attribution of conduct. The United States noted that a relationship between a person and a state may exist *de facto* even where it is difficult to pinpoint a precise legal relationship.[20] Austria was also of an opinion that rules of attribution sufficiently cover acts of natural persons and juridical persons, who, at the time of committing a violation of international law, do not act as state organs but nevertheless act under the authority and control of the state.[21] Similarly, Germany[22] and Mongolia[23] noted the importance of taking into account the fact that states increasingly entrust persons outside the structure of the state with activities normally attributable to a state. Though not supported

and against Nicaragua, is to be treated as a general principle, Crawford's First Report, 43, para 213. As for the term 'effective control', which was employed by the ICJ, Judge Ago required nothing less than specific authorization of the wrongful conduct itself, Crawford's First Report, 40, para 200.

18 Crawford First Report, 38, para 183.

19 Yearbook of the International Law Commission, A/CN.4/SER.A/1998/Add.1 (Part 1) (ILC 1998), 277, para 2 of commentary to art 7.

20 Yearbook of the International Law Commission, A/CN.4/SER.A/1998/Add.1 (Part 1), 108, United States' comment to Article 8 (Attribution to the State of the conduct of persons acting in fact on behalf of the State).

21 Official Records of the General Assembly, Fifty-second Session, Sixth Committee, 23rd meeting (A/C.6/52/SR.23), and corrigendum, 6, para 31.

22 See Yearbook of the International Law Commission, A/CN.4/SER.A/1998/Add.1 (Part 1), 105, for Germany's comment to chapter 2 as a whole of the draft.

23 See Yearbook of the International Law Commission, A/CN.4/SER.A/1998/Add.1 (Part 1), 107, for Mongolia's comment to Article 8 (Attribution to the State of the conduct of persons acting in fact on behalf of the State).

by the ILC, France's position was that the term 'state organ' is too restrictive and the better term would be 'any state organ or agent'.[24]

To summarize, the general rule of attribution under Article 4 of the ARSIWA is based on a person's formal status as an 'organ' in the official structure of the state. Situations when a person who is not part of the state machinery, nevertheless acts on behalf of the state, are addressed in other articles. Conduct of persons who act on behalf of the state but are not part of its formal structure is only attributed to the state if there is some additional element: empowerment to carry governmental authority by the state (Article 5) or direction and control by the state (Article 8). According to Crawford, there can be substantive differences between the two cases. For example, unauthorized acts of organs are to be attributed to the state, whereas different considerations may apply to unauthorized acts of agents.[25]

4.2.2 *The ARIO Framework*

The ARIO framework, which otherwise closely follows the structure of the ARSIWA, provides a conceptually different approach to attribution of conduct. While the general rule of attribution under the ARSIWA is based on the structural relationship between a person and a state, the ARIO employs a functional approach. The source of the functional test employed by the ILC is the advisory opinion in the *Reparation for Injuries* case, where the International Court of Justice (ICJ) stated that what matters for a person to be regarded as an agent is not his or her character as an official but the fact that he or she is a '*person through whom [the organization] acts*'.[26] According to Gaja, when a person was entrusted by an organization in his or her official capacity with a mission, that person acted for the organization.[27]

24 See Yearbook of the International Law Commission, A/CN.4/SER.A/1998/Add.1 (Part 1), 105, para. 1, for France's comment to Article 5 (Attribution to the State of the conduct of its organs).

25 Crawford First Report, 35, para 162.

26 Yearbook of the International Law Commission, A/CN.4/SER.A/2004/Add.1 (Part 2) (ILC 2004), 49, para 5, commentary to Article 4. The ILC cites p 177 of the Advisory Opinion in the *Reparation for injuries suffered in the service of the United Nations*.

27 Summary Record of the 2800th Meeting, A/CN.4/SR.2800, 67, para 5. The phrase to express the link between a person and an international organization, as chosen by the Drafting Committee, was 'conduct of an organ or agent in the performance of the functions of that organ or agent' as opposed to an alternative 'in the performance of their official functions'. The chosen phrase had to solve the problem of the burden of proof since the solution was that a complainant simply had to prove that the conduct of the organ or agent had occurred in the performance of its functions, and not that the function was also the function of the organization, Summary Record of the 2800th Meeting, A/CN.4/SR.2800, 136, para 8.

Making a U-turn from the approach held by both Ago and Crawford with respect to states, Gaja maintained that there is little reason for distinguishing between persons who had the formal status of an 'organ' and other persons who did not have that official status. In his Second Report on the ARIO, Gaja thus argued in favour of a broad general rule of attribution which '*would cover most cases in which a person was entrusted with part of an international organization's functions or whose conduct was directed or controlled by an international organization*'.[28] Gaja referred to 'organs, agents and officials' without differentiating between them and stressed the importance for attribution of external boundaries rather than the internal boundaries between those categories.[29] According to the drafters of the ARIO, the distinction between organs and agents does not appear to be relevant for the purposes of attribution of conduct to an international organization since conduct of both is attributable to it.[30] Given that some international organizations criticized this approach,[31] the ILC noted that in exceptional cases, a person or entity could be considered as having been entrusted with functions of the organization, even if this was not in accordance with the rules of organization.[32] The ILC noted that most international organizations act through their organs (whether so defined or not) and a variety of agents who carry out functions of an organization.[33]

In line with Gaja's approach and in accordance with the ICJ's interpretation of agent in the *Reparations for Injuries* case '*in the most liberal sense*',[34] the

[28] Summary Record of the 2800th Meeting, A/CN.4/SR.2800, 68, para 12.

[29] Summary Record of the 2803rd Meeting, A/CN.4/SR.2803 (ILC 2004), 92, para 49.

[30] Yearbook of the International Law Commission, A/CN.4/SER.A/2004/Add.1 (Part 2), 48, para 5, commentary to Article 4.

[31] The ILO referred to Article 8 of ARSIWA and noted that 'if not based on the rules of organizations, the conduct of a person or entity could be attributable to an organization only if acting on its instruction, or under its direction or control'; see Comments A/CN.4/568, 130, sect E. INTERPOL stated that the National Central Bureau is to be considered as either an organ or agent of INTERPOL; however, due to a lack of effective control over these bodies, their conduct will normally not be attributed to INTERPOL; see Comments A/CN.4/556, 37.

[32] Yearbook of the International Law Commission, A/CN.4/SER.A/2004/Add.1 (Part 2), 49, para 9, commentary to Art 4.

[33] Yearbook of the International Law Commission, A/CN.4/SER.A/2004/Add.1 (Part 2), (2004), 48, para 4. The ILC refers to the decision of the Swiss Federal Council of 30 October 1996, which stated: 'As a rule, one may attribute to an international organization the acts and omissions of its organs of all rank and nature and of its agents in the exercise of their competences' (translation form the original French, document VPB 61.75, published on the Swiss Federal Council's website: www/vpb.admin.ch).

[34] Advisory opinion in the *Reparations for injuries suffered in the service of the United Nations*, 177.

Drafting Committee adopted a broad concept of the general rule of attribution. The Drafting Committee preferred the term 'agent' on account of the importance attached to it by the Advisory Opinion of the ICJ.[35] According to the Drafting Committee, the reason for including the latter element was to ensure that the draft articles do not exclude the possibility that an organization could confer certain functions on an organ or agent without clear statement to that effect in the organization's rules as well as cases of 'apparent authority'.[36] A narrow rule would require identifying the various natural and legal persons through whom an organization performs its functions, which was a complicated undertaking due to a variety of international organizations.[37] The term 'agent' provided in the ARIO is thus wide enough to cover situations enshrined in Articles 5 and 8 of the ARSIWA.[38] It may even be argued that Article 8 of the ARIO, which states that *ultra vires* conduct of organs and agents is attributed to an international organization, is superfluous. If there is no requirement for formal status, empowerment or control by the organization for the purposes of attribution of conduct, there can be no exceeding of its authority – what does not exist, cannot be measured.

Gaja's approach was welcomed by other members of the ILC,[39] some of whom noted the conceptual difference of the general rule under the ARIO with that of the ARSIWA.[40] Due to the broad scope of the general rule of attribution under Article 6 of the ARIO, the ILC considered it unnecessary to

35 Comment by Cedeño, chairperson of the Drafting Committee, Summary Record of the 2810th Meeting, A/CN.4/SR.2810 (ILC 2004), 136, para 6. At the outset the Committee also considered the term 'official', but it was later agreed to refer to 'organs and agents' only since the latter term covered officials.

36 Summary Record of the 2810th Meeting, A/CN.4/SR.2810, 136, para 11.

37 Comment by Cedeño, chairperson of the Drafting Committee, Summary Record of the 2810th Meeting, A/CN.4/SR.2810, 135, para 5. Similarly, it was decided to replace the phrase 'in the structure of the organization', as suggested by Gaja, with 'in the organization' because it was more suited to the broad definition of an organ or agent which was adopted by the Committee, Summary Record of the 2810th Meeting, A/CN.4/SR.2810, 136, para 9.

38 Yearbook of the International Law Commission, A/CN.4/SER.A/2004/Add.1 (Part 2), 49, paras 12–13, commentary to Art 4.

39 For comments by Cedeño, see Summary Record of the 2801st Meeting, A/CN.4/SR.2801, 81, para 74; for comments by Galicki, see Summary Record of the 2803rd Meeting, A/CN.4/SR.2803, 86, para 3. But see comments by Dugard who noted that while he cannot see how the drafting can be improved, he nevertheless wished to reiterate that the whole question of who was an agent of the UN remained an unexplored area and that the UN practice was not clear on the subject, Summary Record of the 2803rd Meeting, A/CN.4/SR.2803, 91, para 42.

40 For comment by Galicki, see Summary Record of the 2803rd Meeting, A/CN.4/SR.2803, 86, para 5; for comment by Pellet, see Summary Record of the 2801st Meeting, A/CN.4/SR.2801, 74, para 8.

include rules equivalent to Articles 5 and 8 of the ARSIWA. Both conduct by persons empowered to exercise elements of (governmental) authority (the ARSIWA Article 5) and conduct of persons acting on the direction and control (the ARSIWA Article 8) fall under the scope of the general rule of attribution laid down in Article 6 of the ARIO.

Some international organizations met the general rule of attribution with apprehension and noted that they have no practice of external persons acting on their behalf. The World Health Organization (WHO) and the World Trade Organization (WTO) remarked that their internal rules contained no provisions regarding persons acting on behalf of the organization.[41] The International Labour Organization (ILO) similarly expressed a concern over a wide scope of the definition of the term 'agent' which '*includes officials and other persons or entities through whom the organization acts*'.[42] According to the ILO, in its reference to the Advisory Opinion in *Reparation for Injuries*, the ILC used only the last part of the definition of 'agent' and left out an important qualification '*charged by an organ of the Organization*' and so expanded the scope of the term 'agent' beyond the limits established by the rules of organization.[43] The ILO claimed that it was difficult to foresee under what circumstances conduct of external entities could be attributed to the organization. According to the ILO, besides acts of officials or experts on missions performed in their official capacity, only conduct of persons or entities operating in fact on the instruction, or under the direction and control of an organization, could be attributed to the latter.[44]

The United Nations Educational, Scientific and Cultural Organization (UNESCO) raised concern that the reference to 'functional link' as a parameter to determine whether the conduct of entities through which an organization acts is attributed to it is not sufficiently developed to clearly delimit the category of 'agents'.[45] It gave the example of private contractors

41 Comments A/CN.4/545, 34, sect 4 para 1 for comment by the WHO and sect 5 for comments by the WTO.

42 Comments A/CN.4/568, 130, sect E.

43 Comments A/CN.4/637, 17, para 2 comments by the ILO. The ILO questioned whether it was the intention of the ILC that situations of state representatives performing temporarily functions for the organization but in their national capacity, such as the chairperson of meetings and organs, the members of various bodies such as the Commission itself, or judges of administrative and international criminal tribunals, trigger responsibility of the organization concerned; see Comments A/CN.4/637 (n 28), 18, para 3.

44 Comments A/CN.4/568, 131, sect E.

45 Comments A/CN.4/568, 130, sect E.

who perform various operational activities of similar nature to those carried out by UNESCO officials. According to UNESCO, contractual relations with such persons exclude attribution of their conduct to UNESCO.[46] Similarly, the International Monetary Fund (IMF) noted that in its Articles of Agreement it employs the term 'officials' to refer to officials, agents and other persons acting on its behalf.[47] Under the internal rules of the IMF, the criteria for attribution of acts of officials are consistent with the criteria used to determine whether or not the conduct of IMF officials constituted acts performed by them in their official capacity to which the IMF immunities apply.[48] Without providing a clear definition, the IMF differentiates officials from external entities.[49] As to the latter, the IMF noted that it is not aware of cases in which an act of an external entity had been attributed to the IMF, and, in its view, no act of an entity external to the IMF could be attributable to the IMF unless an appropriate IMF organ ratified or expressly assumed responsibility for that act.[50]

Nevertheless, the drafters of the ARIO adopted a broad functional approach to the general rule of attribution according to which acts of any organ, agent or official, whether part of the official structure of the organization or as *de facto* agents, can be attributed to the organization if they carryout one of its functions.

To reiterate the introductory point made earlier, the ILC framework speaks only in the language of general categories. That the ILC has adopted a broad concept of organ and agent is useful to the present analysis but does not allow to definitively differentiate between organs/agents of the EU and its Member States for the purposes of determining exclusive responsibility. The following section thus look at how the concept of an organ and agent is defined by the EU itself and whether its approach finds support in international dispute-settlement practice.

4.3 A *DE FACTO* ORGAN OF THE EU

Separating the conduct of the EU and its Member States in situations where there is a breach of joint obligations through the exercise of their shared sovereignty is complex. To provide an illustration of the many scenarios that may arise, the following questions must be considered. Are Member

46 Comments A/CN.4/568, 131, sect E.
47 Comments A/CN.4/545, 33, para 1.
48 Article IX, sect. 8 of the IMF Articles of Agreement.
49 Comments A/CN.4/545, 33, sect 3 para 1.
50 Comments A/CN.4/545, 34, sect 3 paras 1–4.

States' customs authorities acting as EU organs when they implement EU customs decisions, resulting in attribution of conduct to the EU? Should the EU, rather, be attributed responsibility because it adopts decisions binding its Member States? If so, what about Member States' discretion? Klabbers rightly notes that a breach of an international agreement will usually stem from the conduct of an organ of the EU or Member State in compliance with some sort of EU regulation.[51] But that does not tell us all that much. Putting aside official EU institutions like the European Commission and the Council, juridical categorization of the EU's executive governance is not straightforward.

Attempts have been made to disentangle this complex relationship. Titi, for example, explores the complex web of institutional ties and decision-making processes in relation to financial assistance during the Eurozone crisis.[52] However, as the author herself admits, the discussion is about *potential* responsibility only because international dispute-settlement practice in the area of the Eurozone financial crisis does not (yet) exist.[53] A comprehensive analysis on the topic can be found in the recent work of Wessel and Dekker who provide insight into the many identities of a state which is a member of an international organization.[54]

As has been noted in the beginning of this chapter, the ARIO rules do not provide relevant answers. The general rule of attribution stated in Article 6 refers to '*[t]he conduct of an organ or agent of an international organization*' without specifying which organ or agent is an organ or agent of an organization. The second paragraph of the ARIO Article 6 states that the rules of organization apply in the determination of the functions of its organs and agents. Though the provision does not say so expressly, it seems that the answer as to who is an organ or agent of the EU and its Member States is to be sought in the rules of organization.

In its comments during the drafting of the ARIO, the European Commission took the view that when implementing a binding act of the EU, Member States act as *de facto* organs of the EU, so that '*the conduct of the organ of a member State would be attributed [to the EU]*'.[55] The EU's approach relates to the doctrine of *dédoublement fonctionnel*, which may be

51 Klabbers 2009, 279.

52 Catharine Titi, 'Aspects of the EU's Responsibility in International Investment Disputes', in Marise Cremona, Anne Thies and Ramses Wessel (eds), *The European Union and the International Dispute Settlement* (Hart Publishing 2017).

53 Titi 2017.

54 Wessel and Dekker 2017.

55 Gaja Seventh Report, 12.

interpreted as meaning that Member States' authorities perform a dual role.[56] Member States implement their own law and at the same time they are functionally organs of the EU. This, according to Delgado Casteleiro, is the main consequence of the adoption of executive federalism within the EU.[57] The argument may be traced to an obligation of the Member States to fulfil all measures of national law necessary to implement legally binding Union acts stated in Article 291(1) of the Treaty on the Functioning of the European Union (TFEU).

Talmon interprets the general rule of attribution laid down in Article 6 of the ARIO as being wide enough to accommodate the EU's claim that Member States' authorities act as *de facto* organs or agents of the EU when they exercise Community functions.[58] A number of scholars, however, doubt as to whether the EU's approach sits comfortably with Article 6. Kuijper and Paasivirta, for example, suggest that Article 6 '*does not capture the core features of the EU action, since the Member States are seen as remaining sovereign and not constituting organs of the organization in a formal sense. Consequently, the Member States would always be responsible, as the immediate actors, should acts be attributed on purely organic lines*'.[59] Delgado Casteleiro, whose study provides the most extensive analysis on the normative control of the EU to date, also concludes that Article 6 does not deal with EU normative control scenarios.[60]

To reiterate an argument made earlier, however, the question of who are the EU's organs should not be interpreted through the prism of whether they are covered by Article 6 – the general rule of attribution does not tell us who should be considered as EU organs. It only tells us that *if* an organ is an EU organ, its conduct is attributed to the EU. The content of 'if' is not addressed in the ILC framework. In this context, we may only look at the ILC framework as a source of general legal theory, not as governing law.

The EU's argument that Member States' organs act as its *de facto* organs for the purposes of attribution of conduct is flawed in that such arrangement

56 Higgins 1995.

57 Andrés Delgado Casteleiro, *The International Responsibility of the European Union: From Competence to Normative Control* (Cambridge University Press 2016), 43.

58 Stefan Talmon, 'Responsibility of International Organizations: Does the European Community Require Special Treatment?', in Maurizio Ragazzi (ed), *International Responsibility Today* (Martinus Nijhoff 2005), 412.

59 Pieter Jan Kuijper and Esa Paasivirta, 'EU International Responsibility and Its Attribution: From the Inside Looking Out', in Malcolm Evans and Panos Koutrakos (eds), *The International Responsibility of the European Union: European and International Perspective* (Hart Publishing 2013), 54.

60 Delgado Casteleiro 2016, 71.

lacks some of the common institutional characteristics. The EU cannot exert its decisions on Member States' authorities directly, but it has to do so through the Member States. This is the essence of the EU's executive federalism.[61] Neither are Member States' authorities part of the institutional structure of the EU, similarly to EU organs such as the European Commission. However, given that the drafters of the ARIO interpreted the term agent and organ broadly and did not consider it necessary that they be part of the official structure of the organization, the ILC doctrine of international responsibility does not prevent the EU's claim that Member States' authorities may act as its *de facto* organs for the purposes of attribution of conduct. But does the EU's approach find support in international dispute settlement practice?

Some interpret the WTO Panel's report in the *EC – Geographical Indications* dispute as a landmark decision which established the principle that the EU bears international responsibility on behalf of its Member States because the latter act as *de facto* organs of the EU when they implement Union decisions.[62] In paragraph 7.269 of its Report, the Panel noted that '*Community laws are generally not executed through authorities at Community level but rather through recourse to the authorities of its member States which, in such a situation, 'act de facto as organs of the Community, for which the Community would be responsible under WTO law and international law in general'*.[63]

It is true that under the WTO dispute-settlement regime, the general practice is that the EU represents its Member States. That, however, is based on the nature of their joint participation in mixed agreements, which will be addressed in detail in Part II. To the best of my knowledge, there is nothing in the WTO case law which suggests that the Dispute Settlement Body (DSB) allocates international responsibility to the EU *because* it considers that Member States act as organs of the EU when implementing its decisions.

Reliance on the cited passage in *EC – Geographical Indications* to address the question of shared responsibility is questionable. The Panel's conclusion on the principal/agent relationship between the EU and its Member States is unrelated to the issue of responsibility. The Panel addressed a substantive, not a procedural, aspect of the case.

61 Pieter Jan Kuijper, 'International Responsibility from Mixed Agreements', in Christophe Hillion and Panos Koutrakos (eds), *Mixed Agreements Revisited: The EU and its Member States in the World* (Hart Publishing 2010).

62 For example, Francesco Messineo, 'Attribution of Conduct', in André Nollkaemper and Ilias Plakokefalos (eds), *Principles of Shared Responsibility in International Law: An Appraisal of the State of the Art* (Cambridge University Press 2014), 75, ft 57.

63 *EC – Geographical Indications*, PR, para 7.269.

The issue under consideration was whether the application procedure for registration of geographical indications subjected holders of names of agricultural products and foodstuffs located in a third country outside the EC to a less favourable treatment than that afforded to nationals of Member States. Under the disputed regulation, all applicants were required to submit their applications in the country in which the geographical area was located, that is to the authorities either of an EC Member State or a third country. If authorities which received an application considered that it satisfied the requirements of the regulation, they were to forward it to the EC Commission. The question before the Panel was whether the filing of an application to a Member State authority was equivalent to applying directly to the EC. If this was the case, the argument of the claimant followed, holders of names located in third countries were disadvantaged because their application process included an additional step of review by an intermediary third country authority.

To answer this question, the Panel had to determine whether Member State authorities act as organs of the EC in which case the filing of an application through a Member State authority would mean filing to the EC itself. In that same paragraph 7.269, the Panel thus concluded that

> *any application relating to a geographical area located in an EC member State is filed directly with a 'de facto organ of the Community' which also carries out the initial examination. An application relating to a geographical area located in a third country cannot be filed directly, but must be filed with a foreign government. This is a formal difference in treatment.*

The remark, however, is entirely unrelated to the question of international responsibility and instead addressed a wholly separate issue of the process of registration of geographical names.[64]

The cited statement that Member States can act as organs of the EU has been reiterated in another WTO case, *EC – Selected Customs Matters*. It is true that the DSB acknowledges that in some cases organs of Member States may perform *dédoublement fonctionnel*. The Panel in this case noted that the courts of the Member States may be assigned a dual role – when determining a dispute governed by national law, they form part of the national legal order; however, according to the Panel, the same national courts assume the status

64 In a similar manner, the panel refers to the EU/Member State agency relationship with respect to other substantive issues, for example, in paras 7.725–7.726, to conclude that to the extent that advantages are granted under the disputed regulation by the EC and Member States' authorities exercising powers under the regulation, to the EC's own nationals, those advantages are not granted to the nationals of any other country.

of Community courts when determining a case governed by Community law.[65]

The statement, however, was once again unrelated to the question of attribution of conduct. The dispute arose as to whether the EC's obligation under Article X:3(b) of the General Agreement on Tariffs and Trade (GATT) 1994 to maintain judicial procedures for the prompt review and correction of administrative action relating to customs matters can be satisfied through the Member States' institutional structures. The EC referred to *EC – Geographical Indications* to argue that the judicial authorities of the EC Member States fulfilled that requirement, because Member States' courts are EC courts when it comes to the application and interpretation of EC law.[66] The United States disagreed with the analogy,[67] but the Panel concluded that the EC may comply with its obligations through organs in its Member States[68] because authorities in the Member States act as organs of the EC when they review and correct administrative action taken pursuant to EC customs law.[69] Once again, the statement here relates to a substantive issue, that is whether an obligation to ensure judicial review can be fulfilled through Member States' courts. It is unrelated to the question of international responsibility.[70]

Furthermore, it is questionable whether attributing conduct of Member States' organs to the EU when they implement EU competences is compatible with the principle of independent responsibility. If the EU and its Member States are independently responsible for violations of their joint obligations irrespective of the internal division of competences, how then could conduct of a Member State's organ be attributed to the EU on the basis that it is carrying an EU function? The DSB makes this point as well. It refuses to acknowledge that violations by Member States' organs may be attributed to the EU based on its internal law. The DSB does not release Member States from responsibility for conduct of their organs, irrespective of the internal law of the EU. For example, in *EC – Large Civil Aircraft* the Panel noted that '*[w]hatever responsibility the European Communities bears for the actions of its member*

65 *European Communities – Selected Customs Matters*, WT/DS315/R, PR adopted 11 December 2006 (*EC – Selected Customs Matters*), para 2.23.

66 *EC – Selected Customs Matters*, PR, para 4.385.

67 *EC – Selected Customs Matters*, PR, para 4.705.

68 *EC – Selected Customs Matters*, PR, para 4.552.

69 *EC – Selected Customs Matters*, PR, para 4.553.

70 The EU's reference in para 4.708 of the PR to the ILC rules of responsibility, which state that the responsibility for internationally wrongful acts extends not only to organs of the central government but also to organs of territorial units, is misplaced – the EU is using ARSIWA as a general institutional law of international organizations, which falls outside the scope of the articles.

States does not diminish their rights and obligations as WTO Members, but is rather an internal matter concerning the relations between the European Communities and its Member States'.[71]

EC and Certain Member States – IT Products provides another example of the DSB's refusal to release Member States from responsibility when their organs implement or apply EU law. Instead, the Panel confirmed that EC Member States are WTO members in their own right and that, like all WTO members, they are bound to act consistently with their WTO obligations.[72] According to the Panel, '*if one or more EC member States were found to have applied WTO inconsistent measures, be they enacted by the States themselves or by the European Communities, it could be appropriate to find that the member States have acted inconsistently with their WTO obligations*'.[73] The Panel stated so irrespective of the European Commission's submission that the EC attests that Member States would be required under Community law to apply the implementing measures taken by the EC to meet the Panel's recommendation.[74]

EC – Computer Equipment provides yet another example where the DSB refrains from endorsing the view that authorities of Member States act as organs of the EU when they implement Union law. The case concerned tariff application for certain computer technology by the EU, as well as the customs authorities of the United Kingdom and Ireland. The Panel's reference to 'customs authorities in the European Union' could be read as supporting the EU's proposition that Member States' customs authorities act functionally as EU organs when implementing EU law, and thus responsibility for their conduct should be attributed to the EU.[75] However, such interpretation is unlikely given that the Panel unequivocally states that '*the European Communities, Ireland and the United Kingdom are all bound by their tariff commitments under Schedule LXXX*' and that '*[t]he respondents in these documents are the European Communities, the United Kingdom and Ireland,*

71 *EC – Large Civil Aircraft*, PR, para 7.175.

72 *EC and Certain Member States – IT Products*, PR, para 8.2.

73 *EC and Certain Member States – IT Products*, PR, para 8.2.

74 *EC and Certain Member States – IT Products*, European Communities' response to the panel's Question No. 17. See also the statements of the European Communities at the panel's organizational meeting of 4 February 2009; letter from the Delegation of the Commission (4 February 2009).

75 Gracia Marín Durán, 'The EU and Its Member States in WTO Dispute Settlement: A "Competence Model," or a Case Apart, for Managing International Responsibility?', in Marise Cremona, Anne Thies and Ramses A Wessel (eds), *The EU and International Dispute Settlement* (Hart Publishing 2016).

respectively'.[76] The Panel thus refuses to allocate exclusive responsibility to the EU on the basis that Member States' customs authorities act as *de facto* EU organs. Flett similarly suggests that the Panel did not state that the EU had exclusive responsibility for such matters, but rather that the EU and its Member States would concurrently bear the obligations contained in the WTO Agreements.[77]

Direct application of the reference in *EC – Geographical Indications* to '*de facto* organs of the EU' as a legal basis of the EU's exclusive responsibility is even less convincing given the ambiguous and inconsistent interpretation of this organic relationship by the EU itself. The case-law analysis reveals that the EU characterizes its principal/agent relationship with the Member States in accordance with its defence strategy on a case-by-case basis.

For example, in some cases, the EC denied the existence of any degree of Member States' independence with respect to customs administration. In *EC – Geographical Indications*, the EC argued that the disputed regulation was a measure of the Community and not of its Member States, and therefore only the views of the EC institutions, and not the individual views of the Member States, were relevant for the interpretation of that same regulation.[78] According to the European Commission, it is unclear what the United States means when it says that Member States are '*acting pursuant to an EC*' to the disputed regulation.[79] The European Commission maintained that the EC was the only respondent in this dispute, despite the fact that '*[u]ndoubtedly, the Member States have certain responsibilities in the implementation and execution of [the disputed] Regulation*'.[80] The European Commission's submission thus denies the existence of any degree of Member States' sovereignty when they implement Union law. Similarly, in *EC – Selected Customs Matters* the EC argued that under international law, it was allowed to discharge its obligations through its Member States.[81] It maintained that Member States do not apply their own interpretation of the tariff classification and there

76 *EC – Computer Equipment*, PR, para 8.16.

77 James Flett, 'The Practice of Shared Responsibility in Relation to The World Trade Organization and the European Union and Its Member States in the WTO', in André Nollkaemper and Ilias Plakokefalos (eds), *The Practice of Shared Responsibility in International Law* (Cambridge University Press 2016), 890.

78 *EC – Geographical Indications*, replies to questions of the European Communities after 1st Meeting, Question No. 70, para 173.

79 *EC – Geographical Indications*, second written submission of the EC, 22 July 2004, Annex B-5, B-210, para 255.

80 *EC – Geographical Indications*, second written submission of the EC, 22 July 2004, Annex B-5, B-210, para 255.

81 *EC – Selected Customs Matters*, PR, para 4.705.

can be no inconsistency in the system of the EC's customs administration due to a number of mechanisms which ensure the uniform interpretation and application of its customs laws.[82]

On other occasions, however, the EC has argued in favour of an opposite position that Member States remain responsible for the implementation or application of Union law. For example, in *EC and Certain Member States – IT Products*, the EU refused to release Member States from international responsibility by stating that while the EC is exclusively competent to decide the duty applicable to each product at issue, the 'application' of such duty *'is the sole responsibility of the EC member State customs authority'*.[83] Similarly, in *EC – Selected Customs Matters* the European Commission alluded to GATT Article XXIV:12 which calls for observance of the provisions of GATT by regional and local governments and authorities, thus suggesting that it considered the dispute to be about the observance of the uniform application of customs laws by the Member States, not by itself.[84] In *EC – Geographical Indications* it also submitted that implementation of the disputed regulation is not only the responsibility of the Community but also of its Member States, who, for instance, are responsible for the transmission of applications and objections regarding the registration of geographical names to the Commission.[85]

Similarly, in *EC – Computer Equipment* the EC asserted that Member States have transferred to the Union their sovereignty with respect to customs matters, and therefore the EC has assumed full responsibility for obligations in this field.[86] However, the European Commission at the same time rejected that incorrect classification of customs tariffs by Member States could be considered as its own conduct. According to the Commission, *'it was clear that the EC was not bound vis-à-vis its trading partners by any actions of national authorities which were inconsistent with the EC's position'*.[87] Similarly, the EU refused to accept that the issuance of binding tariff information (BTI)[88] by Member States authorities could have created a legitimate

[82] *EC – Selected Customs Matters*, PR paras 4.757–4.763, also para 4.756.

[83] *EC and Certain Member States – IT Products*, PR, para 6.11.

[84] *EC – Selected Customs Matters*, PR, para 4.454. The United States disagreed, stating that the article is not applicable because the dispute did not concern observance of GATT provisions by regional and local governments and authorities in the EC, but by the EC itself.

[85] *EC – Geographical Indications*, EC's Request for Preliminary Ruling, 24 February 2004, para 31.

[86] *EC – Computer Equipment*, PR, para 4.15.

[87] *EC – Computer Equipment*, PR, para 5.39.

[88] Under EU law, a natural or legal person wishing to know how goods for export or import are classified by the national customs authorities of the Member States through which the goods

expectation for importers as against the EC because '*BTIs did not represent classification decisions of the EC*'.[89]

In *EC – Commercial Vessels* too, the EU separated its conduct from that of the Member States, even though Member States acted in the EU's area of competence. The European Commission disputed that Korea's challenge of the EU state aid scheme in the shipping sector covered individual instances of financing by the Member States. The European Commission stated that '*the member State measures are not implementing measures of the TDM Regulation. They are autonomous decisions on whether or not to make use of the derogation from the prohibition under EC law of contract-related operating aid in the shipbuilding sector*'.[90] The European Commission did not consider Member States' measures to be part of its domain of activity. Importantly, the European Commission stressed that the challenged EU regulation was not a specific authorization and Member States' measures were thus not 'implementing' measures.[91] It concluded that Member States' measures were not covered by the claim against the EU. In this particular dispute, the European Commission has thus suggested that unless Member States are given specific authorizations to implement an EU policy, they are not implementing EU law. Such approach contradicts the EU's claim on other occasions that it is responsible for all activities in its area of competence.

Finally, it is questionable whether the European Commission's claim that Member States' authorities act as *de facto* organs of the EU when they implement Union law for the purposes of allocating international responsibility is compatible with EU law itself. Particularly, I query whether the European Commission's position is consistent with the doctrine of direct actions before the EU Courts against the Member States. Article 258 TFEU provides that the European Commission can start infringement proceedings if it considers that '*a Member State has failed to fulfil an obligation under the Treaties*'. In this context, the Court of Justice of the European Union (CJEU) interprets the notion of 'state' broadly.[92] The Court's case law shows that

will enter the EU market, may request a BTI. A BTI constitutes a commitment of the relevant customs authorities *vis-à-vis* the individual applicant.

89 *EC – Computer Equipment*, PR, para 5.47.

90 *EC – Commercial Vessels*, PR, para 4.22.

91 *EC – Commercial Vessels*, PR, para 4.23.

92 For example, the notion of 'state' has been given a broad definition in the case law on direct effect of directives; see C-188-89 A. *Foster and others* v. *British Gas plc.* [1990] ECR I-3313, para 20.

Member States may incur liability under Article 258 TFEU '*whatever the agency of the State whose action or inaction is the cause of the failure to fulfil its obligations, even in the case of a constitutionally independent institution*'.[93] Accordingly, under EU law, the failure to fulfil a Treaty obligation by a state agent is attributed to the Member States. One may suggest that Article 258 is an internal rule limited to Member States' obligations and does not cover EU obligations, thus distinguishing Article 258 situations from joint obligations of the EU and its Member States under mixed agreements. However, for the purposes of infringement proceedings implementation of EU law is interpreted as a Member States' obligation, contradicting the European Commission's claim that international responsibility follows the division of competences. For example, in the landmark *Commission* v. *France (Strawberries)* case, the French government was held responsible for disruption to free movement of agricultural produce because the French authorities failed to prevent destruction of Spanish and Belgian harvest.[94] Trade in goods is an exclusive EU competence. Under EU law Member States are held liable for the conduct of their organs and agents which violates Treaty obligations in the areas of EU competences. It is thus not clear how the European Commission's claim that Member States' authorities act as *de facto* organs of the EU when they implement Union law is compatible with the CJEU's case law on the attribution of conduct to the Member States in the context of Article 258 TFEU. The European Commission's position that, for example, the conduct of Member States' customs administrations is attributed to the EU in international disputes is unconvincing given that under EU law Member States' are held responsible for the conduct of a wide range of organs and agents in the course of implementation of EU law. While it must be acknowledged that Article 258 TFEU is an internal rule the purpose of which is to ensure that Member States implement Union law, there nevertheless seems to be a contradiction in the European Commission's position in (some) international disputes that Member States have no sovereign control over the implementation of EU law.

In sum, international dispute-settlement practice does not support the European Commission's claim that conduct of Member States' authorities is attributed to the EU when they implement Union law. The position is even less convincing given the inconsistent application of this suggested basis of attribution by the EU itself. Finally, this chapter has also questioned whether

93 C-77/69 *Commission of the European Communities* v. *Kingdom of Belgium* [1970] ECR 237, para 15.

94 C-265/95 *Commission of the European Communities* v. *French Republic* [1997] ECR I-6959.

a claim that Member States' authorities act as *de facto* organs of the EU is consistent with the doctrine of direct actions under EU law.

4.4 CONCLUSION

The Panel's statement in *EC – Geographical Indications* that Member States act as *de facto* organs of the EU indicates the WTO DSB's overall approach to the EC's organizational arrangement. However, as will be explained in detail in Chapter 7, this approach stems from the nature of joint EU/Member State participation in the WTO, not from the EU's claim that Member States' organs act on the EU's behalf. It is unconvincing to extrapolate a legal basis for exclusive responsibility from the Panel's remarks in *EC – Geographical Indications*. Nothing in the case law of the WTO supports the EU's claim that Member States act as its organs when they implement Union law.

The EU's claim that Member States act as *de facto* organs of the EU is further questionable given that the EU itself is not consistent in this approach. Instead, it tends to adapt its arguments depending on the defence strategy, in some cases suggesting that Member States' authorities act as its organs, while on other occasions claiming that implementing acts are independent acts of the Member States.

Direct reliance on the cited paragraph in *EC – Geographical Indications* to qualify Member States' authorities as organs of the EU is even less convincing given that, to the best of my knowledge, there is no decision in international economic law where international responsibility of the EU was determined on the basis of the agency relationship between the EU and its Member States.

If then international dispute-settlement practice does not support the EU's claim that responsibility is to be exclusively allocated to the EU on the basis that Member States' authorities act as *de facto* organs of the EU, there must exist some other rationale for allocating responsibility between an organization and its Member States. After all, Gaja saw no need to devise special rules on attribution in order to assert the organization's responsibility in situations when authorities of Member States implement Union law. According to him, rationales other than attribution of conduct may guide the allocation of responsibility:

> *[the] responsibility of an organization does not necessarily have to rest on attribution of conduct to that organization. It may well be that an organization undertakes an obligation in circumstances in which compliance depends on the*

> *conduct of its member States. Should member States fail to conduct themselves in the expected manner, the obligation would be infringed and the organization would be responsible. However, attribution of conduct need not be implied.*[95]

Part II explores whether, for the purposes of determining exclusive responsibility, (i) attribution of conduct or breach is in fact the legal basis for the allocation of responsibility in a multilayered structure of an international organization and, if not, (ii) what is the appropriate legal basis.

95 Gaja Second Report, 6, para 11.

PART II

FUNCTIONAL INTERNATIONAL RESPONSIBILITY

Part I I examined the legal foundations of the international responsibility of the European Union (EU) and its Member States. Based on deductive reasoning the previous chapters explored the common hypothesis that it is in the International Law Commission's (ILC's) rules of attribution of conduct (direct responsibility) or attribution of breach (indirect responsibility) that these foundations lie.

This hypothesis is not supported by the findings in Part I. It has been suggested in Chapter 2 that the ILC rules of attribution do not determine the allocation of responsibility in the internal structure of a multilayered body like the EU. The subject matter of rules of attribution serves to establish whether an entity *is* internationally responsible, and not to identify the responsible entity in a composite structure where sovereignty is shared among different subjects of international law. This latter task must precede the application of the ILC framework.

Chapter 3 looked at the rules of organization. That the allocation of responsibility is governed by the rules of the organization accords with the preferences of the European Commission, which has pushed the idea of the EU as a *sui generis* entity. According to the European Commission, the international responsibility of the EU is competence-based. The EU is internationally responsible for all breaches in areas of its exclusive competence, irrespective of who carried out the conduct in question. I argued, however, that this approach is not supported by international dispute-settlement practice. Both the EU and its Member States remain independently responsible for their international obligations, irrespective of whether Member States have transferred that competence to the EU. This is so because while a state or a group of states can transfer authority to an international/supranational organization, international obligations are non-transferable. Thus, if both the EU and its Member States are parties to a treaty (i.e. a mixed agreement), they both remain bound by all treaty obligations, even if a Member State has transferred part of its powers to the EU.

The principle that an international organization and its member states are independently responsible for the discharge of their joint obligations does not, however, answer the question of which entity is exclusively responsible in a given situation. One needs to then determine whether the EU, its Member States or both are responsible for a breach of international economic obligations in a particular case. An attempt has been made in Chapter 2 to determine the basis for exclusive responsibility of the EU and its Member States by analysing the concept of an organ and agent of an international organization. While the analysis of the ILC *travaux préparatoires* suggests that the drafters of the Draft Articles on the Responsibility of International Organizations (ARIO) interpret these terms broadly, there is no support in the international dispute-settlement practice for the EU's claim that authorities of Member States act as *de facto* organs of the EU when they implement EU law.

Part II shall examine the extensive international economic dispute-settlement practice which involves the EU and/or its Member States as respondents, primarily World Trade Organization (WTO) disputes and investment arbitration under the Energy Charter Treaty (ECT). Based on inductive reasoning, the following chapters indentify the underlying rationales that international courts and tribunals take into consideration when solving economic disputes involving the EU. The findings call to question whether the determination of international responsibility of the EU and its Member States requires a prior allocation of responsibility for a breach through attribution of conduct or breach, a hypothesis which was central to analysis in Part I.

Drawing on analysis of the case law, Part II suggests a functional approach to international responsibility. It will be argued that the allocation of responsibility for breach to the EU and its Member States is largely irrelevant in the international economic context due to the restorative, as opposed to punitive, function of remedies in this area of international law. International courts and tribunals ask not *who is responsible for a breach* but rather *who is best placed to bear responsibility*. These are essentially different questions. While the former requires identification of a rule of attribution based on some predetermined internal element like competence or normative control, the latter employs an external approach. Accordingly, it is the characteristics of a treaty regime in question that underlie the question of international responsibility of the EU and its Member States. Whether the EU or its Member States are best placed to bear responsibility largely depends on the nature of obligations in question and the system of remedies that protect them. The approach employed here is thus of looking in from outside.

I start my analysis by considering the nature of remedies in international economic law, which is the focus of Chapter 5.

5

The Nature of Remedies in International Economic Law

5.1 INTRODUCTION

The question 'who is responsible?' typically considers the concepts of guilt and retribution: who acted in a particular case or who ordered another to act on his behalf, whose behaviour requires correction and who deserves restriction of rights. The approach stems from domestic criminal law theory where justice is served by the determination of personal fault and imposition of an adequate punishment. There may, of course, be responsibility without guilt, such as in case of strict liability, as there may be punishment without responsibility. But either way the question focuses on the identification of a 'person' who is to be subjected to some form of response. The The International Law Commission (ILC) framework of international responsibility, even though it negated the need for an element of fault in attribution of responsibility, retains a vestige of the orthodox approach that requires an answer to the question '*Who* is responsible for the breach?'.

While responsibility is focused on breach and retribution, even if in this abstract form, in international economic law the term 'responsibility' has a different connotation. Unlike physical and corporate persons under domestic law, states and international organizations are generally not bound by international obligations unless they have expressly consented to them. To follow Vattel's concept of 'voluntary law of nations', states are free to take up international commitments just as they are, in most cases, free to reject them.[1]

[1] Emer de Vattel, *The Law of Nations* (Liberty Fund 2008), 75–76, reprint from Emer de Vattel, *The Law of Nations, Or, Principles of the Law of Nature, Applied to the Conduct and Affairs of Nations and Sovereigns, with Three Early Essays on the Origin and Nature of Natural Law and on Luxury* (1758). The PCIJ in SS Wimbledon famously stated that 'The Court declines to see in the conclusion of any Treaty by which a State undertakes to perform or refrain from performing a particular act an abandonment of its sovereignty. No doubt any convention creating an obligation of this kind places a restriction upon the exercise of the sovereign rights of the State, in the sense that it requires them to be exercised in a certain way. But the right of entering into international engagements is an attribute of State sovereignty'; see *The SS*

As international organizations are composite structures, the intuitive solution is to analyse their independent parts following some fixed normative framework within which to identify the 'responsible' entity. As was discussed in Part I, the topic has often been approached from this internal angle, that is, by attempting to delimit responsibility for a breach of an international obligation between the EU and its Member States in accordance with an internal scheme and power dynamics.

Though logic, this approach misses the point. It fails to raise a question which should precede efforts to extract rules of attribution. One should first ask whether the *allocation of international responsibility for a breach* is practically significant. The answer to this question lies in the nature of remedies in international economic law to which this chapter now turns.

That nations participate in international economic relations voluntarily is crucial to understanding the character of international responsibility for violations of economic treaties. In fact, a lack of consideration of the nature of international economic obligations has resulted in a confusing state of affairs on the issue of international responsibility of the EU and its Member States.

Proceeding from general to specific, this chapter will first discuss remedies in international law, drawing on ILC doctrine (Section 5.1). It will then specify the nature of remedial regimes in international economic law, primarily those under the World Trade Organization (WTO) Agreements (Section 5.2) and the Energy Charter Treaty (ECT) (Section 5.3). Chapter 5 will put forward assumptions about the international responsibility of the EU and its Member States, which will then be tested in Chapters 6–8.

5.2 REMEDIES IN INTERNATIONAL LAW

A remedy is a judicial response to a breach, and so discussion of remedies should start by considering the concept of responsibility.[2] The drafters of the ILC rules of international responsibility have defined 'responsibility' as a consequence of a wrongful act which creates a duty of reparation.[3] Citing the principle articulated by the Permanent Court of International Justice in the *Phosphates in Morocco* case, Special Rapporteur Ago stated that whenever a state is guilty of an internationally wrongful act against another state,

'Wimbledon', United Kingdom and ors v. *Germany*, Judgment, [1923] PCIJ Series A – No. 1, para 35.

2 For a comprehensive analysis of judicial remedies in international law, see the seminal work by Christine Gray, *Judicial Remedies in International Law* (Clarendon Press 1987).

3 Report on International Responsibility, by Mr F. V. García-Amador, Special Rapporteur, A/CN.4/96 (ILC 1956), 180, para 37.

international responsibility is established '*immediately as between two states*'.[4] Ago further noted the various opinions on the nature of this relationship. On the one hand, the wrongful act creates a bilateral relationship in which an obligation of a state which committed an act is set against the subjective rights of the injured state.[5] From another point of view, it creates an authorization to use a sanction against the state in breach.[6] Moreover, it creates different kinds of consequences such as a right to claim reparation or the ability to impose sanctions.[7]

Ago concluded that the commentary to the Articles on Responsibility of States for Internationally Wrongful Acts (ARSIWA) should indicate that the ILC uses the term 'international responsibility' to mean all forms of new legal relationships which may be established in international law by a state's wrongful act, irrespective of whether they are centred on a state's obligation to restore the rights of the injured state and to repair the damage caused, or also involve the ability to impose sanctions.[8] Riphagen, Ago's successor for the ARSIWA project, also supported a wide interpretation of the concept of responsibility.[9] The nature of the new legal relationship established by a wrongful act is determined by the content of an international obligation, not its source.[10] The ILC used the term 'reparation' to refer to all forms of such legal relationship in the early stages of the ILC project.

In sum, all forms of legal relationship created by a wrongful conduct are covered by the concept of 'responsibility'. Responsibility, in turn, calls for a remedy. What, then, are the remedies in international law? Special Rapporteur Arangio-Ruiz introduced the term 'remedy' in his reports in the ARSIWA project. In the following discussion I shall use the terms 'remedy' and 'reparation' will be used interchangeably.

5.2.1 *The System of Remedies in International Law*

The primary purpose of reparation, as set out in the *Chorzów Factory* case, is that '*reparation must, as far as possible, wipe out all the consequences of the*

4 Ago Second Report, 179, para 12, see also para 32, fts 20–21.
5 Ago Second Report, 180, para 15.
6 Ago Second Report, 182, para 17.
7 Ago Second Report, 182, para 18.
8 Ago Third Report, 211, para 43.
9 Preliminary Report on the Content, Forms and Degrees of International Responsibility (Part 2 of the Draft Articles on State Responsibility), by Mr Willem Riphagen, Special Rapporteur, A/CN.4/330 and Corr.1, 2 (French Only) and 3 (ILC 1980), 112, para 28. Riphagen drew three parameters in his attempt to categorize these relationships: new obligations of a guilty state, new rights of injured state and position of third states.
10 Report by Mr R. Ago, chairman of the Sub-Committee on State Responsibility, A/CN.4/291 and Add.1–2 and Corr.1 (ILC 1963), 8 and 10, also p 13, para 32.

illegal act and reestablish the situation which would, in all probability, have existed if that act had not been committed'.[11] The duty to make good the damage as a primary consequence of international responsibility has also been recognized by legal scholars.[12]

The function of wiping out all the consequences of an unlawful act can be achieved through various responses. The ILC distinguishes two main types of reparation: reparation *stricto sensu* and satisfaction.[13] Reparation *stricto sensu* is understood as restitution in kind (restitution *in integrum*) or pecuniary damages,[14] if restitution is impossible.[15] Though the distinction is not formally stated in the commentary to the ILC rules, restitution can be either material (most common in cases of injury to property belonging to an alien) or legal,[16] depending on the nature of the injury in question.[17]

Pecuniary damages differ from restitution in kind – its aim is to compensate for all the consequences of an act or omission contrary to international law and can include interest, expenses and costs as an integral part of indemnity.[18] Cessation, which can be described as restitution by performance, is another form of reparation, though the distinction from other types is not always clear.[19] Cessation may give rise to a continuing and non-derogable obligation, even when return to the *status quo ante* is hardly possible.[20]

Satisfaction is punitive.[21] It differs from restitution in that it is intended to make good a 'political and moral' injury, not as a compensation in its strict sense.[22] Since satisfaction can in some cases take the form of pecuniary

11 *Factory at Chorzów (Germany* v. *Poland)*, Merits, Claim for Indemnity, Judgment No. 13, [1928] PCIJ Series A – No. 17, 47.

12 For example, Clyde Eagleton, 'The Responsibility of States in International Law' (1928) 22 APSR 1004; Dionisio Anzilotti, *Corso Di Diritto Internazionale* (3rd edn, Athenaum 1928), vol I, 416; Crawford First Report (n 33). Third Report on State Responsibility, by Mr. James Crawford, Special Rapporteur (2000) A/CN.4/507 and Add. 1–4, 40.

13 García-Amador Report, 209, para 193.

14 Also referred to as compensation, indemnification, reparation by equivalent.

15 García-Amador Report, 209, para 197.

16 For example, abrogation or modification of a specific provision of an international agreement; see Sixth Report on International Responsibility, by Mr. F. V. García-Amador, Special Rapporteur, A/CN.4/134 and Add.1 (ILC 1961), 17, para 68.

17 Crawford Third Report, A/CN.4/507 and Add. 1–4, 41, para 127, García-Amador Sixth Report, 17, para 67.

18 García-Amador Sixth Report, 18, para 72; see also Crawford Third Report, 57.

19 Crawford Third Report, 43, para 131.

20 Crawford Third Report, 43, para 130. To note a nuance, the objective is to place parties in the *status quo ante*, leaving aside the question of what would the situation have been if the wrong act had not been committed; Crawford Third Report, 40, para 125.

21 García-Amador Sixth Report, 19.

22 García-Amador Sixth Report, 14, para 55.

damages, just like restitution, the main difference lies in its punitive function.[23] According to Special Rapporteur García-Amador, international law traditionally drew no distinction between civil and criminal responsibility (the idea of reparation proper and the idea of punishment), because strictly speaking they were an integral part of one and the same duty to make reparation.[24] International criminal law emerged as a distinct regime after the Second World War. Thus, since 1945, the distinction between punishable acts properly so called and acts or omissions which are merely wrongful has become more pronounced. The international law of responsibility covers both wrongful acts whose remedy is restitution in kind or compensation and punishable acts which call for sanction (satisfaction), though the majority of violations of international law are of the former type.

Accordingly, I suggest to distinguish two groups of remedies in international law according to their central function: restorative and retributive. Restitution, either in kind or in a form of pecuniary damages, is restorative in nature because its purpose is either to return parties to the *status quo ante* or, if that is not possible, to compensate them for the harm caused. That is, restitution aims to restore the order, not to punish the violator. That is why restitution must be adequate to the harm caused. Satisfaction, on the other hand, is retributive in nature – it is a punitive response which aims to reform or deter the violator from the harmful behaviour in the future and give a moral satisfaction to the victim.

5.2.2 *The Function of Remedies in International Law*

The ILC placed the different forms of reparation in a hierarchical structure. It has been undisputed among the special rapporteurs for the ARSIWA project that sanctions with elements of punishment can be imposed for certain violations of international law.[25] Article 34 of the ARSIWA states that

23 Second Report on International Responsibility, by F. V. García-Amador, Special Rapporteur, A/CN.4/106 (1957), 32, para 108.

24 García-Amador Report, 182, para 48.

25 Ago Second Report, 179, para 12, and Fifth Report on State Responsibility, by Mr. Roberto Ago, Special Rapporteur - the Internationally Wrongful Act of the State, Source of International Responsibility (continued) (1976) A/CN.4/291 and Add.1–2 and Corr.1, 43, para 128; Second Report on State Responsibility by Mr. Gaetano Arangio-Ruiz, Special Rapporteur, A/CN.4/425 and Corr.1 and Add.1 and Corr.1 (ILC 1989), 41, para 143; García-Amador Report, 219, paras 241 and 220; see also García-Amador Second Report, 105, para 1 to Art 1. While admitting that reparation can in some cases have elements of punishment in the form of sanctions, García-Amador firmly rejected the possibility of injured states imposing such sanctions unilaterally; see García-Amador Sixth Report, A/CN.4/134 and Add.1, 2, para 6.

reparation for the injury caused by the internationally wrongful act shall take the form of restitution, compensation and satisfaction. Though, according to Special Rapporteur Crawford, reparation by equivalent (i.e. compensation) is the most frequent form of reparation in practice, restitution in kind holds primacy over compensation.[26] Pecuniary damages are available when restitution in kind is no longer possible or feasible.[27] Hindelang also notes that restitution is the very first remedy to be sought among the three forms of reparation (restitution in kind, compensation and satisfaction) as it most closely conforms to the general rule of the law of responsibility according to which the author state is obliged to 'wipe out' all consequences with a view to re-establishing the original situation.[28]

The ILC endorsed the principle stated in the *Lusitania* case that restitution, whether in kind or in a form of compensation, must be adequate and balance, as nearly as may be, the injury suffered.[29] Article 51 of the ARSIWA states that countermeasures must be commensurate with the injury suffered, taking into account the gravity of the internationally wrongful act and the rights in question. Countermeasures under the ILC rules are thus balanced with the harm resulting from the violation. They are not designed to achieve absolute or maximum deterrence of violation.[30] As to compensation, Crawford supported the view that in principle the amount of compensation payable is precisely the value the injured state would have received if restitution had been provided.[31] Accordingly, under the ILC rules of international responsibility, restorative remedies take priority over retributive remedies (though latter ones may be imposed in certain situations).

26 Crawford Third Report, 43, para 135. Arangio-Ruiz advocated for a more strict rule under which injured states could insist on restitution in kind, but this approach was rejected by the members of the ILC as too rigid and inconsistent with practice; see also Christine Gray, 'The Choice between Restitution and Compensation' (1999) 10 EJIL 413.

27 Crawford Third Report, 40, para 125. García-Amador notes that pecuniary damages are used when restitution *in integrum* is not possible for material or legal reasons, or when it is not of itself sufficient to repair all the consequences of the act or omission imputable to the state; see García-Amador Sixth Report, A/CN.4/134 and Add.1, 18, para 70.

28 Steffen Hindelang, 'Restitution and Compensation – Reconstructing the Relationship in Investment Treaty Law', in Hofmann Rainer and Tams Christian (eds), *International Investment Law and General International Law: From Clinical Isolation to Systemic Integration?* (Nomos 2011).

29 Third Report on State Responsibility, by Mr. Gaetano Arangio-Ruiz, Special Rapporteur, A/CN.4/440 and Add.1 (1991), 20.

30 Eric A Posner and Alan O Sykes, *Economic Foundations of International Law* (Harvard University Press 2013), 133.

31 Crawford Third Report, para 148.

Restorative remedies dominate in the context of international economic law. The focus therefore is on the restoration/preservation of the legal order rather than on a personal attack of the violator with a moral claim. This explains why the rules for the admissibility of claims under the WTO regime are flexible and do not focus on the 'victim'. Bartels notes that the requirement of 'substantial interest' to bring a WTO claim includes not only commercial but also systemic interests, which means that in reality all WTO members have a *de facto* right to participate as third parties in WTO dispute-settlement proceedings.[32] Furthermore, in WTO law it does not matter whether the WTO has a legal interest; as long as there is a potential interest, or a future opportunity to compete, the WTO member may initiate consultation.[33] The Appellate Body in the *EC – Bananas III* dispute noted that there is wide discretion whether to bring a case against another WTO member.[34] Such rules of admissibility are not possible in legal regimes which are dominated by punitive remedies, for example, the law of torts.

It seems then that punitive sanctions, while available, are secondary measures under the general law of international responsibility. The main function of remedies is to restore the *status quo ante*, not to bring about retributive justice. Restitution, a primary remedy under international law, must be proportional and carefully calculated so that it is not excessive. Emphasis on restitution, rather than punitive justice, indicates that the primary task of international tribunals is to tailor a response that rebalances the consequences of breach and restores the situation *quo ante*.

The breach must be identified in order to determine whether a subject of international law is internationally responsible.[35] But if the primary function of international adjudicators is restoration rather than retributive justice, performing attribution of breach in the internal structure of an organization may not be necessary. This gives an indication, though at this point of analysis only in the form of an assumption, that allocation of responsibility for a breach between the EU and its Member States may be irrelevant, or largely irrelevant, to purposes of adjudication in international economic law. This proposition is

32 Lorand Bartels, 'Procedural Aspects of Shared Responsibility in the WTO Dispute Settlement System' (2013) 4 JIDS 343, 354, ft 64. Bartels notes that from 1996–2012, 170 of 182 panel proceedings and 102 of 109 Appellate Body proceedings included third parties.

33 Andrés Delgado Casteleiro and Joris Larik, 'The "Odd Couple": The Responsibility of the EU at the WTO', in Malcolm Evans and Panos Koutrakos (eds) *The International Responsibility of the European Union: European and International Perspectives* (Hart Publishing 2013), 246.

34 WTO Appellate Body Report, *European Communities – Regime for the Importation, Sale and Distribution of Bananas*, WT/DS27/RW/USA, and WT/DS27/AB/RW/USA and Corr.1, adopted 9 September 1997 (*EC –Bananas III*), para 132.

35 ARSIWA Art 4, ARIO Art 4.

further supported by the character of the liability rule under international economic law which the next section will consider.

5.2.3 *The Liability Rule in International Economic Law*

The previous section addressed remedies from a functional perspective. It was suggested that the primary role of responsibility for violation of international economic obligations is to restore the *ex ante* (pre-breach) status. The next question is how restoration is to be achieved in international economic law. In the following analysis this question will be addressed through liability and property rules, a distinction articulated by the law and economics literature.[36] The protection of international obligations under international economic regimes in most cases reflects the liability rule under which parties are in effect allowed to pay their way out of international obligations. Because most economic obligations are not punishable acts properly so called but merely wrongful acts or omissions, the ordering of 'pay-outs' is as far as international courts and tribunals can often go in their quest to restore balance. In investment treaties the clearest example of a liability rule is to be found in expropriation provisions, where states are allowed to seize assets from foreign investors in certain circumstances.[37]

The property rule is associated more closely with the 'European' school of international law which maintains that the optimal level of protection is the strongest, whereas the 'US' school considers the maximum level of freedom of action to be the most desirable way to organize international obligations (the liability rule).[38] Under the property rule the court issues an injunction ordering the infringing party to desist.[39] Under the liability rule the tribunal

36 The distinction between the property and the liability rules was noted in the study related to domestic law by Calabresi and Melamed; see Guido Calabresi and Douglas A Melamed, 'Property Rules, Liability Rules, and Inalienability: One View of the Cathedral' (1972) 85 Harv. L. Rev. 1089. The distinction was later adopted by international economic lawyers, for example, see Joel P Trachtman, *The Economic Structure of International Law* (Harvard University Press 2008), 138.

37 Jonathan Bonnitcha, Poulsen Lauge and Michael Waibel, *The Political Economy of the International Investment Regime* (Oxford University Press 2017), 16.

38 For the difference between liability and property rules, see Bonnitcha, Lauge and Waibel 2017, 16. See also Joost Pauwelyn, *Optimal Protection of International Law: Navigating between European Absolutism and American Voluntarism* (Cambridge University Press 2008), 16–24. Pauwelyn refers to the European thought as 'European absolutism' and the American as 'American voluntarism' while himself arguing for the middle path between the two schools; see p 45.

39 Carl Shapiro, 'Property Rules vs. Liability Rules for Patent Infringement' [2016] Available at SSRN: https://ssrn.com/abstract=2775307 or http://dx.doi.org/10.2139/ssrn.2775307, 1.

allows continuance of infringement so long as the party pays compensation. Schwartz and Sykes employ contract theory to explain the division. According to them, under the liability rule performance is induced through the mechanism of expectation damages when it is efficient and breach when it is not.[40]

The distinction between measures which are directly and immediately capable of involving reparation *stricto sensu* and those which constitute a right in a state to act contrary to its obligations subject to paying compensation has been noted by Special Rapporteur García-Amador at the early stages of the ARSIWA project.[41] According to him, the first type of measure constitutes an unlawful act in the true sense of the word, whereas the second is merely an arbitrary act for which the only remedy is compensation in the proper amount and form.[42] For example, if a state has an obligation that is qualified by an alternative performance, such as to refrain from polluting or clean up the pollution, it cannot be said that there is a strict obligation to refrain from pollution.[43] In some cases the primary rule itself may indicate the legal consequences of certain conduct. For example, the primary rule that expropriation must be accompanied by appropriate compensation suggests that it is the non-payment of the compensation, not the act of expropriation itself, that creates legal consequences.[44]

Under the liability system a party wishing to deviate from its commitments may do so without the need to secure the permission of any adversely affected party but is liable for the resulting damage.[45] Most trade and investment treaties provide for compensation or an equivalent remedy, but an injunction is not available. For example, investment standards under most investment treaties are enforced through compensation which is then merely a 'price' for doing what is regulated.[46] Compensation is also typically a remedy for noncompliance with trade obligations in the association agreements between the EU and its neighbours, for example, the Moldova-European Union Association

40 Alan O Sykes and Warren F Schwartz, 'The Economic Structure of Renegotiation and Dispute Resolution in the WTO/GATT System' (2002) 143 John M. Olin Program in Law and Economics Working Paper, 4.

41 García-Amador Sixth Report, 39, para 154.

42 García-Amador Sixth Report, 39, 154 and 156.

43 The example was provided by Trachtman 2008, 138.

44 Preliminary Report on the Content, Forms and Degrees of International Responsibility (Part 2 of the Draft Articles on State Responsibility), by Mr. Willem Riphagen, Special Rapporteur, A/CN.4/330 and Corr.1, 2 (French Only) and 3, 124, para 81–82; Crawford Third Report, 42, para 128. This relates to the distinction of lawful and unlawful expropriation – only expropriation which is not accompanied by adequate compensation is unlawful.

45 Sykes and Schwartz 2002, 4.

46 Pauwelyn 2008, 172.

Agreement[47] and the EU-Ukraine Association Agreement.[48] The WTO system similarly protects its commitments through another 'price' measure, compensation (and, in some cases, retaliation). The following sections will return to trade and investment regimes. Property rules, on the other hand, call for specific performance by the promisor.[49]

The discussion of why states agree to liability-type treaty regimes where promisors can simply pay their way out of obligations is extensive and will thus be noted here only briefly. According to Posner and Sykes, the primary interest of states is cooperation, which reduces international externalities.[50] They argue that the welfare of each state is affected by the policies of other states, and thus without cooperation each would adopt policies to maximize its own welfare, creating a non-cooperative equilibrium.[51] As a result a state of affairs will arise in which all nations are worse off than they would be if the externalities were addressed through cooperation.[52] A good illustration of non-cooperation drawn from a domestic setting are the pictures of numerous oil rigs crammed next to each other during the Pennsylvania oil rush and other oil booms in the late nineteenth century where, due to a lack of regulation, private parties rushed to over-extract oil.[53] The same result would likely be seen on the high seas if there were no rules governing mineral extraction at sea.

In international economic law there is thus a strong self-enforcement element instigated by interest in a community-wide order. States may 'leave' international law when they consider that it no longer serves their interests. That international rules are based on voluntary adherence of states has been particularly apparent in recent years with a series of withdrawals from multilateral treaties, including that of the United States' withdrawal from the Paris Climate Agreement adopted under the United Nations Framework Convention on Climate Change (UNFCCC), withdrawal by a number of Latin American states from their bilateral investment treaties (BITs), the United Kingdom's referendum vote to leave the EU, termination by the United States and Brazil of their relationship with the World Health Organization following its response to the COVID-19 pandemic and the

47 Art 393.
48 Art 315.
49 Sykes and Schwartz 2002, 4.
50 Trachtman, for example, suggests other reasons for compliance, such as fear of reputational damage; see Trachtman 2008, 140.
51 Posner and Sykes 2013, 19.
52 Posner and Sykes 2013, 19.
53 Daniel Yergin, *The Prize: The Epic Quest for Oil, Money, and Power* (Simon & Schuster 1990).

blocking by the United States of judges to the WTO Appellate Body. Crawford notes that *'it is a question of policy rather than law whether or not to withdraw'*.[54]

What keeps the international system intact is, then, not a legal code but collective interest. Multilateral treaties can only remain in force to the extent that they are able to convince their signatories that 'nation first' will benefit from 'community first'. If the treaty regime fails to do so, the thin ice of the international legal order will break, especially so with respect to international trade regimes.

Often the greatest incentive for state compliance is the threat of reciprocal deviation from commitment.[55] For example, a state might retaliate by overfishing if another violates an agreement governing access to their adjacent pools. Such deviation must be calibrated carefully so that it is neither too high nor too low. Somewhat reminiscent of Vattel's concept of 'voluntary law of nations', Goldsmith and Posner argue that states enter into international obligations out of self-interest and without such interest international law would be unable to pull states into compliance.[56] They are sceptical that genuine multinational collective action problems can be solved by treaty, especially when a large number of states are involved.

To Goldsmith and Posner, multilateral treaties reflect multilateral prisoners' dilemmas rather than coordination games because rules themselves are insufficient to ensure compliance.[57] They go as far as to suggest that *'the strength of a state's commitment to an agreement is not a function of its legality, but of the strength and uniformity of public and elite preferences'*.[58] A party which loses a General Agreement on Tariffs and Trade (GATT) adjudication will not invariably bring its trade policy into

54 James Crawford, 'The Current Political Discourse Concerning International Law' (2018) 81 MLR 1, 6.

55 Posner and Sykes 2013, 128. Goldsmith and Posner suggest that fear of retaliation is the simplest explanation why a state might comply with a treaty; Jack L Goldsmith and Eric A Posner, *The Limits of International Law* (Oxford University Press 2005), 100.

56 Goldsmith and Posner 2005, 7. Trachtman criticizes this position, calling it too romantic. According to him, it is not true that in order for a rule to be called law, individuals must comply with it for intrinsic, internalized reasons. Instead, Trachtman argues that the formal binding nature of treaty derives from the customary law rule of *pacta sunt servanda*; see Trachtman 2008, 122. Anne van Aaken also identifies some of the limits to Goldsmith and Posner's approach, including a narrow definition of state preferences; see Anne van Aaken, 'To Do Away with International Law? Some Limits to 'The Limits of International Law' (2006) 17 EJIL 289.

57 Goldsmith and Posner 2005, 87.

58 Goldsmith and Posner 2005, 95.

compliance with GATT rules – that will depend on the reason for which it violated GATT.[59] If the reason or motive was not merely that of 'cheating' but that of changed circumstances or the domestic, political gains from non-compliance, they argue, the defendant might not bring its behaviour into compliance even if the injured state retaliates. For example, European countries ignored the GATT adjudication system in the decade after the creation of the EC Community and the United States circumvented the system in the 1980s when it preferred to use unilateral methods of enforcement.[60] The current trade war between the United States and China is yet another example of how swiftly states may change their international trade policies.

The need for cooperation is especially clear in international trade and investment law. The primary role of an international trade agreement is to avoid high tariffs and non-tariff barriers, which can result from unilateral trade policies. Multilateral trade agreements which set an optimal trade tariff are thus self-enforcing.[61] Goldsmith and Posner suggest that multilateral bargaining may be superior to bilateral cooperation because states gain from trade agreements only if they obtain concessions in return for their commitments, and thus every trade deal is vulnerable to a subsequent trade agreement that results in trade diversion.[62]

If international economic relations are interest-driven, the primary function of treaty dispute resolution must be to keep those interests intact. Since the 'social contract' underpinning international economic relations is an equilibrium of interests, the institution of responsibility serves as a set of scales which balances national policies against the benefits of collective order. Dispute-settlement bodies must apply a complex algorithm which calculates the effects of a state's conduct on the global order protected by international law. The purpose of remedies is not retributive justice, but the restoration of balance to the order. Accordingly, remedies are not predetermined but are carefully crafted and adjusted on a case-by-case basis. A number of international economic treaties, including the EU-Canada Comprehensive Economic and Trade Agreement (CETA)[63] and the EU's association agreements such as that

59 Goldsmith and Posner 2005, 154.
60 Goldsmith and Posner 2005, 154.
61 Kyle Bagwell and Robert W Staiger, *The Economics of the World Trading System* (MIT Press 2002). They argue that the optimal trade tariff is set through a repeated game of reverting to Nash equilibrium whenever the other party is cheating until the limits on the amount of tariff cooperation that is self-enforcing are set.
62 Goldsmith and Posner 2005, 145.
63 CETA Art 29.14.

with Moldova[64] and the Agreement on European Economic Area,[65] specify that remedies for non-compliance must be proportionate and temporary.

If, then, international economic commitments are mostly self-enforcing and if remedies for breach stop short of injunctions, it seems that international actors abide by their economic commitments so long as they deem it beneficial to remain within the realm of a system of reciprocal commitment. If that is no longer the case, they may choose to dishonour their commitments and pay a proportionate price instead or withdraw from the treaty altogether. If they fail in the latter, the ultimate detriment is to reputation and reciprocity of commitment from trading partners.

This brings the present analysis to another important distinction. If liability-type systems in effect allow breaches subject to some form of a payout, it must be true that responsibility is focused not on the breach but on the payout itself. This is still *responsibility* – payouts *are* remedies. That breaches of international economic obligations have a 'price tag' does not mean that they result in impunity. As Ago correctly noted, whichever form of feedback is created, they are all part of the same general concept, that of 'reparation'.[66]

While we are still in the realm of responsibility and remedies, one may nevertheless question whether *allocation of responsibility for breach* between the EU and its Member States has practical relevance in the international economic context. If breaches are, while recognized as wrongful, effectively permitted, is it necessary to engage in the complex task of identifying the violator in the multilayered structure of an international body? What is perhaps more important in international economic law is that 'pay-outs' are delivered, be it by an organization itself or its Member States. But that is a different question. It is unrelated to the allocation of responsibility for breach in the sense of some predetermined structural basis like attribution of conduct, normative control or division of competences, say within the EU. To illustrate this point with the analogy of a joint loan to two borrowers, if one borrower fails to pay due to the actions of the other borrower, a bank will not bother to determine who defaulted. It will focus on securing payment, whoever delivers it.

I am speaking here in the language of assumptions because the discussion so far is based on theory, not practice. The decisions of international courts

64 Art 381 of the EU-Ukraine Association Agreement calls for temporary compensation or suspension of obligations at a level equivalent to the nullification or impairment caused by the violation.

65 Art 112(2) of the EEA Agreement provides that 'safeguard measures shall be restricted with regard to their scope and duration to what is strictly necessary in order to remedy the situation'.

66 Ago Fifth Report, 27, para 82.

and tribunals will be the focus of the following chapters. For now, the remaining sections will specify the earlier discussion on the nature of remedies in international economic law by considering in more detail the remedial systems under the WTO Agreements and investment treaties.

5.3 REMEDIES UNDER THE WTO REGIME

Before and after the Uruguay Round negotiation, debate on the most effective WTO remedial system was and has been extensive. Some suggest, for example, that WTO decisions, the imposition of fines and membership sanctions would prove to be efficient remedies.[67] Others argue that sanctions should be replaced by a compensation mechanism.[68] Mavroidis and Brimeyer, by contrast, suggest that for violations of WTO rules punitive measures should be available.[69] Yet others are content with the existing regime. For example, Lamy, the then trade commissioner of the EU – one of the several repeat players against whom retaliation has been used in practice – supports the current system.[70] Evaluation of the remedies available under the WTO system is beyond the scope of this book. The following discussion will analyse the regime as it currently stands without engaging in the debate on the optimal remedy under the WTO dispute-settlement system.

5.3.1 *The WTO's Liability Rule*

Article 19.1 of the WTO Dispute Settlement Understanding (DSU) provides that where a panel or the Appellate Body concludes that a measure is inconsistent with a covered agreement, it shall recommend that the member concerned bring the measure into conformity with that agreement. If, after

[67] Steve Charnovitz, 'Rethinking WTO Trade Sanctions' (2001) 95 AJIL 792, 824.

[68] For example, Andrew T Guzman, 'The Cost of Credibility: Explaining Resistance to Interstate Dispute Resolution Mechanisms' (2002) 31 J. Legal Stud. 303; Steve Charnovitz, 'Should the Teeth Be Pulled? An Analysis of WTO Sanctions', in Daniel LM Kennedy and James D Southwick (eds), *The Political Economy of International Trade Law: Essays in Honor of Robert E. Hudec* (Cambridge University Press 2002).

[69] 'Petros Mavroidis, 'Remedies in the WTO Legal System: Between Rock and a Hard Place' (2000) 11 EJIL 763; Benjamin L Brimeyer, 'Bananas, Beef, and Compliance in the World Trade Organization: The Inability of the WTO Dispute Settlement Process to Achieve Compliance from Superpower Nations' (2001) 10 Minn J Global Trade 133.

[70] Pascal Lamy's speech 'US-EU: The Biggest Trading Elephants in the Jungle – But will they Behave?', delivered at the Economic Strategy Institute, 7 June 2001.

a reasonable period,[71] the member does not so comply, compensation and the suspension of concessions and other obligations are available against that member.[72] Thus, the WTO dispute-settlement system sets a two-step process: a recommendation to comply and, if compliance is not forthcoming, retaliation. A number of recently concluded economic treaties have adopted a near identical or similar dispute-resolution mechanism to that established in the WTO dispute-settlement system, for example, Chapter 29 of CETA and Chapter 28 of the Comprehensive and Progressive Agreement for Trans-Pacific Partnership (CPTPP).

Scholars agree that the WTO remedial system reflects the liability rule.[73] The primary goal of the WTO dispute-settlement system is to induce compliance and promote distributive rather than retributive justice.[74] The system aims to restore the balance of concessions, not to punish the violator.[75] Since the interest of WTO members is to maximize their mutual gains from trade, the system of adjudication allows deviation from obligations without the permission of affected parties whose only available response is the withdrawal of substantially equivalent concessions after the lapse of reasonable time.[76] The only type of reparation that WTO panels can award is cessation, that is, they can recommend a member comply with its WTO obligations.

According to Trachtman, states that violate WTO obligations are not subject to enforceable specific performance-type remedies, nor do they suffer any penalty beyond the possible authorization or withdrawal of

71 DSU Art 21.3. According to Posner and Sykes, the system even allows a so-called 'three-year free pass', that is a violator can cheat for some time, get caught, drag out litigation, slowly correct its behaviour and ultimately pay no price; see Posner and Sykes 2013, 184.

72 DSU Art 22.1.

73 For an example of a minority view, John H Jackson, 'The WTO Dispute Settlement Understanding—Misunderstandings on the Nature of Legal Obligation' (1997) 91 AJIL 60.

74 Nicolas DiMascio and Joost Pauwelyn, 'Nondiscrimination in Trade and Investment Treaties: Worlds Apart or Two Sides of the Same Coin?' (2008) 102 AJIL 48, 53–54.

75 DiMascio and Pauwelyn 2008, 53–54. See also Reto Malacrida, 'Towards Sounder and Fairer WTO Retaliation: Suggestions for Possible Additional Procedural Rules Governing Members' Preparation and Adoption of Retaliatory Measures' (2008) 42 JWT 3.

76 Sykes and Schwartz 2002, 2. See also Brooks E Allen, 'The Use of Non-Pecuniary Remedies in WTO Dispute Settlement: Lessons for Arbitral Practitioners', in Michael E Schneide and Joachim Knoll (eds), *ASA Special Series No. 30: Performance as a Remedy: Non-monetary Relief in International Arbitration* (JurisNet, LLC 2011), 288. It should be noted that Art 4.7 of the SCM Agreement refers to withdrawal of inconsistent measures without delay, while the DSU uses somewhat different language, i.e. bringing a measure into conformity. In *EC – Commercial Vessels*, Korea noted that the language in the SCM Agreement is simply a particular application of DSU Art 19.1 in the context of prohibited subsidies case which is in contrast with Art 7.8 of the SCM Agreement which provides for an additional remedy of removal of the adverse effects; see WTO Panel Report, *EC – Commercial Vessels Commercial Vessels*, para 4.14, ft 9.

equivalent concessions.[77] Similarly, Schwartz and Sykes suggest that a party found to be in violation of its obligations may, if it so chooses, continue to violate them, the ultimate price being suspension of equivalent concessions to its detriment.[78] They may, similarly, choose to delay implementation of policies the WTO recommends in an attempt to support, for example, influential economic sectors. To Hudec the ultimate 'remedy' which made the GATT dispute-settlement procedure successful is the force of community pressure.[79] Another feature of the WTO regime, which reflects the liability rule, is that Article 12.2 DSU allows parties to a dispute to suspend proceedings at any time if they decide to return to the negotiation table, thus avoiding adjudication.

5.3.2 *Compliance*

Due to the liability-type nature of WTO obligations, its dispute-settlement system gives maximum autonomy to the member concerned in ensuring compliance with panel recommendations, leaving it up to them to choose the way in which they bring their measures into conformity with the WTO rules.[80] Though under Article 21.5 of the DSU the panel may later decide whether the member in question has in fact complied with the ruling, it cannot direct how a respondent is to modify its trade practices.

That the Dispute Settlement Body (DSB) leaves it to the respondent party to choose the method of compliance explains why, in most cases, it does not engage in allocation of responsibility for breach to the EU or its Member States. Panel reports rarely specify whether the EU or its Member States should take remedial action. EU law, not the WTO Agreements, dictates that in most cases the EU is the representative of the bloc in WTO dispute settlement. While the WTO Agreement is a mixed treaty with both the EU and its Member States formally and independently responsible for all WTO obligations, the EU's internal arrangement that it holds exclusive competence in trade translates into its exclusive external competence in trade matters and disputes. The EU and its Member States participate in the WTO system as

77 Joel P Trachtman, 'Building the WTO Cathedral' [2006] Available at SSRN: https://ssrn.com/abstract=815844 or http://dx.doi.org/10.2139/ssrn.815844, 23.

78 Sykes and Schwartz 2002, 11.

79 Robert A Hudec, 'Broadening the Scope of Remedies in the WTO Dispute Settlement', in Friedl Weiss (ed), *Improving WTO Dispute Settlement Procedures: Issues & Lessons from the Practice of Other International Courts & Tribunals* (Cameron May 2000), 376.

80 Under Art 21.5 panels may later review whether the member in question has in fact complied with the ruling.

one bloc. The usual arrangement during the meetings of the Ministerial Conference and the General Council of the WTO is for Member States and the EU to have their delegates seated in a cluster, with the Union speaking on behalf of the Member States, the latter rarely intervening. The WTO system affords wide discretion to the EU in representation of the Member States in dispute-settlement proceedings as well. The practice of EU Members States and the EU is such that representatives of the Member States concerned form part of the EU delegation and can be designated as 'Approved Persons' with access to Business Confidential Information and Highly Sensitive Business Information submitted in the dispute. Submissions and communications themselves are invariably made by the officers of the Legal Service of the Commission.[81] Thus, from the Union's perspective its participation in WTO Agreements is of a *de facto* bilateral nature, with duties and benefits owned by the EU/Member State bloc as against third parties. That the DSB defers to such internal arrangement supports the claim that WTO dispute settlement is a liability-based system.

The underlying reasons for the primary role of the EU under the WTO dispute-settlement system will be examined in Chapter 7. Suffice it to note here that under the WTO regime the method of compliance is left to be decided by the respondent, which is consistent with the liability rule. If compliance is not secured, an injunction is not available. Instead, retaliation is the next response available to the claimant.

5.3.3 *Retaliation*

GATT Article XXIII provides for a system of compensation and retaliation under the WTO regime. Article 22.1–22.2 DSU foresees the possibility of negotiating compensation in lieu of retaliation within the twenty-day period following the expiration of the reasonable period of time.

The system of compensation and retaliation under GATT Article XXIII supports the purposes of the liability rule. The parties are not burdened with specific performance obligations and compensation and retaliation are 'pay-outs' from their obligations.[82] The GATT drafters typically avoided using the term 'sanction' – the standard portrayal of Article XXIII was as

81 Such was the arrangement, for example, in *EC – Large Civil Aircraft*, PR, para 7.173.

82 It is unclear when the term 'retaliation' was adopted in relation to the WTO remedial system. Initially, there was an intention to use the word 'sanction', but some countries, for example those belonging to the Arab League, were opposed to the term; see Charnovitz 2001, 801–802.

a rebalancing of concessions, which reflects the restorative function of remedies in the international economic context.[83]

According to Trachtman, through the system of cross-retaliation WTO Agreements have an embedded political linkage to the dispute-settlement system. For example, in case of a breach of the Agreement on Trade-Related Aspects of Intellectual Property (TRIPS), if the complaining state cannot satisfactorily retaliate by withdrawing TRIPS concessions, it may be permitted to withdraw concessions in other areas, such as in market access to agricultural products.[84]

The essential feature of compensation and retaliation under the WTO regime, which gives a clear indication that it is based on liability, is that retaliation must be equivalent to the harm caused. The need to ensure correspondence of response and avoid punishable sanctions was a driving force in the elimination of the so-called 'consensus' rule. Under this rule DSB were not adopted unless all parties agreed to them, including the party against whom that decision was made. Accordingly, the injured party was left with self-help in the form of unilateral retaliation.[85] According to Posner and Sykes, the elimination of the 'consensus rule' was aimed at reducing rather than increasing the penalty for cheating.[86] It eliminated unilateral retaliation, and any sanctions must now be authorized and approved by the DSB. The primary purpose of the sanctions' review process is to avoid excessive responses and ensure that 'pay-outs' are adequate. As Schwartz and Sykes put it '*instead of having to buy their way out in a world of unilateral threats and counter-threats unconstrained by central oversight, the new system ensures that the price for non-compliance will be set by an honest and unbiased effort to assess harm*'.[87]

The elimination of the consensus rule with the establishment of the WTO thus further supports the restorative rather than retributive nature of remedies under the WTO regime. The role of the arbitrators in limiting excessive sanctions was revealed, for example, in the *EC – Bananas III* dispute where the EU challenged the US sanctions as excessive. Replying to the US argument that the purpose of sanctions was to enforce the property rule and that careful calibration of sanctions was unnecessary, the Arbitrators stated that '*it*

[83] Charnovitz 2001, 801–802. For specification of retaliation with respect to individual commitments, see Pauwelyn 2008, 134.

[84] Trachtman 2008, 198.

[85] In fact Schwartz and Sykes argue that violations have been more often caused by good faith clashes over ambiguous terms of the bargain rather than interest in flagrant cheating; see Sykes and Schwartz 2002, 24; see also Posner and Sykes 2013, 272.

[86] Posner and Sykes 2013, 284.

[87] Sykes and Schwartz 2002, 28.

is the purpose of countermeasures to induce compliance. But this purpose does not mean that the DSB should grant authorization to suspend concessions beyond what is equivalent to the level of nullification or impairment. In our view there is nothing in the relevant provisions [of the DSU] that could be read as a justification for countermeasures of a punitive nature'.[88] According to Schwartz and Sykes, excessive sanctions reminiscent of punishment are detrimental to the system because any greater level of reciprocal withdrawal of concessions would raise the price of non-performance above the costs to the disadvantaged promises.[89]

The purely compensatory nature of retaliation under the WTO regime explains why the DSB is not preoccupied with the allocation of responsibility, a finding that was address in detail in Chapter 6. Instead, it focuses on ensuring that concessions are rebalanced. When it comes to retaliation, the territory of the EU in its entirety, not only of a specific Member State, can be a target of countermeasures. Even if an inconsistent measure is linked to a particular Member State, the WTO member whose rights have been impaired or nullified can direct its retaliation towards commitments of any EU Member State. In case of cross-retaliation, a so-called 'carousel retaliation' applies – goods and Member States which are targeted by cross-retaliation rotate so that consequences are not concentrated in one Member State and with respect to one product.[90]

Another reason why allocation of responsibility for a breach is less, if at all, relevant under the WTO regime is that remedies are forward-oriented. The relief afforded by the WTO panels is prospective in nature and calls for consistent behaviour in future. The emphasis is not on compensation for past injury but on the inducement of compliance going forward.[91]

5.3.4 *The Primacy of Compliance over Retaliation*

The Arbitrators in *United States – Continued Dumping and Subsidy Offset Act of 2000* said that '*it is not completely clear what role is to be played by the suspension of obligations in the DSU and a large part of the conceptual*

88 *EC –Bananas III*, WT/DS27/ARB, Decision of the Arbitrators adopted 9 April 1999, para 6.3.

89 Sykes and Schwartz 2002, 10.

90 Anne Thies, *International Trade Disputes and EU Liability* (Cambridge University Press 2013), 168.

91 DSU Art 3.7 provides that the provision of compensation should be resorted to only if the immediate withdrawal of the measure is impracticable and as a temporary measure pending the withdrawal of the measure which is inconsistent with a covered agreement, whereas suspension of concessions should be a measure of last resort; see also Allen 2011, 288.

debate that took place in these proceedings could have been avoided if a clear "object and purpose" were identified'.[92]

To reiterate the point already made, the liability-type system of the WTO remedies means that breaches of WTO commitments are not punishable acts properly so-called but are merely wrongful measures. WTO members can in effect choose to breach their commitments and suffer proportionate retaliation without encountering a punitive response. Retaliation and compensation have, however, rarely been used under the WTO regime.[93] GATT and TRIPS cases generally result in the timely withdrawal of inconsistent measures.[94] While two members – the EU and the United States – have been subject to retaliation, there is a clear primacy of compliance over retaliation under the WTO dispute-settlement system.[95]

Article 3.7 DSU establishes primacy of compliance over other forms of remedies by noting that '*in the absence of a mutually agreed solution, the first objective of the dispute settlement mechanism is usually to secure the withdrawal of the measures concerned if these are found to be inconsistent with the provisions of any covered agreement*'. The role of retaliation as a compliance-inducing tool is clear from Article 22.8 DSU which states that the suspension of concessions shall be temporary and shall be applied until such time as the measure found to be inconsistent has been removed. The purpose of the WTO dispute settlement system is, however, to avoid these types of payouts and bring an inconsistent measure into compliance with WTO obligations. Retaliation, by raising barriers to trade, is detrimental to the injured party as well.[96]

92 Recourse to Arbitration by Brazil under Article 22.6 of the DSU – Decision by the Arbitrators (31 August 2004) WT/DS217/ARB/BRA, 6.4. See also Gregory Shaffer and Daniel Ganin, 'Extrapolating Purpose from Practice: Rebalancing or Inducing Compliance', in Chad P Bown and Joost Pauwelyn (eds), *The Law, Economics and Politics of Retaliation in WTO Dispute Settlement* (Cambridge University Press 2010). See also Joost Pauwelyn, John H Jackson and Alan O Sykes, 'The Calculation and Design of Trade Retaliation in Context: What Is the Goal of Suspending WTO Obligations?', in Chad P Bown and Joost Pauwelyn (eds), *The Law, Economics and Politics of Retaliation in WTO Dispute Settlement* (Cambridge University Press 2010); Charnovitz 2001.

93 According to the 2009 data presented by Davey, in 75 per cent of trade remedy cases, the typical result has been the modification of the measure; see William J Davey, 'Compliance Problems in WTO Dispute Settlement' (2009) 42 Cornell Int'l L J 119, 120.

94 Davey 2009, 120.

95 The EU has been subject to retaliation in *EC – Bananas III*; *US – Continued Suspension of Obligations in the EC – Hormones Dispute*, WT/DS320/AB/R; the United States has been subject to retaliation in *US – Foreign Sales Corp*, WT/DS108/ARB; *US – Byrd Amendment*, WT/DS234/ARB/CAN.

96 Bernard Hoekman and Petros C Mavroidis, 'WTO Dispute Settlement, Transparency and Surveillance' (2000) 30 World Economy 527.

Accordingly, in the WTO system compensation and retaliation serve as subordinated remedy to compliance.[97] Though the liability rule helps attract international cooperation in the field of international economic law and prevents holdout problems, payouts from commitments which call out retaliation are disfavoured under the DSU.[98] According to Jackson, the DSU creates a strong preference for changing the offending measure over compensation.[99] Though compensation and reparation[100] serve as a form of monetization of a breach, their primary aim is to induce compliance.[101] The ultimate role of compliance, as stated in Article 21.1 DSU, is to ensure effective resolution of disputes to the benefit of all members.

Article 22.1 DSU suggests that 'compliance' means the bringing of a measure into conformity with the covered agreement. Accordingly, the primary remedy under the WTO dispute-settlement system is the modification of a member's legal framework in a way that it becomes compliant with its WTO obligations. Positive actions are often necessary to achieve this purpose, for example, reclassification of a customs tariff, suspension of subsidies, the amendment of a procedure for the registration of trademarks and geographical indications, the elimination of a regulatory restriction.

Chapter 6 will return to the significance of compliance as a primary remedy. At this point it will only be assumed that compliance-oriented remedial systems must focus on the overall regulatory framework rather than on *application* of that framework in a particular case. As has been noted earlier, the purpose of the WTO dispute-settlement system is future-oriented compliance

97 DSU Art 3(7) provides that a 'solution mutually acceptable to the parties to a dispute and consistent with the covered agreements is clearly to be preferred. In the absence of a mutually agreed solution, the first objective of the dispute-settlement mechanism is usually to secure the withdrawal of the measures concerned if these are found to be inconsistent with the provisions of any of the covered agreements. The provision of compensation should be resorted to only if the immediate withdrawal of the measure is impracticable and as a temporary measure pending the withdrawal of the measure which is inconsistent with a covered agreement'.

98 DSU Art 22.1 expressly states that 'neither compensation nor the suspension of concessions or other obligations is preferred to full implementation of a recommendation to bring a measure into conformity with covered agreements'.

99 Jackson 1997.

100 Compensation and retaliation under the WTO regime are often referred to as 'sanctions'. According to Charnovitz, when a trade measure is used against a country to change its behaviour towards conformity with international obligations, that is properly called a 'sanction'; see Charnovitz 2001, 804.

101 The impact of retaliation in inducing compliance has been questioned, for example, by Davey who suggests that the overall good record of the system is due mainly to the good faith desire of WTO members to see the dispute-settlement system work effectively; see Davey 2009, 125.

rather than elimination of an isolated past injury which suggests that the target of the dispute settlement must typically be the EU-wide regulatory regime. That goal cannot be fulfilled by removing specific instances of application of an inconsistent measure at the Member States' level but by leaving the inconsistency in the EU-wide framework intact. This feature of the remedial system under WTO law differentiates it from remedies under investment treaties to which this chapter now turns.

5.4 REMEDIES UNDER INVESTMENT TREATIES

The difference in remedial regimes under investment treaties and the WTO dispute-settlement system stems from the difference of rights protected under these two frameworks. As Demirkol notes, typically investment treaties do not protect the essence of the right.[102] He suggests that they establish an additional layer of protection that precludes the host state from acting in a certain manner.[103] Because the role of investment tribunals is limited to evaluating the behaviour of the host state rather than national laws themselves, they do not have the power to order revocation or modification of those laws. Investment treaties are thus not rules-based legal frameworks in that they do not establish a regulatory regime as such. Instead, they set standards of behaviour when a state exercises its regulatory powers.

Remedies under the investment treaty regime, similarly to the WTO system, are based on the liability rule. In most cases, an injunction is not available and host states which violate rights of foreign investors are subject to pay adequate compensation. However, while both regimes are liability-type, the system of remedies for breaches of investors' rights differs from the one for violations of trade rules. The primary remedy under investment treaties is compensation as opposed to regulatory compliance under the WTO system.

Restitutio in integrum is often divided into two categories, legal (order by a tribunal for the repeal or alteration of a measure) and material (an order for the restoration or repair of property unlawfully seized). First-generation investment treaties[104] rarely specify either type of *restitutio in integrum* in arbitration agreements but leave open a possibility to award them.[105] Article 54 of the Convention on the Settlement of Investment Disputes between States and

102 Berk Demirkol, 'Remedies in Investment Treaty Arbitration' (2015) 6 JIDS 413.

103 Demirkol 2015, 413.

104 By 'first-generation' investment treaties I mean BITs concluded by the Member States as opposed to investment chapters under the recently concluded EU FTAs.

105 Gray 1987, 13. Gray suggests that legal restitution raises the problem of the relationship between international and municipal law.

Nationals of Other States (ICSID Convention) allows a claimant to have only pecuniary obligations recognized and enforced in national courts as final judgments. The ECT allows the disputing party to elect to pay monetary damages in lieu of any other remedy granted.[106] Article 1135(1) of the North American Free Trade Agreement (NAFTA) limits the choice of remedies to pecuniary damages and restitution of property (and even then, monetary damages may be paid in lieu of restitution).

Similarly to the first-generation treaties,[107] pecuniary damages are also a central remedy under the new-generation investment treaties. Monetary damages are listed as a primary remedy under the recently concluded EU free trade agreements (FTAs). For example, Article 8.39 of CETA provides that tribunals may only award monetary damages (and interest) and/or restitution of property, in which case the respondent may still opt to pay monetary damages representing the fair market value of the property. Monetary damages and restitution of property as the only available remedies are similarly indicated in Article 9.24 of the The European Union-Singapore Free Trade Agreement (EUSFTA) and, to refer to a non-EU example, Article 9.29(1) of CPTPP. In addition, while first-generation treaties were silent on this point, new-generation treaties typically expressly state that punitive damages are not available.[108]

Whether the choice of remedies is limited to compensation or not, in practice compensation is the primary remedy under investment regimes. Gray notes that remedies other than damages for injury to foreign nationals are rare.[109] Hindelang also observes that the vast majority of arbitral awards do not discuss – indeed, fail to even mention – different forms of reparation but turn straight to compensation.[110] His explanation is that investment arbitration is commercial in nature and by the fact that claimants frequently ask the tribunal to award compensation only and hence deselect any other form of reparation.

To note for the purposes of precision, non-pecuniary remedies in the form of specific performance have been afforded in some investment disputes under first-generation investment treaties.[111] For example, in *ATA Construction* v. *Jordan*, the respondent was ordered to terminate the ongoing municipal court proceedings initiated following the wrongful extinguishment

106 ECT Art 26(8).

107 Martins Paparinskis, 'Investors' Remedies under EU Law and International Investment Law' (2016) 17 JWIT 919, 923.

108 A prohibition of punitive damages is established, for example, in Art 9.29(6) of CPTPP.

109 Gray 1987, 11.

110 Hindelang 2011.

111 For an in-depth analysis of non-pecuniary remedies in investment law, see Demirkol 2015, 229.

of an arbitration agreement by a national law provision and determined the entitlement of the investor to proceed to commercial arbitration.[112] In *Desert Line* v. *Yemen*, the Tribunal declared that a settlement agreement between the investor and the host state was concluded under duress and was thus declared to have no international effect.[113] *Nykomb v. Latvia* serves as another example.[114] The case concerned the alleged loss of sales income on electric power due to changes of the purchase price. The Tribunal noted that the potential loss by the investor was too uncertain and speculative to form the basis for an award of monetary compensation.[115] Accordingly, the Tribunal concluded that it would be '*a continuing obligation upon the Republic to ensure the payment at the double tariff for electric power delivered under the Contract for the rest of the eight-year period*'.[116] Most notably, the Tribunal in *CMS* v. *Argentina* noted that restitution was '*by far the most reliable choice to make the injured party whole as it aims at the reestablishment of the situation existing prior to the wrongful act*'.[117] Though the arbitrators ultimately decided to award compensation, it did note that renegotiation of contractual relations between the parties was the proper remedy.[118]

Irrespective of these cases, the award of non-pecuniary damages in investment claims is an exception rather than a rule. Accordingly, unlike trade disputes where regulatory compliance is the purpose of adjudication, investment tribunals typically neither recommend nor order compliance with a specific regulatory scheme. In most cases investment tribunals instruct the host state to compensate an investor when its rights are affected.

One may argue that arbitral tribunals cannot order a host state to modify national rules because they lack jurisdiction. Though investment treaties are signed between states (and the EU in case of new-generation FTAs), the primary obligation is owed to a non-state entity.[119] This in itself makes rights private in nature. An investor can only require certain conduct from a host state, and if a host state violates this commitment, it can request

112 *ATA Construction* v. *The Hashemite Kingdom of Jordan* (Award, 18 May 2010) ICSID Case No ARB/08/2.

113 *Desert Line Projects LLC* v. *The Republic of Yemen* (Award, 6 February 2008) ICSID Case No ARB/05/17, para 194.

114 *Nykomb Synergetics Technology Holding AB* v. *The Republic of Latvia*, (Award, 16 December 2003), SCC (*Nykomb* v. *Latvia*).

115 *Nykomb* v. *Latvia*, Award, 41, sect 5.2.

116 *Nykomb* v. *Latvia*, Award, 41, sect 5.2.

117 *CMS Gas Transmission Company* v. *Argentina* (Award 12 May 2005), ICSID Case No. ARB/01/8 (*CMS Gas* v. *Argentina*), para 406.

118 *CMS Gas* v. *Argentina*, Award, para 407.

119 Para 4 of the Commentary to Art 33. The Commentary notes that while a situation when a primary obligation is owed to a non-state entity falls outside the scope of the ILC rules, such protection is possible under special rules, such as investment treaties.

compensation. An investor cannot, however, call for modifications of general rules because those concern rights and obligations of other persons.

This explains why remedies for violation of the same right may differ depending on whether the holder of that right is a state or private person. For example, remedies for violation of the most-favoured-nation clause differ under the WTO regime and investment treaties. A member of the WTO can request (though short of requesting an injunction) another member to modify its framework so that it does not discriminate against foreign actors. A foreign investor, on the other hand, cannot do so under investment treaties. New-generation FTAs, which cover both state-to-state and investor-to-state obligations, highlight this difference by setting out separate dispute-resolution mechanisms. For example, Chapter 29 of CETA establishes a dispute-resolution mechanism for state-to-state claims which closely resembles that of the WTO two-step regime of compliance and retaliation. Investor-to-state dispute resolution, set out in Chapter 8, by contrast, focuses on compensation.

The difference in remedies depending on whether they are available to a person or a state has been known since early international cases. In the *Chorzów Factory* case the Permanent Court of International Justice stated that '*[r]ights or interests of an individual the violation of which causes damage are always in a different plane to rights belonging to a State, which rights may also be infringed by the same act. The damage suffered by an individual is never therefore identical in kind with that which will be suffered by a State; it can only afford a convenient scale for the calculation of the reparation due to the State*'.[120] Non-pecuniary obligations are not enforceable under investment protection regimes, one reason being, according to Douglas, that the adoption of specific judicial acts to comply with a tribunal's order may be complicated by the constitutional norms of the host state or by competing rights of third parties.[121]

Given that compensation is central to investment arbitration, it follows that the focus of tribunals must be on the damage caused by the unlawful conduct of the host state. This is essentially different from the WTO regime, which places regulatory compliance at the heart of its dispute-settlement system. At least in most cases the WTO DSB focuses on the regulatory framework as such, whereas investment tribunals are tasked with calculating damages arising from the unlawful conduct of the host state.

[120] *Factory at Chorzów (Germany* v. *Poland)*, Merits, Claim for Indemnity, Judgment No. 13, [1928] PCIJ Series A – No. 17, 28.

[121] Zachary Douglas, *The International Law of Investment Claims* (Cambridge University Press 2009), 101.

5.5 CONCLUSION

Two findings follow from the aforementioned analysis of the nature of remedies in international economic law in relation to the question of international responsibility of the EU and its Member States.

First, liability-type remedies under trade and investment treaties indicate that the allocation of responsibility for breach between the EU and its Member States may not be relevant in the international economic law context. A state may in effect choose to dishonour its international economic obligations and pay adequate damages. Preference for compliance under the WTO system is consistent with the liability rule – compliance cannot be enforced, it can only be recommended. The choice whether to comply rests with the WTO member. If breaches of economic obligations are, while wrongful, subject to adequate payouts, determining *who* breached an obligation in a multilayered structure like the EU is not relevant. The focus is not on the attribution of breach, but on the payout.

While payouts are primary remedies under investment treaties, they are secondary (though ultimate) remedies under the WTO regime. Compliance is the preferred outcome of WTO adjudication. By contrast, compensation is a central remedy under investment arbitration.

Accordingly, investment tribunals and WTO panels perform different tasks. The former focus on calculation of compensation in accordance to the damage caused, whereas the latter must address inconsistencies in a regulatory framework as such. Upon finding a breach the WTO panels must analyse the overall regulatory framework with the aim of bringing it into compliance with WTO rules. Investment tribunals, on the other hand, seek to identify adequate compensation in relation to a specific instance of application of a general rule. To perform its role the DSB must zoom out its analysis, whereas investment tribunals must zoom theirs in.

Thus, the second finding is that the different tasks performed by trade and investment dispute-settlement bodies are reflected in their treatment of international responsibility of the EU and its Member States. As the purpose of investment law is to compensate investors for violation of their rights caused by the conduct of the host state, the focus of tribunals will be restricted to a particular instance of the application of an unlawful measure. A quest for regulatory compliance under the WTO system, on the other hand, requires investigation and modification of the overall legal framework.

Chapter 6 will explore these findings in detail by looking into trade and investment dispute-settlement practice. The aim of the analysis is to identify the rationales underlying the reasoning of international courts and tribunals when dealing with the responsibility of the EU and its Member States.

6

Identification of the Proper Respondents

6.1 INTRODUCTION

This chapter will examine how international courts and tribunals identify the proper respondents in international economic disputes. The aim is to determine the underlying rationales which guide tribunals in international economic adjudication when faced with situations of shared responsibility.

In Chapter 2 it was argued that the International Law Commission (ILC) rules on international responsibility do not determine the allocation of international responsibility. The ILC framework determines only whether a particular entity *is* internationally responsible. If responsibility is addressed in the context of a multilayered structure like the European Union (EU), where sovereignty is shared between separate legal persons, additional questions arise. Chapter 3 argued that the EU and its Member States are independently responsible for their joint obligations, as in the case of mixed agreements.[1]

This, however, is only a starting point in addressing the question of the allocation of international responsibility within the EU. Nollkaemper and Jacobs rightly note that the principle of independent responsibility in itself provides no basis for the apportionment of responsibility, and, in particular, it does not *answer* the question of who has to pay reparation.[2] That responsibility of both the EU and its Member States *can* be invoked does not tell us whether

[1] To specify, mixed agreements which do not provide a declaration of competences and which contain no 'carve out' of the agreement by allocation of responsibility for areas to the EU and Member States. Accordingly, agreements like UNCLOS and the EU's participation in the Food and Agricultural Organization are outside the scope of discussion.

[2] André Nollkaemper and Dov Jacobs, 'Shared Responsibility in International Law: A Conceptual Framework' (2013) 34 Mich. J. Int'l L. 359, 391. André Nollkaemper, 'Joint Responsibility between the EU and Member States for Non-Performance of Obligations Under Multilateral Environmental Agreements', in Elisa Morgera (ed), *The External Environmental Policy of the European Union* (Cambridge University Press 2012), 330.

the EU, its Member States or both *will* be responsible in a given situation. We are faced with the complex task of determining exclusive responsibility.

It is often assumed that shared responsibility is distributed in accordance with the attribution of breach. It was argued in Chapter 4, however, that there is no support in international dispute-settlement practice for the European Commission's claim that authorities of Member States' act as *de facto* organs of the EU when they implement Union law. It was then suggested in Chapter 5 that attribution of conduct or breach, or allocation of responsibility for a *breach* more generally, is unnecessary in international economic law. This is because the liability-type nature of remedies under international economic regimes carries a restorative rather than retributive function. The focus is not on the party *responsible* but on the party *best placed to bear responsibility*. In international economic law, shared responsibility typically raises the question of the proper respondent(s). I argue that whether the EU, its Member States or both are the proper respondents depends on the nature of the treaty regime in question, particularly the system of remedies designed to protect treaty obligations.

Identification of the rationales that underlie the distribution of shared responsibility of the EU and its Member States in international dispute-settlement practice is a complex task. As has been mentioned in the introduction, the patterns discussed later are novel and have been extracted from an extensive analysis of international case law. While many cases have not (yet) resulted in panel reports, often reports and party submissions are of 500 pages have also been analysed. All publicly available procedural documents of investment arbitration under the Energy Charter Treaty (ECT) which involve the EU. Identification of the rationales underlying the tribunals' decisions on the proper respondent was complicated because my findings are counter-intuitive. International courts and tribunals do not allocate responsibility on some static institutional basis, such as normative control or division of competences. Part I has concluded that international courts and tribunals do not distribute shared responsibility among the EU and its Member States on the basis of attribution of conduct (or breach) and there is no basis to support the view that the EU is responsible for the conduct of Member States when they implement Union law. Having determined what tribunals do *not do*, the following chapter will examine how they in fact *do* distribute shared responsibility.

The aim of this chapter is to identify the underlying bases for the identification of the proper respondent(s) in trade and investment disputes while relying on the characteristics of the remedial systems outlined in Chapter 5. Section 6.2 explores the normative grounds for distributing shared responsibility between the EU and its Member States in international economic law. In Section 6.3 I develop 'the positive solution' test for WTO panels to identify the proper respondent(s). It will be argued in Section 6.4 that shared responsibility arising under the ECT is distributed by placing responsibility on the entity which is the proximate cause of the damage to the investor.

6.2 MAPPING THE NORMATIVE FRAMEWORK

This section introduces the normative considerations informing the law of shared responsibility. In addition to other sources the analysis builds on some of the concepts offered by contributors to the Research Project on Shared Responsibility in International Law (SHARES).

The term 'distribution of responsibility' rather than 'distribution of responsibil*ities*' is employed in the following analysis. The SHARES project uses the latter. The term 'responsibilities', however, has a connotation of power or competence. To avoid confusion with competence-based or normative responsibility in the context of the EU and its Member States, reference will be made to 'responsibility'.

The majority opinion is that the question of international responsibility in the context of the EU's executive federalism where Member States implement Union law involves shared responsibility.[3] To borrow Nollkaemper's definition, shared responsibility refers to situations where a multiplicity of actors contribute to a single harmful outcome, and legal responsibility for this harmful outcome is distributed among or deemed to be shared by more than one of the contributing actors.[4] Though the terms 'shared responsibility' and 'joint and several liability' are often used interchangeably, the latter refers to situations when two or more

3 See inter alia, Giorgio Gaja, 'The European Community's Rights and Obligations under Mixed Agreements', in David O'Keeffe and Henry G Schermers (eds), *Mixed Agreements* (Kluwer Law & Taxation Publishers 1983); Eleftheria Neframi, 'International Responsibility of the European Community and of Member States under Mixed Agreements', in Enzo Cannizzaro (ed), *The European Union as An Actor in International Relations* (Kluwer Law International 2002); Marise Cremona, *External Relations of the EU and the Member States: Competence, Mixed Agreements, International Responsibility, and Effects of International Law* (European University Institute 2006); Joni Heliskoski, 'Joint Competence of the European Community and Its Member States and the Dispute Settlement Practice of the World Trade Organization' (1999–2000) 2 CYELS 80.

4 André Nollkaemper, 'Introduction', in André Nollkaemper and Ilias Plakokefalos (eds), *Principles of Shared Responsibility in International Law: An Appraisal of the State of the Art* (Cambridge University Press 2014), 7. Nollkaemper and Jacobs define shared responsibility by four main features: responsibility of multiple actors, which contribute to a single harmful outcome, where contributions cannot be attributed to individuals based on causation and responsibility, is distributed to them separately; see Nollkaemper and Jacobs 2013, 368.

persons who are jointly and severally liable for obligations are each responsible for the whole damage caused to third parties: 'joint' because they take responsibility for each other's wrongs; 'several' because they can be separately sued.[5] Joint responsibility is narrower than shared responsibility because the former stems from 'the same wrongful act', whereas the latter might not.[6]

The Articles on the Responsibility of International Organizations (ARIO) leaves open the possibility of shared, as well as joint responsibility. The primary basis for joint responsibility under the ILC rules is attribution of conduct and/or responsibility.[7] In fact, the Commentary to Article 48 of the ARIO calls for joint responsibility in case of the EU's mixed agreements.[8] Bartels suggests that an act can be attributable both to an organization and one (or more) of its Member States, resulting in a multiple attribution of act(s).[9] Similarly, Messineo notes that international law has no difficulty in treating the same conduct as the act of an individual and of a collective entity.[10] Fry discusses shared responsibility based on a multiple attribution of responsibility rather than conduct. According to him, under mixed agreements the EU or its Member States may be jointly responsible even if breach can be attributed to the other, without determining the attribution of conduct.[11]

As it was argued in Chapter 4, however, we are unable to distribute shared responsibility among the EU and its Member States based on the attribution of

5 Crawford Third Report, 74, para 272.

6 ARSIWA Art 47(1) provides '[w]here several States are responsible for the same internationally wrongful act, the responsibility of each State may be invoked in relation to that act'. See also Nollkaemper in Nollkaemper and Plakokefalos 2014, 10. See also Lewis A Kornhauser, 'Incentives, Compensation, and Irreparable Harm', in André Nollkaemper and Dov Jacobs (eds), *Distribution of Responsibilities in International Law* (Cambridge University Press 2015), 132.

7 The Commentary states that the fact that an international organization is responsible for an internationally wrongful act does not exclude the existence of parallel responsibility of other subjects, for example, in case of conduct which is simultaneously attributed to an organization and a state.

8 ARIO Art 48 addresses responsibility of an international organization and one or more states or international organizations.

9 Lorand Bartels, 'Procedural Aspects of Shared Responsibility in the WTO Dispute Settlement System' (2013) 4 JIDS 343–359. According to Bartels, while it is possible that an act adopted by a WTO member could be defended on the basis that the WTO member is merely implementing an act properly attributed to another international organization, we do not have WTO dispute-settlement practice on this matter.

10 Francesco Messineo, 'Attribution of Conduct', in André Nollkaemper and Ilias Plakokefalos (eds), *Principles of Shared Responsibility in International Law: An Appraisal of the State of the Art* (Cambridge University Press 2014), 62.

11 James D Fry, 'Attribution of Responsibility', in André Nollkaemper and Ilias Plakokefalos (eds), *Principles of Shared Responsibility in International Law: An Appraisal of the State of the Art* (Cambridge University Press 2014), 99.

conduct (or breach, in case of indirect responsibility), because the line separating the conduct of EU organs and Member States' organs is not clear. In any case it is unlikely that any international dispute-settlement body would be willing to engage in the analysis of the complex web of institutional ties within the Union. To the best of my knowledge no tribunal has so far attempted to carry out such an analysis.

Leaving aside the unitary understanding of international responsibility, it is suggested here that there can be an alternative basis for the distribution of shared responsibility other than attribution of conduct and/or responsibility. This book supports the differentialist approach to shared responsibility expressed by various scholars who contributed to the SHARES project. This project does not aim to provide a single normative or conceptual approach to the distribution of shared responsibility in international law, but rather it aims to identify possible approaches to distribution of responsibility, such as moral, political, economic or normative.[12]

In particular, this book finds that the strict distinction between primary and secondary norms is unhelpful[13] and instead adopts, to use the language of Nollkaemper and Jacobs, a holistic and pluralist approach.[14] It is argued here that for the purposes of distributing responsibility between the EU and its Member States in the international economic context, identification of a 'guilty' party through attribution of conduct or breach is irrelevant to the deliberation of dispute-settlement bodies and even to complaining parties. Drawing on the analysis of the nature of international economic obligations in Chapter 5, this chapter argues that the focus is rather on the party best placed to remedy the harm.[15] As Miller rightly notes, it may not matter so much from a plaintiff's point of view, which particular entity is held responsible – there may be many agents who are able to remedy harm, and what matters is that one such agent, or group of agents, provides redress.[16]

12 Nollkaemper in Nollkaemper and Plakokefalos 2014, 8.

13 The distinction between primary and secondary norms can be useful, for example in the context of adopting the ILC articles on responsibility. Crawford noted that the distinction was of a functional nature rather than grounded in a comprehensive theoretical argument; see James Crawford, 'The ILC's Articles on Responsibility of States for Internationally Wrongful Acts: A Retrospect' (2002) 96 AJIL 874, 876–877.

14 André Nollkaemper and Dov Jacobs, 'Shared Responsibility in International Law: A Concept Paper' (2001) ACIL Research Paper No 2011–07 (SHARES Series), 7.

15 Kornhauser refers to the identification of actors who must 'remedy' the harm as legal responsibility; see Kornhauser 2015, 121. While he distinguished legal responsibility from causal and financial responsibility as other bases for distribution, this author is unsure what this categorization adds since legal and financial responsibility are likely to direct to the same actor.

16 David Miller, 'Distributing Responsibilities' (2001) 9 J. Political Philos. 453, 468.

The question is not *who is responsible for a breach* but *who is best placed to bear responsibility*. While counter-intuitive, this approach is practical. Miller, who in his philosophy of responsibility refers to the principle of capacity, suggests that remedial responsibilities ought to be assigned according to the capacity of each agent to discharge them. His justification for this view is that if we want to put a bad situation right, we should give the responsibility to those who are best placed to do the remedying.[17] Using the SHARES terminology, this proposition reflects the consequentialist approach, in which the starting point of analysis is the harm to be repaired.[18] The other side of the spectrum is the deontological vision which focuses on the duty and the moral blame of the perpetrator. As Nollkaemper and Jacobs rightly note, the adoption of a consequentialist approach may lead to an altogether different set of consequences in terms of distribution of responsibility from that of a more orthodox approach which links responsibility to attribution of conduct.[19]

The consequent question is then as follows: How does one identify 'the party best placed to remedy harm', whether it be the EU, its Member States or both?

Drawing on the analysis of international dispute practice, this book argues that the answer to this question lies in the nature of the primary norms underlying the treaty regime in question. By 'the treaty regime in question' I mean the nature of obligations and remedies, and the dispute-settlement mechanism in which the two operate.

Relying on the characteristics of the remedial systems under trade and investment regimes discussed in Chapter 5, the following section will identify the underlying rationales which govern the choice of proper respondent(s). The analysis shall start with the WTO dispute-settlement system and suggest that the DSB adopts 'the positive solution test' that this study develops. The chapter will then proceed to investment practice which reveals that tribunals operating under the ECT focus on the proximate cause of harm.

6.3 THE POSITIVE SOLUTION TEST IN WTO DISPUTES

The WTO dispute-settlement system is open to shared responsibility.[20] Contentions about shared responsibility of the EU and its Member States

[17] Miller 2001, 460.

[18] André Nollkaemper and Dov Jacobs, 'Introduction: Mapping the Normative Framework for the Distribution of Shared Responsibility', in André Nollkaemper and Dov Jacobs (eds), *Distribution of Responsibilities in International Law* (Cambridge University Press 2015), 16.

[19] Nollkaemper and Jacobs in Nollkaemper and Jacobs 2015, 17.

[20] See also, James Flett, 'The Practice of Shared Responsibility in Relation to The World Trade Organization and the European Union and Its Member States in the WTO', in

have arisen in a number of WTO disputes.[21] These cases will be considered in detail in Chapter 8. Suffice it here to note that in these cases WTO panels did not engage in the allocation of conduct or breach to the EU or its Member States but rather focused on the party best placed to restore order, in line with the hypotheses advanced earlier.

As a general rule, indeed, WTO law avoids addressing questions of distribution of responsibility. Flett rightly notes that WTO law is well suited to avoiding issues of shared responsibility altogether, and, in practice, this is what has been happening.[22] According to Flett, the drafting of the WTO Agreement suggests that attribution will not generally be an issue, and this is confirmed by the case law.[23] Bartels further explains that since WTO membership is almost universal and comes with compulsory submission to the WTO dispute-settlement procedure, it will usually be possible to direct the complaint to the party in question.[24] But which party is the 'party in question'?

The analysis of WTO dispute-settlement practice reveals that in order to answer this question the Dispute Settlement Body (DSB) employs what I call 'the positive solution test'. This term of art is novel and has not been identified in legal scholarship. It has, however, been expressly referred to by the WTO panels. The test stems from the primary aim of the WTO dispute-settlement regime which is to ensure regulatory compliance with WTO law.

As has been explained in Chapter 5, compliance is central to the WTO dispute-settlement regime. To ensure regulatory compliance the DSB must identify inconsistencies in the overall regulatory regime. Attribution of conduct (or causation) is largely irrelevant for compliance purposes because the focus of adjudicators is not on identifying the violator but more broadly on evaluating the compatibility of the member's regulatory regime with WTO law. In fact, WTO dispute-settlement proceedings are available not only for violations of WTO law but also for 'non-violation' and 'situation' complaints (though these are rare in practice).[25]

The restorative function of the DSB is set out in Article 3.7 of the DSU. The provision states that the aim of the dispute-settlement mechanism is '*to secure*

André Nollkaemper and Ilias Plakokefalos (eds), *The Practice of Shared Responsibility in International Law* (Cambridge University Press 2016), 852.

21 Bartels 2013, 347.

22 Flett 2016, 859.

23 Flett 2016, 859.

24 Bartels 2013, 346.

25 Bartels 2013, 344, ft 4: Art XXIII:1 of the General Agreement on Tariffs and Trade (GATT 1994) and equivalent provisions in the other WTO Agreements. Special rules apply to the latter two types of complaint: art DSU Art 26. There have been few decisions on 'non-violation' complaints, and, so far, none on 'situation' complaints.

a positive solution to a dispute'. The language employed by the DSU suggests that the objective of dispute resolution can be reached in various ways, for example, through 'prompt settlement',[26] 'satisfactory settlement',[27] 'mutually agreed solution'[28] or 'mutually acceptable solution'.[29] Whatever form is chosen, the goal is to bring the state's conduct into regulatory compliance.

Positive solution to a dispute does not invariably require addressing the DSB's recommendations to all entities involved in the breach. As the primary aim of the WTO dispute-settlement system is compliance rather than retributive justice, the DSB limits its rulings and recommendations to the EU in some cases even when an inconsistency on the part of the Member States has been (or could be) established. The following sections will illustrate this point with case law.

One may argue that such remedy-focused approach reflects the theory of efficient breach in that it does not sanction breaches that are irrelevant to restorative purposes.[30] The simplified version of the theory, the origins of which can be traced to contract law, holds that expectation damages give parties a reason to perform when and only when the performance will increase overall social welfare. To follow Wendell Holmes' reasoning, '*[t]he duty to keep a contract at common law means a prediction that you must pay damages if you do not keep it – and nothing else*'.[31] The theory concerns the distinction noted by Calabresi and Melamed between the property rule and the liability rule, which was addressed in Chapter 5.[32] When the net cost of compliance is higher than the net cost of breach, breach must be tolerated, even promoted, as it serves the social function of maximizing overall welfare.[33] The focus is on those whose action will be required to ensure compliance. In this sense the DSB allows efficient breach and targets only those responsibility-sharing entities that are necessary to achieve a positive solution to the dispute.

26 DSU Art 3.3.

27 DSU Art 3.4.

28 DSU Art 3.6.

29 DSU Art 3.7.

30 Joel P Trachtman, *The Economic Structure of International Law* (Harvard University Press 2008), 144. See also Alan O Sykes and Warren F Schwartz, 'The Economic Structure of Renegotiation and Dispute Resolution in the WTO/GATT System' (2002) 31 J. Leg. Stud. 179, 180.

31 Oliver Wendell Holmes, 'The Path of the Law' (1897) 10 Harv. L. Rev. 457, reprinted in 110 Harv. L. Rev. 991, 995 (1997).

32 Guido Calabresi and Douglas A Melamed, 'Property Rules, Liability Rules, and Inalienability: One View of the Cathedral' (1972) 85 Harv. L. Rev. 1089, n 388.

33 Joost Pauwelyn, *Optimal Protection of International Law: Navigating between European Absolutism and American Voluntarism* (Cambridge University Press 2008), 8.

The WTO case-law analysis reveals three main features of the WTO dispute-settlement regime which reflect the remedy-based distribution of shared responsibility. First, panels address their recommendations only to those persons and cover only those measures which are *necessary* to achieving a positive solution, reflecting the efficient breach doctrine. Second, the DSB postpones determination of the proper respondent until the final stages of adjudication, which allows it to define what is necessary for compliance purposes. Third, there are a number of procedural techniques which enable the DSB to distribute responsibility on a functional basis without attributing breach.

6.3.1 *Efficient Breach*

The DSB does not engage in the attribution of breach to the EU or its Member States. Rather, it focuses its analysis on what is necessary to achieve a positive solution to the dispute. Accordingly, shared responsibility is shifted (and limited) to those *persons* whose actions are relevant to compliance purposes. Also, it restricts its examination to those *measures* which have not yet expired, disregarding breaches that are irrelevant to remedial purposes. The following analysis is structured according to these two points.

6.3.2 *Limitation to Necessary Persons*

EC and Certain Member States – IT Products illustrates the application of the positive solution test to determine whether the EU, its Member States or both are the proper respondents in the dispute.[34] The case, which was brought by the United States, Japan and Chinese Taipei, concerned the tariff treatment that the EC afforded to certain information technology products. The issue before the Panel was whether a series of EC measures was inconsistent with Article II:1(a) and (b) of the General Agreement on Tariffs and Trade (GATT) because they resulted in less favourable treatment accorded to imports of certain products than is provided in the EC schedule.[35] The claimants disputed duties imposed by the customs authorities of Member States on certain IT products. They listed EU regulations through which Member States impose the allegedly wrongful duties. A dispute arose between the EC and

[34] *EC and Certain Member States – IT Products*, WT/DS375/R, WT/DS376/R, WT/DS377/R, PR.

[35] The products under the dispute covered flat panel display devices, set-top boxes with common function and multifunctional digital machines.

the claimants whether the Panel's findings should cover Member States' actions, or whether the case concerned the EC alone.

According to the EC it was the sole respondent in the dispute.[36] The claimants disagreed, stating that both the EC and its Member States are independent members of the WTO and both play a role in the application of customs duties.[37] The Panel stated that it faced the question of whether it should address findings with respect to the actions of the EC Member States and address recommendations to them in this dispute.[38]

The Panel first noted that both Member States and the EU are independently responsible for violations of the WTO obligations, in line with the principle of independent responsibility suggested in Chapter 3.[39] The question then was that of exclusive responsibility, that is, whether the EU alone or its Member States as well were respondents in *this* dispute. The Panel laid out the guiding principle of its analysis.

The Panel referred to Article 3.7 DSU, which states that the aim of the dispute-settlement mechanism is to secure a positive solution to a dispute and noted that its task is to make such findings as will assist the DSB in making the recommendations.[40] The Panel concluded that analysis of Member States' conduct was not necessary because '*findings with respect to the measures adopted by the European Communities will provide a positive solution to the dispute*'.[41]

The Panel's determination as to whether the EU or its Member States are the proper respondents in this dispute rests on the need to achieve a positive solution to the dispute. It places responsibility on the EC because it is the conduct of the EC that will have to be corrected to achieve compliance. The Panel stops short of addressing its recommendations to the Member States, even though their conduct might also have violated the commitments, because (in this particular case) ruling against the EC was sufficient for remedial purposes.

The *EC – Computer Equipment* case provides a second example of the application of the positive solution test to distribute shared responsibility within the EU. The dispute concerned a US challenge of tariff reclassification by the customs authorities of the EC as well as the United Kingdom and Ireland of local area network (LAN) equipment and PCs with multimedia

[36] *EC and Certain Member States – IT Products*, PR, para 7.80.
[37] *EC and Certain Member States – IT Products*, PR, para 7.81.
[38] *EC and Certain Member States – IT Products*, PR, para 7.82.
[39] *EC and Certain Member States – IT Products*, PR, para 7.86.
[40] *EC and Certain Member States – IT Products*, PR, para 7.87.
[41] *EC and Certain Member States – IT Products*, PR, para 8.2.

capability. The United States maintained that not only the EC but also Ireland and the United Kingdom were parties to the dispute. In its request for the establishment of the panel, the United States also requested that the panel specify which of those parties was responsible to the United States for the nullification or impairment.[42] The EC requested that the panel reject claims against the United Kingdom and Ireland, claiming they were not engaged in tariff binding.[43]

Again, the Panel addressed its rulings and recommendations to the EC alone. It referred back to the US complaint which challenged the following measures: (i) the EC's reclassification of LAN equipment,[44] (ii) the UK's and Ireland's reclassification of LAN equipment,[45] (iii) the EC's reclassification of multimedia PCs[46] and (iv) the UK's reclassification of multimedia PCs.[47] The Panel's reasoning is functional because it is focused on the remedy. It noted that since it found that the tariff treatment of LAN equipment by the EC was incompatible with its WTO obligations, it was *unnecessary* to rule on reclassification by the United Kingdom and Ireland.[48] The Panel refrained from ruling on the Member States' reclassification because finding that the EC's reclassification was incompatible with the WTO obligations was sufficient to determine that the classification needed correction. As in the *EC and Certain Member States – IT Products* discussed earlier, the Panel's reasoning likewise reflects elements of efficient breach.

The Panel avoided engaging in the allocation of responsibility for breach with respect to the tariff reclassification of multimedia PCs. On this point it noted that since it did not find a violation, there was no need to decide which of the defending parties (the EC, Ireland or the UK) was or were responsible for the alleged nullification or impairment of benefits to the US.[49] The Panel's approach to the question of international responsibility of the EU and its Member States was thus remedial: its analysis was guided by what is necessary to achieve a positive solution rather than by a quest to identify the wrongdoer(s).

EC – Large Civil Aircraft is a more unusual case in that the EC itself, not the complainant, requested that the Panel identify the proper respondent,

42 EC – *Computer Equipment*, PR, para 3.2.
43 EC – *Computer Equipment*, PR, para 3.3.
44 EC – *Computer Equipment*, PR, para 8.5 (a) and (b).
45 EC – *Computer Equipment*, PR, para 8.5 (d) and (f).
46 EC – *Computer Equipment*, PR, para 8.5 (c).
47 EC – *Computer Equipment*, PR, para 8.5 (e).
48 EC – *Computer Equipment*, PR, para 8.72.
49 EC – *Computer Equipment*, PR, para 8.72.

departing from the EC's usual approach to assert rather than question its exclusive responsibility.[50] The case concerned a challenge of the incentivization scheme for Airbus companies allegedly launched by the EU and applied by Member States. The analysis follows the patterns observed in the previous cases. The EC claimed that it was the proper respondent in this dispute.[51] The United States, which filed a request for consultations with not only the EC but also the governments of Germany, France, the United Kingdom and Spain, maintained that the EC and its Member States had provided unlawful subsidies to Airbus companies.[52] In the usual manner the EC asserted that it '*was the only respondent*' in this dispute and asked the Panel to drop the reference to the Member States in the title of the case.[53]

The Panel's position was that there was in fact no issue to be solved, thus refusing to allocate responsibility for breach.[54] Once again, in line with the principle of independent responsibility, it noted that Member States and the EC are independent members of the WTO with all the rights and obligations under this regime. According to the Panel, the four Member States indicated in the request for the establishment of the panel were respondents in this dispute, irrespective of whether or not they were represented by the EC in accordance to its internal arrangements.[55] It concluded that a decision on whether the Panel would address recommendations to the Member States involved in this dispute would be known only when it had completed the decision-making process.[56] Once again, the Panel avoided prior distribution of shared responsibility based on attribution of breach.

Distribution of shared responsibility on the basis of what is *necessary* to achieve a *positive solution* to the dispute is also reflected in the *EC – Commercial Vessels* dispute. Here, as in the cases discussed earlier, the claimant also argued that Member States should be respondents because there were independent members of the WTO and that internal EC constitutional issues could not adversely affect the rights of Korea or any other WTO

50 *EC – Large Civil Aircraft*, PR, para 7.174 referring to the Letter from the European Communities dated 23 May 2008.
51 *EC – Large Civil Aircraft*, PR, para 7.169 referring to the Letter from the European Communities dated 23 May 2008.
52 *EC – Large Civil Aircraft*, PR, para 7.170.
53 *EC – Large Civil Aircraft*, PR, para 7.172 referring to the Letter from the EC dated 23 Nov, 2005.
54 *EC – Large Civil Aircraft*, PR, para 7.174.
55 *EC – Large Civil Aircraft*, PR, para 7.175.
56 *EC – Large Civil Aircraft*, PR, para 7.176.

member.[57] According to Korea, the dispute covered both the EC regulation and Member States' measures, and thus the Panel had to make findings in relation to the EC and its Member States and recommend that they both bring their measures into conformity with their WTO obligations.[58] The EC followed its usual position and maintained that it was the proper respondent and that it took full responsibility under international law for measures taken by the EC Member States pursuant to the challenged regulation.[59]

The Panel adopted a functional approach to the international responsibility of the EU and its Member States.[60] It first noted the EC's full assumption of responsibility for the challenged measures, including the Member States' measures. This, according to the Panel, meant '*that the European Community accepts responsibility for any actions that may be required to bring into conformity the measure at issue*'.[61] Placing remedy at the centre of its focus, the Panel concluded that it found '*it sufficient, in the circumstances of this case, to address our recommendation to bring the measures at issue into conformity to the European Communities*'. The use of the term 'sufficient' indicates that the Panel's decision on the proper respondent was guided by the needs of the remedy in question, irrespective of allocation of responsibility for a breach.

Though unrelated to the EU, *China – Payment Services* confirms that the DSB's reasoning reflects elements of efficient breach when dealing with international responsibility of separate but related subjects of international law. In this dispute China contended that there was no legal basis for the claims advanced by the United States in relation to the services supplied in Hong Kong or Macao. According to China, Hong Kong and Macao were separate customs territories and each maintained its own rights and obligations under the WTO.[62] The Panel considered that China's commitments covered supply of services not only in China but also to clients in the territory of other WTO Members.[63] The Panel's decision not to consider whether Hong Kong and Macao might also have had obligations in respect of these services was based on the reasoning that such determination could not affect China's own responsibility.[64]

57 *EC – Commercial Vessels*, PR, para 4.24.

58 *EC – Commercial Vessels*, PR, para 7.32, referring to the Response of Korea to Panel Question 4.

59 *EC – Commercial Vessels*, PR, para 93, referring to the First submission of the EC, para. 93.

60 *EC – Commercial Vessels*.

61 *EC – Commercial Vessels*, PR, para 7.33.

62 *China – Payment Services*, WT/DS413/ R, PR, adopted 31 August 2012, para 7.608.

63 *China – Payment Services*, PR, para 7.619.

64 Bartels 2013, ft 18.

6.3.3 Limitation to Necessary Measures

The DSB rules only on those measures which are necessary to achieve a positive solution to the dispute, disregarding 'irrelevant' violations. This point can be seen in the DSB's reasoning on the temporal scope of the claims. The DSB tends to exclude measures which have expired or were not yet in force at the time of an establishment of a panel, if ruling on them is insignificant for compliance purposes.

The DSB has ruled that while the termination of a measure before the commencement of panel proceedings does not deprive it of the authority to make findings on that measure, it will only rule on that measure if it is necessary to secure a positive solution to the dispute.[65] An obligation of the DSB to rule on all matters before it would be incompatible with the principle of judicial economy,[66] whose exercise enables panels to refrain from making multiple findings that the same measure is inconsistent with various provisions when a single or a certain number of findings of inconsistency suffice to resolve the dispute.[67] It is in a panel's discretion to make findings on those measures that are necessary to fulfil the dispute-settlement objective of securing a positive solution to the dispute.[68]

The positive solution test to determine the temporal scope of the claim was applied in the *EC – Biotech Products* dispute. Here the Panel had to decide whether it was to rule not only on the legal framework for biotech product approval as such – in which case the EC alone would be a sufficient

[65] *Chile – Price Band System and Safeguard Measures Relating to Certain Agricultural Products*, WT/DS207, PR adopted 3 May 2002, para 7.115. In *Argentina – Measures Affecting Imports of Footwear, Textiles, Apparel and other Items*, WT/DS56, PR adopted 25 November 1997, para 6.15, the Panel decided not to make findings on WTO-consistency of measures which had been revoked eleven days before the establishment of a panel. Also, in *United States – Standards for Reformulated and Conventional Gasoline*, WT/DS2, PR adopted 29 January 1996, para 6.19, the Panel noted that it had not been the usual practice to rule on measures that, at the time of panel's terms of reference, were fixed and were not, and would not, become effective.

[66] *Canada – Measures Relating to Exports of Wheat and Treatment of Imported Grain*, WT/DS276, ABR adopted 30 August 2004, para 133.

[67] The source of the principle of judicial economy is linked to *United States – Measures Affecting Imports of Woven Wool Shirts and Blouses from India*, WT/DS33, ABR adopted 25 April 1997. The DSB noted that 'if a panel found that a measure was inconsistent with a particular provision of the GATT 1947, it generally did not go on to examine whether the measure was also inconsistent with other GATT provisions that a complaining party may have argued were violated', para 339.

[68] *EC – Measures Affecting the Approval and Marketing of Biotech Products*, WT/DS291, PR adopted 29 September 2006 (*EC – Biotech Products*), para 4.617.

respondent – but also on the *de facto* general moratorium in 2003 caused by the conduct of certain Member States.

The Panel in this dispute concluded that ruling on the general moratorium itself was not necessary and that a qualified recommendation would safeguard and preserve the rights and interests of all parties, thus securing a positive solution to the dispute.[69] The Panel stated that it was '*not convinced, in view of the findings and conclusions offered by us, that a decision on whether the general moratorium ceased to exist would be necessary to enable the DSB to make sufficiently precise recommendations to the European Communities*'. The Panel then explained that its determination on whether it should rule on the general moratorium was guided by the positive solution test. According to the Panel, '*in the circumstances of this case a qualified recommendation would safeguard and preserve the rights and interests of all Parties and hence would be consistent with the aim of securing a positive solution to the dispute*'. In relation to product-specific marketing bans adopted by certain Member States, the Panel was not persuaded that a product-specific finding '*is necessary to "secure a positive solution to [the] dispute" between Argentina and the European Communities*' because these applications had been withdrawn prior to the establishment of a Panel.[70] It was unnecessary to distribute responsibility to the Member States despite the fact that their conduct might have been inconsistent with WTO law.

The distribution of shared responsibility through the application of the positive solution test to determine the temporal scope of a dispute is also reflected in *EC – Selected Customs Matters*.[71] Here, the EC argued that expired customs measures and those not yet in force could not be part of the claim because they were irrelevant to the purpose of reaching a positive solution to the dispute.[72] The United States disagreed with the EC and suggested that measures of Member States' customs administration that pre-dated or post-dated the establishment of the panel remained relevant to the panel's analysis inasmuch as they provided context for the examination of particular instances of alleged violation.[73]

The Panel first stated that it was competent to make findings and recommendations on Member States' measures in existence at the time of its establishment.[74] The latter time is thus critical in relation to the scope of

69 EC – *Biotech Products*, PR, para 7.1318.
70 EC – *Biotech Products*, PR, para 7.1653.
71 EC – *Selected Customs Matters*, PR, para 5.158.
72 EC – *Selected Customs Matters*, PR, para 6.18.
73 EC – *Selected Customs Matters*, PR, para 6.19.
74 EC – *Selected Customs Matters*, PR, para 6.20.

judicial scrutiny. Accordingly, expired measures might properly be subject to findings and recommendations by the Panel '*only to the extent that they affect the operation of a covered agreement at the time of establishment of a panel*'.[75] The Panel further stressed its functioning approach to the scope of its analysis, emphasizing that its analysis covers inconsistencies '*particularly if such findings and recommendations are necessary to secure a positive solution to the dispute*'.[76] Thus, from a temporal perspective Member States' conduct is covered inasmuch as it is relevant to ensure compliance with WTO obligations. Whether Member States' measures are covered by a dispute directly correlates with whether they shall be respondents in a particular dispute.

A similar line of reasoning can be observed regarding the inclusion of Member States as co-respondents in *EC – Commercial Vessels*. Here the question was whether expired Member States' aid schemes for certain shipyards were covered by the claim. The Panel first noted that it was inappropriate to make a recommendation within the meaning of Article 19 of the DSU in respect of a measure that no longer existed.[77] At the same time it noted the difficulty of determining the exact meaning of the term 'exists' and considered all possibilities for non-compliance had it made no ruling against Member States' measures.[78] Accordingly, where national aid schemes have expired, no new application for aid can be submitted. On the other hand, however, the Panel noted that it cannot be determined with certainty whether and to what extent it is possible that subsidies continue to be provided pursuant to applications made before the expiry of those schemes. The Panel thus considered that its recommendation did not apply to the Member States' schemes that had expired, except to the extent that those schemes continued to be operational.[79] Once again responsibility follows the remedy: Member States are responsible for bringing their measures into compliance to the extent that their schemes may prevent a positive solution of the dispute.

The positive solution test to determine whether Member States' measures fall within the scope of the claim – and accordingly whether Member States

75 EC – *Selected Customs Matters*, PR, para 6.20.

76 EC – *Selected Customs Matters*, PR, para 7.36, referring to *US – Subsidies on Upland Cotton*, WT/DS267, PR, para 261; *Chile – Price Band System*, ABR, paras 126–144; *EC – Boneless Chicken*, ABR, para 156.

77 *US – Import Measures on Certain Products from the European Communities*, WT/ DS165, ABR, para 129.

78 EC – *Commercial Vessels*, PR, para 8.4.

79 EC – *Commercial Vessels*, PR, para 8.4.

are proper respondents in a dispute – is also applied in relation to *amendments* to challenged measures. In the *EC – Boneless Chicken* dispute, the Panel refused to include an amendment to the challenged measure because the measure identified in the request for the establishment of a panel was specific and narrow and did not appear to anticipate inclusion of any measures in addition to those expressly identified.[80] At the same time the Appellate Body in *Chile – Price Band System* identified two conditions which were necessary for an amendment to be covered by a dispute, namely, that the measure at issue is defined broadly and that ruling on an amendment is necessary to secure a positive solution to the dispute.[81] In a similar manner, in the *EC and Certain Member States – IT Products* case the Panel applied the positive solution test to determine whether amendments to the challenged measures were included in the dispute.[82]

6.3.4 *Timing of the Determination of the Proper Respondent*

Another feature which attests to the DSB's functional approach to international responsibility is its tendency to leave the decision on the proper respondents to the final stage of adjudication. That the WTO panels often postpone identification of the proper respondent until the final stages of its analysis supports a hypothesis presented here that international adjudicators are not preoccupied with the allocation of international responsibility for a breach between the EU and its Member States but rather seek to identify the party best placed to ensure compliance.

For example, in *EC and Certain Member States – IT Products* the Panel concluded that it did '*not consider it necessary to determine at the outset whether to rule on the claims directed against the EC member States*'. The Panel maintained that it would consider the extent to which the EC and its Member States had failed to comply with obligations in the context of EC commitments set forth in the EC Schedule. According to the Panel, to the extent that Member States apply a WTO measure inconsistent with another enacted by the EC, there is a reasonable basis to conclude that they have acted

80 *EC – Boneless Chicken*, ABR, para 6.13.

81 *Chile – Price Band System*, ABR, para 144. The AB noted, that 'If the terms of reference in a dispute are broad enough to include amendments to a measure—as they are in this case—and if it is necessary to consider an amendment in order to secure a positive solution to the dispute—as it is here—then it is appropriate to consider the measure as amended in coming to a decision in a dispute'.

82 *EC and Certain Member States – IT Products*, PR, para 7.139.

inconsistently.[83] The Panel then stated that it refrains from '*ruling at the outset whether findings against a particular EC member State would be necessary to secure a positive solution to the dispute*'.[84]

Similarly, in *EC – Computer Equipment* the Panel first noted that not only the EC but also Ireland and the United Kingdom are bound by their tariff commitments under Schedule LXXX, irrespective of the internal transfer of power.[85] It refrained from establishing at the outset the addressee of its rulings and recommendations and noted it would '*revert to this issue in light of the conclusions of that examination*'.[86]

The *EC – Large Civil Aircraft* Panel followed a similar approach. It noted that the decision as to whom its recommendations would be addressed to '*will be known only when we have completed our decision-making process*'.[87]

The functional approach to shared responsibility set out earlier operates through procedural techniques embedded in the WTO dispute-settlement regime which the following section will now address. These techniques concern the joinder of co-respondents, indispensable party rule and the application of countermeasures.

6.3.5 *Procedural Techniques*

The functional approach to responsibility, as opposed to responsibility based on attribution of conduct or breach, is reflected in some of the system's procedural rules. There is no limit to the number of possible substantial causes of injury or to the number of candidates sharing responsibility. Nevertheless, Flett concludes '*that there are certain aspects of WTO law capable of giving rise to issues of shared responsibility, and equally capable of resolving them; but also certain aspects of WTO law that lend themselves nicely to avoiding issues of shared responsibility. In practice, the latter is what is happening, and this is likely to continue*'.[88] I list a number of procedural techniques that allow the DSB to decide disputes without engaging in questions of attribution.

An important feature of the WTO dispute-settlement regime, which distinguishes it from investment arbitration, is that compliance is prospective. That restorative measures are forward-looking explains why panels do not focus on allocation of breach which is backward-looking. The causing of an

83 *EC and Certain Member States – IT Products*, PR, para 7.89.
84 *EC and Certain Member States – IT Products*, PR, para 7.90.
85 *EC – Computer Equipment*, PR, para 8.16.
86 *EC – Computer Equipment*, PR, para 8.16.
87 *EC – Large Civil Aircraft*, PR, para 7.177.
88 Flett 2016, 850.

adverse impact is subject to a rebuttable presumption under Article 3.8 DSU. The test is that of genuine and substantial nexus of cause and effect.[89] The presumption, however, has never been successfully challenged.

A second feature of WTO dispute resolution which gives flexibility to panels when dealing with distribution of shared responsibility concerns the WTO rules on co-respondents. WTO law does not expressly provide for a plurality of respondents. Bartels notes, however, that while DSU Article 6.2 on the establishment of panels is silent on identifying the party(ies) to whom acts are attributed, practice supports multiple co-respondents.[90] The possibility of joinder of co-respondents exists, even without consent of respondents, both under standard and non-standard terms of reference.[91] Removing a co-respondent is also unlikely to pose problems as panels are able to exclude parties from their rulings and recommendations at any stage of proceedings. In fact the title of a dispute neither indicates nor limits its respondents. Equally, citing co-respondents does not imply shared responsibility in WTO law. It seems that consent of the parties to a dispute is equally unnecessary either to adding or to removing a respondent from proceedings. The Panel's approach in *EC and Certain Member States – IT Products* suggests that Member States can be brought in at the request of a complainant even if the EU assumes responsibility on behalf of its Member States. Similarly, the EU may be called to conduct negotiation in disputes between its Member States and other members of the WTO, even if it was not a party to the dispute itself.

Neither does the indispensable third parties rule as articulated by the International Court of Justice in the *Monetary Gold* judgment preclude the WTO from ruling against the EU alone, without delving into the complex question of attribution.[92] The issue of indispensable parties generally does not arise in WTO dispute resolution. Panels' reports are automatically adopted upon request, unless appealed. Thus, if there exists an indispensable third party and the complaining member wishes to pursue the matter, it may simply cite the third WTO member as co-respondent in a new proceeding.[93] Even if the citation of co-respondents were possible, the principles of Article 9 of the

89 EC – *Large Civil Aircraft*, ABR, n 170, paras 1231–1233.

90 Bartels 2013, 351.

91 Bartels refers to two cases which involved the EU and its Member States, namely *EC – Computer Equipment* and *EC and Certain Member States – IT Products*, see Bartels 2013, 351–352.

92 *Monetary Gold (Italy/France, UK and US) (Preliminary Question)* [1954] ICJ Rep 19, 30–33.

93 Flett 2016, 868.

DSU would apply and the rights and obligations of the parties, including the co-respondents, would have to remain unaffected.[94]

In relation to countermeasures (i.e. mainly suspension of concessions), which may be authorized in cases when the WTO-inconsistent measure has not been withdrawn, attribution could be necessary in order to ensure that they are equivalent to the harm caused by the respondent. To calculate equivalent[95] countermeasures it is necessary to apply econometric models which separate causation from the non-attribution factors (other causes).[96] Countermeasures, however, can be applied *de jure* or *de facto* against any part of the territory (and on any product) of the defending member. In case of the EU the so-called 'carousel retaliation' allows the complainant to suspend concessions in any of the Member States and in relation to any of the products. This eliminates the need to draw a precise line between the conduct of the EU and its Member States and to attribute responsibility. It is sufficient to hold the EU responsible because countermeasures can be applied anywhere in the territory of the EU.

The above procedures allow avoidance of questions of attribution of conduct or breach in WTO law. Instead, shared responsibility is distributed to the party(ies) whose restorative actions are necessary to ensure compliance.

To conclude, the proper respondent is that entity which is best placed to achieve a positive solution to the dispute. In the WTO dispute-settlement regime shared responsibility is distributed to the party(ies) whose restorative actions are necessary to achieve compliance, whereas compensation and retaliation are secondary remedies. This is because the aim of interstate trade dispute resolution is to restore the regulatory order rather than to compensate for damage. It is precisely because the WTO dispute-settlement system is orientated towards a rebalancing of future concessions that the DSB rules on matters before it to the extent this is necessary to ensure compliance. Efficient breach is allowed in the sense that panels refrain from ruling on those inconsistencies which are not relevant to remedial purposes, irrespective of their contribution to the breach. Panels are entitled to pick and choose issues which will be addressed in their recommendations. Furthermore, the decision on what is necessary for remedial purposes is postponed to the final stages of adjudication, in line with the restorative rather than retributive nature of

94 Flett 2016, 868. See further Catherine Gascoigne, 'Causation in the Law of the World Trade Organization' (PhD book, University of Cambridge 2018).

95 WTO Arbitration Panel Report, *US – Tax Treatment for 'Foreign Sales Corporations'*, WT/DS108, adopted 30 August 2002, n 15 is an exception. Here authorization was given to 'appropriate' rather than 'equivalent' countermeasures; see Flett 2016, 867.

96 Flett 2016, 866.

adjudication. A number of procedural techniques applied in the dispute-settlement regime allow panels to avoid the allocation of responsibility for breach and instead focus on what is necessary to a positive solution to the dispute.

6.4 THE PROXIMATE CAUSE IN INVESTMENT DISPUTES

It was suggested in Chapter 5 that the remedial system under investment treaties, including the ECT, differs essentially from that under the WTO regime. The purpose of investment claims is to protect the rights of private persons who have suffered damage as a result of violation of an investment protection standard. Challenges under the ECT thus focus on particular instances of application of law rather than regulatory compliance as such, which dominates interstate dispute resolution under the WTO regime. Typically, the function of the investment protection regime is to compensate an investor for damage caused as a result of a host state's unlawful conduct. The primary remedy here – compensation – is orientated towards past behaviour. An obligation to comply does not arise in an investor-to-state adjudication where the new relationship created by a wrongful conduct is owned to a private party, not the investor's home state.[97]

Wittich notes that situations of shared responsibility are rare in investment arbitration practice, mainly because investment law is characterized by strictly bilateral relationships between states, or between a host state and an investor.[98] Hence, in virtually all cases these relationships exist between two parties without the involvement of a third. However, the question of shared responsibility can be raised in the context of the joint participation of the EU and its Member States in the ECT dispute-settlement system.

What does the nature of the remedial system under investment arbitration tell us about the distribution of shared international responsibility in a multilayered structure like the EU?

The discussion later in the chapter leaves aside questions concerning the transfer of competence in the field of foreign direct investment from the Member States to the EU under the Treaty of Lisbon. Nor does it engage in analysis of the new investment chapters under new-generation free trade agreements (FTAs) recently concluded by the EU. These treaties will be

97 Zachary Douglas, *The International Law of Investment Claims* (Cambridge University Press 2009), 95.

98 Stephan Wittich, 'International Investment Law', in André Nollkaemper and Ilias Plakokefalos (eds), *The Practice of Shared Responsibility in International Law* (Cambridge University Press 2017), 826.

addressed in Chapter 9. Analysis here is limited to identification of an underlying reasoning which explains the distribution of shared international responsibility between the EU and its Member States under the ECT. The focus here is on the ECT due to its mixed form which provides a useful context in which to analyse the distribution of responsibility for joint obligations in the context of multidimensional structures with elements of shared sovereignty. The following analysis suggests a novel approach to distribution of shared responsibility in investment disputes which, to the best of my knowledge, has not been identified in legal scholarship to date. It will be argued, on the basis of an extensive case law analysis, that Member States have so far been exclusive respondents in investment disputes because their conduct constitutes the proximate cause of (alleged) harm to investors. Since compensation is typically the primary remedy under investment treaties, it is (in most cases) sufficient to determine the existence of a breach without identifying its scope and root causes.

6.4.1 *The Concept of Proximate Cause*

It has been noted in the introductory remarks to this section that the private nature of investment claims defines the tasks of arbitral tribunals. The primary function of investor-to-state dispute resolution is to compensate investors for violation of their rights. Damage is thus central to investment claims.

Damage is not, however, an element necessary to a finding of international responsibility under the ILC framework which only refers to conduct attributable to the state (or international organization) and breach of that obligation. However, the ILC's draft articles do not exclude damage which may be an element under primary norms. According to Crawford, whether such elements as damage are required depends on the content of the primary obligation.[99] The Commentary to Article 29 of the Articles on Responsibility of States for Internationally Wrongful Acts (ARSIWA) also notes the relevance of primary norms in the determination of international responsibility: '*As a result of the internationally wrongful act, a new set of legal relations is established between the responsible State and the State or States to whom the international responsibility is owned. But this does not mean that the pre-existing legal relation established by primary obligation disappears*'.

[99] Crawford 2002, 84; see also James Crawford, 'Revising the Draft Articles on State Responsibility' (1999) 10 EJIL 435, 438.

Castellanos-Jankiewicz elegantly disaggregates the two levels of relationship created by primary and secondary norms. He notes that the consequences of an internationally wrongful act acquire an existence independent of the obligation that has been violated and so, according to him, a new legal interest arises from breach, which is distinct from the legal interest in safeguarding the rights acquired by the primary norm.[100] In this sense, secondary norms serve a sort of a public interest of protecting the norm itself – the existence of a wrongful conduct in itself creates a new relationship. A private interest, such as that of an investor, rather, stems from rights acquired under primary norms.

Precisely because investment arbitration is a forum for the protection of private interests, damages are central to investment disputes.[101] As the Tribunal in *Merrill & Ring Forestry LP* v. *Canada* noted, '*a finding of liability without finding of damages would be difficult to explain in the context of investment arbitration and would be contrary to some of its fundamental tenets*'.[102] Douglas considers damages to be a constituent element of all forms of delictual responsibility towards foreign nationals, both under the general international law[103] and under the special regime for responsibility established by investment treaties.[104] Article 33 of ARSIWA carves out international responsibility under these, to follow Douglas's terminology, 'distinct regimes' from the ILC's secondary rules of international responsibility. Damage is an element under a number of investment treaties,[105] including the investment chapters under new-generation FTAs.[106]

The element of damage will arise at different times depending on the delict.[107] Douglas rightly notes that with respect to the international minimum

100 León Castellanos-Jankiewicz, 'Causation and International State Responsibility' (2012) 7 SHARES Research Paper, 14. Douglas refers to the interest acquired through the primary norm as a 'secondary consequence of a breach', Douglas 2009, 95.

101 According to Douglas, there would be no requirement for damages in any state/state proceedings under the investment treaties; Zachary Douglas, 'International Responsibility for Domestic Adjudication: Denial of Justice Deconstructed' (2014) 63 ICLQ 867, 894, ft 115.

102 *Merrill & Ring Forestry LP* v. *Canada*, (Award, 31 March 2010), ICSID Case No. UNCT/07/1, para 245.

103 For example, Art 1 of the Draft Articles on Diplomatic Protection refers to injury caused by an internationally wrongful act of the state to a natural or legal person. For a different view, see Martins Paparinskis, 'Investment Treaty Arbitration and the (New) Law of State Responsibility' (2013) 24 EJIL 617, 629.

104 Douglas 2014, 893.

105 For example, Art 24(1)(A)(II) of US Model BIT, Art 82(1) of 2002 Japan/Singapore FTA.

106 For example, CETA, Article 8.18(1)(b) refers to breach of investment protection standards 'where the investor claims to have suffered loss or damage as a result of the alleged breach'.

107 Douglas 2014, 894.

standard or failure to accord full protection and security, the damage occurs simultaneously with the misfeasance or nonfeasance. A violation of the Fair and Equitable Treatment (FET) standard does not automatically eliminate the investment but rather consists of a series of events which cause damage to (and decline of) business.[108] Because of the fluid, temporal nature of breaches of an FET standard, it is not always easy to identify the exact moment when the damage occurs.

However, leaving aside nuances of FET, if the very existence of breach of investment standards gives rise to damage (and a right to compensation), it means that the focus of investment tribunals is limited to identifying the *occurrence* of a breach. It must be then that the *scope* and nature of a breach is in most cases irrelevant. A hypothetical example illustrates this argument: if an investor's rights are violated because it was unlawfully denied a licence to extract mineral resources by ministry X, it is entitled to compensation for damage to its business. The investor is not entitled to *more* compensation because ministry X denied the licence while implementing a decision of the European Commission. Here lies an important difference between the responsibility regimes under the WTO and the ECT. The source and nature of breach is relevant in the WTO context because overall regulatory compliance requires the elimination of the source of inconsistency. It is in most cases irrelevant in investment arbitration where the focus is on the existence of the breach, not on its roots or scope.

The thesis of this book is that the aforementioned difference directly correlates with the distribution of shared responsibility among the EU and its Member States. Precisely because the right to compensation for breach of investment standards arises upon the very *fact* of the violation of an investor's rights, arbitral tribunals are less (or not at all) preoccupied with identifying the broader regulatory context. Accordingly, if a Member State's implementation of an EU policy results in a violation of investor's rights, the tribunal will focus on the Member States' conduct and will likely ignore the implications of the wider EU policy.

This argument holds true because compensation for damage does not depend on the scope of the violation. Most investment treaties have adopted the so-called Hull formula of 'prompt, adequate and effective' compensation. A 'fair market value',[109] 'genuine value', 'market value' and other standards are

108 Kaj Hobér, 'Remedies in Investment Disputes', in Andrea K Bjorklund, A Ian Laird and Sergei Ripinsky (eds), *Remedies in International Investment Law: Emerging Jurisprudence of International Investment Law* (BIICL 2009), 12.

109 As a general rule a fair market value of property is calculated at the time of expropriation and represents the lower limit of the amount of expropriation. No lower limit exists for an FET violation.

also applied. Under the ECT, for example, compensation is calculated by reference to lost profits.[110] Compensation is thus calculated according to the (past or future) value of an investment, not according to the extent and nature of breach. Douglas even notes a tendency of investment tribunals to altogether disregard the type of investment standard under consideration when calculating compensation and focus on the existence of the breach. According to him, '*tribunals are drawing a line under their decisions on whether a breach of an investment treaty obligation has occurred and, by resorting to the distinction between primary and secondary rules, they are purporting to start afresh with a clean slate in deciding upon the remedial consequences for a breach*'.[111] In other words, once the occurrence of a breach has been established compensation is calculated without taking into consideration the nature of the violation but solely on Chapter II of Part Two of the ARSIWA's articles on 'Reparation for Injury'. This, according to Douglas, results in the factual elimination of difference between standards like FET and expropriation.

We are entering here the complex question of causality in the law of international responsibility. While causality is generally not a necessary condition under the secondary rules of international responsibility,[112] Castellanos-Jankiewicz and Pusztai agree that it can be an element of responsibility under primary norms which establish damage as a condition of liability.[113] The discussion here, however, is narrow.[114] This section does not aim to answer the question whether causality is or should be an element of international law, nor other related questions, such as whether/what role it plays in the disputed typology between obligations of means and obligations of result.[115] This section does not refer to causality as an 'element' of responsibility. It looks at it from a remedial perspective – what must a tribunal determine to fulfil its adjudicative function?

[110] ECT Art 13.

[111] Douglas 2009, 104.

[112] Causation appears as an element of responsibility under some secondary norms, namely ARSIWA Art 31, Art 34 and Art 36(1). For difference between causation and attribution, see Ilias Plakokefalos, 'Causation in the Law of State Responsibility and the Problem of Overdetermination: In Search of Clarity' (2015) 26 EJIL 471, 479; Fry 2014, 100.

[113] Dávid Miklós Pusztai, *Causation in the Law of State Responsibility* (University of Cambridge 2017), 48; Castellanos-Jankiewicz 2012, 25.

[114] For a comprehensive analysis of causation in the law of international responsibility, see Pusztai 2017 and Castellanos-Jankiewicz 2012.

[115] The typology was initially suggested by Ago, Sixth Report on State Responsibility, by Mr Roberto Ago, Special Rapporteur – the Internationally Wrongful Act of the State, Source of International Responsibility (continued) (1977) A/CN.4/302 and Add.1–3. Crawford proposed to eliminate the distinction; see Crawford Second Report, para 90. For a critical analysis of this typology, see Pusztai 2017, 51–54.

The argument then is that if investment tribunals are focused on damage and damage (in most cases) occurs simultaneously with a violation of an investment protection standard, it must be true that tribunals are only concerned with the *existence* of a breach. If A causes B and B causes C and C causes breach, investment tribunals need only look at C – the proximate cause of violation. The roots of C's measures are (in most cases) irrelevant to the determination of damage (or calculation of compensation). This is different under the WTO regime where regulatory compliance cannot be achieved by targeting C's measures without also determining the effect of A's and B's measures.

My reference to 'proximate cause' is not aimed at prescribing a causal test for responsibility arising out of investment treaties, especially since scholarship and practice in relation to causal tests is diverse and inconsistent.[116] Once again, the aim of this section is modest, and the language I chose to employ to refer to a standard of causality is remedial rather than normative. What is meant here is that investment tribunals look at the last necessary link in the chain of measures, whatever one calls it.[117] The dissenting judgment in the famous New York decision in *Palsgraf* v. *Long Island Railroad Co.* can be used by analogy to express the very essence of my argument: '*What we do mean by the word "proximate" is, that because of convenience, of public policy, of a rough sense of justice, the law arbitrarily declines to trace a series of events beyond a certain point. This is not logic. This is practical politics*'.[118] Returning to Douglas's statement about the tendency of investment tribunals to disregard the extent and nature of breach in calculating compensation, there seems to be no need to explore causal ties between various events which led to the breach.

What does this say about the distribution of shared international responsibility for violation of joint investment obligations in the context of a multilayered structure like the EU? This study argues that if it is sufficient to determine a proximate cause of a violation in order to award compensation, tribunals can afford not to trace the roots of the challenged measure. Thus, even if treatment afforded by a Member State stems from an EU law or decision, the EU dimension may not be relevant in investment disputes. The following sections will provide support for this hypothesis drawing from the dispute-settlement practice under the ECT.

116 For discussion on various tests, see Plakokefalos 2015.

117 One of the most widely used tests is the *sine-qua-non*, also known as the but-for test.

118 *Palsgraf* v. *Long Island Railroad Co.*, 248 N.Y. 339 (1928), at 352–353 (Andrews J. dissenting opinion).

6.4.2 *Proximate Cause in Practice*

This section is a result of an extensive analysis of publicly available investment disputes which involve EU Member States. It identifes a number of disputes under the ECT system which demonstrate that tribunals focus on Member States' treatment of investors, leaving aside, though often acknowledging, the existence of a related EU measure. In most cases such an EU measure is a source of Member States' conduct, and its binding nature often leaves no discretion to the Member State in question. The existence of an EU law dimension, however, does not shape the tribunals' decisions on the proper respondents which are typically (in fact almost exclusively) Member States.[119] Tribunals rarely engage in the complex analysis of the relationship between the EU and Member States' measures, nor do they consider causality between the EU conduct and an alleged violation. Instead, tribunals limit the scope of the claim to the Member States' treatment of an investment. Disputes examined later in the chapter support a finding that a determination of the *existence* of breach through a proximate event (Member States' treatment of investment), leaving aside its root causes (an EU law dimension), is typical of investment arbitration under the ECT framework precisely because their role is to award compensation, not to ensure regulatory compliance. The analysis thus supports functional international responsibility.

The following analysis is structured by differentiating between three types of EU measures: (i) those which are binding on Member States, (ii) those which authorize Member States' conduct and (iii) those which require Member States to adopt certain conduct.

6.4.2.1 First Category: Binding EU Decisions

Electrabel v. *Hungary* provides a well-known example where a challenged measure was adopted under a binding EU decision. This section suggests a novel reading of the tribunal's approach to international responsibility by arguing that it is remedy-based. While the tribunal acknowledges that a Member State's violation stems from an EU-wide law, it leaves the EU measure out of its analysis and instead focuses on the proximate cause of harm, which is the conduct of the Member State. This is so, because the relief sought by the claimant is monetary compensation.[120]

119 I acknowledge that there may be investment arbitrations where the EU is a respondent, which are not publicly available.

120 *Electrabel* v. *Hungary*, Award, ICSID Case No ARB/07/19, 25 November 2015 para 1.47 states, inter alia, that the claimant seeks declaration that the termination of the Agreement

The case arose as a result of Hungary's decision to terminate a power purchase agreement between an investor and Hungary taken under a binding decision of the EU.[121] Despite the presence of an EU law dimension to this dispute, the Tribunal upheld the claimant's objection to the European Commission's claim that the EU was the proper respondent in this dispute.[122]

The relevance of EU law in this dispute was noted by Hungary itself. In its defence, Hungary argued that '*the obvious question, therefore, is whether Hungary can be condemned under the ECT for doing precisely that which it was ordered to do, by a supranational authority whose decisions the Claimant's own expert concedes were absolutely binding on Hungary*'.[123] Hungary's statement suggests that Member States are not responsible for conduct carried out in accordance to EU law requirements. The Tribunal disagreed with this approach, instead holding Hungary independently responsible for its conduct, irrespective of whether it constitutes implementation of EU law. This supports the independent responsibility of the EU and its Member States for violation of their joint obligations, which is argued for in Chapter 3.

The Tribunal first acknowledged that Member States may be bound internally to implement Union policies. It referred to Article 1(3) of the ECT which states that EU Member States are legally bound by certain decisions of EU organs under EU law. It accordingly noted that investors can have no legitimate expectation in regard to the consequences of the implementation by a Member State of any such decision by the European Commission, because '*the possible interference with a foreign investment through the implementation by an EU Member State of a legally binding decision of the European Commission was and remains inherent in the framework of the ECT itself*'.[124] The claimant, according to the Tribunal, is not protected from the enforcement by Hungary of a binding EU decision.[125] This statement suggests that the tribunal acknowledges that an EU Member State may be obliged to carry out certain conduct on the basis of EU law.

constitutes unlawful expropriation in breach of Article 13(1) Energy Charter Treaty ('ECT') and full compensation has not been paid.

121 *Electrabel* S.A. v. *Hungary*, Claimant's Memorial and Amended Memorial, para 287 as reproduced in the Decision on Jurisdiction, para 4.23. The agreement was terminated following a European Commission's investigation of the Hungarian electricity system following which the Commission requested to end the agreement as it constituted 'unlawful and incompatible state aid to the power generators'.

122 *Electrabel* S.A. v. *Hungary*, Decision on Jurisdiction, para 4.33.

123 *Electrabel* S.A. v. *Hungary*, Respondent's Rejoinder, para 192, as reproduced in the Decision on Jurisdiction, para 4.63.

124 *Electrabel* S.A. v. *Hungary*, Decision on Jurisdiction, para 4.142.

125 *Electrabel* S.A. v. *Hungary*, Decision on Jurisdiction, para 4.169.

The claimant was also supportive of the principle of independent responsibility. It maintained that Member States may not circumvent their obligations on the basis that they are implementing EU law. The claimant did not dispute that the European Commission's decision was legally binding on Hungary under EU law. It nevertheless rejected the claim that Hungary was not a proper respondent in this dispute.[126] Electrabel did not contest that Hungary had no discretion but to implement European Commission's binding decision, but rather it focused on the *manner* in which Hungary went about implementing that decision.[127] In other words, the claimant focused not on the decision itself but on a specific instance of its application which pointed to the Member States rather than the EU.

The Tribunal agreed with the claimant's reasoning. In line with the principle of independent responsibility, it emphasized that if Hungary were bound by a legally binding decision of the EU, this would not, by or of itself, entail the international responsibility of Hungary as it can only be responsible for its own acts.[128] According to the Tribunal, however, this case was not about the legally binding decision of the EU. The scope of the claim was limited to whether Hungary's own acts[129] in terminating the power purchase agreement violated the ECT.[130] Accordingly, Hungary was the right party and, as pleaded, the claim could not be brought against the EU.[131] The claim challenged Hungary's conduct, and it was thus Hungary, not the EC, which had to remedy the breach.

The Tribunal's reasoning is functional. First, it reinforces the principle of independent responsibility by acknowledging the existence of a relevant binding decision of the EU and at the same time refusing to release Member States from responsibility for breaches which occur in the course of implementation of EU law. Second, it limits the scope of its analysis to the proximate cause of harm. It does so by detaching EU law from (the manner of) implementation of that law by Hungary. This supports a hypothesis that if the *occurrence* of a breach is evidenced by the last link in the chain of regulatory events, the Tribunal will focus on the proximate cause of harm without ruling on the EU law dimension. In other words if C (binding EU law) causes B (Hungary's

126 *Electrabel* S.A. v. *Hungary*, Decision on Jurisdiction, para 2.24.

127 *Electrabel* S.A. v. *Hungary*, Decision on Jurisdiction, para 4.38.

128 *Electrabel* S.A. v. *Hungary*, Decision on Jurisdiction, para 6.72.

129 The basis of illegality of Hungary's conduct when terminating the power purchase agreement is listed in paras 6.21–6.27 of the Decision on Jurisdiction.

130 *Electrabel* S.A. v. *Hungary*, Decision on Jurisdiction, para 5.34. The changes in the incentivization scheme were introduced by several legal instruments. First, the Royal Decree 1565/2010 promulgated on 19 November 2010.

131 *Electrabel* S.A. v. *Hungary*, Decision on Jurisdiction, para 5.35.

implementation of binding EU law) and B causes harm to the investor, the tribunal's approach is to focus on B because a finding that B resulted in injury is sufficient to award compensation. To reiterate the distinction between the remedial systems under the WTO and the ECT, it would not be sufficient for the DSB to rule on B only, because elimination of B without eliminating C would not ensure overall regulatory compliance with the WTO law and would thus not achieve a positive solution to the dispute.

The case thus illustrates a functional approach to international responsibility – the Tribunal focuses on what is necessary for remedial purposes, which depends on the system of remedies under a given treaty regime. Importantly, attribution of breach is not relevant in this context. If identifying the latter were central to the distribution of shared responsibility, the European Commission's decision would have been covered by the adjudication because it (might have) constituted a violation of investor's rights.

6.4.2.2 Second Category: Authorized by the EU

A similar pattern of tribunals focusing on the proximate cause of harm may be extrapolated in cases arising from a measure which was authorized by the EU. The *Charanne* v. *Spain* arbitration illustrates how an investment tribunal operating under the ECT regime narrowed the scope of its analysis to a Member State's conduct, ignoring that this conduct was authorized by the EU. Once again, distribution of responsibility is remedy-based and does not focus on the attribution of conduct or breach.

The case is one of the many disputes under the ECT which arose in relation to incentive measures in the form of feed-in tariffs to photovoltaic energy producers. As a way of achieving renewable energy targets set out by the European Commission, Spain introduced various incentives for solar energy producers. The system was based on the EU directive which provides for support systems involving direct payments to producers of electricity from renewable energy sources.[132] Mainly due to subsequent overproduction of solar energy,[133] the governments of Member States adjusted their incentive

[132] In 2005 the Spanish government approved the 2005–2010 Renewable Energy Plan which contained the government's policy regarding the renewable energy sector's compliance with the EU targets set out in Directive 2001/77, see *Charanne and Construction Investments* v. *Kingdom of Spain* (Final Award, 16 March 2017), SCC Case No. V 062/2012 *(Charanne* v. *Spain)*, para 96.

[133] Other factors may also have played a role, such as the financial crisis and the burden of subsidies on Spanish public expenditure.

systems, which resulted in a long list of claims filed by investors under the ECT. Spain had established, *inter alia*, a system of premiums and regulated tariffs to remunerate solar energy producers. The claimants argued that after attracting their investment in the photovoltaic generation sector, Spain had unlawfully amended the special regime regulating the industry, causing losses to their business.[134]

Some of the changes introduced were authorized under EU law. In particular, the disputed requirement to pay a toll for access to the transport and distribution network was applied by Spain '*with reference to the framework established by the valid regulations of the European Union*'.[135] Similarly to the pattern observed in *Electrabel* v. *Hungary*, the *Charanne* v. *Spain* Tribunal also acknowledged the existence of the link between the Spanish measures and EU-wide laws. It noted that the challenged charge for the use of access to the transport and distribution network was implemented '*according to the European standards*'.[136]

Despite the presence of an EU-law dimension, the Tribunal yet again did not focus on the EU-wide framework for the incentivization of solar production. There is nothing in the Tribunal's analysis to suggest that it sought to determine the source of Spain's measures. While the Tribunal acknowledged that EU law authorized limitations to the incentivization scheme for production of solar energy, its examination did not extend to the measures adopted at the EU level. Repeating the pattern observed in *Electrabel* v. *Hungary*, the Tribunal focused on the proximate cause of harm, that is, measures adopted by Spain, while EU law is noted as a context rather than an object of adjudication in itself.

A similar approach was taken by arbitrators in the *RREEF Infrastructure* v. *Spain* dispute, which also concerned the Spanish incentivization schemes for photovoltaic energy production. Here the Tribunal again refused to engage in the analysis of the EU regulatory framework for renewable energy, rejecting the European Commission's application to intervene as a non-disputing party.[137]

[134] *Charanne* v. *Spain*, Final Award, para 80. The claimants based their claim on two points: the elimination of regulated tariffs for photovoltaic facilities and the introduction of a series of additional requirements for energy production; see paras 148–149 of the Final Award. Moreover, on 23 December 2010 the Royal Decree 14/2010 introduced further changes: established a limit of operating hours of photovoltaic facilities and introduced an obligation to pay charges for the use of electricity transportation and distribution network; see Final Award, paras 156–158.

[135] *Charanne* v. *Spain*, Final Award, paras 167–168.

[136] *Charanne* v. *Spain*, Final Award, para 537.

[137] The European Commission filed an application to intervene as a non-disputing party on 10 November 2014 which was rejected by the tribunals' Procedural Order No 2 of

The aforementioned cases with the underlying reasoning of the DSB which were extrapolated from the WTO case law are instructive. The focus under the latter regime is on the rules of general application (i.e. EU law) because eliminating inconsistencies at the EU level is in most cases necessary in order to ensure overall compliance with the WTO regime. Investment treaties, on the other hand, do not seek compliance but are aimed at compensating for harm, which explains why arbitral tribunals often ignore the EU-wide inconsistency. Responsibility in both trade and investment disputes is functional. It is not static but dynamic in that distribution of responsibility shifts from one holder of joint obligations to another, in accordance with the system of remedies under a given treaty regime. This study finds that a dispute based on identical facts may point to the EU or its Member State as the proper respondent, depending on whether it is adjudicated as a trade or investment case.

6.4.2.3 Third Category: Required by EU Law

Nor do arbitral tribunals engage in the analysis of the EU dimension where, though short of a binding EU decision, Member State conduct is nevertheless required by EU law.

Under the ECT dispute-settlement system EU law requirements are treated as facts, the accuracy of which is rarely examined by tribunals as independent challenges. *AES Summit* v. *Hungary* provides an example. The dispute concerned the imposition by Hungary of caps on the price charged for electricity generation.

AES Summit had invested in Hungary's power generation sector following the privatization in the mid-1990s by purchasing electricity power stations and coal-fired power stations. Subsequently Hungary agreed an electricity-pricing schedule with AES Summit. In 2006, two years after Hungary joined the EU, the Hungarian Parliament amended the 2001 Electricity Act by reintroducing a regime of administrative prices for generation of electricity. As a result the agreed formula under which AES Summit was selling its electricity was no longer applicable. In 2007 it filed a request for arbitration, alleging that Hungary had violated its obligations under the ECT by reintroducing administrative pricing.[138]

5 February 2015, *RREEF Infrastructure* v. *Spain*, Decision on Jurisdiction, ARB/13/30, paras 16 and 20.

138 *AES Summit* v. *Hungary*, Award, para 5.1.

Hungary suggested that the Union's competition law must be taken into account in the dispute in question.[139] Hungary argued that it could not ignore the Union law requiring that prohibited state aid be minimized or eliminated.[140] It further contended that AES Summit could not legitimately expect that Hungary would never consider, as a rational vehicle for addressing the Union's concerns, the temporary reintroduction of administrative price controls.

Hungary's attempt to hide behind the veil of its membership of the EU was rightly criticized by Eeckhout whose Expert Opinion rejected Hungary's claim that EU law was part of that applicable in this dispute.[141] Furthermore, he challenged the interpretation provided in the Counter-Memorial that EC competition law is part of the notion of public order, which could justify Hungary's conduct. According to him, Hungary's reference to the ECJ's judgment in the *Eco-Swiss* case, where the Court confirmed that the ordinary courts of the Netherlands have power to review arbitral awards for consistency with EC competition law,[142] was misplaced. Eeckhout's interpretation thus supports the argument which is laid out in Chapter 3 that the EU and its Member States are independently responsible for their joint obligations, including Member States implementing Union law.

While there is nothing in the Tribunal's ruling which would contradict the principle of independent responsibility, it nevertheless excludes EU's measures from the scope of the adjudication. Precisely because the dispute arose in the area which falls within the regulatory framework of the EU, the Union sought to intervene in the dispute. The Tribunal issued a procedural order which allowed the European Commission to participate as a non-disputing party.[143] This attests that the Tribunal acknowledged the relevance of Union law in this dispute. According to the Tribunal, '*[h]ad Hungary been motivated to reintroduce price regulation with a view to addressing the EC's state aid concerns, there is no doubt that this would have constituted a rational public policy measure*'.[144] However, instead of examining the compatibility of

139 *AES Summit* v. *Hungary*, Award, para 7.2.4.

140 *AES Summit* v. *Hungary*, Award, para 7.2.5.

141 Expert Opinion of Prof Piet Eeckhout, 'The Law Applicable to the Dispute under the Energy Charter Treaty 1994', *AES Summit* v. *Hungary*.

142 Case C-126/97, *Eco Swiss* v. *Benetton International* [1999] ECR I-3055, para 36.

143 On 3 September 2008, the Legal Service of the European Commission filed an application under the ICSID Arbitration Rule 37 as a non-disputing party.

144 After having engaged in substantive analysis, the tribunal concluded that the Union imposed no binding state aid decision, and so Hungary's conduct was not required by EU law, *AES Summit* v. *Hungary*, Award, para 10.3.16. Arbitrator Stern, on the other hand, considered that pressures from the European Commission certainly weighed on the Hungarian authorities'

measures of the EU, which is an independent member of the ECT, the Tribunal treated Union law as fact. It concluded that *'the Respondent's acts/measures are to be assessed under the ECT as the applicable law but that the EC law is to be considered and taken into account as a relevant fact'*.[145] Leaving the deliberations on the status of EU law under the ECT framework aside, the aforementioned statement illustrates that the Tribunal did not examine the legality of EU law as an independent object of adjudication. As Hungary's measures were the proximate cause of harm, it was not necessary to subject EU measures to judicial scrutiny to determine whether the investor's rights had been violated.

The now settled *Vattenfall I* v. *Germany* arbitration provides yet another illustration of distribution of shared responsibility on the basis of the proximate cause of harm.[146] In 2009 the Swedish energy company Vattenfall challenged the adoption of an environmental restriction. The restriction was imposed on the company's coal-fired power plant which was under construction along the banks of the Elbe River. Vattenfall claimed that the imposition of the restriction was in breach of the ECT's investment protection standards.

Plans for the construction of the coal-fired power plant were announced by Vattenfall in 2004 and provoked controversy due to environmental concerns.[147] Despite opposition to this large-scale project, a provisional contract with Vattenfall was concluded in 2007 and was followed by the issuance of a preliminary permit. The City of Hamburg issued final permission in 2008, which contained certain environmental restrictions. These restrictions formed the basis for Vattenfall's claim.

Germany claimed that the imposed restrictions were required under EU law. Hamburg explained that it was striving to meet the EU's Water Framework Directive, which requires all EU Member States to ensure certain levels of water quality.[148] Vattenfall alleged, however, that by imposing a more

mind when they decided to reintroduce price regulation. In her view, it appears from the record that the European Commission had made abundantly clear to Hungary that the pricing formula applied to AES Summit was in contradiction with the European free market policies. She concluded that the European Commission's position cannot be separated from the motivation that was behind the disputed decision; see *AES Summit* v. *Hungary*, Award, para 10.3.19.

145 *AES Summit* v. *Hungary*, Award, para 7.6.12.

146 *Vattenfall AB, Vattenfall Europe AG, Vattenfall European Generation AG* v. *Federal Republic of Germany* (Award 11 March 2011) ICSID Case No. ARB/09/6 (*Vattenfall I* v. *Germany*).The case was settled pursuant to the Agreement of 25 August 2010.

147 Nathalie Bernasconi, 'Background paper on *Vattenfall* v. *Germany arbitration*' www.iisd.org/pdf/2009/background_vattenfall_vs_germany.pdf, accessed 31 July 2018.

148 Council Directive 2000/60/EC of the European Parliament and of the Council establishing a framework for the Community action in the field of water policy [2000] OJ L327/1.

stringent standard in the final construction permit, Hamburg had breached its obligations under the ECT.[149] On 28 October 2009 the European Commission sought to intervene.

Even though a detailed analysis of the dispute cannot be carried out due to the lack of publicly available information, it may be concluded that the case had an EU law dimension. Due to its focus on compensation rather than restoration of the legal order, the Tribunal yet again prioritized the application of a challenged measure, not the broader regulatory regime.

Nor did the Tribunal in *Nykomb* v. *Latvia* examine the link between the respondent's measure and Union law. Here the challenged measures had also been adopted in order to comply with the mandatory EU law. The Tribunal noted that the main purpose of the challenged Energy Programme was to integrate the Latvian electricity market with the EU and to harmonize Latvian legislation with EU directives and regulations.[150] Exactly what impact these EU directives and regulations had in relation to the damage to the investor, were left unexamined.

A detailed discussion on whether EU law is applicable under the ECT regime falls outside the scope of this book. Suffice it to say that such a view is not convincing. A claim that there is a special relationship between the ECT and EU law is,[151] while of historical significance, irrelevant from the legal perspective. Eeckhout rightly notes in his Expert Opinion that applicable law, which is defined in Article 26(6) ECT, does not extend to Union law.[152]

What is important for the present purposes is that under the ECT the question of EU law as applicable law is a question of the justification of Member State conduct. That EU law is considered a fact which can exempt treatment of Member States rather than an independent object of judicial evaluation further supports a finding, argued earlier, that tribunals do not typically examine the legality of EU law. The Union law dimension is not considered a link in the chain of causal events which lead to the harm. It is presumed legal and is thus not subject to examination. The compatibility of

149 The claim of Vattenfall was directed at the City of Hamburg but the claim was brought before Germany as it was a party to the ECT.

150 *Nykomb* v. *Latvia*, Award, para 3.1.

151 For example, Professor Sloth in his Expert Report in *AES Summit* v. *Hungary* suggested that the ECT 'should be interpreted as much as possible in harmony with EC law', Expert Report, para 175. In its Counter-Memorial in the same dispute Hungary claimed that the ECT was 'the brainchild of the European Union' and so the ECT could not be read independently from EU law, Counter-Memorial, para 306.

152 Expert Opinion of Prof Piet Eeckhout, 'The Law Applicable to the Dispute under the Energy Charter Treaty 1994', *AES Summit* v. *Hungary*, para 21.

EU law with obligations under the ECT is not in itself an independent object of adjudication.

To conclude, the analysis of investment arbitration suggests that the approach of arbitral tribunals to shared responsibility under the ECT is similar to that under the WTO dispute-settlement system in that questions of attribution of conduct or breach generally do not arise. The commercial nature of investment arbitration directs the focus of tribunals to damage. The proximate cause of harm allows panels to establish the existence of the breach, determination of which is sufficient to award of compensation. Furthermore, the special status afforded to EU law in some disputes is a second reason why the EU dimension is excluded from judicial scrutiny. In this respect the ECT regime differs from that of the WTO where the focus on compliance typically calls for the DSB to determine the legality of the overall regime, including EU measures.

6.4.3 *Regulatory Compliance Claims*

In It was noted in Section 5.3 of Chapter 5 that while compensation is the primary remedy under investment arbitration, in a limited number of cases parties do seek specific performance. In these latter situations the adjudicative function of investment tribunals resembles that of the WTO dispute-settlement bodies where regulatory compliance is the primary goal of adjudication. If then this study's central argument that distribution of shared responsibility depends on who is best placed to remedy the breach holds true, it must be that in case of investment arbitrations in which the parties seek regulatory compliance of an EU measure rather than monetary compensation for the damage caused by the implementation of that measure, the proper respondent is the EU, not the Member States. In other words, distribution of shared responsibility between the EU and the Member States must be different in cases when parties seek compensation to when they seek regulatory compliance. In these latter situations when an investor is seeking a change of rules adopted by the EU, the Union must be the proper respondent as it is better placed to ensure compliance of (allegedly) inconsistent rules. The investment arbitration claim brought by Nord Stream 2 AG against the EU over the amendments of the Third Energy Package supports this argument.

The claim arose following the adoption in April 2019 of the Directive 2019/692 which amended the Directive 2009/73/EC concerning common rules for the internal market in natural gas (the Gas Directive). The Directive 2019/692 has been adopted following a confusion as to whether gas market liberalization rules apply to Nord Stream 2 pipeline which is to transport Russian gas to Germany via the seabed of the Baltic Sea. Nord Stream 2 AG, the pipeline operator, claimed that the original version of the Gas Directive did not apply to 'import' pipelines like Nord Stream 2 because it only covered 'interconnections' between the Member States of the EU, not pipelines coming from third countries. The Directive 2019/692 not only clarified that transmission lines between a Member State and a third country fall under the scope of the Gas Directive but also provided for a Nord Stream 2-tailored exception from the possibility to apply for derogation from liberalization obligations under Article 49(a).[153] This effectively meant that Nord Stream 2, unlike its predecessor Nord Stream 1 or other pipelines from third countries which have been completed before 23 May 2019, had to meet strict ownership unbundling,[154] certification and regulated tariffs requirements. Following the adoption of the amendments the transmission system operator Nord Stream 2 AG, which is a Swiss company fully owed by Gazprom OAO, brought an action for annulment before the General Court of the EU which was declared inadmissible due to a lack of standing.[155] The company then filed a notice of arbitration in accordance with Article 3 of the Arbitration Rules of the United Nations Commission on International Trade Law 1976. The Nord Stream 2 AG claims that its exclusion from the scope of Article 49(a) results in discrimination prohibited under the ECT.

Differently from the usual practice of the EU Member States acting as respondents in investment claims, even when an alleged violation has originated or was otherwise related to an EU measure (as discussed earlier), the Nord Stream 2 AG brought its claim against the EU, not a Member State. That is so because in this specific case the investor is seeking regulatory compliance, not compensation. Specifically, Nord Stream 2 AG is seeking a declaration of breach and injunctive relief in connection with the EU's discriminatory introduction and enactment of Directive 2019/692.[156] An obligation to comply with liberalization requirements would make the Nord Stream 2 project,

[153] Under Art 49(a), derogations from liberalization obligations may be granted to in respect of gas transmission lines between a Member State and a third country completed before 23 May 2019.

[154] Art 9 of the Gas Directive requires to separate ownership of transmission system operators from those of supply and distribution.

[155] *Nord Stream 2 AG and Nord Stream AG* v. *Parliament and Council*, Orders of the General Court in Cases T-526/19 and T-530/19 of 20 May 2020. The General Court found both a lack of individual and direct concern of the Nord Stream 2 AG.

[156] Notice of Arbitration, 26 September 2019, Nord Stream 2 AG and the European Union, para 3, available at: https://jusmundi.com/en/document/pdf/Other/IDS-NS2-26092019-01/en/en-nord-stream-2-v-european-union-notice-of-arbitration-thursday-26th-september-2019 (last visited 7 June 2020). The claimant reserved the right to seek, in addition or in the alternative, pecuniary compensation.

which is due to be completed in 2021, economically not viable for Gazprom OAO (which is both an operator and supplier for the Nord Stream 2 pipeline) as it was based on the company's assumption that the EU's internal market rules do not apply to the project.[157] Given that the amending Directive 2019/692, which brought the project under the scope of the Third Energy Package, has been adopted by the EU, the claim to declare the amendments unlawful has been brought against the EU. It is likely that if the primary relief sought by the investor was compensation, it would have brought the claim against Germany which, being the first connection point of the transmission line with an EU Member State's network, is charged with making the decision whether or not to grant the Nord Stream 2 AG a derogation under Article 49(a) (in fact, Germany has refused to grant such derogation[158]). While it is not yet clear whether the tribunal will confirm the EU as the proper respondent in this dispute, the investor's choice of the claimant supports the argument that responsibility is distributed to the EU when it is best placed to remedy the (alleged) breach.

6.5 CONCLUSION

In international economic law responsibility for violation of international obligations is restorative rather than punitive. The focus is not on the identification of an entity which has carried out unlawful conduct but on the subject which is best placed to remedy harm. In other words the focus is not on the responsible party, but on that which is best placed to bear responsibility.

Both WTO and investment case law under the ECT reveal a functional approach to international responsibility of the EU. The aim of the WTO regime is to bring about compliance. The positive solution test under the WTO guides panels in their determination of who the proper respondents are in a given dispute. The regime allows efficient breach, and the proper respondents are those who are necessary to ensure compliance. Entities whose conduct is inconsistent with the framework may be left out of the panels' recommendations if their actions are unnecessary for compliance purposes.

157 Nord Stream 2 AG, 'Questions and Answers, Nord Stream 2: A New Natural Gas Pipeline through the Baltic Sea', p 12, available at: www.nord-stream2.com/media/documents/pdf/en/2018/07/brochure-questions-answers-en.pdf (last accessed on 7 June 2020).

158 S&P Global Platts, 'German Regulator Formally Rejects Request from Nord Stream 2 for EU Law Waiver', 15 May 2020, available at: www.spglobal.com/platts/en/market-insights/latest-news/natural-gas/051520-german-regulator-formally-rejects-request-from-nord-stream-2-for-eu-law-waiver, last accessed on 8 June 2020.

The aim of investment arbitration, on the other hand, is to compensate private investors for the damage suffered as a result of breach of investment standards. In most cases damage occurs simultaneously with breach. The proof of the *existence* of breach is sufficient for the right to compensation to arise. Investment tribunals thus focus on the proximate cause of harm and often exclude the broader EU dimension from judicial scrutiny.

It may thus be concluded that international responsibility for violation of economic obligations is functional. Distribution of responsibility is not predetermined on the basis of some constant but is dynamic in that distribution of responsibility shifts from one holder of joint obligations to another, in accordance with the system of remedies under a given treaty regime. International responsibility is allocated to the EU or its Member States, depending on the nature of the economic regime in question.

7

The Optimal Respondent

7.1 INTRODUCTION

It was argued in Chapter 3 that the European Union (EU) and its Member States are independently responsible for their international obligations, irrespective of the internal transfer of competence(s). That responsibility of both the EU and its Member States *can* be invoked, however, does not tell us whether the EU, its Member States or both will be responsible in a given situation. It is thus necessary to determine exclusive responsibility. There is no support in international dispute-settlement practice for the European Commission's claim that conduct of Member States' authorities is attributed to the EU in the areas of Union competence(s) (Chapter 4).

Chapter 5 questioned whether attribution of breach is at all relevant to the allocation of responsibility for violation of economic obligations. It was suggested that the primary function of remedies in international economic law is restorative rather than retributive. Accordingly, investment tribunals focus on identifying the entity which is best placed to restore order rather than on attribution of responsibility for the breach. The question of shared responsibility is in effect the question of the proper respondents.

It was argued further in Chapter 6 that determination of whether the EU, its Member States or both are the proper respondents in trade and investment disputes depends on the nature of the treaty regime in question. Analysis of an extensive body of case law allows to identify the underlying rationales for the distribution of shared responsibility between the EU and its Member States. The the World Trade Organization (WTO) panels follow 'the positive solution test' which shifts responsibility to the entity whose conduct is necessary to compliance. Investment tribunals, on the other hand, focus on the proximate cause of harm which is sufficient to merit compensation.

In WTO and Energy Charter Treaty (ECT) adjudication the question of the proper respondent is rarely controversial. The tests for the distribution of shared responsibility identified in Chapter 6 place either the EU or its Member States as the default respondent. The usual pattern is that the EU is a respondent in WTO disputes, whereas Member States have so far been the primary respondents for violations of ECT obligations. The aim of this chapter is to answer the question 'why?' It aims to explain the central role of the EU in the WTO dispute-settlement system on the one hand, and of Member States in investment disputes under the ECT on the other. These patterns will be referred to as the optimal respondent. It will be suggested that the optimal respondent in a given treaty regime depends on the nature of that regime.

Section 7.2 explains the correlation between the nature of the WTO regime and the role of the EU as the primary respondent in WTO disputes. It will be argued that the EU's participation in the framework through mixed treaty-making in most cases allows WTO panels to address their recommendations to the EU alone. Revealing the opposite trend, Section 7.3 will shift focus to investment protection in order to explain why the primary respondents are Member States rather than the EU. The nature of investment protection obligations determines that Member States are the optimal respondents under the ECT regime.

An important caveat is in order. Unlike investment arbitration, where Member States have been not only the optimal but also the exclusive respondents (in publicly available disputes), the pattern is not as clear-cut in WTO disputes. There are a number of cases where panels address their recommendations not only to the EU but also to (some) Member States. The present discussion examines the general pattern and does not aim to explain why in some cases it is necessary to address the recommendations not only to the EU but also to Member States. Discussion of the latter question is reserved to Chapter 8.

7.2 THE EU AS THE OPTIMAL RESPONDENT IN WTO DISPUTES

It was argued in Chapter 6 that the DSB distributes shared responsibility on the basis of what is necessary to achieve a positive solution to the dispute. In most cases this requires the elimination of regulatory inconsistencies and ensuring that the rules of general application comply with WTO law. It has become customary for the EU to represent its Member States in most disputes concerning violation of WTO law.[1] It is usual for the EU to assure the DSB

[1] Gaja noted a tendency to assume that, whenever the EU was responsible, conduct by Member States had to be attributed to the Union; see Summary Record of the 2803rd Meeting, A/CN.4/SR.2803, 92, para 47. In *EC – Large Civil Aircraft*, the EC drew an ambiguous distinction

that it will bear responsibility on behalf of its Member States by affirming that all steps necessary to comply with the ruling will be taken. Presumably the EU's motive for such policy is its exclusive competence in the field of trade.[2] The aim of this section is to explain why the EU is in most cases best placed to achieve a positive solution in WTO disputes.

A number of cases analysed in Chapter 7 suggest that the DSB does not object to the EU's assumption of responsibility and often considers it sufficient to address its rulings and recommendations to the EU alone. For example, in *EC – Computer Equipment* the EC stated that it would respond to all US claims, including those addressed to Ireland and the United Kingdom.[3] The Panel rejected the EC's claim that it was the only respondent in the dispute, noting that both Ireland and the United Kingdom were bound by their tariff commitments.[4] However, though the tariff classification of Ireland and the United Kingdom was found to be inconsistent with the legitimate expectations of the United States, the Dispute Settlement Body (DSB) accepted the EC's assumption of responsibility on behalf of Ireland and the United Kingdom and addressed its recommendations to the EC alone.[5] Similarly, in *EC and Certain Member States – IT Products* the Panel noted that the EC had assured it that, to the extent the panel were to find that any of the measures specified in the joint panel request were in breach of WTO obligations, the EC would bear full responsibility for such breach.[6]

In some cases the EC goes as far as to assume international responsibility for Member States' measures which the EC itself considers to be autonomous decisions rather than implementation of EC law. For example, in *EC – Commercial Vessels* a question arose as to whether individual disbursements of aid by the Member States for certain shipyards were covered by the

between representation of Member States and the taking of responsibility for the actions of Member States. According to the EC, it 'has never said that it "represents" its member States but takes full responsibility in these proceedings for the actions of its member States', see *EC – Large Civil Aircraft*, PR, para 7.171.

2 The Union's quest to be a sole party to these agreements is motivated by the strengthening of its negotiating power through a one-voice approach. Eeckhout also suggests that the EU's willingness to assume responsibility on behalf of its Member States is most probably related to its quest for integration and for international confirmation; see Piet Eeckhout, 'The EU and Its Member States in the WTO: Issues of Responsibility', in Lorand Bartels and Federico Ortino (eds), *Regional Trade Agreements and the WTO Legal System* (Oxford University Press 2006), 457.

3 *EC and Certain Member States – IT Products*, PR, para 4.10. For third-party perception of the EU's assumption of responsibility, see INTERPOL's comments, Comments A/CN.4/556, 42.

4 *EC – Computer Equipment*, PR, para 8.16.

5 *EC – Computer Equipment*, PR, paras 9.1–9.2.

6 *EC and Certain Member States – IT Products*, PR, para 8.2, ft 1937, citing Letter from the Delegation of the European Commission dated 4 February 2009.

Agreement on Subsidies and Countervailing Measures (SCM Agreement). The EC disputed Korea's inclusion of these measures in its claim and noted that Member States' measures were not implementing measures of the challenged regulation but rather autonomous decisions on whether or not to make use of the derogation from prohibition of state aid under EC law.[7] However, despite its lack of normative control over Member States' measures, the EC indicated that if the national aid measures were to be found inconsistent with the WTO Agreement, the EC would bring those measures into conformity.[8] The Panel accepted the EC's assumption of responsibility, emphasizing its focus on the requested remedy. The Panel noted that it understood the EC's declaration that it assumes full responsibility for Member States' measures as the EC's acceptance of responsibility for '*any actions that may be required to bring into conformity the measures at issue*'. It concluded that '*it is sufficient, in the circumstances of this case, to address our recommendations to bring the measures at issue into conformity to the European Communities*'.[9]

Importantly, the EC's assumption of responsibility for its Member States does not relieve the latter of their WTO obligations, consistent with the principle of independent responsibility addressed in Chapter 3. *EC – Large Civil Aircraft* illustrates this point. In this case the EC stated that it takes full responsibility for the conduct of the Member States.[10] The Panel did not object to the EC making all submissions and communications in this dispute on behalf of Member States.[11] According to the Panel it was up to the Member States to choose whether to appear and actively defend their interests before the Panel. Importantly, however, the Panel noted that the internal arrangement of the EC and Member States did not alter their status as respondent in this particular dispute.[12]

It is suggested here that the DSB does not object to the EU's assumption of international responsibility on behalf of its Member States when the conduct of the latter is covered by the claim. While in such cases the DSB does not release Member States from their responsibility, it does not object to the

7 *EC – Commercial Vessels*, PR, para 4.22. The panel also noted that Member States' decisions to grant aid were not implementing EC law, because Member States were not under an obligation to introduce aid schemes in accordance to the challenged regulation, para 7.53.

8 *EC – Commercial Vessels*, PR, para 7.10, also para 7.54.

9 *EC – Commercial Vessels*, PR, para 7.33.

10 *EC – Large Civil Aircraft*, PR, para 7.171. referring to the Letter from the European Communities dated 6 October 2005.

11 *EC – Large Civil Aircraft*, PR, para 7.173. The panel noted that representatives of the EC Member States in question (France, Germany, Spain and the United Kingdom) appeared before the panel at several meetings but did not speak or make any submissions.

12 *EC – Large Civil Aircraft*, PR, paras 7.174–7.176.

Union's affirmation that it will ensure Member States' compliance. The following sections will explain that the DSB's acceptance of such arrangement stems from the internal interdependency of the EU and its Member States in mixed treaty-making. Before addressing mixed treaty-making, a note on a related aspect – the EU's exclusive competence in trade – is in place.

7.2.1 *The EU's Exclusive Competence in Trade*

The WTO Agreements establish rules of general application for the liberalization of trade. The purpose of the WTO dispute-settlement system is to safeguard the rules-based international trading system. Because it is an interstate forum where claims are filtered by governments, challenges to measures of general application form the basis of most claims under the WTO.

The WTO dispute-settlement system is focused on future compliance. The Panel in *US – Superfund* noted that the provisions of the GATT 1947 are intended not only to protect current trade but also to create predictability needed to plan future trade.[13] According to the Panel the WTO regime is *'intended to protect not only existing trade but also the security and predictability needed to conduct future trade. This objective would be frustrated if instruments setting out rules or norms inconsistent with a Member's obligations could not be brought before a panel once they have been adopted and irrespective of any particular instance of application of such rules or norms'*.[14]

The EU has competence in the field of trade and is thus the primary actor when it comes to amending rules of general application. In the seminal *Opinion 1/94* the European Court of Justice (ECJ) noted that the Union had exclusive competence to conclude international treaties on trade in goods, whereas competence in relation to the General Agreement on Trade in Services (GATS) and Agreement on Trade-Related Aspects of Intellectual Property Rights (TRIPS) was shared with Member States. Much has been written on the EU's competence in relation to the WTO, and the analysis will thus not be reiterated here.[15] Suffice it to say that while the EU does not have sufficient competence to conclude the WTO Agreements alone, its exclusive competence in trade is nevertheless central to the framework.

[13] *US – Taxes on Petroleum and Certain Imported Substances*, BISD 34S/136, PR adopted 17 June 1987 (US – Superfund).

[14] *US – Superfund*, PR, para 5.2.2.

[15] See, for example, Hilf Meinhard, 'The ECJ's Opinion 1/94 on the WTO – No Surprise, but Wise?' (1995) 6 EJIL 245; Pierre Pescatore, 'Opinion 1/94 on "Conclusion" of the WTO Agreements: Is There an Escape from a Programmed Disaster' (1999) 36 CML Rev. 387.

The EU's exclusive competence in trade explains the active role played by the EU itself in WTO disputes. The EU is the optimal respondent because it has the necessary competence to ensure compliance with trade rules of general application in the EU. It is the source of EU trade law, and thus inconsistencies with the WTO regime are best addressed through measures at Union level. Kuijper rightly notes that the EU is best placed to carry out the restitution that has been ordered by panels or the Appellate Body and ensures that such conformity will come about.[16] According to Kuijper the EU is the relevant entity in WTO dispute resolution because it has exclusive competence in the fields of customs and trade which, especially since the Lisbon Treaty, are coterminous with, if not broader than, the terrain covered by the WTO Agreements.[17]

I would like to emphasize a significant nuance. As has been noted in other chapters, the European Commission as well as a number of legal scholars approach the question of the international responsibility of the EU through the division of competence between the Union and its Member States. The competence-based model of responsibility of the European Commission has been in Chapter 3. In their seminal work Kuijper and Paasivirta discussed the competence model on which responsibility should basically lie where the competence is.[18] They explain that EU legislation sets out the basis for assessment of the legality of Member States' conduct and that it is ultimately controlled by the EU judiciary through the exercise of 'normative control'.[19] Delgado Casteleiro's study provides a comprehensive and persuasive analysis of the concept of normative control in the context of international responsibility of the EU.[20] Without attempting to give fair voice to Delgado Casteleiro's analysis,[21] I note his argument that by examining which competences are listed in Article 3 of Treaty on the Functioning of the European Union (TFEU) the areas in which the EU

16 Pieter Jan Kuijper, 'Attribution – Responsibility – Remedy Some Comments on the EU in Different International Regimes' [2014] Available at SSRN: https://ssrn.com/abstract=2405028, 9.

17 Kuijper 2014, 8.

18 Pieter Jan Kuijper and Esa Paasivirta, 'EU International Responsibility and Its Attribution: From the Inside Looking Out', in Malcolm Evans and Panos Koutrakos (eds), *The International Responsibility of the European Union: European and International Perspectives* (Hart Publishing 2013), 54.

19 Kuijper and Paasivirta 2013, 55.

20 Andrés Delgado Casteleiro, *The International Responsibility of the European Union: From Competence to Normative Control* (Cambridge University Press 2016).

21 For a more comprehensive overview, see my review of Delgado Casteleiro's book, Emilija Leinarte, '"International Responsibility of the European Union: From Competence to Normative Control" by Andrés Delgado Casteleiro', Book review (2017) 42 *ELR* 6, 918.

would bear responsibility could be established.[22] Delgado Casteleiro suggests that if there is exclusive competence, the EU should bear exclusive responsibility; if competence is shared, so should the responsibility.[23]

It is true that the division of competences between the EU and its Member States is relevant to the question of international responsibility. As will be argued this section, the EU's exclusive competence explains the primary role of the EU in the WTO dispute-settlement system. However, as discussed in Chapter 3, nothing in the WTO case law indicates that panels allocate responsibility to the EU on the *basis* that it holds exclusive competence in trade. Exclusive competence is not in itself a ground for distribution of shared responsibility. Instead distribution is based on the identification of those best placed to restore order. Allocation of responsibility to the EU in areas of its exclusive competence is an outcome of the application of this basis, not the basis itself. The difference is significant: the EU bears responsibility under WTO law not because it holds competence in the field of trade but because it is best placed to ensure compliance, given its competence in the field of trade. Interpreting the division of competences as the basis for allocating responsibility would negate the principle of independent responsibility of the Member States discussed in Chapter 3. Furthermore, the competence-based model is insufficient to explain cases where the DSB identifies Member States as the proper respondents alongside the EU, despite the EU's exclusive competence (these special cases of multiple respondents will be addressed in Chapter 8).

If, on the one hand, this book argues that the EU is the optimal respondent in WTO disputes because its exclusive competence in trade makes it best placed to ensure compliance and, on the other hand, it maintain that Member States remain independently responsible for their conduct, why then does the DSB allow the EU to assume international responsibility on behalf of Member States? The Panel stated its approach in *EC – Large Civil Aircraft*: '*The fact that four of those Members are member States of the European Communities, which is itself a Member of the WTO, does not affect their individual status as Members of the WTO against whom another Member, the United States, has brought claims of violation of various provisions of the WTO Agreements. Whether these four WTO Members choose to appear and actively defend their interests before the Panel separate from the actions of the European Communities is a matter entirely within their discretion, subject to the obligations of their status as member States of the European Communities*'.[24] If the DSB does

[22] Delgado Casteleiro 2016, 26.
[23] Delgado Casteleiro 2016, 26.
[24] *EC – Large Civil Aircraft*, PR, para 7.174.

not release Member States from their independent responsibility, why does the DSB empower the EU to bring its house in order?

The EU's exclusive competence in trade provides only a partial explanation of the primary role of the EU in the WTO regime. It does explain why the EU itself is a proper respondent in most disputes under the WTO regime. However, it remains to be examined why panels allow the EU to assume responsibility on behalf of Member States who remain independently responsible for their violations. The answer lies in the interdependency of the EU and its Member States in mixed agreements.

7.2.2 *The Internal Interdependency under Mixed Agreements*

It is well established in WTO law that when an inconsistency between a challenged legal measure and WTO obligations is found, it is up to the respondent to decide how it will bring its inconsistent measure(s) into compliance. Since the central remedy under the WTO dispute-settlement regime is the elimination of regulatory inconsistencies, the manner in which the measure is to be brought into conformity is directly linked to the substance of WTO obligations.[25] As has been argued in Chapter 6, this is not the case in investment arbitration where the correlation between the type of standard breached and compensation is (mostly) irrelevant.

If under WTO law the substance of obligations breached defines compliance, the division of competences between the EU and Member States could in effect provide guidance on the optimal respondent. However, the WTO regime does not contain a declaration of competences, and even if there were one, its usefulness could be doubted.[26] The apportionment of competences between the EU and its Member States would be too complex a task for an external adjudicator, especially in relation to GATS and TRIPS where the dividing line is not clear.[27] Nor is the DSB obliged to follow such delimitation of competences which is of a purely internal nature.[28] The panels are, however, released from the task by the very nature of the EU's participation in the WTO regime through mixed treaty-making.

25 *EC – Selected Customs Matters*, PR, para 7.17.

26 Peter M Olson, 'Mixity from the Outside: The Perspective of a Treaty Partner', in Christophe Hillion and Panos Koutrakos (eds), *Mixed Agreements Revisited: The EU and Its Member States in the World* (Hart Publishing 2010), 337.

27 Eeckhout is of the same opinion, see Eeckhout 2006, 459.

28 Christian Tomuschat, 'Liability for Mixed Agreements' in David O'Keeffe and Henry G Schermers (eds), *Mixed Agreements* (Kluwer Law & Taxation Publishers 1983), 125.

7.2.3 *The WTO as a Mixed Treaty*

The WTO Agreement is a mixed treaty – both the EU and its Member States are parties to it. Mixity is a technique which aggregates powers of the EU and Member States to enable them to undertake commitments *vis-à-vis* non-member states which none of them could enter alone due to a lack of competence.[29] In his seminal work on mixity, Heliskoski described the use of mixed agreements as a technique for organizing international relations of the Union and its Member States.[30] This technique, according to Schermers, is employed in relation to any treaty to which an international organization, some or all of its Member States and one or more third states are parties and for execution of which neither the organization nor its Member States have full competence.[31]

The lack of competence arises because the Union is a separate legal person with limited capacity and therefore enjoys only those powers which Member States have conferred on it.[32] The dynamism of competence allocation under the internal structure of the EU calls for mixity. Generally, the Union is entitled to conclude international agreements on its own only if it enjoys exclusive competence in all matters covered by that treaty. Therefore, even if the Union has competence for subject matter of the agreements but that competence is shared with Member States,[33] the latter may become parties

29 Jean Groux and Philippe Manin, *The European Communities in the International Order* (Office for Official Publications of the European Communities 1985), 61. The system of mixed agreements is different from that chosen by federal states in which a single entity enters into agreements binding on both the Union and Member States regardless of the internal allocation of competences; see Olson 2010, 334.

30 Joni Heliskoski, *Mixed Agreements as a Technique for Organizing the International Relations of the European Community and Its Member States* (Kluwer Law International 2001). Ehlermann notes that the concept of mixed agreements has been created for internal reasons rather than being called for by third states; see CD Ehlermann, 'Mixed Agreements: A List of Problems', in David O'Keeffe and Henry G Schermers (eds), *Mixed Agreements* (Kluwer Law and Taxation Publishers 1983), 3–21.

31 O'Keeffe and Schermers 1983, 25.

32 Though the Union's legal personality has been recognized early on, it is only the Treaty of Lisbon which, in Art 47 TEU, explicitly recognizes the legal personality of the EU, making it an independent entity in its own right. This should be read in conjunction with Art 5 TEU which establishes the principle of conferral and Art 4 TEU which states that competences not conferred upon the Union in the Treaties remain with the Member States. On the typology of competence allocation, see Allan Rosas, 'The European Union and Mixed Agreements', in Alan Dashwood and Christophe Hillion (eds), *The General Law of E. C. External Relations* (Sweet & Maxwell 2000), 203.

33 Areas of shared competence can become exclusively the Union's competence once the EU exercises that competence and the exercise of parallel competence by the Member States could affect the common rules or alter their scope.

alongside the EU, should they wish to do so.[34] It should be noted, however, that Advocate General Wahl in *Opinion 3/15* suggested that the choice between a mixed agreement or an EU-only agreement, when the subject matter of the agreement falls within an area of shared competence (or of parallel competence), is generally a matter for the discretion of the EU legislature.[35] According to him, the Union enjoys wider discretion to conclude EU-only agreements in areas which involve political, economic and social choices on its part and in which it is called upon to undertake complex assessments. On the other hand, a mixed agreement would be required, generally, where an international agreement concerns coexistent competences: that is, it includes a part which falls under the exclusive competence of the Union and a part which falls under the exclusive competence of the Member States, without any of those parts being ancillary to the other.[36]

Aside from competence-related rationales, Member States favour mixity for political reasons, such as visibility and prestige.[37] Mixity can also result from the inclusion of the so-called subordination clauses in international agreements. For example, many environmental treaties include a subordination clause which obliges the EU to conclude these agreements as mixed.[38] Finally, the ECJ has been flexible and generous in recognizing Member States' quest for mixity.[39] In *Opinion 2/15* which concerned the EU-Singapore free trade agreement (FTA) case the ECJ established that the EU lacks sufficient competence in relation to the investor-to-state dispute-resolution

34 Heliskoski 2001, 67.

35 Opinion procedure 3/15, Opinion of Advocate General Wahl, delivered on 8 September 2016, 19.

36 Opinion procedure 3/15, Opinion of Advocate General Wahl, delivered on 8 September 2016, 122.

37 Pieter Jan Kuijper and others, *The Law of EU External Relations Cases, Materials, and Commentary on the EU as an International Legal Actor* (2nd edn, Oxford University Press 2015).

38 For example, UNCLOS Annex IX Art 2 states that an international organization may sign the Convention if a majority of its Member States are signatories to it. For more on subordination clauses in environmental agreements, see Lena Granvik, 'Incomplete Mixed Environmental Agreements of the Community and the Principle of Bindingness', in Martti Koskenniemi (ed), *International Law Aspects of the European Union* (Kluwer Law International 1998), 260.

39 Robert Schütze, 'Federalims and Foreign Affairs: Mixity as a (Inter)National Phenomenon', in Christophe Hillion and Panos Koutrakos (eds), *Mixed Agreements Revisited: The EU and its Member States in the World* (Hart Publishing 2010), 82. This is by no means to say that the CJEU ignores legal rules for competence allocation, for example in *Portugal* v. *Spain*, Case C-268/94, concerning the Union's agreement for cooperation with India, the Court took a restrictive position and noted that the use of mixity is to be determined by analysing the essential object of the agreement (in this case, development cooperation) and not with respect to individual clauses which are merely ancillary.

mechanism and so new-generation FTAs will likely be mixed.[40] A number of authors therefore agree that the use of mixed agreements is only going to increase in the future.[41]

From the perspective of third parties, mixity can be regarded as a safeguard that the agreement binds an actor with relevant powers.[42] If an agreement is concluded by the EU alone, a third party may be unable to bring a claim against a Member state because it is not a party to an agreement. Even though Member States would be bound internally, a conclusion of an agreement by the EU alone does not by itself mean that Member States become parties implicitly or are bound from the international law perspective.[43] In addition, unlike their ties to the EU, third parties have long-standing relationships with Member States and therefore do not usually object to mixity.[44] Rather, their interest is in achieving clarity and ensuring that all parties necessary to compliance are bound by the agreement. It is therefore correct to suggest that analysis of mixity should incorporate not only the Union and its Member States but also their treaty partners,[45] a point which is often ignored.

The complexity of the joint participation of the EU and its Member States in the WTO poses little contention because mechanisms are in place which allow the EU to assume responsibility without posing risks to third parties. The following sections will explain procedural safeguards that can achieve this objective – which explain why panels deem it sufficient to leave it to the EU to ensure compliance with its rulings.

7.2.4 *The EU–Member States Bloc*

The WTO Agreement is a multilateral treaty ratified by 164 members. Each member, including the EU and its Member States, is an independent signatory, as is reflected in Article XI:1 of the WTO Agreement.[46] The WTO is

40 Opinion 2/15 *Free Trade Agreement with Singapore* [2017]; Opinion of AG Sharpston delivered on 21 December 2016. AG Sharpston concluded that the EU does not have exclusive competence over the area of the FTA and the treaty was thus mixed.

41 For example, see Rosas 2000, 371.

42 Groux and Manin 1985, 67; Olson 2010, 334.

43 I Macleod, ID Hendry and S Hyett, *The External Relations of the European Communities* (Oxford University Press 1996), 126.

44 Groux and Manin 1985, 68. Resistance towards mixity is more likely to be motivated by political reasons, for example, as was the case when mixed agreements of the European Communities were opposed by the USSR, see p 70–71.

45 Heliskoski 2001, 8.

46 According to Gaja, agreements that impose obligations separately on the Community and also grant the Community separate rights, may consider the Community's participation as completely independent from the Member States. Under this type of agreement, the Community

a multilateral treaty because it establishes relationships in respect of rights and obligations between each of its members.[47] In this regard it differs from bilateral treaties such as the Lomé Convention which, although concluded with several non-Member States, confers rights and obligations only between the Union and its Member States and each of the non-members, but not between the latter states themselves.[48]

As was discussed in detail in Chapter 3, the EU and Member States are independently responsible for discharging all obligations to other members of the WTO, irrespective of the internal division of competences between them.[49] Importantly, the EU and its Member States participate in mixed agreements as one bloc in that they do not acquire rights and duties in respect of each other.[50] Some commentators suggest that from the Union's perspective, the conclusion of a multilateral agreement by the EU in a mixed form should be viewed as 'concealed bilateralism' because the EU and its Member States stand before other members as one party.[51]

That the EU and Member States form one block in the WTO system is reflected in the EU's participation in the treaty. Article IX:1 of the WTO Agreement provides that the EU shall have a number of votes equal to the number of their Member States which are members of the WTO.[52] The EU

and Member States hold parallel positions and can be viewed as entirely separate contracting parties; see Giorgio Gaja, 'The European Community's Rights and Obligations under Mixed Agreements', in David O'Keeffe and Henry G Schermers (eds), *Mixed Agreements* (Kluwer Law & Taxation Publishers 1983), 138.

47 Rosas defines multilateral agreements as those involving parallel competences between the Union and the Member States, meaning that the EU adherence would not, in principle, be different from the separate participation of some or all of the Member States; see Rosas 2000, 206.

48 Groux and Manin 1985, 60.

49 The WTO does not contain the EU's declaration of competences, and thus there is no separability of the parts of the agreement which imposes obligations and gives rights to the Union from the other parts of the same agreement; Groux and Manin 1985, 139. Similarly, from an international law perspective, a Union agreement does not bind those Member States which are not parties to it; see for example UNCLOS Art 4(5) of Annex IX which states that 'Participation of such an international organization shall in no way confer any rights under the Convention on member States of the organization which are not State Parties to this Convention'. For incomplete mixity issues, see Ehlermann 1983.

50 Kuijper and others 2015, 171.

51 Philip Allott, 'Adherence to and Withdrawal from Mixed Agreements', in David O'Keeffe and Henry G Schermers (eds), *Mixed Agreements* (Kluwer Law and Taxation Publishers 1983), 106. Groux and Manin also note a bilateral nature of such agreements, suggesting that in such cases decisions are adopted unanimously by the 'European Party' on the one hand, and the contracting non-member countries on the other; see Groux and Manin 1985, 61.

52 Voting arrangements in mixed agreements are sometimes a subject of contention inside the EU, for example, regarding a right to vote in the UN Food and Agriculture Organization Conference on the adoption of an Agreement to Promote Compliance with International

voting arrangement in the WTO resembles that under the United Nations Convention for the Law of the Sea (UNCLOS).[53] Similarly, the joint nature of membership of the EU and its Member States is also evident from their participation in the regime by way of common positions for the implementation of mixed agreements.[54] The implementation of the WTO Agreement is conditional on the adoption of official common positions since the EU became party to the treaty, though action through *de facto* common positions was a reality even before the EU's accession to the WTO when the Union held observer status.[55] Furthermore, the freedom to regulate the negotiation and implementation of a mixed agreement in accordance with the EU's internal principles allows respect for the internal division of competences.[56]

7.2.5 *The Duty of Cooperation*

The building block for the joint participation of the EU and its Member States in the WTO regime is based on the duty of cooperation. Article 216(2) of the TFEU states that Union agreements are binding on the institutions of the Union and on Member States.[57] Member States are under an obligation to respect the mixed agreement which stems from a general obligation not to jeopardize the attainment of the objectives of the Treaties.[58] That Member States have shared competence with the EU is secondary to their duty of cooperation.

Arguably the EU is entitled to take infringement action against Member States which violate an international agreement, even if within the sphere of

Conservation and Management Measures by Fishing Vessels on High Seas. The decision of the EU Council to allocate the rights to vote to Member States, despite the EU's exclusive competence in this area, was annulled by the ECJ; see in Case C-25/94 *Commission of the European Communities* v. *Council of the European Union* [1996], ECR I-01469.

53 UNCLOS Art 4(4) of Annex IX states that participation of an international organization should not entail an increase in decision-making rights; for more see Ehlermann 1983, 12. Recently, third parties have required that the EU does not have more than one vote; see Antarctic Convention Art 12(4).

54 For the counting of votes for amendments of the WTO Agreements, see Frank Hoffmeister, 'Institutional Aspects of Global Trade Governance from an EU Perspective', in Bart Van Vooren, Steven Blockmans and Jan Wouters (eds), *The EU's Role in Global Governance* (Oxford University Press 2013), 147.

55 Groux and Manin 1985, 54.

56 Granvik 1998, 268. For a detailed account of the negotiation of mixed agreements, see Heliskoski 2001, 71–100.

57 Member States are bound by the duty of cooperation already during the negotiations for the conclusion of an international agreement; see Macleod, Hendry and Hyett 1996, 148–150.

58 Art 4(3) TEU, see also Gaja 1983, 140.

shared competence.[59] Once the Union enters into an international agreement Member States are subject to the duty of cooperation to facilitate the implementation of obligations under that agreement even in areas of shared competence and are prevented from acting unilaterally.[60] In his Opinion in *EDF* AG Jacobs noted that the exact limits of that duty could not be laid down in the abstract but depended on the agreement in question.[61] This duty of cooperation is an essential element of regional integration, as it would be futile to enter into cooperation if at the same time individual states were able to act contrary to the common interest. The EU's monist approach to international economic law allows international obligations to be enforced inside the EU.[62] The DSB has also recognized the duty of cooperation under EU law.[63]

Stemming from the general duty of cooperation is a more particular duty of unity of representation in international affairs laid down in Article 4 TEU. The ECJ has ruled that Member States have a duty to secure performance of international agreements to which the Union is a party.[64] Even though the duty has often been regarded as an internal obligation,[65] the Court has interpreted it as also binding the EU *vis-à-vis* third states.

The duty is owned to the Union which assumes responsibility for the due performance of the agreement.[66] Member States are precluded from taking action which is capable of affecting or altering the scope of the agreement.[67] The purpose of unity of representation is to present a common, coherent approach and Union action should not be hampered or undermined by the

59 C-239/03 *Commission of the European Communities* v. *French Republic (Étang de Berre)* [2004] EU:C:2004:598; Ehlermann 1983, 20–21.

60 See Rosas 2000, 197.

61 Opinion of Advocate General Jacobs delivered on 10 November 1993, I-641 in Case C-316/91, *Parliament* v. *Council of the European Union* [1994] ECR 661.

62 See C-21-24/72, *International Fruit Company NV et autres contre Produktschap voor Groenten en Fruit* [1972] ECR. For more on the EU's monist approach to international obligations, see Schütze 2010, 77–80. The situation may be different outside economic law, as was evidenced by the Kadi saga, Joined Cases C-402 & C-415/05P, *Kadi & Al Barakaat Int'l Found.* v. *Comm'n* [2008] ECR. I-6352; Joined Cases C-584, C-593, and C-595/10P, *Comm'n* v. *Kadi* [2013].

63 For example, see *EC – Selected Customs Matters*, PR, paras 2.13–2.14, where the panel noted that the Union's principle of executive federalism is based on the principle of subsidiarity, the functioning of which is based on the duty of sincere cooperation.

64 C-104/81 *Hauptzollamt Mainz* v. *C.A. Kupferberg & Cie KG a.A.* [1982] ECR 3641, 11–13.

65 See Schütze 2010, 76; Macleod, Hendry and Hyett 1996, 126.

66 Macleod, Hendry and Hyett 1996, 126.

67 The ECJ has confirmed this duty in its case law; see for example, C-425/01 *Ospelt* v. *Schlössle Weissenberg Familienstiftung* [2003] ECR I-9743, para 24. The Court recalled that even though the systems of ownership fall under the Member States' competence, they remain subject to fundamental rules of Community law.

countervailing action of Member States.[68] According to Dolmans, the fewer discretionary powers Members States have to decide on the content of engagements with third parties, the more cooperation and coordination is necessary.[69] This could explain why a duty of cooperation applies with respect to the WTO Agreement, which mainly falls within exclusive EU competence. Cooperation between the EU and Member States is often managed through the so-called Codes of Conduct, though no such conduct was adopted in relation to the WTO Agreement due to lack of internal agreement.[70]

To conclude, the EU's central role in the WTO dispute-settlement system results from the WTO's rules-based framework, the purpose of which is to protect rules of general application and thus achieve a positive solution in WTO disputes which is aimed at compliance. The EU is in most cases the optimal respondent because it is best placed to ensure compliance. As for the EU's assumption of international responsibility on behalf of its Member States when the conduct of the latter is also covered by the claim, the interdependency of Member States and the EU through mixed treaty-making allows the EU to assume international responsibility on behalf of its Member States. Third parties are safeguarded through the duty of cooperation which obliges Member States to comply with the DSB's rulings and recommendations. The existence of the internal mechanisms to bind Member States explains why panels refrain from interfering in the EU's quest to provide compliance itself even in cases where Member States' conduct is found to be inconsistent.

The following section focuses on investment disputes, where Member States have so far been exclusive respondents.[71] Contrary to the WTO regime, where consistency of rules of general application with WTO law is often at the centre of adjudication, investment claims are focused on the *application* of inconsistent measures in a specific case. As has been suggested in Chapter 6, investment tribunals focus on the proximate cause of harm because it is sufficient for determining award of compensation. Analysis of the content of investment protection obligations reveals that Member States are the optimal respondents because they are in most cases the proximate cause of harm to investors' rights.

68 CWA Timmermans, 'Organizing Joint Participation of E.C. and Member States', in Alan Dashwood and Christophe Hillion (eds), *The General Law of E. C. External Relations* (Sweet & Maxwell 2000), 241.

69 Maurits JFM Dolmans, *Problems of Mixed Agreements: Division of Powers Within the EEC and the Rights of Third Parties* (Asser Instituut 1985), 45.

70 A draft Code of Conduct was published in Inside US Trade, 23 September 1994, at 14. See Meinhard 1995, 248; Kuijper and others 2015, 171.

71 I acknowledge that there may be disputes not publicly accessible where the EU has been a respondent.

7.3 MEMBER STATES AS THE PRIMARY RESPONDENT IN INVESTMENT DISPUTES

Revealing a trend opposite to that observed under the WTO regime, Member States have been the primary actors in investment arbitration. There are practical reasons for this pattern. The EU is not a party to the International Centre for Settlement of Investment Disputes (ICSID) Convention and claims against the EU cannot be brought before ICSID tribunals. This may change with the implementation of the Multilateral Investment Court (MIC), currently under construction by the European Commission.[72] Setting aside the institutional aspects, it will be suggested that the central role of Member States in investment disputes stems mainly from the nature of investment protection standards.

Before engaging in the analysis, a preliminary observation is in place. Since 2009 when the Treaty of Lisbon came into force, the EU has held competence in the field of investment protection. Under the new ordering of EU external relations, the EU common commercial policy (CCP) was placed in the category of exclusive EU competences. As a result the area of foreign direct investment (FDI) was transferred from the sphere of competences of Member States to that of the Union. This flows from Article 207 and Article 3(1) TFEU: Article 207 provides that FDI is now one of the areas covered by the CCP, whereas Article 3(1) states that CCP is an area of exclusive EU competence. Article 206 of the TFEU further provides that in establishing the customs union the EU shall contribute, in the common interest, to the progressive abolition of restrictions on international trade and protection of FDI.

This chapter does not address the transfer of competences in the area of FDI to the EU. Specifically, it does not discuss investment chapters in new-generation FTAs which the EU has concluded or is in the process of concluding. These treaties will be addressed in Chapter 9. The present analysis focuses on ECT practice without touching upon the implications of the new division of competences in the field of investment between the EU and its Member States. The ECT provides a relevant context for the analysis of the distribution of shared responsibility for violation of joint obligations which are discharged in the context of shared sovereignty because of its rich practice, and, importantly, it is a mixed agreement which does not contain a declaration of competences.

72 For more on the European Commission's Multilateral Investment Court project, see http://trade.ec.europa.eu/doclib/press/index.cfm?id=1608, last visited 31 July 2018.

Recall the argument in Chapter 6, that investment tribunals are mainly concerned with the proximate cause of harm to investors' rights. Damage, which is an element in determining responsibility under investment treaties, in most cases occurs simultaneously with malfeasance or misfeasance. Since the *existence* of breach calls for an award of compensation, the extent and causes of breach are, while relevant, not necessarily part of the remedial process. The context is essentially different under the WTO regime. The aim of the WTO dispute-settlement system is regulatory compliance, which requires WTO panels to determine the roots of inconsistent measures. If the DSB focused only on the proximate cause of harm, adjudication would not result in a positive solution to the dispute which aims to ensure overall regulatory compliance. Furthermore, while WTO disputes mainly arise from inconsistencies in rules of general application, investment arbitration concerns specific instances of application of law.[73] This is so because damage is an important element of investor-state disputes.

It will be argued in the following sections that Member States are the optimal respondents in investment arbitration because it is their conduct that in most cases constitutes the proximate cause of injury to investors. The nature of investment protection standards is closely tied to acts of Member States, while the EU itself rarely interacts with investors directly. This is so because investment protection treaties are intended to create favourable conditions for foreign investment, which call for an effective normative framework, an impartial judicial system, an efficient and legally restrained bureaucracy, as well transparent decisions.[74] Investment protection regimes set standards for the host state's treatment of investors. They apply to actions and measures of various Member States' institutions and officials, which form the foundation of investment projects.

Precisely because Member States interact directly with investors it is their conduct which gives rise to investors' claims. Member States engage in bilateral relations with investors and adopt measures which affect the development of investment projects. The ECT practice provides a good example. Disputes under the ECT have arisen over a wide variety of Member States' measures adopted by state officials and entities. For example, *Nykomb v. Latvia* concerned the calculation of electric power purchase price by

[73] For data, see Zoe Phillips Williams, 'Risky Business or Risky Politics: What Explains Investor-State Disputes?' (PhD book, Hertie School of Governance, Berlin Graduate School for Transnational Studies, 2016), 43.

[74] Robert D Sloane and Michael Reisman, 'Indirect Expropriation and Its Valuation in the BIT Generation' (2003) 73 BYIL 115, 117.

a state-owned company.[75] *Hrvatska Elektroprivreda* v. *Slovenia* arose due to a state's measure affecting the ownership and operation of an electric power plant.[76] *Plama Consortium* v. *Bulgaria* involved *inter alia* a sudden amendment of an environmental law.[77]

The following section will take a closer look at the content of investment protection standards and investment arbitration practice. Analysis of the content of investment obligations provides insight into the key actors and objects forming investment claims. The analysis reveals that, if applied by analogy to the EU legal order, measures and actions of Member States' institutions and officials, not the EU, are more likely to constitute the proximate cause of the alleged injury to foreign investors. The following section discusses the Fair and Equitable Treatment (FET) standard, expropriation as well as umbrella clauses, to the extent that they support this thesis.

7.3.1 *Fair and Equitable Treatment*

An FET is a central investment protection standard. It is a broad obligation which may be violated in the course of a wide array of Member States'

75 *Nykomb* v. *Latvia*, Award. A dispute concerned a contract between Latvenergo, a company whose 100 per cent shares were owned by the Government of Latvia, and a Swedish company Nykomb for the construction of a cogeneration plant in Bauska. A purchase price of the electric power was agreed in the contract. Nykomb alleged that Latvenergo applied a different price calculation formula than was agreed upon in the contract between the parties, claiming that this amounted to indirect expropriation. At the time of the dispute Latvia was not yet a member of the EU, which she entered in 2004. However, the case serves as an example of a regulatory measure which formed the basis of a dispute and the ECT.

76 *Hrvatska Elektroprivreda d.d.* v. *Republic of Slovenia* (Award, 17 December 2015) ICSID Case No. ARB/05/24. The dispute arose between the Croatian company and Slovenia who, prior to declaration of independence in 1991 from the Yugoslavia bloc, constructed a commonly financed power plant sharing the ownership equally. The claimant alleged that after the declaration of independence, Slovenia disconnected electricity deliveries to the claimant and issued a decree which affected its rights. After a failure to solve the differences through the signing of a 2001 agreement for financial arrangements in relation to modernization of the plant, the dispute was brought before the ICSID arbitration. Similarly to *Nykomb* v. *Latvia*, the dispute arose prior to Slovenia's membership in the EU. It nevertheless serves as an example of possible Member State measures brought before international arbitral tribunals.

77 *Plama Consortium Limited* v. *Republic of Bulgaria* (Award, 27 August 2008) ICSID Case No. ARB/03/24, para 149. Claimant, a company incorporated in Cyprus engaged in oil refining, alleged that Bulgarian Government, the national legislative and judicial authorities and other public authorities and agencies deliberately created numerous grave problems for the company's business and refused or unreasonably delayed the adoption of adequate corrective measures upon the initiation of bankruptcy proceedings against the claimant, para 72.

conduct. FET obligation can be found in virtually any investment protection regime. A study shows that 90 per cent of investment treaties contain an FET provision and violations of FET constitute the most common challenge in investment arbitration.[78] Though highly significant in relation to investors' rights, an FET is a broad standard which has typically been left undefined in order to give it broad scope and leave room for judicial interpretation. Thus, the majority of investment treaties do not spell out the scope or content of this obligation.[79] New-generation FTAs to some extent limit the scope of FET by expressly referring to conduct which constitutes breach of FET. For example, the now abandoned Transatlantic Trade and Investment Partnership (TTIP)[80] and currently provisionally applied EU-Canada Comprehensive Economic and Trade Agreement (CETA)[81] provide almost identical open-ended lists of categories of measures that violate FET: denial of justice in criminal, civil or administrative proceedings; fundamental breach of due process in judicial and administrative proceedings; manifest arbitrariness or targeted discrimination on manifestly wrongful grounds; and harassment, coercion and abuse of power.[82]

While this chapter not dispute that a violation of an FET standard may be caused by the adoption of an EU measure as such, Member States are the primary actors in this context. Damage resulting from a violation of FET will in most cases stem from the host state's treatment of investment. The content of FET primarily concerns direct bilateral relations between a host state and an investor. Since the EU generally does not interact with investors directly, measures falling within its sphere of influence will rarely be subject to an FET challenge. The content of FET is discussed here by considering its three main

78 Jonathan Bonnitcha, Poulsen Lauge and Michael Waibel, *The Political Economy of the International Investment Regime* (Oxford University Press 2017), 94, tables 4.1 and 4.2.

79 Jeswald W Salacuse, *The Law of Investment Treaties* (2nd edn, Oxford University Press 2015), 253; Katia Yannaca-Small, 'Fair and Equitable Treatment Standard', in Katia Yannaca-Small (ed), *Arbitration under International Investment Agreements: A Guide to the Key Issues* (Oxford University Press 2010), 394. The 2004 U.S. Model BIT and a number of US free trade agreements stipulate that FET includes the obligation not to deny justice in criminal, civil or administrative adjudicatory proceedings in accordance with the principle of due process embodied in the principle of legal system of the world (Art 5(2)(a) of 2004 Model U.S. BIT).

80 TTIP Art 3(1) of Ch III.

81 CETA Art 8.10(2).

82 The differences in the wording are as follows: the draft TTIP Art 3(2) of Chapter 3 lists 'obstacles to effective access to justice' as a possible breach of due process, whereas the relevant CETA provision does not include this element. Also, abusive treatment in draft CETA text is a general term (coercion, duress and harassment are listed as possible forms of abusive treatment). The respective general term in TTIP is 'similar bad faith conduct' (Art 3(2)(e)). A third difference is the addition of 'duress' in the list of abusive treatment under Art X.9, which is not stated in TTIP provision.

components: denial of justice and due process, arbitrary and discriminatory treatment and frustration of legitimate expectations.[83]

7.3.2 *Denial of Justice and Due Process*

Actions or omissions of the Union's quasi-judicial and administrative entities may amount to a breach of due process in a variety of settings, for example through its state aid decisions. However, a host state's judicial and administrative organs interact directly with individual investors to a much greater extent than those of the Union. Decisions of Member States' authorities directly affect the realization of investors' projects.

Denial of justice is closely related to domestic judicial and administrative systems. It is a category of deficiencies in the host state's governmental organs, particularly those involved in the administration of justice.[84] Denial of justice can arise from either procedural or substantive deficiency. The primary actors in this context are courts and state agencies.[85] In relation to international investment law, denial of justice has in most cases manifested itself in connection with the improper administration of civil and criminal justice, for example, denial of access to courts.[86] Tribunals have found denial of justice in cases where an investor was not given proper notification of a hearing or was prevented from participation in an administrative process directly concerning its rights.[87]

Closely related to denial of justice are due process infringements.[88] A wide variety of judicial, legislative or executive deficiencies can amount to a breach

[83] Bonnitcha, Lauge and Waibel 2017, 109–111.

[84] James Crawford, *Brownlie's Principles of Public International Law* (8th edn, Oxford University Press 2012), 619. Paparinskis states that denial of justice unquestionably applies to administration of justice, Martins Paparinskis, *The International Minimum Standard and Fair and Equitable Treatment* (Oxford University Press 2013), 181. Third Restatement of the Foreign Relations Law of the United States § 711 adopts a narrower approach to the scope of denial of justice by referring only to injury consisting of, or resulting from, denial of access to courts, or denial of procedural fairness and due process in relation to judicial proceedings.

[85] Salacuse 2015, 265.

[86] In *Waste Management, Inc.* v. *United Mexican States* ('Number 2') (Award, 30 April 2004), ICSID Case No. ARB(AF)/00/3.

[87] For example, *Metalclad Corporation* v. *The United Mexican States* (Award, 30 August 2000) ICSID Case No. ARB(AF)/97/1. A construction permit was denied to the investor at a municipal meeting of which the investor received no notice and before which it was given no opportunity to appear; in *Middle East Cement Shipping and Handling Co. S.A.* v. *Arab Republic of Egypt*, (Award, 12 April 2002) ICSID Case No. ARB/99/6, an investor complained that an Egyptian government seized and auctioned its ship without a proper notice.

[88] Rudolf Dolzer and Christoph Schreuer, *Principles of International Investment Law* (Oxford University Press 2008), 142.

of due process, and it is therefore more viable to list examples than provide a typology of relevant measures.[89] In *Petrobart* v. *Kyrgyz Republic* the Tribunal found a breach of due process when a host state failed to execute a judgment of a local court rendered in favour of an investor by transferring assets of a liable state entity and declaring it bankrupt.[90] In *Tecmed* v. *Mexico* arbitration, due process was breached because the environmental regulatory authority had failed to notify the investor of its intentions, which deprived the investor of the opportunity to state its position.[91] A miscarriage of justice due to a gross failure to afford due process during trial proceedings and failure to protect an investor from nationality-based prejudice was affirmed (though obiter only) by the *Loewen* v. *United States* Tribunal.[92]

Denial of justice and due process infringements by Member States, though in a context other than investment protection, has manifested itself in numerous forms and instances, as is attested by the case law of the European Court of Human Rights (ECtHR). The Court has found denial of justice by Member States on a variety of grounds: denial of right of access to a court,[93] lack of an impartial court system[94] or fair trial.[95]

Due process infringements are most likely to appear at Member State level of decision-making where measures of all branches of government influence the development of investment projects. Investors are often the direct addressees of institutional policies which, accordingly, may be the proximate cause of injury.

89 In *Waste Management* v. *Mexico*, Award, para 98, the tribunal provided a general description of due process requirement: '[th]e minimum standard of treatment of fair and equitable treatment is infringed by conduct attributable to the State and harmful to the claimant if the conduct is arbitrary, grossly unfair, unjust or idiosyncratic'.

90 *Petrobart Limited* v. *The Kyrgyz Republic* (Award, 29 March 2005) SCC Case No. 126/2003, 82.

91 *Técnicas Medioambientales Tecmed, S.A.* v. *The United Mexican States* (Award, 29 May 2003) ICSID Case No. ARB (AF)/00/2.

92 *Loewen Group, Inc. and Raymond L. Loewen* v. *US* (Award, 26 June 2003) ICSID Case No. ARB(AF)/98/3.

93 For example, denial of access to court was addressed in *Kreuz* v. *Poland* and *Hadjianastassiou* v. *Greece* App no 12945/87 (ECtHR, 16 December 1992) (concerning procedural obstacles on access); *Arnolin* v. *France*, *Legrand* v. *France*, *Maggio and others* v. *Italy* App no 61145/16 (ECtHR, 22 February 2017) and others regarding finality of decisions; *Užkurėlienė and others* v. *Lithuania* App no 62988/00 (ECtHR, 7 April 2005) for timely execution of awards.

94 For example, *Piersack* v. *Belgium*; *H.* v. *Belgium* App no 8692/79 (ECtHR, 10 January 1982).

95 For example, *Monnell and Morris* v. *the United Kingdom* App no 9562/81; 9818/82 (ECtHR, 2 March 1987). For a detailed account of ECtHR case law in relation to denial of justice, see Dovydas Vitkauskas and Grigoriy Dikov, *Protecting the Right to a Fair Trial under the European Convention on Human Rights Council of Europe Human Rights Handbooks* (Council of Europe 2012).

7.3.3 *Arbitrary and Discriminatory Treatment*

As is the case with denial of justice and breach of due process, a wide variety of host state's judicial, executive and legislative actions may fall within the arbitrary and discriminatory measures category. As noted by Salacuse, the discrimination element of an FET standard is highly fact-specific – it calls for determination whether in a given situation the particular action of a government in respect of an individual investor within a framework of a relationship that is complex and long-standing is actually discriminatory and arbitrary.[96] Member States, under whose jurisdiction a particular investor operates, are best placed to respond to specific fact-driven challenges.

Furthermore, faced with claims based on discriminatory measures, tribunals are often required to balance investors' interests against those of a host Member State. This calls for close analysis of various social, economic or political circumstances that have informed a host state's decision.[97] Member States, whose system and particularities in this context form the essence of a dispute, are in most cases the optimal respondents.

To avoid an overly broad discussion of the discrimination element of an FET standard, it is helpful to look at discriminatory or arbitrary treatment arising from tax measures, which frequently form a ground of investors' claims.[98] In the legal order of the EU Member States have retained competence to regulate taxation, as long as national rules are consistent with the Union's principles, such as the general prohibition of discrimination.[99] In this context Member States' tax administrators are the key actors. The degree of

96 Salacuse 2015, 261.

97 For example, in *LG&E Energy Corp., LG&E Capital Corp., and LG&E International, Inc* v. *Argentine Republic* (Decision on Liability, 3 October 2006) ICSID Case No. ARB/02/1, the tribunal had to weigh measures taken by Argentina in the midst of its economic and financial crisis with investor's interests. Similarly, in *Alex Genin and others* v. *Republic of Estonia* (Award, 25 June 2001) ICSID Case No. ARB/99/2, the tribunal considered whether political and economic transition occurring in Estonia at the time justified heightened scrutiny of the banking sector.

98 Some investment protection treaties expressly exclude tax administration from the coverage of the FET obligation. Examples of cases where tribunals found such a limitation of the FET standard include *Marvin Roy Feldman Karpa* v. *United Mexican States* (Award, 16 December 2002) ICSID Case No. ARB(AF)/99/1, para 109; *EnCana Corp* v. *Republic of Ecuador* (Award, 3 February 2006) London Court of International Arbitration (LCIA) Case No. UN3481, para 140. However, in *Occidental Exploration* v. *Ecuador Occidental Exploration and Production Company* v. *The Republic of Ecuador* (Award, July 1, 2004) LCIA Case No. UN3467, paras 185–187, the tribunal determined that the denial of VAT rebate was the result of a failure to provide predictable environment to the investor and thus constituted a violation of FET obligation.

99 Case C311/97 *Royal Bank of Scotland plc* v. *Greece* [1999] ECR I2651.

deference to be afforded to tax administrators, who interact directly with investors and take measures as well as provide interpretative guidance, is often at the centre of discrimination challenges. A host state is entitled to apply various measures in relation to an investor, such as source withholding or punishment for failure to comply.[100] As Tietje and Kampermann note, taxation, by its very nature, is predestined to offer alternative, more subtle measures to squeeze foreign investors out of the country.[101] Measures such as collection and asset freezing are of utmost importance to investors whose projects depend on cash flows.[102] Accordingly, actions or omissions of a host Member State's tax administrators may be the proximate cause of alleged harm.

7.3.4 *Legitimate Expectations*

Member States are also the optimal respondents in disputes over frustration of investors' legitimate expectations. Member States deal directly with investors for various administrative purposes related to their projects' realization and are thus the key providers of representations which form legitimate expectations. The EU rarely plays a central role in this regard because specific investment projects are subject to the host Member State's domestic regime.

A claim that a host state frustrated an investor's legitimate expectations is based on a duty of consistency. An investor has a right to expect that representations made to it by the state and on which it relied in making its business decisions are not unreasonably frustrated. Claims of inconsistency on behalf of a state have arisen in a variety of forms and factual circumstances. One common feature is often a claim by an investor that it had received some form of official approval on which an investor was entitled to rely.[103] An essential aspect in this context is the specificity of a representation – an investor has to show that it received specific formal assurances that visibly display an official

100 The arbitration in the Yukos case provides an example of a tribunal ruling that reporting requirement was enforced too rigidly, *Yukos Universal Limited (Isle of Man)* v. *The Russian Federation* (Final Award, 18 July 2014) UNCITRAL, PCA Case No. AA 227.

101 Christian Tietje and Karoline Kampermann, 'Taxation and Investment: Constitutional Law Limitations on Tax Legislation in Context', in Stephan W Schill (ed), *International Investment Law and Comparative Public Law* (Oxford University Press 2010), 581.

102 An asset freeze was in dispute under Yukos arbitration, because an investor claimed the measure was not necessary since the company had available liquid assets sufficient to cover liability, *Yukos Universal Limited (Isle of Man)* v. *The Russian Federation*, Final Award.

103 Danielle Morris, 'The Regulatory State and the Duty of Consistency', in Shahleza Lalani and Rodrigo Polanco Lazo (eds), *The Role of the State in Investor-State Arbitration* (Brill Nijhoff 2015), 49.

character.[104] Accordingly, the conduct of Member States' officials who directly interact with investors often constitutes a proximate cause of injury stemming from inconsistent executive action. For example, in *Metalclad* v. *Mexico*, a claim arose in relation to representations by federal government officials who assured the investor that it could proceed with the construction and operation of a landfill.[105] In *Tecmed* v. *Mexico*, in dispute was the replacement of an unlimited licence with that of limited duration by state officials.[106]

Sudden and inconsistent departures from established administrative practice by tax administrators provide another example of sources of misrepresentation.[107] A frequent reason for a change of treatment by state authorities is a change in government.[108] A change in policy also often results in amendments to tax regimes.[109] Moreover, not only the change in policy itself but also the treatment of an investor during the process of regulatory change may form the basis of an investor's claim.[110] For example, in *Plama Consortium* v. *Bulgaria* the claimant argued that a sudden change in Bulgarian environmental regulation resulted in an unexpected financial burden being placed on the company.[111] Member States, who legislate and apply tax regimes, are the optimal respondents in claims over alleged injury through tax measures.

Another category of complaints where Member States' conduct may constitute a proximate cause of injury to investors is the frustration of a host state's contractual obligations. Though there is debate in the literature as to the extent to which FET protection extends to observance of obligations arising from contract,[112] some authors suggest that breaches of contract by state authorities in their official capacity can amount to frustration of legitimate

104 Jan Paulsson and Zachary Douglas, 'Arbitrating Foreign Investment Disputes: Procedural and Substantive Legal Aspects', in Norbert Horn (ed), *Indirect Expropriation in Investment Treaty Arbitration* (Kluwer Law International 2004), 157.

105 *Metalclad* v. *Mexico*, Award.

106 *Tecmed* v. *Mexico*.

107 Paul B Stephan, 'Comparative Taxation Procedure and Tax Enforcement', in Stephan W. Schill (ed), *International Investment Law and Comparative Public Law* (Oxford University Press 2010), 603.

108 NAFTA case *International Thunderbird Gaming Corporation* v. *Mexico* (Award, 26 January 2006) IIC 136 provides an example. Investor's gaming facilities, which were operated with a permission of a preceding government, were declared illegal after a new government took over the power.

109 Bonnitcha, Lauge and Waibel (n 389). Ch. 9.

110 *Franck Charles Arif* v. *Republic of Moldova* (Award, 8 April 2013) ICSID Case No. ARB/11/23, para 555.

111 *Plama Consortium* v. *Bulgaria*, Award, para 198.

112 Dolzer and Schreuer 2008, 140.

expectations.[113] Key actors in these disputes are once again authorities of host Member States who are involved in contractual relations with investors. Case law analysis reveals a wide variety of state officials whose actions have formed a basis of investors' claims of a breach of contractual obligations, for example local city councils,[114] ministers[115] and quasi-governmental regulatory bodies.[116] Inconsistency of action between two arms of the same government in relation to contractual obligations is yet another ground for claims.[117] With respect to case law involving European countries, *Plama Consortium* v. *Bulgaria* concerned *inter alia* an alleged breach of a debt-settlement agreement by a state-owned bank.[118] Breach of a contractual agreement entered into by the claimant and a state-owned company Latvenergo in relation to the formula for the calculation of an electric power purchase price was at issue in *Nykomb* v. *Latvia*.[119] *Electrabel* v. *Hungary* concerned the termination of a power purchase agreement by Hungary.[120]

Closely related to the frustration of legitimate expectations is a claim that host states fail to provide a transparent environment for the realization of investment projects. Transparency means that the legal framework for the investor's operations is readily apparent and that any decision affecting the

113 Salacuse 2015, 259. A restrictive approach that only *puissance publique*, that is activity beyond that of an ordinary contracting party, can amount to frustration of legitimate expectations was affirmed by the tribunal in *Impregilo S.p.A.* v. *Islamic Republic of Pakistan* (Decision on Jurisdiction, 22 April 2005) ICSID Case No. ARB/03/3, paras 266–270. Position that only breaches in sovereign capacity can amount to frustration of legitimate expectations was also taken by tribunal in *Consortium RFCC* v. *Royaume du Maroc* (Award, 22 December 2003) ICSID Case No. ARB/00/6, paras 33–34. Dolzer and Schreuer suggest that it is yet too early to determine whether a restrictive or broader approach will prevail; see Dolzer and Schreuer 2008, 142. They also note that even if the underlying relationship is clearly commercial, the motives of a government for a certain act may still be governmental.

114 For example, in *Waste Management* v. *Mexico* at dispute was a failure by the City of Acapulco to make payments under the concession agreement.

115 Such was a case in *Eureko BV* v. *Poland* (Partial Award, 19 August 2005) IIC 98, where the investor claimed that the Minister of Treasury of Poland wilfully refused to sell shares to an investor it had previously agreed.

116 *CME Czech Republic BV* v. *Czech Republic* (Final Award, 14 March 2003) IIC 62 concerned interference with contractual obligations by the Czech Media Council, which reversed its previous position on the legal situation of an investor as a licence holder.

117 In *MTD Equity Sdn. Bhd. and MTD Chile S.A.* v. *Republic of Chile* (Award, 25 May 2004) ICSID Case No. ARB/01/7, investor signed an investment contract with Chile's Foreign Investment Commission. However, the project was disrupted once zoning authorities discovered that it was in breach of zoning requirements.

118 The claimant alleged that various breaches of a Debt Settlement Agreement which it was obliged to enter due to accrual of significant debts owed to a state-owned bank; for more details see *Plama Consortium* v. *Bulgaria*, Award, Sect C.5.

119 *Nykomb* v. *Latvia*, Award, para 4.2.

120 *Electrabel* v. *Hungary*, Award, para 51.

investor can be traced to that legal framework.[121] Transparency claims target the host state's legal framework and its implementation practices. The legal framework consists first and foremost of assurances by national authorities of the Member States, rather than EU actors. For example, in *Occidental* v. *Ecuador*, an investor's claim was directed at inconsistent practice of the host state's tax administrators in reimbursing VAT.[122] The Tribunal in *CMS Gas Transmission Company* v. *Argentina* dealt with adoption of emergency laws and regulations that caused loss to the investor.[123] In *Bayindir* v. *Pakistan* the tribunal stated that an obligation to maintain a stable framework applies not only to the regulatory framework as such but also to the goal of the relevant policies and to administrative practices.[124] Executive actions that affect investors are primarily acts of Member States and not of general Union legislation.[125]

To conclude, the nature of challenges of denial or maladministration of justice and due process, discriminatory measures and failure to fulfil legitimate expectations explain why Member States are the optimal respondents in FET disputes. It is the acts and measures of their officials and entities that may be and often are the proximate cause of FET violations. It is of course acknowledged that there can be instances when acts of EU organs are the source of investment claims, for example if the ECJ were to annul a patent. However, in most cases the Union does not hold sufficient power to ensure the application of an FET standard in the Member States' jurisdiction since state sovereignty prevents them from intruding into national judicial and administrative systems.

7.3.5 *Expropriation*

The prohibition of unlawful expropriation is another major element of investment protection. New-generation FTAs of the EU are no exception.[126] The

121 Dolzer and Schreuer 2008, 133.

122 *Occidental Exploration* v. *Ecuador Occidental Exploration and Production Company* v. *The Republic of Ecuador*, (Award, 1 July 2004) LCIA Case No. UN3467.

123 *CMS Gas Transmission Company* v. *The Republic of Argentina* (Award, 12 May 2005) ICSID Case No. ARB/01/8.

124 *Bayindir Insaat Turizm Ticaret Ve Sanayi A.S.* v. *Islamic Republic of Pakistan* (Decision on jurisdiction, 14 November 2005) ICSID Case No. ARB/03/29, para 240.

125 For example, in *Plama Consortium* v. *Bulgaria*, the claimant alleged that Bulgaria failed to create stable, equitable, favourable and transparent conditions for making the investment (Award, para 73) by a number of actions and omissions of the government, the national legislative and judicial authorities and other public authorities and agencies deliberately creating numerous, grave problems for NovaPlama and/or refused or unreasonably delayed the adoption of adequate corrective measures (Award, para 73).

126 For example, protection against unlawful expropriation is provided in CETA Art 8.12.

provisions cover protection against both direct and indirect expropriation.[127] Member States are the optimal respondents in challenges to both types of expropriation.

A typical form of direct expropriation is acquisition by the state of property for public infrastructure or to pursue national economic policies.[128] Member States are the proper respondents in disputes alleging unlawful direct expropriation because it is Member States that must ensure the legality of direct takings by, first and foremost, paying adequate compensation to an investor.[129] The EU's influence in this respect is limited. Article 345 TFEU states that the Treaties shall in no way prejudice Member States' rules governing the system of property ownership. It is suggested by some that usually investment treaties do not prohibit host states from expropriating assets of foreign investors but rather place certain conditions upon the exercise of a state's right to expropriate.[130] Dimopoulos points to the limits of Article 354 TFEU, suggesting that it preserves the power of the Member States to decide whether and when expropriation occurs, not the conditions under which it takes place.[131] Nevertheless, in most cases Member States not only decide on the system of property but also place conditions on its use because property falls within domestic jurisdiction.

The essence of indirect expropriation disputes is that not all host state's measures which harm investments are expropriatory and carry with them an obligation to compensate.[132] General regulatory measures[133] adopted in the

127 CETA Annex 8-A defines direct and indirect expropriation.

128 An example of direct expropriation is a case *Marvin Roy Feldman Karpa* v. *United Mexican States* (Award, 16 December 2002), ICSID Case No. ARB(AF)/99/1 para 100, where the tribunal noted: 'Recognizing direct expropriation is easy: Governmental authorities take over a mine or factory, depriving the investor of all meaningful benefits of ownership and control'.

129 Even though in the pre-EU membership era, a case against Latvia provides an example. Latvia was brought before an investment tribunal by a Swedish investor who claimed that believing he had an agreement with appropriate Latvian authorities, he purchased and renovated a ship to be used as a floating trade centre. Latvian authorities, without providing a notice to the owner, removed the ship from the port and sold it in auction. Tribunal ruled that such actions by the Latvian authorities were direct expropriation, *Swembalt AB, Sweden* v. *The Republic of Latvia*, (Award, 23 October 2000) UNCITRAL, para 38.

130 Vidal Puig, 'Scope of the New Exclusive Competence of the European Union with Regard to Foreign Direct Investment' (2013) 40 LIEI 133, 146.

131 Angelos Dimopoulos, 'The Common Commercial Policy after Lisbon: Establishing Parallelism between Internal and External Economic Relations' (2008) 4 CYELP 101, 116. Similarly, Eeckhout notes that the ECJ tends to interpret the scope of Art 345 TFEU. Restrictively; see Piet Eeckhout, *EU External Relations Law* (2nd edn, Oxford University Press 2011), 65.

132 Dolzer and Schreuer 2008, 109.

133 Some tribunals have used a term 'police powers' which is common in the United States, for example *Tecmed* v. *Mexico*, Award, para 119.

exercise of functions that are generally considered to be among the government's powers to regulate public welfare do not lead to an obligation to compensate.[134] The complexity of expropriation disputes in most cases lies in the difficulty of drawing a line between non-compensable public policy regulations and expropriation which calls for compensation.[135] The host states' regulatory powers are thus at the heart of expropriation disputes. Tribunals are required to balance a state's regulatory actions and investors' interests; therefore, the manner of a host state's exercise of its sovereign powers is at the centre of such disputes.

While it is not disputed that the EU's conduct may lead to indirect expropriation claims, for example, through adoption of an unlawful state aid decision, it is nevertheless Member States who are the optimal respondents in virtually all indirect expropriation cases.[136] Challenges alleging unlawful indirect expropriation in most cases concern executive action of the host Member State.

It is impossible to provide a full typology of Member States' regulatory measures capable of leading to indirect expropriation. As was noted by the Tribunal in *Feldman* v. *Mexico*, the way in which governmental authorities may force a company out of business, or significantly reduce the economic benefits of its business, are many.[137] Some first-generation bilateral investment treaties (BIT) have enumerated certain types of measure that can be expropriatory, including taxation, the freezing or blocking of assets or funds,

[134] For example, such approach was taken by tribunals in *Telenor Mobile Communications A. S.* v. *The Republic of Hungary*, (Award, 13 September 2006) ICSID Case No. ARB/04/15, para 78. In *Saluka Investments B.V.* v. *The Czech Republic* (Partial Award, 17 March 2006), paras 254–255, the tribunal stated that deprivation can be justified if it results from the exercise of regulatory actions aimed at the maintenance of public order. For a different approach, see *Compañía del Desarrollo de Santa Elena, S.A.* v. *Republic of Costa Rica* (Award, 17 February 2000) ICSID Case No. ARB/96/1, para 72.

[135] Andrew Newcombe and Lluís Paradell, *Law and Practice of Investment Treaties. Standards of Treatment* (Kluwer Law International 2009), 30; Tarcisio Gazzini, 'States and Foreign Investment: A Law of the Treaties Perspective', in Lalani Shahleza and Rodrigo Polanco Lazo (eds), *The Role of the State in Investor-State Arbitration* (Brill Nijhoff 2015), 29.

[136] For example, claims alleging expropriation were initiated against Lithuania by OAO Gazprom which claimed that implementation of the ownership unbundling model in the energy sector had an effect of expropriation. Lithuania chose complete ownership unbundling provided as an alternative in the EU Third Energy Package, i.e. Directive 2009/72/EC concerning common rules for the internal market in electricity and repealing Directive 2003/54/EC and Directive 2009/73/EC concerning common rules for the internal market in natural gas and repealing Directive 2003/55/EC.

[137] *Feldman Karpa* v. *United Mexican States* (Award, 16 December 2002) ICSID Case No. ARB(AF)/99/1, para 103.

compulsory sales and deprivation of management.[138] Among the measures which could lead to expropriation claims, Christie lists the blocking of factory entrances on the pretext of maintaining public order, the setting of wages for local labour at prohibitively high rates, the denial of visas to foreign technical personnel, interference with occupation of real property and appointment of conservators, managers or inspectors who might interfere with the free use of premises and facilities.[139] Effectively any area of a host state's regulatory action could give rise to expropriation claims.[140] Salacuse groups case law into broad categories and suggests the following list of regulatory areas that most commonly form the subject of expropriatory disputes: interference with contract rights, revocation or denial of government permits or licences, disproportionate tax increases and interference with management of an investment.[141] Actions or omissions concerning these measures involve direct interaction between the host state and investors. Accordingly, Member States are the primary actors in this regard.

In relation to interference with contractual rights, for example, contractual obligations in question are in most cases those assumed by Member States, not the EU. Often investment decisions are protected by specific contractual obligations assumed by the host state, which cover matters such as taxation, customs regulation, right and duty to sell at a certain price to the host state or

138 Kenneth J Vandevelde, *United States Investment Treaties: Policy and Practice* (Kluwer Law and Taxation Publishers 1992), 117–138. For example, Art 5 of the Protocol of the Congo, Democratic Republic Of (Kinshasa) BIT (1984) provides that expropriation '[…] may include the levying of taxes equivalent to indirect expropriation, the compulsory sale of all or part of an investment, or the impairment or deprivation of the management, control, or economic value of an investment'.

139 George C Christie, 'What Constitutes a Taking of Property under International Law' (1962) 38 BYIL 307.

140 To illustrate the diversity of measures addressed in expropriation cases, see the following examples: in *Biloune and Marine Drive Complex Ltd.* v. *Ghana Investments Centre and the Government of Ghana* (Award on Jurisdiction and Liability, 27 October 1989) UNCITRAL. At dispute was the issuance of a stop work order by the local government authorities as well as arrest and expulsion of investor. To provide another example, *S.A.R.L. Benvenuti & Bonfant* v. *People's Republic of the Congo* (Award, 8 August 1980) ICSID Case No. ARB/77/2 concerned *inter alia* interference with the marketing of investor's products by fixing sales prices dissolving a marketing company, constituting criminal proceedings against the investor who then left the country.

141 Salacuse 2015, 328. Art 3 of the 1967 OECD Draft Convention on the Protection of Foreign Property describes non-compensable measures as 'normal and lawful regulatory measures short of direct taking of property rights, but rather, to misuse of otherwise lawful regulation to deprive an owner of the substance of his rights'. Art 4(b) then lists possible misuses of lawful regulation: excessive or arbitrary taxation, prohibition of dividend distribution complied with compulsory loans, imposition of administrators, prohibition of dismissal of staff, refusal of access to raw materials or of essential export or import licences.

pricing questions.[142] Contractual rights form part of the term 'investment' under most investment protection treaties.[143] New-generation FTAs also provide protection of contractual rights.[144]

A related ground for indirect expropriation challenges is that of decisions to revoke licences and permits issued by the host state.[145] Investment projects often depend on various licences, and therefore revocation of a licence or modification of its terms may harm investors' projects. In the EU legal order regulatory licences, permits and authorizations are issued mainly by Member States. For example, in the energy sector national governments issue permits for various activities, such as the extraction of natural resources, electricity and gas distribution and supply, as well as construction of wind turbines. Member States set the conditions and procedure for the issuance of these authorizations. To give an example, the EU may announce financial bids, such as NER 300 for carbon capture and storage and other similar projects, but even in such cases the issuers of licences for CO_2 storage are the Member States.[146] Similarly, Member States are the issuers of authorizations in the telecommunications and other sectors.[147]

142 Dolzer and Schreuer 2008, 116.

143 For example, ECT Art 1(6)(f) provides that the term 'investment' includes 'any right conferred by law or contract or by virtue of any licences and permits granted pursuant to law to undertake any Economic Activity in the Energy Sector'. Similarly, NAFTA Art 1139(h) states that 'investments' inter alia cover interests arising from the commitment of capital or other resources in the territory of a party to economic activity in such territory, such as under (i) contracts involving the presence of an investor's property in the territory of the party, including turnkey or construction contracts, or concessions or (ii) contracts where remuneration depends substantially on the production, revenues or profits of an enterprise.

144 CETA Art 8.1 defines investment, *inter alia*, as (f) an interest arising from (i) a concession conferred pursuant to domestic law or under a contract, including to search for, cultivate, extract or exploit natural resources (ii) a turnkey, construction, production or revenue-sharing contract or (iii) other similar contracts.

145 For example, *Antoine Goetz et consorts* v. *République du Burundi* (Award, 2 September 1998) ICSID Case No. ARB/95/3 and *Middle East Cement Shipping and Handling Co. S.A.* v. *Arab Republic of Egypt* (Award, 12 April 2002) ICSID Case No. ARB/99/6) both concerned claims that a host governments' revocation of investors' free-zone status (and benefits) had expropriatory effects. Another landmark case is *Tecmed* v. *Mexico*, which concerned a refusal of the host government to renew authorization to operate a hazardous waste landfill. The tribunal found a refusal to renew the authorization by the host state's agency to amount to expropriation, para 151. An example of a refusal to grant licence by a local municipality authority is provided in *Metalclad* v. *Mexico* arbitration where the tribunal found such refusal to show elements of indirect expropriation.

146 For more on NER 300 see here: https://ec.europa.eu/clima/policies/lowcarbon/ner300_en (last visited 16 September 2018).

147 General guidance on authorizations is provided in the Directive 2002/20/EC of the European Parliament and of the Council of 7 March 2002 on the authorization of electronic

As mentioned earlier, another regulatory area which has caused a number of investors to file complaints against host governments is disproportionate taxation measures. Taxation in general is a form of appropriation which is non-compensable.[148] At the same time excessive taxation has proved to be one of the most intensive intrusions into investors' property as it is a means of rendering the economic value of an investment worthless.[149] At the centre of disputes concerning disproportionate taxation is the difficult task of drawing a line between a legitimate state regulatory power to tax and taxation which shows elements of expropriation. In *Link Trading* v. *Moldova* the tribunal considered tax measures to be expropriatory when they amounted to an 'abusive taking'.[150] The famous *Yukos* v. *Russia* case demonstrated the magnitude of claims arising out of state-taxing powers.[151] As has been mentioned in relation to the discussion of an FET standard, taxation is regulated primarily by Member States' rules and managed by its tax administrators, whereas EU powers in this area are limited.

To conclude, analysis of measures which have given rise to claims for unlawful expropriation reveals that the acts of Member States' officials and entities are of central importance. Accordingly, in their claims for compensation, investors focus on Member States' measures because they are the proximate cause of alleged injury.

7.3.6 *Umbrella Clauses*

Finally, this section will briefly explain why Member States are also the optimal respondents in claims of violation of umbrella clauses. For the

communications networks and services as amended by Directive 2009/140/EC. The national rules in relation to the enforcement mechanisms for authorization holders and procedures aimed at addressing breaches of an authorized operator follow the general line of the director, but generally Member States follow their own framework in this context; see Report for the European Commission 'MSS Authorisation Regimes, Authorisations and Enforcement in the EU Member States', available at: https://ec.europa.eu/digital-single-market/en/news/mss-authorisation-regimes-authorisations-and-enforcement-eu-member-states-call-tenders-20130013, 3, (last visited 1 August 2018).

148 Newcombe notes that taxes of 50 per cent or 60 per cent are common in some countries and international authorities are clear that a significant tax burden may be imposed on an investment, Andrew Newcombe, 'The Boundaries of Regulatory Expropriation in International Law' (2005) 20 ICSID Review-FILJ 36.

149 Tietje and Kampermann 2010, 590.

150 *Link Trading Joint Stock Co* v. *Moldova* (Award, 18 April 2002) UNCITRAL, paras 64–91. For analysis of the concept of 'abusive' fiscal measures, see also *Burlington Resources Inc.* v. *Republic of Ecuador* (Decision on Liability, 14 December 2012) ICSID Case No. ARB/08/5, para 394.

151 *Yukos Universal Limited (Isle of Man)* v. *The Russian Federation*.

development of investment projects host states often enter into various commitments based on which an investor makes his business decisions. Such commitments are embodied in a variety of legal instruments, for example bilateral agreements such as investment accords, development contracts, public service concessions and tax stabilization agreements, or multilateral acts such as foreign investment legislation, licences and regulatory permission.[152] Taking into consideration the importance of such undertakings to foreign investors in the development of their projects, around 45 per cent of investment agreements include the so-called umbrella clauses, which provide protection from breach by the host state of its commitments.[153]

Depending on the precise formulation in a given treaty, the effect of umbrella clauses is that host states become obliged under international law to respect state concession contracts to operate public services, government permits to operate landfills, tax exemptions promised in foreign investment codes and even representations made by ministers to investors during investment promotion 'road shows'.[154] Therefore, umbrella clauses impose on a host state a direct obligation under international law to honour obligations into which they have entered with the investors.[155]

One effect of umbrella clauses is that they introduce domestic law, which governs the nature and scope of a commitment in question, directly into investment arbitration proceedings. It should be noted here that umbrella clauses do not transform a contractual obligation governed by domestic law into an obligation governed by international law. The source, nature and scope of the obligation remain to be governed by the law under which it was originally created, that is, in most cases, the law of host states.[156] This point has been underlined by the *SGS* v. *Philippines* Tribunal, which stated that the clause addresses not the scope of the commitment entered into with regard to specific investments but the performance of these obligations, once they are ascertained.[157]

The distinction is important for the present discussion. It suggests that if a tribunal is asked to determine the (non)performance of a Member State

152 Salacuse 2015, 299.
153 Bonnitcha, Lauge and Waibel 2017, 94, table 4.2.
154 Salacuse 2015, 306.
155 James Crawford, 'Treaty and Contract in Investment Arbitration' (2008) 24 Arbitration International 3, 351.
156 Salacuse 2015, 303.
157 *SGS* v. *Philippines* (Decision, 29 January 2004) ICSID Case No. ARB/02/6, para 126. In para 128 of the Decision, the tribunal reasserted that it makes a breach of the BIT for the host state to fail to observe binding commitments, including contractual commitments, which it has assumed with regard to specific investments.

commitment, it will have to take into consideration that Member State's national law which governs the obligation in question. Member States are thus the optimal respondents in cases involving umbrella clauses because they are best placed to redress violation of commitments under such clauses.

In conclusion, analysis of the content of investment obligations suggests that Member States are (in most cases) central and necessary parties to investment disputes. The body of case law on FET, expropriation and umbrella clauses reveals that the majority of measures and actions challenged in investment disputes would, if applied by analogy, be those of the Member States, not the EU. Accordingly, the nature of investment protection obligations organically places Member States as optimal respondents in investment disputes. EU law, even if it is a source of an unlawful Member State measure, is in most cases irrelevant because tribunals focus on proximate cause of harm.

7.4 CONCLUSION

The purpose of this chapter was to explain the correlation between the optimal respondents and the nature of the international economic regime in question. The characteristics of the treaty regime in question determine whether the EU or its Member States are best placed to ensure compliance.

It was suggested that the central role of the EU in WTO disputes stems from the rules-based character of the WTO regime, the purpose of which is to protect rules of general application. The EU holds exclusive competence in trade and is thus best placed to ensure regulatory compliance. Its participation in the WTO through mixed treaty-making allows it to assume responsibility on behalf of its Member States without creating risks to complainants. The interdependency between the EU and its Member States under mixed treaties provides safeguards for compliance which explains the deference afforded by the DSB to the EU's quest to assume international responsibility.

Member States, by contrast, are the optimal respondents in investment disputes. Member States and investors enter into direct bilateral relations for the development of investment projects. Investors depend on various measures of host states, such as the issuance of licences and contracts, and a transparent and just judicial and administrative system. The executive machinery of the host Member State interacts with investors who rely on investment protection standards to conduct their business. Violations of investment standards by host Member States are in most cases the proximate cause of injury, proof of which prompts an award of compensation.

The following chapter will examine the special cases in WTO dispute settlement where the DSB deems it necessary to direct their recommendations not only to the EU but also to Member States. The aim of Chapter 8 is to explain why in some cases the DSB deviates from the general pattern in its choice of the EU as the optimal respondent discussed earlier and instead calls for multiple respondents. Findings addressed in Chapter 8 further support functional international responsibility.

8

Multiple Respondents in WTO Dispute Settlement

8.1 INTRODUCTION

Chapter 7 explained patterns in the selection of optimal respondents in trade and investment disputes. It was suggested that the central role of the European Union (EU) in the World Trade Organization (WTO) dispute-settlement stems from its exclusive competence in trade, which allows it to ensure that its legal framework complies with the WTO regime. The interdependency of the EU and its Member States, woven into their joint participation in mixed treaties, allows panels to shift shared responsibility to the EU without engaging in attribution of conduct. The previous chapter also examined the opposite trend in the investment regime, where the optimal respondents are Member States. It was argued that Member States are the primary respondents in investment disputes because their measures in most cases constitute the proximate cause of (alleged) injury to investors. Whether the EU or its Member States are the optimal respondents thus depends heavily on the nature of a given treaty regime.

Chapter 7 also made a brief remark that in some disputes under the WTO dispute-settlement system the Dispute Settlement Body (DSB) addresses its recommendations not only to the EU but also to some of its Member States. The aim of this chapter is to examine these specific WTO cases of multiple respondents. The following sections are based on the results of an extensive review of WTO cases which involve the EU. Analysis of practice reveals a correlation between, on the one hand, the scope of the claim and remedy in a given dispute and, on the other, the distribution of shared responsibility between the EU and its Member States.

The findings of this analysis are novel and, to the best of my knowledge, have not been identified in the literature. They support the thesis of this book that responsibility in the international economic context is distributed on a remedial basis rather than through attribution of conduct or breach. Whether the EU alone or also its Member States will be the addressees of panels' recommendations depends on whether Member States' actions are necessary for compliance purposes. To put it simply, the argument is that the scope of the claim defines the remedy which, in turn, points either to the EU or (also) to its Member States. The findings of the present discussion add an additional layer to the conclusions assessed in Chapter 7 by explaining particular cases where the general pattern of sole EU responsibility is modified by Member States' participation in dispute settlement.

As has already been noted in the introduction to this book, identifying rationales that underlie the determination of international responsibility of the EU and its Member States in WTO law is complex and time-consuming. The findings presented herein are counterintuitive in that the DSB does not distribute shared responsibility on a predetermined basis stemming from the institutional arrangement between the EU and its Member States. Rather, distribution varies on a case-by-case basis, depending on what is necessary to achieve a positive solution to the dispute. Accordingly, it is difficult to pinpoint the factors that are decisive in the DSB's decision on the proper respondent(s). These novel patterns were identified by putting together multiple pieces of the DSB's reasoning scattered throughout the reports which were not expressed directly in relation to identification of respondent.

One remark is timely. As was suggested in Chapter 7, the EU is the optimal respondent in WTO disputes because in most cases it takes it upon itself to ensure compliance with the panels' reports. A question may arise as to how panels differentiate between situations where the EU is allowed to assume responsibility on behalf of its Member States (Chapter 7) and special cases examined in this chapter where the panels deem it necessary also to address their recommendations to the Member States.

It seems that there is no particular rationale for the different treatment of the two situations and the approach is somewhat random. Panels do tend to address the question of multiple respondents in those disputes where complainants insist that the DSB determine whether Member States' conduct is to be also included in judicial scrutiny. However, even in such cases the DSB may decide to shift responsibility to the EU if the EU gives assurance that it will ensure compliance on behalf of its Member States, as was suggested in Chapter 6. Marín Durán notes that joint EU-Member State membership of the WTO is becoming much more visible in dispute-settlement practice post-Lisbon Treaty as complaints addressed jointly to the EU and one or more of its Member States are no longer the exception but almost as common as complaints directed against the EU alone.[1] This observation supports the finding

[1] Gracia Marín Durán, 'The EU and Its Member States in WTO Dispute Settlement: A "Competence Model," or a Case Apart, for Managing International Responsibility?', in

presented in this book that distribution of shared responsibility does not follow the internal division of competences because the Lisbon Treaty expanded rather than reduced the scope of the EU's competences in the area of common commercial policy.

The following analysis will start by considering the correlation of the scope of claims and remedies under the WTO system (Section 8.2). It will then identify the difference between two types of claims – claims 'as such' and claims 'as applied' (Section 8.3). Finally, Section 8.4 will explain how that correlation plays out in the DSB's identification of multiple respondents.

8.2 CORRELATION OF CLAIMS AND REMEDIES

Article 6.2 of the Dispute Settlement Understanding (DSU) provides in relevant part that '*[t]he request for the establishment of a panel shall … identify the specific measures at issue and provide a brief summary of the legal basis of the complaint sufficient to present the problem clearly*'. The 'measure at issue' stated in the request for establishment of a panel plays a pivotal role in WTO dispute-settlement proceedings because it constitutes the matter referred to the DSB which forms part of a panel's terms of reference under Article 7.1 of the DSU. Terms of reference define the scope of a dispute.[2]

Importantly, it is the 'measure at issue' identified in the request for the establishment of a panel, and consequently stated in the terms of reference, that must be brought into conformity in case it is found to be in violation of WTO Agreements. This flows from Article 19.1 of the DSU which states that if the Appellate Body concludes that a measure is inconsistent with a covered agreement, that measure must be brought into conformity with that agreement. Thus, there is an interlinkage between the reference to the term 'measure' in Article 19.1 of the DSU and the term 'measure at issue' in Article 6.2 of the DSU.[3] In other words the DSU establishes a direct link between the challenged measure and the remedy – in case of a violation of a WTO obligation, a measure which will have to be brought into consistency will be the same measure which the complainant challenged. This is different from investment arbitration where, as was argued in Chapter 7, tribunals focus on the existence of breach, whereas the scope and roots of a challenged

Marise Cremona, Anne Thies and Ramses A Wessel (eds), *The EU and International Dispute Settlement* (Hart Publishing 2016), 257.

[2] *US – Countervailing Duties on Certain Corrosion-Resistant Carbon Steel Flat Products from Germany*, WT/DS213, ABR adopted 28 November 2002, para 126.

[3] *EC – Selected Customs Matters*, PR, para 7.14.

measure are largely irrelevant because compensation is calculated in accordance to the harm.

A 'measure' should not, however, be understood as a specific law or regulation, that is, a Member State is free to implement the DSB recommendations through *legal instruments* different from those in dispute, as long as they bring the challenged *measure* into conformity with its WTO obligations.[4] This corresponds to the central goal of the WTO remedial system, which is to restore the balance of concessions.

If the measure identified in the request for the establishment of a panel is defined broadly, the remedy will have a corresponding scope. In some cases the system can even encourage the complaining party to draft their requests broadly. For example, in *EC – Geographical Indications* the Panel refused to declare a violation of an obligation to accord a certain treatment under Article 22.2 Agreement on Trade-Related Aspects of Intellectual Property Rights (TRIPS)[5] based on the regulation identified in the request, because the obligation could have been implemented by other legal instruments which were not identified in the request.[6] It remains unclear whether the result would have been more favourable to the complainant had it attacked the legal regime of protection of geographical indications as a whole. Similarly, in *EC – Selected Customs Matters* the Panel also noted that while there is nothing in the DSU that would prevent a complaining party from challenging a responding member's system as a whole,[7] the complainant was precluded from so challenging the EC customs administration system in this dispute because the complainant's request was restricted to specific areas of customs administration.[8]

As to how broadly the 'measure at issue' may be defined by the complainant, the DSB sets no limit but requires that the request be not vague. In the *EC – Bananas III* dispute the Panel rejected the claim against the EU's banana import 'regime', stating that the request was too vague and did not identify specific measures.[9] According to the Panel, as long as the complaining party does not expand the scope of the dispute, it hesitates to impose too rigid a standard for the 'precise and exact' identification of a request.[10] In-depth

4 *EC – Geographical Indications*, PR, para 7.746.
5 An obligation to protect geographical indications.
6 *EC – Geographical Indications*, PR, para 7.747.
7 *EC – Selected Customs Matters*, PR, para 7.44.
8 *EC – Selected Customs Matters*, PR, para 7.46.
9 *EC – Bananas III*, PR, para 2.9.
10 *EC – Large Civil Aircraft*, PR, para 7.121, referring to *US – Subsidies on Upland Cotton*, WT/DS267.

analysis of the scope of claims falls outside the ambit of present discussion. Suffice it here to note that both specific regulatory measures and an overall regulatory system can be challenged under the WTO regime, provided that the claim is precise.

While the remedy cannot exceed the scope of the claim, panels are not obliged to make findings and recommendations with respect to all the measures and claims identified in a request for the establishment of a panel.[11] The rationale behind the discretion afforded to the DSB in this regard is based on the principle of judicial economy which has been widely endorsed under the WTO dispute-settlement system.[12] Thus, consistent with the analysis in Chapter 6, panels are vested with a *discretion* only to rule on those matters *necessary to secure a positive solution* to a dispute.[13]

The Appellate Body in the *Australia – Salmon* case clarified when judicial economy can be exercised so that it does not result in a partial resolution of the matter at issue. According to the Panel, the principle of judicial economy has to be applied keeping in mind the aim of the dispute-settlement system, which is to resolve the matter at issue and to secure a positive solution to the dispute.[14] The DSB must address those claims on which a finding is '*necessary in order to enable the DSB to make sufficiently precise rulings as to allow (for) prompt compliance by a Member with those recommendations and rulings in order to ensure effective resolution of disputes to the benefit of all members*'.[15]

The aforementioned analysis draws three conclusions regarding the scope of claims under the WTO system. First, measures identified in the complainant's request for the establishment of a panel correspond to the measures which will have to be brought into compliance if the claim is upheld. Thus, the scope of the claim determines the scope of the remedy. Second, a measure identified in the request can be defined broadly, provided it is not vague. Third, subject to the principle of judicial economy, the DSB enjoys discretion

[11] See, for example, *EEC – Quantitative Restrictions against Imports of Certain Products from Hong Kong*, BISD 30S/129, PR adopted 12 July 1983, para 33.

[12] *Canada – Wheat Export and Grains Imports*, ABR para 133; *EC – Biotech Products*, PR, para 6.81.

[13] *EC – Selected Customs Matters*, PR, para 7.42. DSU Art 3.4 provides that recommendations or rulings by the DSB must be aimed at achieving a satisfactory settlement of the 'matter'. The matter to be settled is the matter referred to the DSB for settlement; see *Guatemala – Anti-Dumping Investigation Regarding Portland Cement from Mexico*, WT/DS60, ABR adopted 2 November 1998, para 72.

[14] *Australia – Measures Affecting Importation of Salmon*, WT/DS18, ABR adopted 20 Oct 1998, para 223.

[15] *Australia – Salmon*, ABR, para 223.

only to rule on those matters which are necessary to secure a positive solution to the dispute.

It is suggested here that in the special cases (as opposed to the general pattern identified in Chapter 7 where the EU acts as the optimal respondent) when the DSB addresses the question whether the EU, its Member States or both should be respondents in a given dispute, it determines the proper respondent in light of the cumulative effect of the three rules identified earlier. Panels look at the scope of the request for the establishment of a panel and decide which measures must necessarily be brought into compliance to achieve the balance of concessions. In so doing the DSB determines whose actions are necessary to ensure compliance with WTO obligations. Thus, instead of engaging in a complex analysis of attribution of breach, panels either include or exclude Member States from the addressees of its recommendations according to whether their action(s) is necessary for remedial purposes. As will be seen from the following analysis, an actor whose conduct constitutes a breach of WTO rules and an actor whose conduct is necessary to eliminate the inconsistency are not always the same entity.

Before considering the rationales underlying the DSB's reasoning on the proper respondent, it is necessary to distinguish between two types of claim under the WTO dispute-settlement regime – claims 'as such' and claims 'as applied' – in order to provide a normative framework for the case-law analysis.

8.3 CLAIMS 'AS SUCH' AND CLAIMS 'AS APPLIED'

The nature and scope of claims under the WTO system play a crucial role in the determination of whether a ruling and recommendation will be addressed to the EU, its Member States or both. In this regard two main types of claims are decisive. Claims 'as such' challenge laws and other legal instruments on their face, whereas claims 'as applied' contest specific instances of application of such laws. As will be seen later, the typology is reflected in the case law.

It was argued in Chapter 7 that the EU is the optimal respondent under the WTO regime because WTO disputes often target rules of general application. Claims alleging inconsistency of rules of general application are claims 'as such'. The EU will typically be the optimal respondent in 'as such' disputes because the EU is the main source of trade rules of general application and is best placed to ensure they are brought into conformity with the WTO regime. Member States are drawn into the dispute when the claim (also) covers specific instances of application of such rules, that is, claims 'as applied'. The EU reflects the system of executive federalism where Member States implement Union law. Accordingly, if a claim covers instances of application of inconsistent laws, panels will often decide to address their rulings and recommendations to the Member States as well because those Member States' restorative action will be necessary for compliance purposes. Though, to the best of my knowledge, the typology has remained unnoticed by scholars exploring the distribution of shared responsibility between the EU and its Member States, it is suggested here that the nature of claims is decisive in this context.[16]

The DSB itself distinguishes between challenges to rules of general application and claims 'as applied'.[17] For example, the Panel in *EC – Commercial Vessels* noted that the disputed EC authorizations of subsidies apply to the aid scheme 'as such', not to the grant of aid in individual cases pursuant to the aid scheme.[18] Flett rightly notes that the choice between bringing claims 'as applied' and claims 'as such' may in some cases be dictated by WTO law itself.[19] For example, Article 17.4 of the Anti-Dumping Agreement states that a member may refer to the DSB a final action taken by the administrative authorities of the importing member to levy definitive anti-dumping duties or to accept price undertakings. Under EU law those types of decision are taken by the Member States and constitute application of anti-dumping rules. The case law shows that the United States has argued (albeit unsuccessfully) that 'final liquidations' in US anti-dumping law are not caught by Article 17.4, which would explain why they have not attacked identical Member States' measures when bringing cases against the EU.

It must be acknowledged, however, that the distinction between claims 'as such' and claims 'as applied' does not always square with the differentiation between EU and Member States' measures. For example, in relation to trade remedies, a measure adopted at EU level may relate to a specific WTO complaining member and/or to a specific product and impose a specific duty or other constraint. In such cases a challenge to an EU measure could be regarded as a claim 'as applied'. This is also true of EU treaty provisions.[20] Panels have in some cases also found the distinction between 'as such' and 'as

16 James Flett, 'The Practice of Shared Responsibility in Relation to The World Trade Organization and the European Union and Its Member States in the WTO', in André Nollkaemper and Ilias Plakokefalos (eds), *The Practice of Shared Responsibility in International Law* (Cambridge University Press 2016), notes the distinction.

17 For example, in *US – Tax Treatment for 'Foreign Sales Corporations'*, WT/DS108, PR adopted 8 October 1999, the panel noted that it examined the 'FSC scheme' as a whole, that is the existence and operation of the scheme itself rather than individual instances of application of the scheme by particular corporations; see Panel Report, paras 7.98–7.101. See also *Canada – Wheat Exports and Grain Imports*, PR, paras 22 and 27.

18 *EC – Commercial Vessels*, PR, para 7.51.

19 Flett 2016, 884.

20 Flett 2016, 894.

applied' claims to be irrelevant.[21] Though the typology is not straightforward, the distinction is nevertheless helpful for present purposes.

Importantly, with respect to 'as such' challenges, claimants are not required to adduce evidence of specific instances of application of a measure under dispute. The systematic application of a challenged rule or norm can be evidence of its general and prospective application, but such evidence is not required to substantiate an 'as such' challenge of a particular rule or norm.[22] For example, in *US – Tax Incentives for Large Civil Aircraft*, a claim brought by the EU against the United States concerning tax incentives for large civil aircraft, the Panel noted that the distinction between 'as such' claims and claims 'as applied' is important because the former is not directed against the application of tax measures at any given time or in any particular instance.[23] According to the Panel, although evidence of the actual use of certain fiscal incentives may support or confirm its findings, it is not required for 'as such' claims.[24] That a measure imposed inconsistently with GATT could nullify or impair benefits accruing under the GATT before they were actually applied to specific imports had also been recognized in *Japanese – Measures on Imports of Leather*.[25] Here the Panel stated that the existence of a quantitative restriction should be presumed to cause nullification or impairment not only because of any effect it had had on the volume of trade but also for other reasons.[26] The requirement to show evidence of application of a challenged measure in 'as applied' claims should not be confused with the presumption of nullification or impairment of benefits. While the latter concerns the admissibility of claims, the former is a rule of evidence.

21 For example, in *Thailand – Restrictions on Importation of and Internal Taxes on Cigarettes*, WT/DS10/R-37S/200, PR adopted 7 November 1990, para 19, the United States noted that implementation of the import licencing system set forth in Tobacco Act of 1996 acted as a *de facto* prohibition on imports from the SY and other Contracting Parties. See also *US – Measures Affecting the Production and Sale of Clove Cigarettes*, WT/DS406/R, PR adopted 2 September 2011, para 7.18, where the panel refused to afford any relevance to the 'as such' and 'as applied' distinction of a claim.

22 *EC and Certain Member States – IT Products*, PR, para 7.1168, ft 1538.

23 *US – Tax Incentives for Large Civil Aircraft*, WT/DS487/R, PR adopted 28 November 2016, para 7.154.

24 *US – Tax Incentives for Large Civil Aircraft*, PR, para 7.154. The United States agreed with such interpretation, by stating that where a Member asserts that a financial contribution exists in the abstract, there is no need to establish actual receipt of the subsidy under examination, US Second Written Submission, para 85.

25 *Japanese – Measures on Imports of Leather*, BISD 31S/113, PR adopted 15/16 May 1984.

26 *Japanese – Measures on Imports of Leather*, PR.

If both types of claims exist in WTO law, in what circumstances can a measure be challenged 'as such' and when is it necessary to show that it has been applied? Case-law analysis reveals that the DSB has developed a so-called 'mandatory/discretionary legislation' doctrine to determine whether a measure in question can be challenged 'as such'.[27] As formulated by the Panel in *US – Malt Beverages*, the test states that legislation mandatorily requiring the executive authority to take action inconsistent with WTO Agreements violates the WTO regime irrespective of whether or not the legislation was currently implemented, whereas legislation merely allowing the executive to act inconsistently, does not, by itself, constitute a violation.[28] The Panel in this dispute concluded that the mandatory laws of Massachusetts and Rhode Island by their terms treated imported beer and wine less favourably than similar domestic products, and they were thus inconsistent with GATT Article III:4, irrespective of the extent to which they were being enforced.[29]

Similarly, the Panel in *Thailand – Cigarettes* concluded that legislation mandatorily requiring the executive authority to impose internal taxes discriminating against imported products was inconsistent with Article III:2 of GATT, irrespective of whether or not an occasion of its actual application had yet arisen.[30] The Panel in *US – Tobacco* stated that legislation which mandated action inconsistent with the GATT could be challenged *per se*, whereas legislation which merely gave discretion to the executive authority to act inconsistently could not be challenged as such. Only the actual application of such legislation could be the subject of a claim.[31]

In *US – Superfund* Canada and the EEC considered it appropriate to challenge the US legislation establishing a tax which was not in operation, because it could affect the decision on investment and supply contracts before more serious trade damage had occurred. The Panel agreed with the complainants and suggested that '*the very existence of mandatory legislation providing for an internal tax without being applied to a particular imported product should be regarded as falling within the scope of Article III:2, first sentence*'.[32] The Appellate Body in *US-AntiDumping Act of 1919* rejected the United

[27] The burden of proof in 'as such' is on the claimant. In *US – Carbon Steel*, ABR, para 157, noted that a measure is considered WTO-consistent until proven otherwise.

[28] *US – Malt Beverages*, WT/DS23/R-39S/206, PR, adopted 19 June 1992, para 5.57.

[29] *US – Malt Beverages*, PR, para 5.60.

[30] *Thailand – Restrictions on Importation of and Internal Taxes on Cigarettes* WT/DS10/R – 37S/200, PR adopted 7 November 1990, para 84.

[31] *US – Measures Affecting the Importation, Internal Sale and Use of Tobacco*, WT/DS44/R, PR adopted 4 October 1994, para 118.

[32] *US – Superfund*, PR, para 5.2.2.

States' claim that the 'mandatory/discretionary legislation' test is relevant only in those cases where the challenged legislation has never been applied.[33]

Additionally, the Panel in the *US – Tyres (China)* dispute explained that in practice the import of the mandatory/discretionary distinction is most pronounced in cases where, although a member's law appears to be WTO-inconsistent on its face, there is sufficient discretion to allow national authorities to apply the law in a WTO-consistent manner.[34] For example, the Panel in *EEC – Regulation on Imports of Parts and Components* concluded that the anti-circumvention provision under the EC anti-dumping law did not mandate the imposition of duties or other measures but merely authorized the European Commission and Council to take certain actions.[35] The Panel noted that although it would be desirable for the EC to withdraw the anti-circumvention provision, the EC would meet its obligations under the GATT if it were to cease to apply the provision in respect of the contracting parties.[36]

While the distinction between claims 'as such' and claims 'as applied' is not always clear-cut, the general pattern which can be drawn from the EU's executive federalism is that the Union is in most cases the legislator of trade rules which are implemented by Member States. Accordingly it may be assumed that the EU is the proper respondent in claims 'as such', whereas Member States are necessary parties in claims 'as applied' precisely because their action will be necessary to eliminate the inconsistency. Taking the aforementioned normative considerations a step further, the following sections will consider the case law which supports my hypothesis. It will be shown that the DSB refers to the type of a claim (and accordingly the respective remedy) in the identification of whether the EU, its Member States or both are the proper respondents in a given dispute.

8.4 IDENTIFICATION OF MULTIPLE RESPONDENTS

Claims 'as such' dominate WTO dispute settlement, which explains why the EU is the optimal respondent in WTO law (Chapter 7). The WTO dispute-settlement regime provides a state-to-state forum which is why in most cases WTO members bring claims 'as such' to challenge laws, regulations or other

33 *US – Anti-Dumping Act of 1916*, WT/DS 136/AB/R, WT/DS 162/AB/R, ABR adopted 26 September 2000, para 93.

34 *US – Measures Affecting Imports of Certain Passenger Vehicle and Light Truck Tyres from China Tyres (China)*, WT/DS399/R, PR adopted 13 December 2010, para 7.118.

35 *EEC – Regulation on Imports of Parts and Components*, L/6657-37S/132, PR adopted 16 May 1990, para 5.25.

36 *EEC – Regulation on Imports of Parts and Components*, PR, para 5.26.

instruments of general and prospective application. The purpose of such claims is to prevent members *ex ante* from engaging in certain conduct and the DSB considers 'as such' claims to be more serious than 'as applied' claims.[37] Unlike investment protection treaties which aim to compensate harm already caused, the WTO dispute-settlement system focuses on prospective trade relations. The central focus of the WTO dispute-settlement system is the preservation of the regulatory order established by WTO Agreements. Claims 'as such' prevent future violation because they eliminate '*the root of WTO-inconsistent behaviour*'.[38] Explanation for the active role of the EU in 'as such' disputes is straightforward: if the validity of a norm rather than its application in specific instances is at issue, it will be the EU which in most cases will be best placed to bring that regulation into conformity with the WTO obligations. This brings the analysis back to the EU's exclusive competence in trade, discussed in Chapter 7. Matters such as customs, antitrust law and import and export restrictions are regulated by the EU, and it is the Union bodies that are best placed to make laws WTO-consistent in accordance with recommendations of the DSB. The EU is a more frequent respondent under claims challenging laws and norms themselves, rather than their application, because it is the proper party to ensure the necessary regulatory changes. Member States, on the other hand, are better placed to respond to 'as applied' claims because they implement Union trade law.

An important observation is that the subject of the dispute does not necessarily correspond to what a claimant asks for. For example, a dispute may focus on Member States' conduct which serves as evidence of a systematic failure in the legal framework itself. If the claim challenges a legal system as such, Member States' conduct will be treated as a fact, not as an independent object of a claim. Member States will thus not be treated as respondents because the remedy will call for removal of the inconsistencies in the legal system by the EU, not the Member States, because the EU is (in most cases) the legislator of general rules. Conversely, a claimant may focus on the unlawfulness of a rule to assert that its application violates its rights. This further supports the

37 *US – Sunset Reviews of Anti-Dumping Measures on Oil Country Tubular Goods from Argentina*, WT/DS268, ABR adopted 29 November 2004, para 172. The AB stated 'By definition, an "as such" claim challenges laws, regulations, or other instruments of a Member that have general and prospective application, asserting that a Member's conduct—not only in a particular instance that has occurred, but in future situations as well—will necessarily be inconsistent with that Member's WTO obligations. In essence, complaining parties bringing "as such" challenges seek to prevent Members ex ante from engaging in certain conduct. The implications of such challenges are obviously more far-reaching than "as applied" claims'.

38 *US – Sunset Review of Anti-Dumping Duties on Corrosion Resistant Carbon Steel Flat Products from Japan*, WT/DS244/AB/R, ABR adopted 15 December 2003, paras 81–82.

hypothesis that attribution of conduct is not decisive for the distribution of shared responsibility in international economic disputes.

As will be discussed later, claims 'as applied' are common under the WTO regime. In fact, claims brought before the DSB are often composite, that is they cover both 'as such' and 'as applied' measures. WTO members challenge not only an EU legal instrument in isolation but also various systems, regimes and processes.[39] Claims tend to be broadly defined and often involve Member States' measures which either implement or apply Union law. The task of identifying whether Member States are necessary respondents in a given dispute is complex because of the composite structure of claims under the WTO regime.

The task, however, is decisive to the distribution of shared responsibility between the EU and its Member States. In a factually identical situation, the EU, its Member States or both may be the proper respondent(s), depending on the target of the claim and the respective remedy. Neither the division of competences between the EU and its Member States nor attribution of conduct provides a sufficient basis for the allocation of responsibility between an organization and its Member States. The EU, its Member States or both may be the proper respondent(s) in exactly the same dispute covering exactly the same competences. Which of them will bear responsibility depends on the object of the disputing party's claim and the remedy it seeks.

EC – Geographical Indications provides a good example. The dispute concerned an EC regulation which set out procedure for the individual product designation of origin and geographical indications. Under the disputed regulation applicants for registrations had to submit their applications to authorities in the country of the geographical area, that is Member States (or third countries).[40] The United States argued that the registration procedure on its face did not afford equal treatment to the nationals of the EC and other WTO members because it did not allow applications for geographical indications located in third countries to be filed directly with the competent authorities in Europe. It challenged the procedure 'as such', not specific instances of product registration. Thus, while the conduct concerned is that of Member

39 *US – Sunset Review of Anti-Dumping Duties on Corrosion Resistant Carbon Steel Flat Products from Japan*, ABR, paras 81–82. Note, that DSU Art 6.2 requires inclusion of the laws, regulations, decisions alleged to be administered in a manner that is in violation of Article X:3(a) GAT; see para 7.27. There is a special duty of diligence on the part of a claimant to set out 'as such' claims in their panel requests as clearly as possible, *US – Oil Country Tubular Goods Sunset Reviews*, ABR, paras 172–173.

40 *EC – Geographical Indications*, PR, para 7.271.

States, the issue before the Panel was a legal instrument itself, not its application in a particular case.

In fact, provisions concerning the protection of geographical indications under consideration have never been applied[41] and parties were not aware of any application for registration of a name of an area in a third country outside the EU ever having been filed with authorities of a third country.[42] Since the focus was on the regulatory scheme as such, the EC was the proper respondent because it was best placed to bring the regulation into compliance with the recommendations of the DSB. The Panel itself noted that one way in which the EC could implement recommendations was to amend the challenged EC regulation in such a way that registration of geographical names located in other WTO members was not subject to different procedures.[43]

That Member States are entities which designate geographical indications was irrelevant in this particular dispute because compliance was focused on amending the legal instrument rather than correcting consequences which flowed from an incorrect application of that instrument. Nor is the division of competences between the EU and its Member States decisive in this context. Had the claimant challenged specific designations of geographical indications, it is probable (as will be seen later) that the relevant Member States would have been assigned respondent status, even though trade is an area of EU competence.

The following sections will provide further support for this thesis. For purposes of clarity the discussions structured by grouping disputes in accordance to their subject matter.

8.4.1 *Customs Disputes*

As was suggested earlier, attribution of conduct is not helpful in distributing responsibility between the EU and its Member States in the WTO context (as well as in international economic law in general). Moreover, tracing conduct may be misleading for the determination of the proper respondent. The *EC – Selected Customs Matters* illustrates this point. In this case litigation focused on Member States' conduct, but the claim challenged a regulatory system as such, leaving it up to the EC to ensure compliance. The United States contested 'the manner' in which the EC administered its laws, regulations,

41 EC – *Geographical Indications*, PR, para 7.52.
42 EC – *Geographical Indications*, PR, para 7.266.
43 EC – *Geographical Indications*, PR, para 8.5.

decisions and rulings in relation to the customs union.[44] This function is carried out by Member States. According to the United States, Member States' administrations *'do not always treat the [binding tariff information] issued by another Member State as binding'*.[45]

In this particular dispute the United States was concerned with the way in which the EC customs authorities administered the customs framework.[46] The emphasis is on the actions of customs authorities of the Member States, whereas, by contrast, there is no mention of actions taken and/or procedures and institutions existing at EC level.[47] The Panel concluded that it was authorized to examine particular cases or instances of the administration of customs laws expressly identified in the United States' request.[48] The case thus concerned conduct of Member States which, following the doctrine of attribution of conduct, points to the Member States rather than the EU as proper respondents in this dispute.

Yet, while the case was *about* Member States' conduct, the remedy sought directed the Panel to the EU as the proper respondent. The United States claimed that the regime itself was flawed and was not designed systematically to achieve uniform administration, thus resulting in a breach of Article X:3 of the GATT 1994.[49] It sought changes in the way the EU administered its customs law, not to remedy the consequences of particular instances of misapplication of customs law by Member States.[50] Particular instances of alleged incorrect administration by Member States[51] served as factual evidence to show that inconsistencies did occur (and so the system as such had to be improved), rather than as independent challenges.[52]

44 EC – *Selected Customs Matters*, PR, para 4.546.

45 EC – *Selected Customs Matters*, PR, para 4.602. The United States claimed that it challenges the design and structure of the EC system of customs administration 'as such', see para 7.51.

46 EC – *Selected Customs Matters*, PR, para 7.59.

47 EC – *Selected Customs Matters*, PR, para 7.60.

48 EC – *Selected Customs Matters*, PR, para 7.64.

49 EC – *Selected Customs Matters*, PR, para 4.34.

50 Obligation for uniform administration of customs laws under GATT Art X:3(a) GATT does not require harmonization of laws at sublevels as long as a certain minimum degree of predictability and security is ensured. In other words, the United States went after the EC's obligation of an overall administration, not of particular laws of Member States.

51 Different interpretations by national authorities of complex nomenclature system, para 4.9; failure of customs authorities to abide by binding customs classifications rulings, para 4.12; exercise of discretionary powers by the Member States with respect to revocation of binding tariff information etc.

52 Similarly, the EC claimed that the dispute did not concern the correctness of individual classifications, but rather the question of uniform administration of customs regime, EC – *Selected Customs Matters*, PR, para 4.627.

As a result the Panel identified a number of gaps in the system of customs administration, such as absence of a duty to consult other Member States before adopting binding decisions, of a system to inform of revocations and of a duty in Member States to consult the binding tariff information database.[53] It called for a *restitutio in integrum* type of remedy, suggesting that if the manner in which laws and regulations are administered was found to lack uniformity, there would be a need to amend the legal regime of customs administration itself.[54] It was then up to the EC, not the Member States, to fill the gaps in the legal framework, which explains why the Panel addressed its rulings and recommendations to the EC alone. Member States' conduct was investigated by the Panel as evidence of a problem, but the solution to it was to come from the EC.

Taking the facts of this case by analogy, the result could have been different had the claim focused on correcting Member-State conduct itself rather than the system in which Member States' operate. For example, had the United States complained not about the structural gaps in the EC customs regime but about the actual tariff classification by a Member State, the panel might have addressed its rulings and recommendations to that Member State.

EC – Computer Equipment sustains this claim. This dispute concerned reclassification of certain computer equipment by the European Commission and, accordingly, United Kingdom and Irish authorities. The United States and Japan argued that Member States, specifically the United Kingdom and Ireland, were respondents in this dispute in addition to the EC because they were independent members of (the) GATT and bound by corresponding obligations.[55] The reasoning of the parties with respect to Member States' responsibility was focused on the remedy. For example, Chinese Taipei, which was acting as a third party in this dispute, sought to challenge Member States in lieu of the EC on the rationale that if the DSB recommendations were not addressed to the Member States, they might continue to breach and thus the positive solution to the dispute would fail.[56] The identification of the United Kingdom and Ireland in the request for establishment of a panel was most likely based on the fact that these countries were the US

53 *EC – Selected Customs Matters*, PR, paras 7.159–7.170.

54 *EC – Selected Customs Matters*, PR, para 7.21.

55 *EC and Certain Member States – IT Products*, PR, para 7.81. The EC did not agree with such position and argued that the United States and Japan may not challenge the application of duties by the Member States because they have not challenged the measures on an 'as applied' basis. According to the EC the role of customs authorities of EC Member States is limited to applying measures previously enacted by the Union; see para 6.11, also paras 8.1 and 8.6.

56 *EC and Certain Member States – IT Products*, PR, para 6.45.

industry's largest export markets in the EC. The strategic importance of obtaining a remedy not only against the EC but also against the specific instances of tariff classification by the United Kingdom and Ireland explains why tariff treatment of several other Member States (Denmark, the Netherlands and France) served as evidence rather than individual claims.[57]

The complainants acknowledged that they did not challenge any particular prior application of customs duties by particular Member States but claimed that it was appropriate directly to challenge the Member States because it is their authorities that applied customs duties.[58] The Panel agreed and stated that the United Kingdom and Ireland were respondents alongside the EC.[59] Its decision to include Member States as co-respondents can be explained by the United States arguing that its claim concerned not reclassification as such but the actual tariff treatment by the European Commission, the United Kingdom and Ireland.[60]

Theories of competence-based responsibility or normative control would be insufficient to explain the different approach of the DSB to the question of international responsibility of the EU in *EC – Selected Customs Matters* and *EC – Computer Equipment*. Both disputes concerned customs matters subject to the same internal EU normative framework. Explanation of this difference lies in the claim and, accordingly, the remedy requested by the claimant. In the case of the former dispute, the remedy was the filling of gaps in the legal framework of the customs administration, a task to be undertaken by the EU. In the latter case, the United States sought to correct the actual tariff treatment not only by the EU but also by two strategically important Member States. Thus, two disputes covering the same field of competence where conduct is carried out by the same actors (Member States) can result in responsibility of the EU, a Member State or both, depending on the focus of the claimant's request and the remedy it seeks.

Differently from *EC – Computer Equipment*, where the United Kingdom and Ireland were included as respondents in the proceedings, the Panel in *EC and Certain Member States – IT Products* refused to afford that status to the Member States. In line with the analysis in Chapter 6, the Panel noted that its primary objective was a positive solution to the dispute.[61] Accordingly, the claimant challenged customs duties 'as such' without identifying any

57 *EC – Computer Equipment*, PR, para 8.44.

58 *EC and Certain Member States – IT Products*, PR, para 7.85, also para 8.2.

59 *EC – Computer Equipment*, PR, para 8.16.

60 *EC – Computer Equipment*, PR, para 5.3, see also paras 8.58 and 8.12.

61 *EC and Certain Member States – IT Products*, PR, para 7.90.

particular instances of application.[62] It thus concluded that findings with respect to the measures adopted by the EC alone would provide a positive solution to the dispute.[63]

One additional point provides further support for functional approach to international responsibility. The Panel in *EC – Computer Equipment* ultimately decided to exclude two respondents, the United Kingdom and Ireland, from its recommendations and instead address its recommendations to the EU alone. According to the Panel, having determined an inconsistency on the part of the EU, it was unnecessary also to address its ruling to the United Kingdom and Ireland.[64] The DSB did not provide its reasoning for omitting the two respondents and instead resorted to judicial avoidance techniques. A likely explanation for this approach was that in this particular case, declaring unlawful an EU measure automatically resulted in the inapplicability of the United Kingdom and Irish measures.[65] It was unnecessary to rule against the Member States because elimination of an inconsistency on the EU's part was sufficient to achieve a positive solution to the dispute. Leaving out of a ruling respondents whose measures are found inconsistent but who add nothing to compliance is consistent with my argument that responsibility in international economic law carries a restorative rather than retributive function, in line with the argument in Chapter 5.

8.4.2 *Subsidies Disputes*

Subsidies decisions differ from customs measures in that the EU does not oblige Member States to grant subsidies, whereas Member States are bound by customs regulation. Nevertheless, subsidies cases reveal a pattern in the DSB's reasoning analogous to that discussed earlier. This further supports the view that panels are concerned neither with attribution of conduct nor with the untangling of organizational ties and power dynamics within an organization when faced with the task of distribution of shared responsibility.

EC – Commercial Vessels provides an illustration. In this dispute the parties held different views as to whether Member States were parties to the

62 *EC and Certain Member States – IT Products*, PR, para 7.89. Interestingly, the request for the establishment of a panel did refer to 'applied measures' in a reference attached to the main text. However, in the Report of the panel reference to 'applied measures' had disappeared, most probably as a technical error.

63 *EC and Certain Member States – IT Products*, PR, para 8.2.

64 *EC – Computer Equipment*, PR, paras 8.15–8.16 and 8.72.

65 The claim challenged an EU regulation classifying computer equipment as 'telecommunications apparatus' and two subsequent binding tariff information letters, one by Irish customs authorities and one by UK authorities.

proceedings. Member States were not initially cited as co-respondents in the request for the establishment of a Panel and the question of multiple respondents arose during the adjudicative phase. The dispute concerned a Council regulation governing the granting of state aid to certain shipyards as well as national aid schemes adopted in line with the regulation.[66] Under this scheme, and subject to a decision of the European Commission, Member States could grant individual subsidies to certain shipyards.

The EC argued that the claim did not cover individual Member States' grants of subsidies and that Korea's claim was limited to the subsidy scheme as such.[67] According to the EC, Member States' measures were autonomous decisions on whether to provide state aid.[68] Such a position departs from the EU's claims in other disputes that responsibility follows the division of competences because competition matters fall within the exclusive EU competence. According to the Union, the importation of individual disbursements of funds by the Member States into the dispute would have severely hampered its due process rights because such disbursements are granted by the Member States, leaving no time to obtain the relevant evidence from them.[69]

Korea's reasoning that Member States' grants of subsidies were not separate measures but mere applications of the disputed regulation was compliance-focused.[70] It was concerned that if the EC's general measures were to be found inconsistent while any specific applications were excluded unless individually listed in the claim, the result would seem to be that such applications could continue, at least to the extent that they had been committed, but not paid prior to the panel's rulings and recommendations.[71] According to Korea, Member States implementing the challenged regulation, including Denmark, France, Germany, the Netherlands and Spain, equally violated WTO obligations and directed its arguments regarding illegality of the EC's regulation *mutatis mutandis* to the Member States implementing these measures.[72] To prevent the circumvention of WTO obligations, Korea asked the panel to clarify whether individual disbursements of funds by Member

66 The Council Regulation (EC) No 1177/2002 of 27 June 2002 concerning a temporary defensive mechanism to shipbuilding.

67 *EC – Commercial Vessels*, PR, para 4.7.

68 *EC – Commercial Vessels*, PR, para 4.22.

69 *EC – Commercial Vessels*, PR, para 4.15.

70 *EC – Commercial Vessels*, PR, para 7.4.

71 *EC – Commercial Vessels*, PR, para 4.14, also para 7.22. Korea was relying on ABR in *Brazil-Aircraft* where the AB noted that to 'continue to make payments under an export subsidy measure found to be prohibited is not consistent with the obligation to "withdraw" prohibited export subsidies', see ABR, para 45.

72 *EC – Commercial Vessels*, PR, para 4.250.

States were covered by the claim because they were part of the implementation of the challenged regulation.[73]

The Panel's analysis supports the argument that distribution of shared responsibility under WTO law is remedy-based. The Panel rejected Korea's request, drawing a distinction between the EC's and Member States' measures. It emphasized that the regulation under consideration did not in itself authorize individual disbursements.[74] Accordingly, the EC regulation provided a legal basis but not an obligation of Member States to make individual disbursements of aid.[75] Moreover, there was no information before the Panel regarding individual instances of application of the national aid schemes.[76] It separated the Member States' application of the disputed regulation and limited the scope of the dispute to an 'as such' claim. The approach supports the thesis that in cases where individual instances of application of general rules are not challenged (or do not exist), the panel will not address its recommendations to the Member States because their actions are not necessary for restorative purposes.

Importantly, the focus of the Panel in this case was on whether ruling on individual disbursements was necessary to provide an effective solution to the dispute, in line with the analysis in Chapter 6. The Panel noted that Article 19.1 of the DSU permitted it only to make a recommendation to 'bring its measures into compliance' but it could not request cessation of further disbursements.[77] Accordingly, individual disbursements of Member States were neither expressly stated in the request nor was ruling on them helpful for purposes of ensuring the effective solution to the dispute. The Member States were thus not afforded a respondent status in this dispute. Furthermore, as was noted in Chapter 7, the EC assured the panel that it would ensure compliance on behalf of its Member States, if necessary.

The Panel's conclusion regarding multiple respondents in *EC – Commercial Vessels* can be contrasted with that in *EC – Large Civil Aircraft*. Unlike *EC – Commercial Vessels*, the claimant in *EC – Large Civil Aircraft* identified various instances of financing. Though drafted in broad terms, the claim alleged more than 300 instances of subsidization over a period of almost

73 *EC – Commercial Vessels*, PR, para 4.22. Korea argued that if disbursements are not covered by the claim, they might continue for a period of years after expiration of the authority under the challenged regulation as long as they were approved before such expiration; see para 4.19.

74 *EC – Commercial Vessels*, PR, para 7.53.

75 *EC – Commercial Vessels*, PR, para 4.53. The panel noted that authorization by the European Commission applies to the aid scheme as such, not to the grant of aid in individual cases pursuant to the aid scheme; see para 7.51.

76 *EC – Commercial Vessels*, PR, para 4.51.

77 *EC – Commercial Vessels*, PR, para 7.24.

forty years by the EC and four of its Member States with respect to large civil aircraft.[78] The United States specifically targeted German, French, Spanish and the United Kingdom's subsidizations of Airbus through the provision of infrastructure grants.[79] The requested remedy *inter alia* expressly included the withdrawal of export subsidies by these four Member States.[80] The EC contested the United States' claim that Member States should be included in the dispute as co-respondents with the EC.[81]

A question arose as to who was the proper respondent in this dispute. In its usual manner the EC claimed that it was the only proper respondent.[82] However, in line with the principle of independent responsibility (Chapter 3), the Panel noted that in addition to the EC, France, Germany, Spain and the United Kingdom were also the proper respondents in this dispute, irrespective of any internal arrangements in the EU.[83]

The Panel's decision to include the four Member States as co-respondents in this dispute was functional Unlike *EC – Commercial Vessels*, the claimant in *EC – Large Civil Aircraft* asked not only that the EC state aid measures as such but also specific instances of funding by certain Member States be declared unlawful. In other words the claim challenged not only legal instruments as such but also specific instances of application, calling for remedial action from both the EC and the four Member States. Addressing the recommendation to the EU alone would be insufficient to achieve a positive solution to the dispute because elimination of an inconsistent measure of general application would not result in elimination of Member States' inconsistent measures.

8.4.3 *Regulatory Measures*

Disputes over regulatory measures also reveal a functional approach to the distribution of shared responsibility between the EU and its Member States.

78 *EC – Large Civil Aircraft*, PR, para 7.1.
79 *EC – Large Civil Aircraft*, PR, para 4.271.
80 *EC – Large Civil Aircraft*, PR, para 3.2.
81 Here the EC contested a broad term 'launch aid' which was used by the United States to refer to the pool of the EC and Member State instances of financing of Airbus. The EC stated that 'rather than using the suggestive and oversimplifying term "launch aid," the EC will refer to each of the member States' measures separately'; WTO Panel Report, *EC – Large Civil Aircraft*, para 4.85.
82 *EC – Large Civil Aircraft*, PR, para 7.169.
83 *EC – Large Civil Aircraft*, PR, para 7.174. Whether or not it will address its rulings and recommendations to the Member States as well will be known, according to the panel, only once its decision-making process is completed; para 7.177.

Though the two disputes differ in their facts, the nature and focus of the claim in *EC – Biotech Products* resembles that in *EC – Geographical Indications* discussed earlier in one relevant respect. As in *EC – Geographical Indications*, the claim in *EC – Biotech Products* was about Member States' measures 'as applied' but it in fact targeted rules of general application. The proper respondent was thus not the Member States but the EC, because the EC was best placed to eliminate the inconsistency.

In this dispute the United States complained that the EC carried out a *de facto* moratorium on the approval of biotech products which was a condition of importing biotech products to the EC. The Panel set out to determine whether there were any grounds for believing that the EC or one of its entities – the Member States, the European Commission or the Council – had intended to suspend biotech product approval.[84] The issue before the Panel was whether these entities could prevent or delay approval.[85] The Panel considered sovereign actions[86] of the Member States which were involved in the process of biotech product approval, including the adoption by the environment ministers of five EC Member States, of a declaration on suspension of authorization, delay in assessment of nine applications at Member-State level[87] and the role of the Council and Member States in the Regulatory Committee.[88] The complainant itself noted that the European Commission's approval of applications for biotech products had consistently been blocked by the five Member States.[89] Thus, the conduct before the DSB was that of the Member States, in addition to that of the EC.

The Panel found that Member States' conduct had violated the claimant's rights. It found a systematic opposition to final approvals of biotech products

84 *EC – Biotech Products*, PR, para 7.460.

85 *EC – Biotech Products*, PR, para 7.466.

86 Under laws governing the approval of biotech products at the time of the dispute, individual Member States had a right to provisionally restrict or prohibit the use and/or sale of an approved biotech product in their own territory if they had detailed grounds for considering that the particular product posed a risk to human health or the environment. In cases where a Member State was to adopt a 'safeguard' measure, it had an obligation to inform other EC Member States and the Commission of the action it has taken and a decision of the Member State 'safeguard' measure then had to be taken at Community level, Directive 2001/18/EC, O. J. 17.4.2001 L106/1 and Regulation (EC) No. 258/97, O.J. 14.2.1997 L043/1.

87 *EC – Biotech Products*, PR, paras 4.150–4.151. The European Commissioner David Byrne stated that the reluctance of Member States to approve the placing on the market of new biotech products has resulted in a complete standstill in the current authorizations and a *de facto* moratorium, *EC – Biotech Products*, PR, para 4.146.

88 *EC – Biotech Products*, PR, paras 4.200–4.204.

89 *EC – Biotech Products*, PR, para 4.586.

by certain Member States who formed a 'blocking minority'.[90] Moreover, it acknowledged that the European Commission sought to introduce the 'interim approach', the purpose of which was to resume the authorization process, but it lacked political support from the Member States.[91] It is thus clear from the facts of the case that the failure to approve biotech products was caused by the actions of specific Member States, not the EU itself.

However, despite the inconsistencies on the part of the Member States, the question before the Panel was not whether certain Member States had or had not approved biotech products, but whether the system of approval itself could lead to an outright ban of approvals.[92] In other words the claim was about deficiencies in the system as such. Accordingly, it was not necessary to rule on the general moratorium itself (i.e. Member States' conduct) in order to reach a positive solution to the dispute.[93] The focus of the Panel was on the process of approval as such, whereas Member States' conduct was regarded as a way of proving that an outright ban was in fact possible within the current framework and was thus improper. The claimant's request was not to eliminate inconsistent Member States' conduct but to trigger changes in the general regulatory process. In this respect the dispute resembles *EC – Geographical Indications* in that Member States' conduct is examined in order to determine inconsistencies of the rules as such. Similar to the conclusions with respect to that case, the decisive factor in the determination of multiple respondents is the remedy requested by the claimant, not attribution of conduct under consideration. This approach explains why the respondent in this dispute was the EC itself, not the Member States, and supports the argument that attribution of conduct is not a decisive factor in international economic disputes.

EC – Asbestos, another regulatory dispute involving the EU and its Member States, was decided prior to *EC – Biotech Products*. Though the exact reasoning of the parties in *EC – Asbestos* is not known, it seems that the focus on the remedy had been the driving force in the choice of bringing a claim against the EC, even though the challenge targeted a national measure. In *EC – Asbestos* the EC was the respondent in a case brought by Canada regarding a French

90 *EC – Biotech Products*, PR, para 7.493.

91 *EC – Biotech Products*, PR, para 4.586.

92 Irrespective of the different effect of the European Commission the Member States in the creation of the general moratorium, the delays at the Community level and those at Member States' level were merged into what the tribunal referred to as a 'general moratorium'; see *EC – Biotech Products*, PR, para 7.1340.

93 *EC – Biotech Products*, PR, paras 6.79–6.83.

ban on chrysotile fibre.[94] France, which imported two-thirds of its chrysotile fibre from Canada, imposed a ban in 1996 by decree, and various other EC Member States had also introduced restrictions on the use of asbestos since the 1980s. Several years later in 1999 the EC had adopted legislation banning asbestos products which were to enter into operation in 2005.[95] Thus, at the time of the claim in *EC – Asbestos* case, the EU measure was not yet in force.

The *EC – Asbestos* case reveals a functional compliance-focused approach to international responsibility of the EU and its Member States. The primary interest of the claimant in this case was the ban on asbestos products. At the time of the claim, the EC ban had not yet been in force, only a national measure. The inability to bring a legal challenge against an EC-wide measure must have been the reason why Canada requested that the panel recommend France to make its domestic measure compatible with its WTO obligations.[96] At the same time, since the EU-wide regulation was underway at the time of the panel proceedings, the claim was directed against the EC (note: not against an EC measure). The result of such procedural tactic was a somewhat confusing case study of international responsibility: a claim against the EC challenging a French measure of general application. This conundrum can be explained by the fact that the time when the EC had adopted its common policy banning asbestos coincided with the timing of the dispute proceedings. A ruling on the French measure would not have achieved compliance and so would have failed to achieve a positive solution to the dispute since the later EU-wide ban would have been intact. Placing the EC in a respondent status pre-empted its ability to enforce the EC-wide ban even before it became law proper. The *EC – Asbestos* dispute is thus a rather extreme example of functional approach employed by the DSB to achieve a positive solution to the dispute, in line with the analysis in Chapter 5.

The cases described in the chapter illustrate functional international responsibility adopted in the WTO dispute settlement. Determination of multiple respondents is based on whose actions are necessary to ensure compliance with WTO law. That in turn depends on the scope and nature of the claim. The EU, its Member States or both may be respondents in a particular dispute based on what is necessary for remedial purposes, irrespective of the internal division of competences or attribution of conduct.

94 *EC – Measures Affecting Asbestos and Products Containing Asbestos (EC – Asbestos)* WT/DS135, PR adopted 18 September 2000.

95 The EU decision was adopted in on 4 May 1999.

96 *EC – Asbestos*, PR, para 3.3.

8.5 CONCLUSION

It was argued in Chapter 6 that the primary focus of the WTO DSB is to ensure a positive solution to dispute. Since withdrawal of an inconsistent trade rule is a central remedy under the WTO regime and the EU is in most cases the legislator of trade rules of general application, it is the optimal respondent in WTO disputes (Chapter 7). However, in several cases restorative action on the part of Member States was (also) necessary for compliance purposes. These latter disputes were the focus of this chapter.

Analysis of the WTO case law has revealed a correlation of the scope of the claim and the requested remedy on the one hand, and inclusion of Member States as co-respondents on the other. Differentiation between claims 'as such' and claims 'as applied' is useful for this purpose. Challenges 'as such' cover rules of general application, whereas the application of such rules in specific cases constitutes 'as applied' claims.

Close analysis of customs, subsidies and regulatory disputes reveals patterns in the DSB's determination of multiple respondents. The EU is in most cases the proper respondent in 'as such' disputes because it is often best placed to bring measures of general application into compliance with WTO obligations. Member States are commonly necessary parties when disputes also cover specific instances of application of trade rules because restorative action on their part is necessary to ensure a positive solution to the dispute.

The competence-based approach to international responsibility as well as the normative control theory is insufficient to explain why panels decide to address some of their recommendations to the EU, while others (also) to its Member States, when dealing with cases in the same area of competence. This is so because the basis for distribution of shared responsibility is not static and depends on the remedy-defined function of the DSB. The findings of this chapter thus further reinforce functional international responsibility.

9

Normative Implications for the EU's Free Trade Agreements

9.1 INTRODUCTION

It was argued in Part I that the EU and its Member States are independently responsible for their joint obligations. It was further concluded that international dispute-settlement practice provides no support for the theory that adjudicators follow some predetermined structural basis in deciding exclusive responsibility within the European Union (EU). International trade and investment case law does not support the EU's claim that responsibility follows the internal division of competences or that the conduct of Member States' authorities is attributed to the Union when they implement EU law.

Part II developed the concept of functional international responsibility of the EU and its Member States in international economic law. It was argued that distribution of shared responsibility is remedy-based. Responsibility is shifted to the entity which is best placed to restore order and eliminate wrong. Because of the restorative rather than retributive nature of remedies in international economic law, distribution of shared responsibility typically raises the question of the proper respondent(s). Whether the proper respondent is the EU, its Member States or both in a given dispute depends heavily on the nature of the treaty regime in question. It was suggested that the system of remedies for the protection of obligations under a given treaty is decisive for how international courts and tribunals will distribute shared responsibility within the EU.

The above findings are the result of an in-depth case-law analysis, primarily under two multilateral economic treaties which were concluded in a mixed form with both the EU and its Member States holding joint obligations – the international trade regime under the World Trade Organization (WTO) Agreements and the investment regime under the Energy Charter Treaty (ECT).[1] The WTO

[1] Three main reasons guided this choice. First, both the WTO Agreements and the ECT are mixed treaties with the EU and its Member States as parties. Secondly, neither agreement

case law analysis revealed that the Dispute Settlement Body (DSB) employs what is called 'the positive solution test' to identify the proper respondent(s). WTO panels address their recommendations to the party (or parties) which is necessary to ensure compliance with WTO law. Investment tribunals, on the other hand, focus on the proximate cause of harm which enables them to award compensation. An analysis both of the substantive nature of obligations and relevant procedural aspects of participation of EU/Member States in the WTO regime and the ECT was conducted in order to explain why the EU is the optimal respondent in WTO claims, whereas investment claims have so far been typically brought against Member States. Finally, an additional WTO case-law analysis to identify the special cases of multiple respondents in WTO law was also carried out. It was suggested that the inclusion of Member States in the dispute-settlement proceedings varies depending on the object of the disputing party's claim.

The following analysis will attempt to apply the aforementioned normative outcomes to new-generation free trade agreements (FTA) that the EU has recently concluded or is in the process of negotiating. Analysis is based on the extensive discussions in the autumn of 2017 with a number of officials involved in the negotiation of the new FTAs, including representatives of the Legal Service of the European Commission, the Directorate General for Trade, the EU Mission in the WTO, the Mission of Canada to the EU and the United States Trade Representative. These discussions provided insight into the process of negotiation of the dispute-settlement mechanism under the new FTAs and the approach to the distribution of shared responsibility of the EU and its Member States adopted by both the EU and its trading partners.

The here is not to provide a policy evaluation of the normative outcomes of this book. The analysis is limited to identification of the rationales that govern the allocation of international responsibility in the EU. The conclusions in Chapter 10 will nevertheless note some of the critical questions that lead to further debate on functional international responsibility in international economic law.

Section 9.2 will outline the application of the normative findings of this book to dispute resolution under the EU's new-generation FTAs. It will then discuss the mechanism for the determination of the proper respondent for investment claims under new investment chapters (Section 9.3). Section 9.4 of this chapter will consider procedural safeguards which serve as a guarantee to third parties that the Union will not use its discretion to determine the proper respondent as a way of obstructing adjudication.

contains a declaration of competences which would separate EU obligations from those of the Member States. The third reason was the availability of dispute- resolution practice.

9.2 APPLICATION OF THE NORMATIVE FINDINGS TO NEW-GENERATION FTAS

The Treaty of Lisbon gave new impetus to the EU's external action in the area of common commercial policy. Among other things the Treaty of Lisbon transferred competences in the field of foreign direct investment (FDI) from Member States to the Union and integrated it in the EU's common commercial policy. Empowered with these new powers, the EU has started to negotiate a number of FTAs with third countries which, in addition to trade liberalization, also cover investment protection. The Union has recently signed treaties with several countries, including the EU-Canada Comprehensive Economic and Trade Agreement (CETA), the EU-Singapore Free Trade Agreement (EUSFTA) and the EU-Japan Economic Partnership Agreement (EPA).[2] Investment chapters under these FTAs are replacing the web of bilateral investment treaties (BIT) that the EU Member States have concluded with third parties. Accordingly, investment arbitration regimes under the Member States' treaties are being gradually replaced by the dispute-resolution mechanism established in the new FTAs.

The purpose of this chapter is to apply the normative findings of this book to the dispute-resolution mechanisms under new-generation FTAs. The question of mixity of these FTAs provides a significant contextual point for further analysis.

9.2.1 *The Question of Mixity*

Until May 2017, it was unclear whether future EU's FTAs would be mixed or EU-only agreements. If Member States were not party to new-generation FTAs, they would not be bound by these agreements from the international law perspective. Accordingly, the question of the distribution of international responsibility between the EU and its Member States would have been moot (though the question of the internal allocation of financial responsibility would have remained). Such outcome was likely if one were to follow the position that the EU holds exclusive competence to conclude future investment treaties. In Opinion 2/15, delivered on 16 May 2017, the European Court of Justice (ECJ) concluded that the EU does not hold sufficient exclusive competence to conclude new-generation FTAs which include a regime for investment arbitration and that Member States' consent is necessary. This is not to say, however, that all

[2] For a list of the EU's FTAs, see Overview of FTA and other trade negotiations at http://trade.ec.europa.eu/doclib/docs/2006/december/tradoc_118238.pdf, last visited 1 August 2018.

FTAs must be mixed treaties. An example of an EU-only FTA is the EU-UK Trade and Cooperation Agreement (TCA) which governs post-Brexit EU-UK relationship. The TCA does not include investment arbitration. This chapter does not address EU-only treaties like the TCA and is focused on mixed FTAs. Accountability under the former raise additional complex questions.

Much has been written about *Opinion 2/15*, though often only in the form of blog posts or other short formats.[3] The dispute concerned the EUSFTA which, according to the European Commission, could be concluded as an EU-only agreement because the Union held all necessary powers to do so.[4] The European Parliament supported the European Commission's claim of exclusive competence.[5] The Council and certain Member States, on the other hand, contended that parts of the treaty cover areas of shared competence and thus called for a mixed form of treaty-making.[6] The ECJ, upon reviewing the agreement chapter by chapter, concluded that the EU lacks the necessary exclusive competence to conclude the agreement alone.[7] Importantly, the ECJ rules that setting out an investor-state dispute settlement (ISDS) mechanism is a shared competence and cannot be established without the Member States' consent.[8] The Court also ruled that Chapter 15 of the EUSFTA, which lays out the dispute-settlement mechanism between the parties, cannot be concluded by the EU alone.[9] The ECJ's position echoed the Opinion of AG Sharpston, who considered that not all parts of the agreement fall within the EU's exclusive competence and therefore the agreement cannot be concluded without the participation of all of its Member States.[10]

Opinion 2/15 has important implications for the EU's external economic governance. Following the Court's interpretation, both CETA and EUSFTA

3 For a more in-depth analysis, see David Kleimann, 'Reading Opinion 2/15: Standards of Analysis, the Court's Discretion, and the Legal View of the Advocate General' (2017) 23 EUI RSCAS 1–38.

4 *Opinion 2/15*, para 12. In relation to portfolio investment the European Commission stated that the EU has exclusive competence pursuant to Art 3(2) TFEU because of the overlap between (i) the commitment contained in that agreement concerning those investments and (ii) the prohibition of restrictions on movement of capital and on payments between Member States and third states that is laid down in Art 63 TFEU, see para 16.

5 *Opinion 2/15*, para 18.

6 *Opinion 2/15*, para 19.

7 Among other, the ECJ concluded that the EU does not have exclusive competence in relation to portfolio investments, see *Opinion 2/15*, para 244.

8 *Opinion 2/15*, paras 292–293. The Court reasoned that an investor may decide to submit a dispute to arbitration rather than courts of a Member States, without that Member State being able to oppose this, see para 291.

9 *Opinion 2/15*, para 304.

10 Opinion of AG Sharpston delivered on 21 December 2016.

were concluded in a mixed form, though the main part of CETA negotiations was conducted with a view to it being an EU-only agreement. Like CETA and EUSFTA, it is likely that future EU trade and investment agreements will also be mixed.

Clarification of the mixity of the Union's FTAs will likely be welcomed not only by Member States but also by the Union's trading partners. Though mixed treaty-making inevitably complicates and prolongs the process of treaty ratification,[11] it also ensures that Member States give direct consent to obligations under an FTA. In this way mixity can be considered a tool for organizing both the EU and Member States' internal and external relations.

Clarity on mixity is especially relevant in relation to the dispute-settlement system under the new treaties. Recently concluded EU's FTAs set out two fora for dispute resolution: a general dispute-settlement mechanism for trade measures and a special ISDS forum.[12]

Before examining the application of the normative findings of this book to the dispute-settlement regimes under the new FTAs, one general remark is timely. It was concluded in Chapter 3 that the Union and its Member States remain independently responsible for their joint international obligations, irrespective of the internal division of competences. In the case of mixed agreements which do not contain a declaration of competences, the obligations of the EU and its Member States are joint and they are independently responsible for their violations. The analysis further revealed that while both the Union and Member States are internationally responsible for all obligations under mixed agreements, the proper respondent in a particular case is that best placed to remedy a breach under consideration. The focus is not on the responsible party, but on the party which is best placed to bear responsibility. The principles of independent responsibility and functional international responsibility thus complement each other. Two entities may be independently responsible for their joint obligations, but which of them will bear exclusive responsibility in a given dispute depends on which of them is best placed to restore the order. The coexistence of these two stages in the determination of responsibility (i.e. independent responsibility and remedy-based exclusive responsibility), which was extrapolated from an extensive case-law analysis conducted in Part II, has been set out expressly in new-generation

11 The very recent example of how mixity can complicate the treaty-making process is the rejection by the Walloon government to ratify CETA. Under the federal constitution of Belgium, Walloon approval is necessary for Belgium to be able to ratify the agreement. Upon revision, Wallonia ultimately withdrew its veto.

12 For example, CETA Sect F Ch 8 (investment disputes), Ch 29 (trade disputes); EUSFTA Ch 9 (investment disputes), Ch 15 (trade disputes).

FTAs. For example, Article 1.8 of CETA states that each party is fully responsible for the observance of all provisions of this agreement. This provision is novel as it has not been provided in other mixed treaties, such as the WTO or the ECT. It expressly lays down the principle of independent responsibility of the EU and its Member States in mixed agreements. At the same time Article 8 of CETA establishes a mechanism for the determination of the respondent, which is applied on a case-by-case basis. Accordingly, the normative findings on the principle of independent responsibility and functional international responsibility suggested in this book are expressly reflected in new-generation FTAs.

9.2.2 *Application of the Normative Findings to Trade Disputes*

Trade disputes under the new FTAs are covered by the general treaty dispute-settlement mechanism which closely follows the WTO dispute-resolution model.[13] In fact, both agreements address a possible overlap with WTO obligations through choice of forum provisions. Article 29.3 of CETA and the parallel Article 15.21 of the EUSFTA provide that if an obligation is equivalent in substance under CETA and the WTO Agreement, a party may not seek redress for the breach of such an obligation in the two fora.

Application of the normative findings of this book to trade disputes under the new FTAs is straightforward. It is suggested here that trade disputes will follow the pattern of the optimal respondent in WTO law which were identified in Chapter 7 of this book.[14] To reiterate, it is likely that the EU will be the proper respondent in *trade disputes* under the new FTAs. In most cases the EU is best placed to ensure compliance with trade obligations. In addition, the internal interdependency of the EU and its Member States inherent in mixed treaty-making will allow third parties and tribunals to accept the EU's assumption of international responsibility on behalf of its Member States, similarly to the DSB's approach in WTO dispute-settlement.

The conclusions differ with respect to the special cases of multiple respondents addressed in Chapter 8. That chapter identified a correlation of the scope of a claim and the DSB's decision to address its recommendations to Member States in addition to the EU. It was suggested that the EU is the proper respondent in claims 'as such', whereas Member States are the necessary parties in challenges 'as applied'. It was argue that it is unlikely that the

[13] For example, the dispute-settlement laid out in CETA Ch 29.

[14] Rules for the choice of forum between the WTO and CETA are provided in CETA Art 29.2.

patterns identified and discussed in Chapter 8 will be repeated in new-generation FTAs.

As was suggested in Chapter 7, from an international law perspective the relationship between the EU/Member States on the one hand, and other members of the WTO on the other, is *de facto* bilateral. In practice the EU and its Member States participate in the WTO as one bloc (e.g. they have special voting arrangements), but they each constitute separate and independent members of the WTO. Though considered during the negotiations, a disconnection clause, which would exclude the application of the WTO obligations from the inter-Member States relations, has not been included in the WTO Agreements. Accordingly, from a purely external perspective, the Union and its Member States are unrelated and independent members of the WTO.

Thus, the new FTAs are different from the WTO Agreements – they are *de jure* bilateral because the EU and its Member States are expressly defined as one party (referred to as the 'EU Party').[15] Unlike under the WTO system, where from an international law perspective intra-EU disputes are *de jure* possible, the new FTAs do not establish Member States' obligations to each other. It should be noted that the definition of the parties in, for example, Article 29.2 of CETA specifies that the 'EU Party' covers both the 'EU *and* its Member States' and the 'EU *or* its Member States'. While the second prong does refer to the separateness of the two entities and thus reinforces the principle of independent responsibility discussed in Chapter 3 of this book, challenges to Member States are unlikely. This is so because Article 29.2 also provides that the EU and its Member States are parties to the treaty '*within their respective areas of competence as derived from the Treaty on European Union and the Treaty on the Functioning of the European Union*'. This novel generalized declaration of competences[16] allows the EU to claim that it is the proper respondent in all trade disputes. It is likely that, because of the expressly bilateral nature of the new treaties and the reference to the internal division of powers, the number of special cases of both the EU and its Member States as co-respondents will be, at most, rare.

While the discussion here is limited to future *trade* disputes under the new FTAs to the aforementioned, the new *investment* chapters beg a more

[15] For example, CETA Art 1.1 provides that 'Parties means, on the one hand, the European Union or its Member States or the European Union and its Member States within their respective areas of competence as derived from the Treaty on European Union and the Treaty on the Functioning of the European Union (hereinafter referred to as the "EU Party"), and on the other hand, Canada'.

[16] For more on declaration of competences, see Sect 3.2 of Ch 3 above.

nuanced analysis and will thus be the focus of this chapter. The dispute-resolution mechanism under the new treaties reveals a combination of Part II normative findings attributed to both the WTO and the ECT.

9.2.3 *Application of the Normative Findings to Investment Disputes*

Application of the normative findings of this book to investment disputes under the new FTAs is nuanced. On the one hand, in line with Chapter 7 analysis, the substantive nature of investment obligations under the new FTAs points to Member States as the proper respondents in investment disputes. As was suggested, Member States' actions are commonly the proximate cause of harm to investors. On the other hand, the new FTAs are innovative in that they oblige third parties to allow the Union internally to determine the proper respondent.[17] Allocation of responsibility is governed by Regulation (EU) No. 914/2014 of the European Parliament and of the Council of 23 July 2014 establishing a framework for managing financial responsibility linked to investor-to-state dispute settlement under international agreements to which the EU is a party (Regulation No. 914/2014).[18] This latter mechanism for the allocation of responsibility set out in the Regulation No. 914/2014 will be examined in the following sections of this chapter. Suffice it here to say that the EU's rules place the Union, not the Member States, at the centre of investment-dispute resolution, contrary to the general pattern observed in Chapter 7. This relates back to the Treaty of Lisbon which transferred competence in the area of FDI from Member States to the EU. Accordingly, it is argued that the new FTAs establish primacy of procedural rules, which place the EU at the forefront of dispute resolution, over investment obligations and the system of remedies designed to protect them.

The discussions with the negotiators of the new FTAs reveal that in exchange for empowering the EU with a discretionary right to modify the general pattern of Member States as the optimal respondents in investment disputes due to their being the proximate cause of harm (Chapter 7), third parties negotiated a number of procedural safeguards. These guarantee that the award will be complied with, irrespective of whether the Member States are respondents in a given investment dispute. Procedural rules effectively transform the internal interdependency of the EU and its Member States into an external interdependency, thus allowing third parties to rest assured that the

[17] A similar mechanism was provided in the ECT, albeit only on a voluntary basis.
[18] For more on the Regulation No. 914/2014, see Armin Steinbach, *EU Liability and International Economic Law* (Hart Publishing 2017).

'EU party' will not circumvent its obligations by hiding behind the institutional veil. Thus, under the new FTAs the internal interdependency, which was discussed in the WTO context in Chapter 7, is elevated to the domain of international law. Though not yet tested in practice, the new FTAs demonstrate how the EU's international responsibility can be constructed through procedural mechanisms.

The following section will examine the mechanism for the determination of respondents in investment disputes under the new FTAs.

9.3 THE MECHANISM FOR THE DETERMINATION OF RESPONDENTS UNDER THE NEW-GENERATION FTAS

Under new FTAs both the EU and Member States can be respondents in investment disputes.[19] New-generation FTAs also provide a mechanism for determining the proper respondent(s) in disputes involving the EU.[20] Article 8.21 of CETA, titled 'Determination of the respondent for disputes with the European Union or its Member States', was drafted at a time when both negotiating teams considered the new treaty to be an EU-only agreement; thus, the relevance of the provision only increased with the ultimate choice of mixity. Under Article 8.21(1) the claimant shall deliver notice to the EU requesting a determination of the proper respondent. The EU shall, upon its decision, inform the investor as to whether the EU, its Member States or both shall be the proper respondent(s) in a given case.

The scheme for the determination of respondents negotiated under the new FTAs is not novel. Pursuant to Article 26(3)(b)(ii) of the ECT[21] the EC Council and European Commission submitted a statement which addressed *inter alia* the determination of the respondent in investor-state disputes under the ECT.[22] The statement established that the EC and their Member States have both concluded the ECT and are thus internationally responsible for the fulfilment of the obligations contained therein, in accordance with their respective competence. The statement further provides that the EC and its Member States shall, if necessary and on an investor's request, determine

19 Art 8.1 provides that respondent means Canada or, in the case of the EU, either the Member State of the EU or the EU pursuant to Art 8.21.

20 For example, determination of the respondents in EUSFTA Art 9.15, CETA Art 8.21.

21 Art 26(3)(b)(ii) required each Contracting Party that is listed in Annex ID to provide a written statement of its policies, practices and conditions, Annex 1 to the Final Act of the European Energy Charter Conference (adopted 16–17 December 1991, opened for signature 17 December 1994) (1994) 34 ILM 360.

22 Statement submitted by the European Communities to the Secretariat of the ECT, OJ L 336, 23 December 1994, 115.

among them who is the proper respondent. The mechanism, however, is yet to be used. As was mentioned earlier, Member States have been respondents in all publicly available disputes under the ECT, including those with an EU dimension. Such was the choice of investors themselves who opted not to follow the procedure, allowing the EU to determine a proper respondent internally, as provided in the statement. The statement did not constitute a procedural technique powerful enough to override the content of investment obligations which, as was suggested in Chapter 7, is closely related to Member States' conduct and thus organically called for Member States' participation. It is likely that this is so partly because the EC statement was provided in the form of a letter annexed to the main body of the ECT rather than its main text and partly because its mandatory force was further diminished by a qualification that the statement is without prejudice to the investor's right to initiate proceedings against both the EC and its Member States.

Unlike the ECT, the scheme which allows the EU to determine the proper respondent internally is mandatory under the new FTAs. It is provided in a form of a legally binding provision in the main body of the treaty, and thus investors have an obligation rather than choice to request the EU to determine the respondent. The loose language in the EC's statement under the ECT, that the EC and Member States shall determine the respondent 'if necessary' is replaced by the obligatory verb 'shall' in the new FTAs.[23] The new treaties eliminate the investor's choice of respondent by obliging it to send its request for consultation concerning an alleged breach to the EU.[24] The system established under the new FTAs is not without ambiguities, however. For example, Article 8.19 of CETA provides that consultations concerning a dispute take place in Brussels if measures challenged include a measure of the EU, or in Member States if they are exclusively measures of that Member State. It remains unclear how an investor is to determine whether conduct is that of the EU or its Member State beforehand and how Article 8.19 corresponds to the EU's rights and obligation to determine the proper respondent under Article 8.21. It is likely that for practical reasons all consultations will take place in Brussels.

In addition to the establishment of a mechanism under which the EU itself will determine whether it will act as respondent in a given dispute, the new FTAs also provide a forum where it will in fact be able to act as such. One of

[23] CETA Art 8.21(1) provides that 'the investor shall deliver to the European Union a notice requesting a determination of the respondent'.

[24] CETA Art 8.19(7).

the practical and procedural reasons which prevented the EU's participation in dispute settlement under the ECT was that the EU is not a party to the International Centre for Settlement of Investment Disputes (ICSID) Convention and could not become one unless changes were introduced which allowed international organizations to become parties to the Convention. The EU's new FTAs were accompanied by calls for reform of ISDS. Among the major developments are plans to create the Investment Court System (ICS) which is increasingly gaining speed and form.[25] The European Commission is currently working on the Multilateral Investment Court (MIC) project.[26] It is expected that by the time CETA takes full effect, a new and improved ICS will replace the current investor-state dispute-settlement mechanism with respect to the EU's investment treaties.

It follows then that investment arbitration under the new FTAs allows the EU to place itself as respondent in investment disputes. Differently from BITs and the ECT, new-generation investment treaties also establish a dispute-resolution forum where the EU's participation will be practically possible. A question then is whether and how these novel arrangements will redefine the distribution of shared responsibility of the EU and its Member States in investment arbitration.

To reiterate the normative findings of this book, it was noted in Chapter 7 that Member States have so far been the exclusive respondents in investment disputes under the ECT, even though it is a mixed agreement which binds both the EU and its Member States. This this pattern was explained by suggesting that the content of investment obligations is closely linked to Member States' conduct. From a functional perspective, a wider EU law dimension, even if present, is in most cases insignificant. Differently from the WTO system, where the primary aim is overall regulatory compliance, the aim of investment disputes is compensation. Compensation is triggered by the existence of a breach and is calculated on the basis of harm, not according to the scope of regulatory inconsistency. Thus, from the investor's perspective, it is sufficient to challenge a measure which is the proximate cause of harm. It was suggested that in most situations it is the host Member State's conduct which constitutes the proximate cause of harm because Member States have

[25] CETA Art 8.9 provides that the parties shall pursue with other trading partners the establishment of a multilateral investment tribunal and appellate mechanism for the resolution of investment disputes. Before the multilateral investment tribunal is established, CETA provides for a possibility to submit a claim under ICSID, ICSID Additional Facility Rules, or any other rules on agreement of disputing parties, see Art 8.23(2) CETA.

[26] For more on the European Commission's Multilateral Investment Court project, see http://trade.ec.europa.eu/doclib/press/index.cfm?id=1608, last visited 1 August 2018.

a direct relationship with investors. That the source of a challenged Member State measure is an EU-wide policy is essential to WTO panels that are called to identify regulatory inconsistencies and are not required to calculate damage (unless non-compliance calls for retaliation). Investment tribunals, on the other hand, perform an entirely different task as their focus is the determination of the degree and extent of damage, not the investigation of an overall regulatory system.

The new FTAs reverse this pattern through a negotiated construct which allows the EU itself to determine the proper respondent in a given dispute. As will be discussed later, it is likely that under the new system the EU will become a key respondent in investment disputes. The question arises as to why third parties have agreed to this new arrangement.

The answer to this question recalls Chapter 7's analysis of the internal interdependency of the EU and its Member States in the WTO regime. It was explained that in WTO law the EU is in most cases allowed to assume international responsibility on behalf of its Member States because these are internally bound to the EU's international commitments. This reduces the risk of circumvention of obligations and allows the DSB to address their rulings to the EU even when Member State compliance is necessary to ensure a positive solution to a dispute. In other words, provided there are sufficient procedural safeguards, the DSB typically leaves the matter to be determined in accordance with the internal rules of the EU (though in some cases it will still call for Member States to act as co-respondents, as was explained in Chapter 8). These same considerations form the basis of the third-party position under the new FTAs. The EU's partners under the recently concluded FTAs have accepted the arrangement which will place the decision to determine the proper respondent with the EU precisely because the new FTAs provide sufficient procedural safeguards to ensure that a remedy will be delivered. In addition, while interdependency of the EU and its Member States in the WTO context is internal (i.e. binding under EU law), the system of safeguards under the FTAs is binding *vis-à-vis* contracting third states. The following section examines these safeguards.

9.4 PROCEDURAL SAFEGUARDS UNDER THE NEW-GENERATION FTAS

The new FTAs contain several procedural safeguards aimed at providing additional security to third parties in case the EU fails to determine the proper respondent or otherwise hinders third parties from exercising their right to judicial protection. These procedural safeguards allow third parties to leave it to the EU to decide how it participates in the negotiations. For example, during the negotiations of CETA Canada showed deference to the Union's internal constitutional arrangement by allowing the EU to fully represent its Member States. In fact, in contrast to Canada's large delegation which included representatives of provinces, EU Member States were not present at all during negotiations of the treaty as they were represented by the EU Directorate General for Trade. Revealing a functional approach, the focus of third parties is not whether and how Member States participate in treaty negotiations but on whether there are sufficient procedural safeguards which ensure that Member States are bound by the treaty.

9.4.1 *Safeguards against Inadmissibility Defence*

When it comes to the scheme under which the EU itself determines the proper respondent, one of the central concerns of third parties was that the arbitral process could be blocked by a delay in EU decision-making. In CETA this concern is addressed by Article 8.21(4) which establishes a time of fifty days for the EU's determination of the respondent. The provision states that if no decision is made within this period, a Member State shall be the respondent if the challenged measure is exclusively that of a Member State, whereas if it also includes a measure of the EU, the EU shall be a respondent. It is unclear how an investor would determine the exact nature and scope of the measure, and it is thus likely that in Article 8.21(4) situations all investor claims would be filed against the EU.

Article 8.21(4) was adopted as a procedural safeguard for the treaty partner. It was hoped by third-party negotiators that recourse to it would in practice never be necessary. From an EU law perspective the provision is problematic as it leaves it to the tribunal to decide whether a measure is exclusively that of a Member State or the EU. Under Article 19(1) of the Treaty on European Union (TEU) the CJEU has exclusive jurisdiction to interpret and apply EU treaties, including questions concerning competence. While Article 8.21(4) provides a necessary safeguard for the treaty partner, my discussions with informed officials reveal that there was an intention that this clause is not triggered.[27]

An arguably stronger procedural safeguard for the treaty partner is enshrined in Article 8.21(6) which establishes the 'no inadmissibility' rule. This provision states that if the EU or a Member State is a respondent, neither can object to the claim on the ground that the respondent was not properly determined.

[27] Informal interview conducted on 27 September 2017 at the Mission of Canada to the European Union, Brussels.

The 'no inadmissibility' rule applies both to the determination of a respondent by the EU pursuant to Article 8.21(1) and in the Article 8.21(4) situation when the determination is made by the investor upon the EU's failure to do so within the 50-day period.

The purpose of the 'no inadmissibility' rule is to safeguard third parties from the Union's procedural defence that the claim has been brought against a wrong party. There have so far been no cases where an inadmissibility defence has been employed by the Union, most likely because the EU is seeking to prove itself as a significant global player. A procedural defence of inadmissibility should not be conflated with the substantive defence that a challenged measure is required under Union law. This latter defence has caused confusion in practice, and so I shall discuss it in the following section.

9.4.2 *Safeguards against Micula-type Situations*

The question of legitimacy of intra-EU obligations has been a subject of extensive debate among scholars and practitioners since the Treaty of Lisbon transferred competence in the field of FDI from the Member States to the EU. Analysis of the status of intra-EU BITs falls outside the scope of this book and will thus not be addressed in detail. However, what is important for purposes of the present analysis is the question of the supremacy of EU law over that of international treaties governing investment obligations which has arisen mainly in the context of disputes under intra-EU BITs, including disputes between Member States under the ECT.

The European Commission holds EU law supreme in matters concerning investment protection obligations between Member States. Member States have, on several occasions, employed the notion of primacy as a defence against claims brought by investors. Importantly, the supremacy argument has so far been limited to situations where a claim is brought by an EU-incorporated investor against a host Member State. There is thus no clear indication that the European Commission or Member States would employ the supremacy defence in disputes under the new FTAs with third parties. Nevertheless, as was suggested by those involved in the US Transatlantic Trade and Investment Partnership (TTIP) negotiations, the prospect that supremacy may be invoked is unsettling for third parties.[28] Some of the considerations of arbitral tribunals concerning the relationship between EU law and international investment obligations create ambiguity, if not anxiety, among EU partners as it is not

28 Informal interview conducted on 25 September 2015 at the United States Trade Representative, Washington, DC, United States.

clear whether they target exclusively intra-EU relations. Before addressing the procedural safeguards employed in the new FTAs to give assurance to the EU's treaty partners, it is useful to survey disputes where the supremacy argument has been raised as it reflects more generally on tribunals' approach to the status of EU law in relation to the ECT.

In its submission as a non-disputing party in *Electrabel* v. *Hungary*, the European Commission stated that the Tribunal, established under the ICSID Convention, had no jurisdiction over the claim under consideration.[29] *Electrabel* v. *Hungary* was an intra-EU dispute between Hungary and Electrabel S.A., an energy generation and sales company incorporated under Belgian law. The European Commission cited the *Bosphorus* case, where the European Court on Human Rights (ECtHR) noted that the Convention has to be interpreted in the light of any relevant rules and principles of international law applicable in relations between the Contracting Parties, that is, EU law.[30] In argument reminiscent of Solange-type reasoning the European Commission reiterated the ECtHR's conclusion that if the two bodies of law can be considered equivalent in their protection of individual rights, an act which is in conformity with EU law will be considered to be in conformity with the ECHR.[31] The European Commission further maintained that in case of contradiction between the ECT and EU law, the latter prevails.[32] Accordingly, an award that substituted compensation for state aid unlawful under EU law would not be enforceable because it would be equivalent to a judgment of a national court of an EU Member State made in contradiction of EU law.[33] The Tribunal noted that the European Commission did not explain precisely how this defence to recognition or enforcement of an award could be made in respect of an ICSID award before the national courts of a non-EU Member State.[34] The analysis of the Tribunal's approach is relevant to the new FTAs as it discusses the relationship between the ECT and other agreements, including EU treaties.

Though the Tribunal noted from the outset that there was no inconsistency between the EU law and the ECT,[35] it nevertheless went on to provide a theoretical analysis of a situation where such inconsistency does in fact arise. It first noted that there is no rule of international law compelling

29 *Electrabel* v. *Hungary*, Decision on Jurisdiction, para 4.101.
30 *Electrabel* v. *Hungary*, Decision on Jurisdiction, para 4.102.
31 *Bosphorus*, para 150.
32 *Electrabel* v. *Hungary*, Decision on Jurisdiction, para 4.109.
33 *Electrabel* v. *Hungary*, Decision on Jurisdiction, para 4.110.
34 *Electrabel* v. *Hungary*, Decision on Jurisdiction, para 4.110.
35 *Electrabel* v. *Hungary*, Decision on Jurisdiction, para 4.167.

harmonious interpretation of all existing legal rules.[36] However, the Tribunal noted that if there were an inconsistency between the EU law and the ECT, they should, if possible, be read in harmony.[37] While the implications of the Tribunal's considerations for interpretation of the new FTAs remain unclear, a possibility that investment tribunals may apply the self-imposed principle of harmonious interpretation remains.

The Tribunal then considered a hypothetical situation where there in fact exists a material inconsistency not subject to harmonious interpretation. In a surprising turn, it noted that decisions of the EU which bind the respondent have to be taken into account because the ECT does not protect investors from enforcement by the respondent of a decision of the European Commission binding under EU law.[38] Accordingly, the framework of the ECT recognizes that EU Member States will be legally bound by decisions of the EU under EU law and thus investors can have no legitimate expectation in regard to the consequences of the implementation by an EU Member State of any such decision by the European Commission.[39]

The Tribunal also considered Article 16 of the ECT which *inter alia* states that where contracting parties have entered into a prior or subsequent international agreement whose terms concern provisions related to investment protection and dispute-settlement provisions under the ECT, nothing in the provisions of such international agreements or the ECT shall be so construed as to derogate from reciprocal provisions in another agreement where any such provision is more favourable to the investor. A parallel provision is established in CETA Article 1.5 which states that the parties affirm their mutual rights and obligations under the WTO Agreement and other agreements to which they are party. The Tribunal dismissed the applicability of Article 16 ECT in *Electrabel* v. *Hungary*. According to it nothing in EU law can be interpreted as precluding investor-state arbitration under the ECT and the ICSID Convention simply because the EU law does not deal with investor-state disputes.[40] As for the substantive protections, Article 16 was equally inapplicable because the ECT and EU law do not share the same subject matter.[41]

The Tribunal then proceeded to Article 351 of the Treaty on the Functioning of the European Union (TFEU) which establishes that pre-accession agreements between the Member States and third parties shall not

36 *Electrabel* v. *Hungary*, Decision on Jurisdiction, para 4.173.
37 *Electrabel* v. *Hungary*, Decision on Jurisdiction, para 4.167.
38 *Electrabel* v. *Hungary*, Decision on Jurisdiction, para 4.169.
39 *Electrabel* v. *Hungary*, Decision on Jurisdiction, para 4.142.
40 *Electrabel* v. *Hungary*, Decision on Jurisdiction, para 4.175.
41 *Electrabel* v. *Hungary*, Decision on Jurisdiction, para 4.176.

be affected by the provisions of EU treaties.[42] As interpreted by the ECJ, in relation to treaties between Member States and third parties, the provision resolves the conflict between the two incompatible obligations in favour of the earlier obligation.[43] Article 351 TFEU itself is not directly relevant to the new FTAs as these constitute post-accession obligations.

Similarly, in *RREEF Infrastructure* v. *Spain*, a dispute over photovoltaic energy regulation, Spain argued that the EU is an economic integration area which includes a comprehensive system for promoting and protecting intra-EU investments. This, it said, has primacy over that provided by the ECT.[44] Spain argued that the system of intra-EU investor protection deriving from EU instruments and judicial decisions takes precedence over or displaces that contained in any other international treaty.[45] Spain rejected the relevance of the absence of a disconnection clause in the ECT and instead provided a number of arguments in support of its supremacy argument.[46] The Tribunal rejected Spain's considerations, in line with the previous decision in *Electrabel* v. *Hungary*.[47] However, contrary to the position in *Electrabel* v. *Hungary*, the Tribunal found that to the extent possible the two treaties should be interpreted in such a way as not to contradict each other.[48] It then applied what it called a principle of harmonious interpretation to the present case but found no inconsistency between EU law and obligations under the ECT.

The practical implications of the supremacy of EU law manifested themselves in the *Micula* v. *Romania* arbitration under the Romania-Sweden BIT.

42 The provision has been interpreted by the ECJ as bearing opposite logics in relations between two EU Member States, i.e. that inconsistent earlier treaties between Member States do not survive entry into the EU, see Case 10/61, *Commission* v. *Italy* [1962] ECR 1, 10. See also Jan Klabbers, *Treaty Conflict and the European Union* (Cambridge University Press 2009), 120.

43 This position was followed by the ECJ in its Judgment in Case C-264/09, *European Commission* v. *Slovak Republic* [2011] ECR I-08065, para 41: 'According to settled case-law, the purpose of the first paragraph of Article 307 EC is to make clear, in accordance with the principles of international law, as set out in, inter alia, Article 30(4)(b) of the Vienna Convention on the Law of Treaties of 23 May 1969, that the application of the EC Treaty does not affect the duty of the Member State concerned to respect the rights of non-member countries under a prior agreement and to perform its obligations thereunder (see, to that effect, Case 812/79 *Burgoa* [1980] ECR 2787, para 8)'. This Judgment only reiterates the ECJ's analysis since Case 10/61, *Commission* v. *Italy* [1962] ECR 1.

44 *RREEF Infrastructure* v. *Spain*, Decision on Jurisdiction, para 40.

45 *RREEF Infrastructure* v. *Spain*, Decision on Jurisdiction, para 41.

46 *RREEF Infrastructure* v. *Spain*, Decision on Jurisdiction, paras 40–50. Spain stressed the special status of the EU in the framework of the ECT and the fact that the EU was one of the authors of the ECT.

47 *RREEF Infrastructure* v. *Spain*, Decision on Jurisdiction, para 75.

48 *RREEF Infrastructure* v. *Spain*, Decision on Jurisdiction, para 76.

The dispute arose after the Micula brothers invested in a food production facility in Romania based on an investment incentive scheme in the form of an emergency government ordinance. Romania repealed the tax incentives because it was considered state aid. Investors brought a claim against Romania before the ICSID Tribunal. The Award, which was issued in December 2013, granted the Micula brothers damages equivalent to the assistance which they would have received if the tax incentives had not been repealed.

Enforcement of the ICSID award encountered opposition from the EU which argued that the payment of any compensation to the Micula brothers would constitute unlawful state aid and be invalid under EU law. In 2014 the EU issued an injunction to Romania to restrain its compliance with the Award. Moreover, on 30 March 2015 the EU adopted a Final Decision 2015/1470 which declared that payment of the Award would constitute unlawful state aid and ordered Romania to recover payments already made. The Micula brothers challenged the Final Decision before the General Court of European Union (GCEU). In parallel, the English High Court rejected Romania's application to set aside the Court's 2014 order registering the Award. The Award was registered in the High Court pursuant to the Arbitration (International Investment Disputes) Act of 1996.[49] However, the Court stayed enforcement of the Award in the United Kingdom pending determination of proceedings before the GCEU.

The Court's reasoning was based on the argument that registered ICSID awards are treated in the same way as judgments of the English High Court and so must be in conformity with EU state aid rules. The Court did not dispute the claimant's position that the Award was *res judicata* from the date of its issue.[50] However, the Court reasoned that if it proceeded to enforce the Award, this would contravene the European Commission's Final Decision. Since the issue of whether the Award was *res judicata* is before the GCEU, the Court saw a possibility of inconsistency if it were to decide that the Award could be enforced. Thus, enforcement of ICSID awards was deemed subject to EU law. The Court refused to rule on the effect of Article 351 TFEU, which establishes that international obligations arising from Member

49 The Act implements the ICSID Convention in English law. Registration takes place where a person seeks '*recognition or enforcement*' of an award. Under Art 54 of the ICSID Convention, the Award must be recognized as if it were a final judgment of a Contracting State's own national system.

50 According to the Court as a matter of English law read with Art 54 of the ICSID Convention, an ICSID Convention award achieves finality, and becomes *res judicata*, at the time of the award.

States' pre-accession agreements are not affected by the treaties as this provision was raised in proceedings before the GCEU.

The European Commission has adopted the Micula-type approach in a number of pending investment disputes under the ECT over Spain's incentivization scheme for renewable energy production.[51] Most of the investors that have brought claims against Spain are based in other Member States, and thus the disputes are mainly intra-EU. In November 2017 the European Commission issued a decision in which it stated that any compensation which an arbitration tribunal were to grant to an investor on the basis that Spain had modified the premium economic scheme by the notified scheme would constitute in and of itself state aid.[52] Furthermore, the European Commission maintains that if tribunals award compensation, as in *Eiser* v. *Spain*, or were to do so in the future, this compensation would be notifiable state aid pursuant to Article 108(3) TFEU and be subject to the standstill obligation. According to the European Commission, this decision is binding on investment tribunals and can only be interpreted by the CJEU.

The European Commission's refusal to accept the effects of the intra-EU BITs has been supported by the CJEU's recent judgment in *Slovak Republic* v. *Achmea B. V.*[53] The CJEU ruled that the arbitration clause contained in Article 8 of the 1991 Netherlands-Slovakia BIT has an adverse effect on the autonomy of EU law and was therefore unlawful.

An important safeguard is enshrined in the already mentioned Regulation No. 914/2014 which establishes a framework for managing financial responsibility linked to investor-to-state dispute-settlement under new-generation FTAs to which the EU is party. Regulation No. 914/2014 gives priority to the payment of the award, whereas the internal allocation of financial responsibility can be carried out retroactively. Regulation No. 914/2014 provides that where an award has been issued against the Union, that award should be paid without delay.[54] The legislation calls for a separate line in the Union's budget to cover expenditure resulting from agreements pursuant to provisions on FDI to which the Union is a party and which provide for investor-to-state dispute settlement.[55] Article 20(1) of the regulation states that the European

[51] For the list of disputes, see https://energycharter.org/what-we-do/dispute-settlement/all-investment-dispute-settlement-cases/, last visited 1 August 2018.

[52] European Commission's letter 'State aid SA.40348 (2015/NN) – Spain Support for electricity generation from renewable energy sources, cogeneration and waste', Brussels, 10 November 2017 C(2017) 7384 final, para 165.

[53] C-284/16 *Slowakische Republik* v. *Achmea BV* [2018].

[54] Para 19 of the preamble of the Regulation.

[55] Para 21 of the preamble of the Regulation.

Commission may adopt a decision requiring the Member State concerned to advance financial contributions to the budget of the Union in respect of foreseeable or incurred costs arising from the arbitration. Regulation No. 914/2014 thus establishes a tight link between the EU and its Member States under the new FTAs, with the Union confining itself to paying awards without delay, even if the expense will ultimately have to be covered by the Member State. In other words the Union pledges to pay any adverse award, irrespective of whether it will bear financial responsibility under internal rules. CETA Article 8.41 similarly states that an award issued by an arbitral tribunals shall be binding between the disputing parties and must be complied with without delay.

Whether the combined effect of CETA and Regulation No. 914/2014 is sufficient to protect investors' rights in *Micula*-type situations remains to be seen. It is likely that the European Commission's insistence on the primacy of EU law will be confined to intra-EU disputes. It is doubtful that the EU will be willing to jeopardize its newly acquired role as the negotiator of EU trade agreements by raising concerns about its trustworthiness in the eyes of its foreign partners. It is expected that the European Commission will try to maintain an image of a house in order by abiding to the code of conduct established under Regulation No. 914/2014. The following section considers Regulation No. 914/2014 in more detail.

9.4.3 *The Internal Code of Conduct under Regulation No. 914/2014*

It has been mentioned earlier that the new FTAs leave the determination of the respondent in disputes involving EU measures to the Union itself. To this end the EU has adopted Regulation No. 914/2014 for managing financial responsibility resulting from adverse arbitral awards. Regulation No. 914/2014 applies not only to the new FTAs but also to existing agreements to which the Union is a party, such as the ECT.

In the Explanatory Memorandum to the Regulation No. 914/2014 the European Commission suggested that the regime is based on special rules applicable between an international organization and its members as provided in Article 64 of the Articles on the Responsibility of International Organizations (ARIO), the *lex specialis* rule. In the Explanatory Memorandum the Commission refers to Article 64, stating that '*in the international context, the International Law Commission has recognized the possibility that special rules may apply between an international organization and its member*'. As has been argued in Chapter 2, the ARIO framework does not govern the allocation of international responsibility in a multilayered structure of an international body. The ARIO rules determine whether a subject *is* internationally responsible. If responsibility arises in the context of an international body where sovereignty is shared between the organization and its Member States, additional questions arise which fall outside the scope of the ILC rules. Nor do the rules govern the internal allocation of financial responsibility between the organization and its Member States. Nevertheless, the Commentary to Article 64 refers to special rules which may 'supplement' more general rules (not only replace them). Regulation No. 914/2014 is *lex specialis* in relation to the ARIO framework, especially since the Commentary specifically refers to the special rules which govern attribution to the EU of conduct of Member States when they implement binding acts of the Community.

The framework of responsibility established under Regulation No. 914/2014 differentiates between two types of responsibility, *international* and *financial*.[56] While the term 'financial responsibility' is expressly defined in the Regulation,[57] neither the proposal for Regulation No. 914/2014 nor the legal act itself explains in more detail what is meant by the term 'international responsibility' as opposed to 'financial responsibility'.[58] It seems that under Regulation No. 914/2014 international responsibility concerns questions of settlement of international disputes, especially the status of respondent. International responsibility and financial responsibility are determined on a different legal basis. The motive for the introduction of financial responsibility as a category was the need to protect the Union's budget from the adverse effect of awards which result from conduct of Member States.

The regulation establishes a competence-based principle of *international responsibility*. Paragraph 3 of the preamble states that international responsibility follows the division of competences between the Union and Member States, irrespective of whether the treatment at issue is afforded by the Union itself or by a Member State. *Financial responsibility*, on the other hand, is based on authorship of the treatment in question.[59] In cases where an adverse

[56] In the Explanatory Memorandum the European Commission stated that '[i]t is important to separate the issue of the conduct and management of an investor-to-State arbitration claim from the issue of the allocation of financial responsibility', sect 1.3.

[57] Article 2(g) of the Regulation states that 'financial responsibility' means an obligation to pay a sum of money awarded by an arbitration tribunal or agreed as part of a settlement and including the costs arising from the arbitration.

[58] Proposal for a regulation of the European Parliament and of the Council establishing a framework for managing financial responsibility linked to investor-state dispute-settlement tribunals established by international agreements to which the European Union is party of 21 June 2012, COM(2012) 335 final (Proposal).

[59] Proposal for a Regulation, Explanatory Memorandum, 2.

award flows from treatment afforded by a Member State, that Member State will bear *financial responsibility*, unless the treatment in question is required by Union law.[60] Joint financial responsibility is provided in cases which concern both treatment afforded by a Member State and treatment required by Union law.[61]

It is not clear how the treaty partners and the Union itself will separate Member State 'treatment' from that of the EU itself as it is not defined in Regulation No. 914/2014. The task is not easy, because the conduct of the EU and Member States is inextricably linked, and it is often difficult to draw a dividing line between a Member State's implementation of the Union's measure and the Member States' exercise of discretion. Definition of the term 'required by Union law', provided in Article 1(l) of the Regulation No. 914/2014, will hardly be helpful as it refers to a clear-cut 'with discretion/without discretion' situation, whereas the functioning of the Union is often polychromatic. According to the European Commission officials, the exact meaning of the term 'required' was extensively debated during the adoption of the regulation.[62] It is understood that the definition is narrow in that it refers to situations where no margin of discretion is given to Member States, such as in the case of customs tariff classifications. The definition of 'measure' provided in CETA Article 1.1 is similarly of little relevance as it covers 'any form of measure' by a party.

Guidance on the definition of the term 'required by Union law' may be afforded in the doctrine of direct effect under EU law. Provisions of EU directives may have horizontal direct effect (i.e. may be invoked and relied on by individuals before national courts) if *inter alia* they are sufficiently clear and precise.[63] Whether a provision is sufficiently clear and precise depends on how much discretion a Member State enjoys with respect to its implementation. The Court's case law on what constitutes discretion is, however, complex.[64] It is thus difficult to determine what counts as 'no discretion' under Regulation No. 914/2014. For example, in the controversial *Kortas* decision the ECJ ruled that the possibility of a Member State's derogation from a harmonizing directive did not prevent direct effect and did not preclude an individual from relying directly on its provisions.[65] It may be

60 CH 2 Art 3(1), also para 5 of the preamble.
61 Para 7 of the preamble.
62 Informal interview conducted on 6 October 2017 at the Directorate General for Trade of the European Commission, Brussels.
63 Paul Craig and Gráinne de Búrca, *EU Law: Text, Cases, and Materials* (6th edn, Oxford University Press 2015), 202, ft 71.
64 Craig and de Búrca 2015, 202.
65 Case C-319/97 *Kortas* [1999] ECR I-3143.

assumed that in the context of Regulation No. 914/2014, the term 'required by Union law' will be interpreted broadly so as to cover a wide range of Member States' conduct. This is based on the EU seeking to be an active participant in international adjudication which can be observed in the WTO regime.

It must be noted that the competence-based principle of international responsibility created discomfort among the Member States. They were displeased with an arrangement in which the Union participates in all investment disputes, including those where the award is to be paid by a Member State.[66] Regulation No. 914/2014 thus qualifies the principle of competence-based international responsibility. Paragraph 9 of the preamble provides that a Member State may act as respondent to defend the treatment which it has afforded to the investor. The European Commission thus adopts a treatment-based approach to responsibility which is different from its competence-based stance under the WTO regime. Despite this qualification, the EU equips itself with broad discretion to decide whether a Member State in question will be given a role in the dispute after a '*full and balanced factual analysis and legal reasoning provided to the Member States*'.[67] Joint participation of the Union and Member States in investment disputes involving treatment afforded both by the EU and Member States can be excluded on the basis of a decision of the European Commission.[68] Further exceptions to a Member States' right to act as respondent are provided in Article 9 and include *inter alia* situations when a related case is filed under the WTO dispute-settlement system.

The Explanatory Memorandum to Regulation No. 914/2014 affords even broader discretion to the European Commission. It is suggested that '*rather than set up the mechanisms in a manner reflecting a strict application of the rules on competence, it is more appropriate to put forward pragmatic solutions which ensure legal certainty for the investor . . . the Commission is of the view that Member States should be permitted to act as respondents in order to defend its own actions, except under circumstances where the Union interest requires otherwise*'. The European Commission can thus opt in to act as a respondent in an investor-state arbitration whenever it decides that '*the Union interest so requires*'.[69] Furthermore, Member States may similarly

66 Informal interview conducted on 6 October 2017 at the Legal Service of the European Commission, Brussels.

67 Regulation Art 9(2) and (3).

68 Para 11 of the preamble of the Regulation.

69 For a supporting position as to the Union's right to decide on the naming of a respondent, see Eileen Denza, 'Responsibility of the EU in the Context of Investment', in Malcolm Evans and

transfer the task of respondent to the Union, an option provided in the Regulation itself.[70]

It is yet to be seen whether Member States will be keen to transfer the role of respondent to the European Commission. Given the European Commission's growing expertise in investment dispute settlement, Member States may consider it pragmatic to leave litigation to its Legal Service. Such tendency is evident from WTO dispute-settlement practice, where Member States have shown little interest in getting involved. This may also depend on the size of the EU Member State and its administrative resources. It may also depend on the extent of the Member States' experience in investment arbitration since some states have participated in investment disputes more often than others (e.g. Hungary has been a repeat respondent in investment disputes). On the other hand, the WTO arrangement is different from investment disputes because under the WTO regime Member States do not bear the risk of a direct financial burden in case of an adverse award. In an unlikely event of retaliation, an application of the so-called 'carousel retaliation' would mean that the negative effects of countermeasures would be shared by various Member States. If a WTO-type approach of refraining from dispute resolution repeats itself under the new FTAs, the determination of a respondent mechanism under Regulation No. 914/2014 will become less relevant because the central focus shifts instead to the rules for the allocation of financial responsibility.

Some elements of the model of separating international responsibility and financial responsibility established under Regulation No. 914/2014 can be found in federal systems. The adoption of the regulation was well received by the EU's trade partners, who welcomed the legislation as the EU's housekeeping rules which bring clarity.[71] In fact the inspiration for the adoption of Regulation No. 914/2014 itself came from the gap in the constitutional law of Canada, the EU's CETA partner. Canada, which is a federal state, does not have a mechanism to allocate financial regulation between the federal government and provinces. This has proved to be problematic, for example, in the *Abitibi* v. *Canada* dispute under the North American Free Trade Agreement (NAFTA).[72] The case concerned an expropriation claim by a US incorporated

Panos Koutrakos (eds), *The International Responsibility of the European Union: European and International Perspectives* (Hart Publishing 2013), 232.

70 Regulation Art 9(2).

71 Informal interview conducted on 27 September 2017 at the Mission of Canada to the European Union, Brussels.

72 *AbitibiBowater Inc.* v. *Government of Canada* (Consent Award, 15 December 2010) ICSID Case No. UNCT/10/1.

pulp and paper manufacturer which operated in the Canadian province of Newfoundland. Upon its closure in 2009 Abitibi still retained various property rights and assets which, it claimed, were unlawfully expropriated by the government of Newfoundland and Labrador. The claim was filed against the federal government of Canada which acted as respondent in the dispute. The parties settled the case in 2010 for $130 million, with a final settlement agreement signed between the company and the government of Canada.[73] The province was not involved in the settlement and has so far paid no contribution towards the compensation. It remains unclear how the Canadian government will seek recovery of the settlement money from the province.[74] Similarly, in *Metalclad* v. *Mexico*, concerning a claim brought by the US investors against Mexico under NAFTA, the federal government was also obliged to bear international responsibility for the actions of subnational units.[75] The question of allocation of responsibility between a federal government and provinces has also arisen in the WTO context.[76] Regulation No. 914/2014 thus provides assurance to the EU's partners that the EU has 'its house in order' when it comes to issues of allocating responsibility between the Union and its Member States.

The EU's house-keeping rules are not, however, free of complication. The basis for the adoption of Regulation No. 914/2014 was the 2009 transfer of exclusive competence in the field of FDI from Member States to the EU, which now has exclusive competence to represent the Union in investment disputes. When the treatment in question is that of a Member State, the Union delegates power to participate in the dispute back to the Member State. The reverse delegation is implicit in Article 2(1) TFEU, which provides that Member States can act in the field of an exclusive competence of the EU only if empowered by the Union. Such reasoning, however, suffered a setback by the *Opinion 2/15* that stated that the Union has exclusive competence in

73 *AbitibiBowater Inc.* v. *Government of Canada*.

74 Céline Lévesque, 'Les Rôles et Responsabilités Des Provinces Canadiennes Dans Le Cadre de Procédures d'arbitrage Entre Investisseurs et États Fondées Sur Des Traités Économiques' (2015) 28 Revue québécoise de droit international 107–155. See also Scott H Fairley, 'Internal Accountability for Provincial Violations of Canada's International Obligations: Lessons from Abitibi' (2012) 53 Can Bus LJ 31–62.

75 *Metalclad* v. *Mexico*, Award.

76 For example, see *Canada – Provincial Liquor Boards* (EEC), WT/ DS17/R – 39S/27, PR adopted 18 February 1992; *Canada – Import, Distribution and Sale of Alcoholic Drinks by Canadian Provincial Marketing Agencies*, BISD 35S/37, PR adopted 22 March 1988; *Canada – Provincial Liquor Boards* (US), WT/DS17/R, PR adopted 18 February 1992; *Canada – Import, Distribution and Sale of Certain Alcoholic Drinks by Provincial Marketing Agencies*, BISD 39S/27, PR adopted 18 February 1992.

relation to substantive standards, whereas dispute settlement is part of shared competence. The Court's rejection of exclusive Union competence in relation to dispute settlement placed the European Commission in limbo. One way of solving the conundrum is to suggest that by adopting Regulation No. 914/2014 the European Commission exercised its shared competence which accordingly was transformed into its exclusive competence. Such solution remains ambiguous given that Article 1(1) of the Regulation itself states that its adoption shall not affect delimitation of competences established by treaties. All in all the Court's interpretation may remain theoretical only, since Member States have not expressed objection to Regulation No. 914/2014, which serves their interests by providing clarity as to the consequences of investment dispute.

In conclusion, the new FTAs provide several procedural safeguards which help to ensure that the Union and its Member States will deliver the remedy in a given dispute. In particular, the safeguards protect third parties from an inadmissibility defence in relation to the proper respondent, avoid *Micula*-type situations where awards conflict with EU law and establish an internal mechanism for the allocation of financial responsibility. These safeguards allow third parties to comfortably place the determination of a proper respondent at the Union's discretion. The substantive nature of investment protection obligations, which points to the Member States as essential players, is neutralized by the primacy of procedural rules. As long as these rules ensure that the Union will deliver a remedy, third parties abstain from interfering in the EU's internal constitutional arrangements.

9.5 CONCLUSION

The aim of this chapter was to apply the normative findings of this book to new-generation FTAs recently negotiated between the EU and third countries, primarily CETA. It was suggested that trade disputes under the new FTAs will closely follow the patterns of functional international responsibility laid out in Part II. It was argued that the EU will be the optimal respondent in trade disputes, similarly to its current role in the WTO dispute-settlement regime. This chapter argued that disputes involving multiple respondents, such as those observed in Chapter 8 in the WTO context, will be rare under the new FTAs because of the *de jure* bilateral nature of the new treaties.

With respect to investment arbitration under the new FTAs, distribution of shared responsibility will embody mixed patterns observed in relation to the WTO and the ECT. This is so because dispute resolution under the new FTAs provides mechanisms which will allow tribunals to place the determination of the proper respondent in the hands of the European Commission. The effect of these procedural safeguards will be similar to the internal interdependency of the EU and its Member States in the WTO context that was discussed in Chapter 7.

Accordingly, while the content of investment arbitration suggests that Member States are the optimal respondents in investment disputes, the procedural rules modify this pattern by shifting responsibility to the EU. It is thus concluded that functional responsibility may be structured through procedural mechanisms provided in the treaty framework.

10

Conclusions

The question of the international responsibility of the European Union (EU) is inextricably linked to the allocation of responsibility between the Union and its Member States. Only separate subjects of international law may have international obligations and bear responsibility if they breach them. Organizations and their Member States are separate legal persons, but the transfer of powers between them blurs the line dividing their conduct. Distribution of shared responsibility for violation of joint obligations in a multilayered structure of an international body where sovereignty is shared between the organization and its members has caused confusion among international scholars and practitioners. The aim of this book has been to identify the legal basis for the distribution of responsibility between the EU and its Member States in international economic law. It reached the following findings.

First, this book enquired what law governs the allocation of responsibility between the EU and its Member States. Following an orthodox approach, the starting point of the analysis is the International Law Commission (ILC) framework of international responsibility. Upon reviewing the ILC rules for responsibility of states (the ARSIWA) and international organizations (the ARIO) and their *travaux préparatoires*, the study concludes that the ILC framework does not govern the allocation of responsibility within an international body. The purpose of the ILC rules is to determine whether a subject of international law *is* internationally responsible. If the question arises in a multilayered structure like the EU, the exercise of sovereignty by the organization and its Member States must first be defined. The book suggests to consider the rules of organization.

Second, the book examines the EU's claim that its international responsibility is competence-based, and rejected it. The position of the European Commission that the EU is internationally responsible for all violations that fall within its competence, irrespective of who carried out the conduct in question is explained. The extensive body of international dispute-settlement practice in the areas of human rights, trade and investment protection does not support the competence-based approach to international responsibility. While states are free to transfer their powers to an international organization, their obligations are non-transferable. It is argued that states and international organizations remain independently responsible for violation of their joint obligations, as in the case of the EU's mixed agreements.

Third, the principle of independent responsibility of the EU and its Member States provides only a half-way solution to the EU's responsibility conundrum. That the EU, its Member States or both *may* be held responsible for violation of their joint obligations does not mean that they *will* be held responsible in a given dispute. Having determined independent responsibility, the analysis turned to determining exclusive responsibility. To establish the latter a line between the conduct of the EU and its Member States was drawn. For that purpose the book explored the concept of an organ and agent in ILC doctrine. The analysis suggests that the ILC supports a broad reading of the term 'organ' of an international organization which may effectively cover any person who carries out the functions of an organization. This provides room for the European Commission's interpretation that authorities of the Member States act as *de facto* organs of the EU when they implement Union law. No support for such claim in the international dispute-settlement practice was, however, identified. This book instead suggests that international dispute-settlement bodies do not allocate responsibility between the EU and its Member States on the basis of attribution of conduct.

Fourth, a conclusion is drawn that attribution of conduct (or breach in case of derived responsibility) is irrelevant to the distribution of shared responsibility between the EU and its Member States in international economic law. This conclusion is based on the analysis of the nature of international economic obligations and the system of remedies that protects them, particularly under the WTO and the ECT regimes. Remedies in international economic law have a restorative rather than retributive purpose. Dominance of liability-type obligations suggests that the focus of adjudication is on keeping the international economic order intact rather than on punishing the entity that carried out the (allegedly) unlawful conduct. As the primary purpose of adjudication of economic disputes is restorative, attribution of conduct or breach is irrelevant. It is argued that the question of responsibility typically raises the question of the proper respondent. Responsibility is allocated to that subject of international law which is best placed to restore order.

Fifth, the question then was to determine *how* international courts and tribunals determine whether the EU, its Member States or both are the proper respondents in a given dispute. I noted the essential difference in the system of remedies under the two treaties – compliance under the WTO regime and compensation under the ECT. I confirmed my hypothesis that distribution of shared responsibility correlates with the nature of the remedial regime under a given treaty. In order to test this hypothesis, an analysis of an extensive body of trade and investment disputes, primarily under the WTO and ECT regimes was conducted. It allowed to discover patterns in the reasoning of the WTO DSB and investment tribunals acting under the ECT which have not been identified in legal scholarship. It is suggested that the DSB applies what I called 'the positive solution test' to determine which party is necessary for compliance purposes. The WTO panels shift responsibility to those subjects the actions of which are necessary to ensure removal of inconsistent measures. Investment tribunals, on the other hand, focus on the proximate cause of breach because the determination of the *existence* of breach is sufficient to trigger award of compensation to an investor. Allocation of responsibility is remedy-based. Rather than being predetermined on some structural basis, it varies in accordance with the system of remedies under the treaty regime in question.

Sixth, having determined that allocation of responsibility in international economic law is remedy-based, this study explains why the EU has so far been the optimal respondent in WTO cases, whereas Member States have been exclusive respondents in investment disputes. What makes the EU best placed to remedy violations of trade obligations, and why are Member States the optimal respondents under the ECT? It is argued that the answer lies in the nature of these treaty regimes. In WTO disputes the EU in most cases assumes responsibility on behalf of its Member States. The DSB's acceptance of such arrangement stems from the internal interdependency of the EU and its Member States in mixed treaty-making. On the other hand, the primary role of Member States in investment disputes can be explained by the nature of investment protection standards, which focus on the conduct of the host state, not the EU.

Seventh, while the EU is in most cases the optimal respondent in WTO dispute settlement, there are special cases of multiple respondents. There is a correlation between the scope of the claim (and the requested remedy), on the one hand, and the DSB's decision to address its recommendations to Member States in addition to the EU, on the other. Analysis of WTO disputes reveals that panels distinguish between two types of claim: claims 'as such' and claims 'as applied'. The EU is the optimal respondent in claims challenging measures of general application as such, whereas Member States are necessary respondents when a complaint (also) covers specific instances of application of such measures. This is so because Member States' actions are necessary to correct breaches resulting from the application of EU trade policies. The DSB's reasoning further supports functional international responsibility.

Finally, the aforementioned normative findings were applied to the EU's new-generation FTAs, primarily CETA. The chapter focused on investment chapters in the new treaties, which provide a novel mechanism for the determination of the proper respondent in investment disputes. The analysis suggests that the new FTAs exhibit a mix of characteristics of the WTO and ECT regimes of responsibility addressed in this book. Under the new FTAs the right to determine the proper respondent is afforded to the EU in exchange for procedural safeguards which serve as a guarantee that the EU will not misuse that right to obstruct adjudication. The effect of these procedural safeguards is similar to the internal interdependency of the EU and its Member States in the WTO context, which were also addressed in this book. This study concludes that the new FTAs demonstrate how the EU's international responsibility can be constructed through procedural mechanisms.

OUTLOOK

The aim of this book has been to identify the legal basis for the distribution of shared responsibility for violation of joint economic obligations in the multilayered structure of the EU. This book does not provide a policy evaluation of its findings. It leaves critical assessment of functional international responsibility for future research. I should nevertheless like to make several remarks.

This book has argued that in international economic law shared responsibility is distributed among subjects of international law which are part of a common institutional structure based on which of them is best placed to remedy breach. This is so because the purpose of international economic adjudication is restorative rather than punitive. Allocation of responsibility does not follow attribution of conduct (or breach) but instead depends on the system of remedies available under a given treaty. Allocation of responsibility is thus a dynamic concept which is not tied to breach but rather depends on the nature of the treaty regime in question.

It follows then that the distribution of responsibility in international economic law is to some degree left to treaty negotiations which may lead to fragmentation of international rules of responsibility in this field. Benvenisti notes that new-generation multi-regionals[1] are negotiated following a strategy

[1] In particular, Benvenisti refers to TTIP and TPP. The negotiations of the former are currently on hold, while the latter was transformed into CPTPP upon withdrawal of the United States.

of fragmentation which separates competing groups of state parties and by maintaining secrecy over the content of negotiations.[2] The conclusion of mega-regionals shapes global rules, and so Benvenisti concludes that negotiating such agreements behind closed doors by the world's superpowers denies the voice of 'Global Others'.[3]

As has been explained in Chapter 9, the EU's new-generation FTAs provide almost unhindered freedom to the EU to decide on the internal allocation of responsibility. Differently to both the ECT, where the European Commission's determination of the proper respondent was an option, and the WTO, where the DSB could at any time reject the EU's assumption of responsibility on behalf of its Member States, the new FTAs oblige parties to hand the decision to the EU. Responsibility has thus been 'downsized' to an internal affair of commercial nature. This seems to be the new global rule on international responsibility of organizations, established by the largest organization itself – the EU.

Functional international responsibility may thus enhance fragmentation. The Brexit negotiations illustrate this point. The central principle of the EU's common commercial policy is regulatory equivalence. The extent of frictionless trade with the EU directly depends on an obligation to apply rules equivalent to those of the EU. Furthermore, frictionless trade requires the acceptance of the Court of Justice of the European Union's (CJEU) jurisdiction. For example, the implementation of rights and obligations stemming from the EU-Turkey Customs Union, in so far as they are identical with corresponding provisions of EU Treaties, must be interpreted in conformity to CJEU's case law.[4] And while such reach of the EU's Court does not extend beyond a customs union with the EU, the tendency of the EU to domesticate international law is present. Article 403 of the EU-Moldova Association Agreement provides that the CJEU's rulings are binding on matters of EU law in disputes between the EU and Moldova. Similarly, Article 322 of the EU-Ukraine Association Agreement provides that where a dispute raises a question of EU law, the arbitration panel must request the CJEU's ruling which would be binding on the arbitration panel. Where frictionless trade with the EU calls for regulatory alignment (or at least regulatory harmonization), the role of the CJEU is considerable. The independence of international adjudication of these bilateral relationships is thus reduced. It

2 Eyal Benvenisti, 'Democracy Captured: The Mega-Regional Agreements and the Future of Global Public Law' (2016) 23 Constellations 58.

3 Benvenisti 2016, 62.

4 Art 66 of the Decision No 1/95 of the EC-Turkey Association Council.

seems then that, at least in cases of close economic cooperation, violation of international economic obligations may be decided by an EU court which distributes international responsibility within the EU according to its own internal rules.

If international responsibility is subject to treaty negotiations, whom do the Member States of the EU account to for their conduct? It seems that Member States sit behind a powerful organization which has become the global rule-setter,[5] and which is willing to assume international responsibility on their behalf. For example, as has been explained in Chapter 5 and elsewhere in this book, if a trade rule is violated by one of the Member States, retaliation can be applied to any part of EU's customs territory.[6] Functional international responsibility thus shields Member States from personal responsibility. The more trade powers are transferred to the EU, the less personal responsibility is carried by an individual Member State. This is so because authority points to the EU as best placed to remedy the consequences.

One may be concerned that turning international responsibility into an internal affair may reduce transparency and even disincline Member States to abide by their international obligations. On the other hand, international economic relations are contractual, and they last only so long as there is political will. Perhaps then, it is only reasonable that the nature of the institution of international responsibility in the context of global trade is functional. But that is a subject for further debate.

5 Anu Bradford, 'The Brussels Effect' (2012) 107 NULR 1.
6 The so-called 'carousel retaliation'.

Bibliography

INTERNATIONAL LAW COMMISSION'S DOCUMENTS

Reports of the Special Rapporteurs

Report on International Responsibility, by Mr. F.V. García-Amador, Special Rapporteur, A/CN.4/96 (1956)

Second Report on International Responsibility, by Mr. F.V. García-Amador, Special Rapporteur, A/CN.4/106 (1957)

Sixth Report on International Responsibility, by Mr. F.V. García-Amador, Special Rapporteur, A/CN.4/134 and Add.1 (1961)

Report by Mr. R. Ago, Chairman of the Sub-Committee on State Responsibility, A/CN.4/152 (1963)

Second Report on State Responsibility, by Mr. Roberto Ago, Special Rapporteur – the Origin International Responsibility, A/CN.4/233 (1970)

Third Report on State Responsibility, by Mr. Roberto Ago, Special Rapporteur – the Internationally Wrongful Act of the State, Source of International Responsibility, A/CN.4/246 and Add.1–3 (1971)

Fifth Report on State Responsibility, by Mr. Roberto Ago, Special Rapporteur – the Internationally Wrongful Act of the State, Source of International Responsibility (Continued), A/CN.4/291 and Add.1–2 and Corr.1 (1976)

Sixth Report on State Responsibility, by Mr. Roberto Ago, Special Rapporteur – the Internationally Wrongful Act of the State, Source of International Responsibility (Continued), A/CN.4/302 and Add.1–3 (1977)

Eighth Report on State Responsibility, by Mr. Roberto Ago, Special Rapporteur – the Internationally Wrongful Act of the State, Source of International Responsibility, A/CN.4/318 and Add.1–4 (1979)

Preliminary Report on the Content, Forms and Degrees of International Responsibility (Part 2 of the Draft Articles on State Responsibility), by Mr. Willem Riphagen, Special Rapporteur, A/CN.4/330 and Corr.1, 2 (1980)

Second Report on State Responsibility, by Mr. Gaetano Arangio-Ruiz, Special Rapporteur, A/CN.4/425 and Corr.1 and Add.1 and Corr.1 (1989)

Third Report on State Responsibility, by Mr. Gaetano Arangio-Ruiz, Special Rapporteur, A/CN.4/440 and Add.1 (1991)

First Report on State Responsibility, by Mr. James Crawford, Special Rapporteur, A/CN.4/490 and Add. 1–7 (ILC 1998)

Second Report on State Responsibility, by Mr. James Crawford, Special Rapporteur, A/CN.4/498 and Add. 1–4 (ILC 1999)

Third Report on State Responsibility, by Mr. James Crawford, Special Rapporteur, A/CN.4/507 and Add. 1–4 (2000)

First Report on Responsibility of International Organizations, by Mr. Giorgio Gaja, Special Rapporteur, A/CN.4/532 (2003)

Second Report on Responsibility of International Organizations, by Mr. Giorgio Gaja, Special Rapporteur, A/CN.4/541 (2004)

Third Report on Responsibility of International Organizations, by Mr. Giorgio Gaja, Special Rapporteur, A/CN.4/553 (2005)

Fourth Report on Responsibility of International Organizations, by Mr. Giorgio Gaja, Special Rapporteur, A/CN.4/564 and Add. 1–2 (2006)

Fifth Report on Responsibility of International Organizations, by Mr. Giorgio Gaja, Special Rapporteur, A/CN.4/583 (2007)

Sixth Report on Responsibility of International Organizations, by Mr. Giorgio Gaja, Special Rapporteur, A/CN.4/597 (2008)

Seventh Report on Responsibility of International Organizations, by Mr. Giorgio Gaja, Special Rapporteur, A/CN.4/640 (2009)

Reports of the International Law Commission

Report of the International Law Commission on the Work of Its Twenty-Fifth Session, 7 May – 13 July 1973, Official Records of the General Assembly, Twenty-Eighth Session, Supplement, A/9010/Rev.1 (1973)

Yearbook of the International Law Commission, A/CN.4/SER.A/1998/Add.1 (Part 1) (1998)

Yearbook of the International Law Commission, A/CN.4/SER.A/2001/Add.1 (Part 2) (2001)

Yearbook of the International Law Commission, A/CN.4/SER.A/2004/Add.1 (Part 2) (2004)

Yearbook of International Law Commission, A/CN.4/SER.A/2006/Add.1 (Part 2) (2006)

Comments by Governments and International Organisations

Comments and Observations Received from Governments, A/CN.4/547 (2004)

Comments and Observations Received from International Organizations, A/CN.4/545 (2004)

Comments and Observations Received from Governments and International Organizations, A/CN.4/556 (2005)

Comments and Observations Received from International Organizations, A/CN.4/568 (2006)

Comments and Observations Received from International Organizations, A/CN.4/582 (2007)

Comments and Observations Received from International Organizations, A/CN.4/637 (2011)

Summary Records

Summary Record of the 1210th Meeting, A/CN.4/SR.1210 (1973)

Summary Record of the 1212th Meeting, A/CN.4/SR.1212 (1973)

Summary Record of the 1226th Meeting, A/CN.4/SR.1226 (1973)

Summary Record of the 1253rd Meeting, A/CN.4/SR.1253 (1974)

Summary Record of the 1255th Meeting, A/CN.4/SR.1255 (1974)

Summary Record of the 1258th Meeting, A/CN.4/SR.1258 (1974)

Summary Record of the 1261st Meeting, A/CN.4/SR.1261 (1974)

Summary Record of the 22nd Meeting, A/C.6/59/SR.22 (2004)

Summary Record of the 2800th Meeting, A/CN.4/SR.2800 (2004)

Summary Record of the 2801st Meeting, A/CN.4/SR.2801 (2004)

Summary Record of the 2802nd Meeting, A/CN.4/SR.2802 (2004)

Summary Record of the 2803rd Meeting, A/CN.4/SR.2803 (2004)

Summary Record of the 2810th Meeting, A/CN.4/SR.2810 (2004)

BOOKS

Alvarez JE, *International Organizations as Law-Makers* (Oxford University Press 2010)

Amerasinghe CF, *Principles of the Institutional Law of International Organizations* (2nd edn, Cambridge University Press 2005)

Anzilotti D, *Corso Di Diritto Internazionale* (3rd edn, Rome 1928)

Bagwell K and Staiger RW, *The Economics of the World Trading System* (MIT Press 2002)

Benvenisti E and Downs GW, *Between Fragmentation and Democracy: The Role of National and International Courts* (Cambridge University Press 2017)

Bonnitcha J, Lauge P and Waibel M, *The Political Economy of the International Investment Regime* (Oxford University Press 2017)

Burton W, *Burtons Legal Thesaurus 5th Edition: Over 10,000 Synonyms, Terms, and Expressions Specifically Related to the Legal Profession* (5th edn, McGraw-Hill Education 2013)

Clapman A, (ed), *European Community Law, Collected Courses of the Academy of European Law* (Martinus Nijhoff 1991)

Craig P and de Búrca G, *EU Law: Text, Cases, and Materials* (6th edn, Oxford University Press 2015)

Crawford J, *Brownlie's Principles of Public International Law* (8th edn, Oxford University Press 2012)

Crawford J, *State Responsibility: The General Part* (Cambridge University Press 2013)

Cremona M, *External Relations of the EU and the Member States: Competence, Mixed Agreements, International Responsibility, and Effects of International Law* (European University Institute 2006)

Delgado Casteleiro A, *The International Responsibility of the European Union: From Competence to Normative Control* (Cambridge University Press 2016)

Dolmans MJFM, *Problems of Mixed Agreements: Division of Powers Within the EEC and the Rights of Third Parties* (Asser Instituut 1985)

Dolzer R and Schreuer C, *Principles of International Investment Law* (Oxford University Press 2008)

Douglas Z, *The International Law of Investment Claims* (Cambridge University Press 2009)

Eeckhout P, *EU External Relations Law* (2nd edn, Oxford University Press 2011)

Garner B, *A Dictionary of Modern Legal Usage* (2nd edn, Oxford University Press 1996)

Goldsmith JL and Posner EA, *The Limits of International Law* (Oxford University Press 2005)

Gray CD, *Judicial Remedies in International Law* (Oxford: Clarendon Press 1987)

Groux J and Manin P, *The European Communities in the International Order* (Office for Official Publications of the European Communities 1985)

Heliskoski J, *Mixed Agreements as a Technique for Organizing the International Relations of the European Community and Its Member States* (Kluwer Law International 2001)

Hirsch M, *The Responsibility of International Organizations Toward Third Parties: Some Basic Principles* (Martinus Nijhoff Publishers 1995)

Klabbers J, *An Introduction to International Institutional Law* (2nd edn, Cambridge University Press 2009)

Klabbers J, *Treaty Conflict and the European Union* (Cambridge University Press 2009)

Klabbers J, *An Introduction to International Organizations Law* (Cambridge University Press 2015)

Kuijper PJ, *The Law of EU External Relations Cases, Materials, and Commentary on the EU as an International Legal Actor* (2nd edn, Oxford University Press 2015)

Macleod I, Hendry, ID and Hyett S, *The External Relations of the European Communities* (Oxford University Press 1996)

Newcombe A and Paradell L, *Law and Practice of Investment Treaties. Standards of Treatment* (Kluwer Law International 2009)

O'Keeffe D and Schermers HG (eds), *Mixed Agreements* (Kluwer Law and Taxation Publishers 1983)

Paparinskis M, *The International Minimum Standard and Fair and Equitable Treatment* (Oxford University Press 2013)

Pauwelyn J, *Optimal Protection of International Law: Navigating between European Absolutism and American Voluntarism* (Cambridge University Press 2008)

Posner EA and Sykes AO, *Economic Foundations of International Law* (Harvard University Press 2013)

Salacuse JW, *The Law of Investment Treaties* (2nd edn, Oxford University Press 2015)

Steinbach A, *EU Liability and International Economic Law* (Hart Publishing 2017)

Trachtman JP, *The Economic Structure of International Law* (Harvard University Press 2008)

Vandevelde KJ, *United States Investment Treaties: Policy and Practice* (Kluwer Law and Taxation Publishers 1992)

BOOKS CHAPTERS

Allen BE, 'The Use of Non-Pecuniary Remedies in WTO Dispute Settlement: Lessons for Arbitral Practitioners', in Michael E Schneide and Joachim Knoll (eds), *ASA Special Series No. 30: Performance as a Remedy: Non-monetary Relief in International Arbitration* (JurisNet, LLC 2011)

Allott P, 'Adherence to and Withdrawal from Mixed Agreements', in David O'Keeffe and Henry G Schermers (eds), *Mixed Agreements* (Kluwer Law and Taxation Publishers 1983)

Barros AS, '6 Responsibility, 6.3 Matthews v United Kingdom, ECtHR, App. No. 24833/94, 18 February 1999', in Cedric Ryngaert and others (eds), *Judicial Decisions on the Law of International Organizations* (Oxford University Press 2016)

Barros AS, Ryngaert C and Wouters J, 'Member States, International Organizations and International Responsibility', in Ana Sofia Barros, Cedric Ryngaert and Jan Wouters (eds), *International Organizations and Member State Responsibility: Critical Perspectives* (Brill Nijhoff 2017)

Bleckmann A, 'The Mixed Agreements of the EEC in Public International Law', in David O'Keeffe and Henry G Schermers (eds), *Mixed Agreements* (Liability for mixed agreements 1983)

Charnovitz S, 'Should the Teeth Be Pulled? An Analysis of WTO Sanctions', in Daniel LM Kennedy and James D Southwick (eds), *The Political Economy of International Trade Law: Essays in Honor of Robert E. Hudec* (Cambridge University Press 2002)

Cortés Martín JM, 'European Exceptionalism in International Law? The European Union and the System of International Responsibility', in Maurizio Ragazzi (ed), *Responsibility of International Organizations: Essays in Memory of Sir Ian Brownlie* (Martinus Nijhoff Publishers 2013)

D'Aspremont J, 'A European Law of International Responsibility? The Articles on the Responsibility of International Organizations and the European Union', in Vicky Kosta, Nikos Skoutaris and Vassilis Tzevelekos (eds), *The EU Accession to the ECHR* (Hart Publishing 2014)

Delgado Casteleiro A and Larik J, 'The "Odd Couple": The Responsibility of the EU at the WTO', in Malcolm Evans and Panos Koutrakos (eds), *The International Responsibility of the European Union: European and International Perspectives* (Hart Publishing 2013)

Denza E, 'Responsibility of the EU in the Context of Investment', in Malcolm Evans and Panos Koutrakos (eds), *The International Responsibility of the European Union: European and International Perspectives* (Hart Publishing 2013)

Eeckhout P, 'The EU and Its Member States in the WTO: Issues of Responsibility', in Lorand Bartels and Federico Ortino (eds), *Regional Trade Agreements and the WTO Legal System* (Oxford University Press 2006)

Ehlermann CD, 'Mixed Agreements: A List of Problems', in David O'Keeffe and Henry G Schermers (eds), *Mixed Agreements* (Kluwer Law and Taxation Publishers 1983)

Evans M and Okawa P, 'Approaches to Responsibility in International Courts', in Panos Koutrakos and Piet Eeckhout (eds), *The International Responsibility of the European Union: European and International Perspectives* (Hart Publishing 2013)

Flett J, 'The Practice of Shared Responsibility in Relation to The World Trade Organization and the European Union and Its Member States in the WTO', in André Nollkaemper and Ilias Plakokefalos (eds), *The Practice of Shared Responsibility in International Law* (Cambridge University Press 2016)

Fry JD, 'Attribution of Responsibility', in André Nollkaemper and Ilias Plakokefalos (eds), *Principles of Shared Responsibility in International Law: An Appraisal of the State of the Art* (Cambridge University Press 2014)

Gaja G, 'Some Reflections on the European Community's International Responsibility', in Henry G Schermers, Ton Heukels and Philip Mead (eds), *Non-Contractual Liability of the European Communities* (Martinus Nijhoff Publishers 1988)

Gaja G, 'The European Community's Rights and Obligations under Mixed Agreements', in David O'Keeffe and Henry G Schermers (eds), *Mixed Agreements* (Kluwer Law & Taxation Publishers 1983)

Gazzini T, 'States and Foreign Investment: A Law of the Treaties Perspective', in Lalani Shahleza and Rodrigo Polanco Lazo (eds), *The Role of the State in Investor-State Arbitration* (Brill Nijhoff 2015)

Granvik L, 'Incomplete Mixed Environmental Agreements of the Community and the Principle of Bindingness', in Martti Koskenniemi (ed), *International Law Aspects of the European Union* (Martinus Nijhoff Publishers 1998)

Hindelang S, 'Restitution and Compensation – Reconstructing the Relationship in Investment Treaty Law', in Hofmann Rainer and Tams Christian (eds), *International Investment Law and General International Law: From Clinical Isolation to Systemic Integration?* (Nomos 2011)

Hobér K, 'Remedies in Investment Disputes', in Andrea K Bjorklund, A Ian Laird and Sergei Ripinsky (eds), *Remedies in International Investment Law: Emerging Jurisprudence of International Investment Law* (BIICL 2009)

Hoffmeister F, 'Institutional Aspects of Global Trade Governance from an EU Perspective', in Bart Van Vooren, Steven Blockmans and Jan Wouters (eds), *The EU's Role in Global Governance* (Oxford University Press 2013)

Hudec RA, 'Broadening the Scope of Remedies in the WTO Dispute Settlement', in Friedl Weiss (ed), *Improving WTO Dispute Settlement Procedures: Issues & Lessons from the Practice of Other International Courts & Tribunals* (Cameron May 2000)

Klabbers J, 'Presumptive Personality: The European Union in International Law', in Martti Koskenniemi (ed), *International Law Aspects of the European Union* (Martinus Nijhoff Publishers 1998)

Kornhauser LA, 'Incentives, Compensation, and Irreparable Harm', in André Nollkaemper and Dov Jacobs (eds), *Distribution of Responsibilities in International Law* (Cambridge University Press 2015)

Kuijper PJ, 'International Responsibility from Mixed Agreements', in Christophe Hillion and Panos Koutrakos (eds), *Mixed Agreements Revisited: The EU and its Member States in the World* (Hart Publishing 2010)

Kuijper PJ and Paasivirta E, 'EU International Responsibility and Its Attribution: From the Inside Looking Out', in Malcolm Evans and Panos Koutrakos (eds), *The International Responsibility of the European Union: European and International Perspectives* (Hart Publishing 2013)

Marín Durán G, 'The EU and Its Member States in WTO Dispute Settlement: A "Competence Model," or a Case Apart, for Managing International Responsibility?', in Marise Cremona, Anne Thies and Ramses A Wessel (eds), *The EU and International Dispute Settlement* (Hart Publishing 2016)

Messineo F, 'Attribution of Conduct', in André Nollkaemper and Ilias Plakokefalos (eds), *Principles of Shared Responsibility in International Law: An Appraisal of the State of the Art* (Cambridge University Press 2014)

Morris D, 'The Regulatory State and the Duty of Consistency', in Shahleza Lalani and Rodrigo Polanco Lazo (eds), *The Role of the State in Investor-State Arbitration* (Brill Nijhoff 2015)

Neframi E, 'International Responsibility of the European Community and of Member States under Mixed Agreements', in Enzo Cannizzaro (ed), *The European Union as An Actor in International Relations* (Kluwer Law International 2002)

Nollkaemper A, 'Joint Responsibility between the EU and Member States for Non-Performance of Obligations under Multilateral Environmental Agreements', in Elisa Morgera (ed), *The External Environmental Policy of the European Union* (Cambridge University Press 2012)

Nollkaemper A, 'Introduction', in André Nollkaemper and Ilias Plakokefalos (eds), *Principles of Shared Responsibility in International Law: An Appraisal of the State of the Art* (Cambridge University Press 2014)

Nollkaemper A and Jacobs D, 'Introduction: Mapping the Normative Framework for the Distribution of Shared Responsibility', in André Nollkaemper and Dov Jacobs (eds), *Distribution of Responsibilities in International Law* (Cambridge University Press 2015)

Olson PM, 'Mixity from the Outside: The Perspective of a Treaty Partner', in Christophe Hillion and Panos Koutrakos (eds), *Mixed Agreements Revisited: The EU and Its Member States in the World* (Hart Publishing 2010)

Paulsson J and Douglas Z, 'Arbitrating Foreign Investment Disputes: Procedural and Substantive Legal Aspects', in Norbert Horn (ed), *Indirect Expropriation in Investment Treaty Arbitration* (Kluwer Law International 2004)

Pauwelyn J, Jackson JH and Sykes AO, 'The Calculation and Design of Trade Retaliation in Context: What Is the Goal of Suspending WTO Obligations?', in Chad P Bown and Joost Pauwelyn (eds), *The Law, Economics and Politics of Retaliation in WTO Dispute Settlement* (Cambridge University Press 2010)

Proulx V-J, 'An Uneasy Transition? Linkages between the Law of State Responsibility and the Law Governing the Responsibility of International Organizations', in Maurizio Ragazzi (ed), *Responsibility of International Organizations: Essays in Memory of Sir Ian Brownlie* (Martinus N, Martinus Nijhoff Publishers 2013)

Rosas A, 'Mixed Union – Mixed Agreements', in Martti Koskenniemi (ed), *International Law Aspects of the European Union* (Martinus Nijhoff Publishers 1997)

Rosas A, 'The European Union and Mixed Agreements', in Alan Dashwood and Christophe Hillion (eds), *The General Law of E. C. External Relations* (Sweet & Maxwell 2000)

Schütze R, 'Federalims and Foreign Affairs: Mixity as a (Inter)National Phenomenon', in Christophe Hillion and Panos Koutrakos (eds), *Mixed Agreements Revisited: The EU and its Member States in the World* (Hart Publishing 2010)

Shaffer G and Ganin D, 'Extrapolating Purpose from Practice: Rebalancing or Inducing Compliance', in Chad P Bown and Joost Pauwelyn (eds), *The Law, Economics and Politics of Retaliation in WTO Dispute Settlement* (Cambridge University Press 2010)

Stephan PB, 'Comparative Taxation Procedure and Tax Enforcement', in Stephan W. Schill (ed), *International Investment Law and Comparative Public Law* (Oxford University Press 2010)

Talmon S, 'Responsibility of International Organizations: Does the European Community Require Special Treatment?', in Maurizio Ragazzi (ed), *International Responsibility Today* (Martinus Nijhoff 2005)

Tietje C and Kampermann K, 'Taxation and Investment: Constitutional Law Limitations on Tax Legislation in Context', in Stephan W Schill (ed), *International Investment Law and Comparative Public Law* (Oxford University Press 2010)

Timmermans CWA, 'Organizing Joint Participation of E.C. and Member States', in Alan Dashwood and Christophe Hillion (eds), *The General Law of E. C. External Relations* (Sweet & Maxwell 2000)

Titi C, 'Aspects of the EU's Responsibility in International Investment Disputes', in Marise Cremona, Anne Thies and Ramses Wessel (eds), *The European Union and the International Dispute Settlement* (Hart Publishing 2017)

Tomuschat C, 'Liability for Mixed Agreements', in David O'Keeffe and Henry G Schermers (eds), *Mixed Agreements* (Kluwer Law & Taxation Publishers 1983)

Weiler JHH, 'The External Legal Relations of Non-Unitary Actors', in David O'Keeffe and Henry G Schermers (eds), *Mixed agreements* (Kluwer Law and Taxation Publishers 1983)

Wessel RA and Dekker IF, 'Identities of States in International Organizations', in Ana Sofia Barros, Cedric Ryngaert and Jan Wouters (eds), *International organizations and member state responsibility : critical perspectives* (Brill Nijhoff 2017)

Wittich S, 'International Investment Law', in André Nollkaemper and Ilias Plakokefalos (eds), *The Practice of Shared Responsibility in International Law* (Cambridge University Press 2017)

Yannaca-Small K, 'Fair and Equitable Treatment Standard', in Katia Yannaca-Small (ed), *Arbitration under International Investment Agreements: A Guide to the Key Issues* (Oxford University Press 2010)

JOURNAL ARTICLES

Ahlborn C, 'The Rules of International Organizations and the Law of International Responsibility' (2011) 8 International Organizations Law Review 2, 397

Bartels L, 'Procedural Aspects of Shared Responsibility in the WTO Dispute Settlement System' (2013) 4 Journal of International Dispute Settlement 343

Bartels L, 'The UK's Status in the WTO after Brexit' [2016] Available at SSRN: https://ssrn.com/abstract=2841747

Benvenisti E, 'Democracy Captured: The Mega-Regional Agreements and the Future of Global Public Law' (2016) 23 Constellations 1, 58
Björklund M, 'Responsibility in the EC for Mixed Agreements – Should Non-Member Parties Care?' (2001) 70 Nordic Journal of International Law 3, 373
Brimeyer BL, 'Bananas, Beef, and Compliance in the World Trade Organization : The Inability of the WTO Dispute Settlement Process to Achieve Compliance from Superpower Nations' (2001) 10 Minnesota Journal of Global Trade 1, 133
Castellanos-Jankiewicz L, 'Causation and International State Responsibility' (2012) 7 SHARES Research Paper 7
Charnovitz S, 'Rethinking WTO Trade Sanctions' (2001) 95 American Journal of International Law 4, 792
Chayes A, 'The Role of the Judge in Public Law Litigation' (1976) 89 Harvard Law Review 7, 1281
Crawford J, 'Revising the Draft Articles on State Responsibility' (1999) 10 European Journal of International Law 435
Crawford J, 'The ILC's Articles on Responsibility of States for Internationally Wrongful Acts: A Retrospect' (2002) 96 American Journal of International Law 4, 874
Crawford J, 'The Current Political Discourse Concerning International Law' (2018) 81 Modern Law Review 1, 1
Davey WJ, 'Compliance Problems in WTO Dispute Settlement' (2009) 42 Cornell International Law Journal 1, 119
Demirkol B, 'Remedies in Investment Treaty Arbitration' (2015) 6 Journal of International Dispute Settlement 2, 229
DiMascio N and Pauwelyn J, 'Nondiscrimination in Trade and Investment Treaties: Worlds Apart or Two Sides of the Same Coin?' (2008) 102 American Journal of International Law 1, 48
Dimopoulos A, 'The Common Commercial Policy after Lisbon: Establishing Parallelism between Internal and External Economic Relations' (2008) 4 Croatian Yearbook of European Law and Policy 101
Douglas Z, 'International Responsibility for Domestic Adjudication: Denial of Justice Deconstructed' (2014) 63 International & Comparative Law Quarterly 3, 867
Eagleton C, 'The Responsibility of States in International Law' (1928) 22 American Political Science Review 4, 1004
Fairley SH, 'Internal Accountability for Provincial Violations of Canada's International Obligations: Lessons from Abitibi' (2012) 53 Canadian Business Law Journal 31
George CC, 'What Constitutes a Taking of Property under International Law?' (1962) 38 British Yearbook of International Law 307
Gonzalez MP, 'Les Organisations Internationales et Le Droit de La Responsabilité' (1998) 92 Revue Générale de Droit International Public 63
Gray C, 'The Choice between Restitution and Compensation' (1999) 10 European Journal of International Law 2, 413–423
Guido C and Melamed DA, 'Property Rules, Liability Rules, and Inalienability: One View of the Cathedral' (1972) 85 Harvard Law Review 1089
Guzman AT, 'The Cost of Credibility: Explaining Resistance to Interstate Dispute Resolution Mechanisms' (2002) 31 Journal of Legal Studies 303

Heliskoski J, 'Joint Competence of the European Community and Its Member States and the Dispute Settlement Practice of the World Trade Organization' (1999–2000) 2 Cambridge Yearbook of European Legal Studies 80

Higgins R, 'The Legal Consequences for Member States of the Non-Fulfilment by International Organizations of Their Obligations toward Third Parties', Yearbook of the Institute of International Law (Paris), part I (Session of Lisbon, Preparatory works) (1995) Available at: www.idi-iil.org/app/uploads/2017/06/1995_lis_02_en.pdf

Hoekman B and Mavroidis PC, 'WTO Dispute Settlement, Transparency and Surveillance' (2000) 30 World Economy 527

Hoffmeister F, 'Litigating against the European Union and Its Member States – Who Responds under the ILC's Draft Articles on International Responsibility of International Organizations?' (2010) 21 European Journal of International Law 723

Holmes OW, 'The Path of the Law' (1897) 10 Harvard Law Review 457

Jackson JH, 'The WTO Dispute Settlement Understanding—Misunderstandings on the Nature of Legal Obligation' (1997) 91 American Journal of International Law 60

Kleimann D, 'Reading Opinion 2/15 : Standards of Analysis, the Court's Discretion, and the Legal View of the Advocate General' (2017) 23 EUI RSCAS 1–38

Koers A, 'Participation of the European Economic Community in a New Law of the Sea Convention' (1979) 73 American Journal of International Law 426

Kuijper PJ, 'Amsterdam Center for International Law: Introduction to the Symposium on Responsibility of International Organizations and of (Member) States: Attributed or Direct Responsibility or Both?' (2010) 7 International Organizations Law Review 9

Kuijper PJ, 'Attribution – Responsibility – Remedy. Some Comments on the EU in Different International Regimes' [2014] Available at SSRN: https://ssrn.com/abstract=2405028

Lévesque C, 'Les Rôles et Responsabilités Des Provinces Canadiennes Dans Le Cadre de Procédures d'arbitrage Entre Investisseurs et États Fondées Sur Des Traités Économiques' (2015) 28 Revue québécoise de droit international 107–155

Malacrida R, 'Towards Sounder and Fairer WTO Retaliation: Suggestions for Possible Additional Procedural Rules Governing Members' Preparation and Adoption of Retaliatory Measures' (2008) 42 Journal of World Trade 3

Mavroidis PC, 'Remedies in the WTO Legal System: Between Rock and a Hard Place' (2000) 11 European Journal of International Law 763

Meinhard H, 'The ECJ's Opinion 1/94 on the WTO – No Surprise, but Wise?' (1995) 6 European Journal of International Law 245

Miller D, 'Distributing Responsibilities' (2001) 9 Journal of Political Philosophy 453

Newcombe A, 'The Boundaries of Regulatory Expropriation in International Law' (2005) 20 ICSID Review-FILJ 1–57

Nollkaemper A, 'The European Community and International Environmental Co-Operation: Legal Aspects of External Community Powers' (1987) 14 Legal Issues of European Integration 55

Nollkaemper A and Jacobs D, 'Shared Responsibility in International Law: A Concept Paper' (2001) ACIL Research Paper No 2011–07 (SHARES Series)

Nollkaemper A and Jacobs D, 'Shared Responsibility in International Law: A Conceptual Framework' (2013) 34 Michigan Journal of International Law 359

Noyes JE and Smith BD, 'State Responsibility and the Principle of Joint and Se Veral Liability' (1988) 13 Yale Journal of International Law 225

Paasivirta E, 'Responsibility of a Member State of an International Organization: Where Will It End? Comments on Article 60 of the ILC Draft on the Responsibility of International Organizations' (2010) 7 International Organizations Law Review 49

Paparinskis M, 'Investment Treaty Arbitration and the (New) Law of State Responsibility' (2013) 24 European Journal of International Law 617

Paparinskis M, 'Investors' Remedies under EU Law and International Investment Law' (2016) 17 Journal of World Investment & Trade 919

Pescatore P, 'Opinion 1/94 on "Conclusion" of the WTO Agreements: Is There an Escape from a Programmed Disaster' (1999) 36 Common Market Law Review 387

Plakokefalos I, 'Causation in the Law of State Responsibility and the Problem of Overdetermination: In Search of Clarity' (2015) 26 European Journal of International Law 471

Puig V, 'Scope of the New Exclusive Competence of the European Union with Regard to Foreign Direct Investment' (2013) 40 Legal Issues of Economic Integration 133

Shapiro C, 'Property Rules vs. Liability Rules for Patent Infringement' [2016] Available at SSRN: https://ssrn.com/abstract=2775307 or http://dx.doi.org/10.2139/ssrn.2775307

Sloane RD and Reisman M, 'Indirect Expropriation and Its Valuation in the BIT Generation' (2003) 73 British Yearbook of International Law 115

Sykes AO and Schwartz WF, 'The Economic Structure of Renegotiation and Dispute Resolution in the WTO/ GATT System' (2002) 31 Journal of Legal Studies 179

Temple L, 'The Ozone-Layer Convention: A New Solution to the Question of Community Participation in "Mixed" International Agreements' (1986) 23 Common Market Law Review 157

Trachtman JP, 'Building the WTO Cathedral' [2006] Available at SSRN: https://ssrn.com/abstract=815844 or http://dx.doi.org/10.2139/ssrn.815844

van Aaken A, 'To Do Away with International Law? Some Limits to "The Limits of International Law"' (2006) 17 European Journal of International Law 289

MISCELLANEOUS

European Commission, 'Communication from the Commission to the Council, the European Parliament, the European Economic and Social Committee and the Committee of the Regions: Towards a Comprehensive European International Investment Policy, COM (2010), 343

Eagleton C, 'International Organization and the Law of Responsibility', Collected Courses of the Hague Academy of International Law 76 (Brill 1950), 316

Leinarte E, 'International Responsibility of the European Union: From Competence to Normative Control' by Andrés Delgado Casteleiro (Book Review) (2017) 42 European Law Review 6

Leinarte E, 'EU Liability and International Economic Law' by Armin Steinbach (Book Review) (2018) European Law Review 280–281

Pusztai DM, 'Causation in the Law of State Responsibility' (PhD book, University of Cambridge 2017)

Index

For EU product safety concerns, contact us at Calle de José Abascal, 56–1°, 28003 Madrid, Spain or eugpsr@cambridge.org.

www.ingramcontent.com/pod-product-compliance
Lightning Source LLC
LaVergne TN
LVHW011810200926
848484LV00005B/1128

* 9 7 8 1 1 0 8 8 3 8 8 8 7 *